Julian Grenfell in France, 1915

Hertfordshire Record Publications Volume 20

JULIAN GRENFELL,

SOLDIER & POET:

LETTERS AND DIARIES, 1910-1915

Edited by Kate Thompson

Hertfordshire Record Society

2004

Hertfordshire Record Society

The publication of this volume has
been assisted by generous grants from
The Marc Fitch Fund
Isobel Thornley Bequest
The Scouloudi Foundation
in association with The Institute of Historical Research

ISBN 978-0-9547561-1-6

Printed by Stephen Austin Ltd,
Caxton Hill, Hertford, England

Contents

Illustrations

Introduction

The First World War continues to fascinate and to appal people in equal measure. Interest in the various battles and their participants, in the outcomes and after-effects, seems to increase, rather than diminish, the further in the past the conflict becomes. There are countless books, websites, museums and other sources of information for the war; battlefield tours are particularly popular. The conflict and the literature that it generated are regularly studied in schools. *Oh What a Lovely War*, the drama first produced by Joan Littlewood, continues to draw audiences[1]. In the recently issued DVD of the film version of this production, one of the characters refers to Julian Grenfell by name. She mentions a letter that she has received from him and the subsequent dialogue is based on an actual letter[2]. This letter is just one of the hundreds written by Julian that have survived and that are the subject of this volume.

The Panshanger archive

The letters of Julian Grenfell form part of the Panshanger archive, arguably the most important collection in the care of Hertfordshire Archives and Local Studies. The house called Panshanger, demolished in 1953, was in the parish of Hertingfordbury. Access was from the present B1000, which runs between Hertford and Welwyn Garden City; a modern housing estate bears the name. The Panshanger archive was deposited in the former Hertfordshire Record Office in three stages. The first deposit (reference HALS: **DE/P**), deposited in 1953, consists largely of estate material, although it does include some personal items. The second (HALS: **DE/Rv**), deposited in 1975 and 1978, contains not only the bulk of Julian's letters but also other significant Desborough family material, such as Lady Desborough's diaries, of which DE/Rv/F61 covers 1915 and records Julian's last few days. The third (HALS: **D/EX789**), deposited in 1986, comprises a wide variety of items, including, for example, Julian's diary written up until the day before he was wounded and also, perhaps surprisingly, the contents of his uniform pockets. Most of

---

[1] The script has been published as Theatre Workshop, Charles Chilton and members of the original cast, *Oh What a Lovely War* (1965)

[2] Letter 229, HALS: DE/Rv/C1135/684, 24 Oct 1914; the film was produced by Richard Attenborough and the reference number for the DVD is 5 014437 897534

the material in this deposit relates to Julian and was separated out from the rest of the archive by his family.

In 1992, following the death of the last member of the family who had a direct connection with the Panshanger archive, the documents were offered to the County Council in a private treaty sale. A major fund-raising exercise was launched to meet the asking price of over half a million pounds, after tax deductions. This successful appeal resulted in the largest sum ever (at the time) being raised by a county record office. It is an enormous collection, with the letters alone running into thousands of items. All of the Desboroughs were prolific writers and there are some 869 letters from Julian in the archive, the bulk of them (712) to his mother[3]. They begin when he was about four, written from his home at Taplow Court to his parents when they were away. They continue throughout his education, from his time at Summer Fields preparatory school (near Oxford), at Eton College and then at Balliol College, Oxford[4]. From a historian's point of view, the most interesting letters are those that he wrote whilst serving in the army; he was posted to India and then to South Africa before being sent to the Western Front[5]. Due to the large quantity of his letters, only those written during his army service have been reproduced in this volume.

In the letters from Flanders, he paints a vivid picture of life for an officer in the first year of the Great War: the alternate fear and boredom and the rapid change from optimism to despair. As a cavalry officer, he experienced at first hand changes in tactics and the growing dependence on trench warfare. He considered joining the newly formed (Royal) Flying Corps as an observer, but this came to nothing[6]. On the whole, the letters are in good condition, although Julian's last letter to his mother, as might be expected, is rather the

---

[3] Most of Julian's letters are in DE/Rv, with some additional material in D/EX789. In this introduction, when referring to a particular letter the following details are provided: the number that has been assigned to it in this volume; its HALS reference; and the date on which it was written (if known)

[4] As well as being an avid correspondent, Julian also liked drawing. His letters from Summer Fields contain requests for crayons and paints. Several later letters were illustrated with sketches, some of which have been reproduced in this volume

[5] The significance of the contents of some of the letters, not only those written from Flanders but also from India and South Africa, will be discussed briefly below

[6] Letter 241, HALS: DE/Rv/C1138/29, 19 December 1914

worse for wear[7]. A map of Belgium, found in his pocket after he was wounded, appears to be blood-stained[8]. Some of the letters, especially the later ones, are still stored in their original envelopes.

The following series contain letters from Julian and have been used in this book: DE/Rv/C1133/45-93; C1134/19-21; C1135/513-712; C1137/1; C1138/9-30; C1142/1; C1146/1; D/EX789/F15. There are a number of other items that refer to Julian; some further details can be found in Appendix 3.

Both Julian's diary for 1915 and his mother's covering the period after he was wounded have been included in this book, as Appendix 1[9]. Julian's, as might be expected, is written with a variety of implements and is often difficult to read. The handwriting is much smaller than in his letters and it is not always possible to interpret what he has written. His mother's diary is clearer, but her handwriting is very small and cramped. Both Julian and Lady Desborough used abbreviations, some of which are obvious, but others are unclear.

Julian Grenfell's life

Julian's biography was written by his relative Nicholas Mosley, Lord Ravensdale. It was first published in 1976 and in 1999 it was reissued by a different publisher[10]. For this reason only a brief biography is given here. The eldest son of William (Willy) Grenfell, first Baron Desborough, and his wife Ethel (Ettie), Julian was born at 4 St James's Square, London, on 30 March 1888. His father was a keen sportsman and chairman of the British Committee for the 1908 Olympic Games held in London[11]. He had married

---

[7] Letter 278, HALS: DE/Rv/C1135/712, 14 May 1915

[8] HALS: D/EX789/F22

[9] Their reference numbers are D/EX789/F23 and DE/Rv/F61

[10] Nicholas Mosley, *Julian Grenfell: his life and the times of his death, 1888-1915* (first edition, 1976; second edition, 1999). (The second edition has been used for this introduction.) See also, Angela Bolger, *Julian Grenfell. Soldier-Poet (1888-1915)* (Taplow, 2005); Mark Pottle, 'Grenfell, Julian Henry Francis (1888-1915), army officer and poet', ODNB (2004); Jon Stallworthy, *Anthem for Doomed Youth* (London, 2002), pp22-31

[11] Willy Grenfell was created first Baron Desborough in 1905. For a brief biography, see Ian F W Beckett, 'Grenfell, William Henry, Baron Desborough (1855–1945)', ODNB (online edn, May 2006).

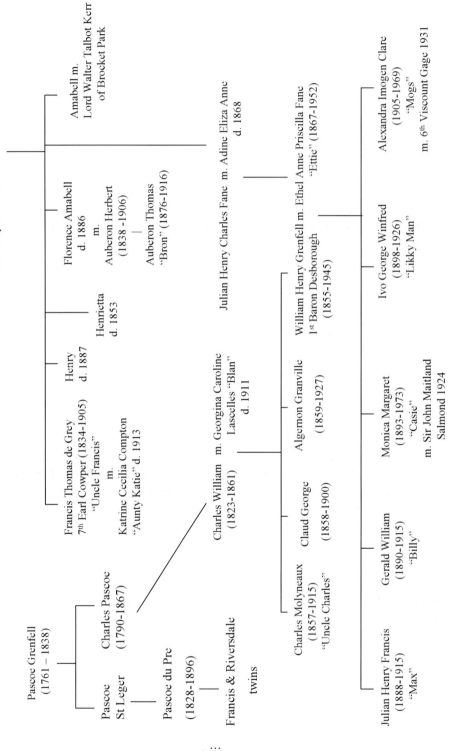

George Augustus Frederick m. Anne Florence de Grey
6th Earl Cowper d. 1856

Amabell m.
Lord Walter Talbot Kerr
of Brocket Park

Pascoe Grenfell
(1761 – 1838)

Pascoe
St Léger

Charles Pascoe
(1790–1867)

Pascoe du Pre
(1828–1896)

Francis & Riversdale
twins

Francis Thomas de Grey (1834–1905)
7th Earl Cowper
"Uncle Francis"
m.
Katrine Cecilia Compton
"Aunty Katie" d. 1913

Henry
d. 1887

Henrietta
d. 1853

Florence Amabell
d. 1886
m.
Auberon Herbert
(1838 -1906)
|
Auberon Thomas
"Bron" (1876-1916)

Charles William   m. Georgina Caroline
(1823–1861)   Lascelles "Blan"
d. 1911

Charles Molyneaux
(1857-1915)
"Uncle Charles"

Claud George
(1858-1900)

Algernon Granville
(1859-1927)

Julian Henry Charles Fane   m. Adine Eliza Anne
d. 1868

William Henry Grenfell m. Ethel Anne Priscilla Fane
1st Baron Desborough   "Ettie" (1867-1952)
(1855-1945)

Julian Henry Francis
(1888-1915)
"Max"

Gerald William
(1890-1915)
"Billy"

Monica Margaret
(1893-1973)
"Casie"
m. Sir John Maitland
Salmond 1924

Ivo George Winfred
(1898-1926)
"Likky Man"

Alexandra Imogen Clare
(1905-1969)
"Mogs"
m. 6th Viscount Gage 1931

INTRODUCTION

Ettie Fane in 1887, the Prince of Wales being one of their witnesses[12]. Willy and Ettie were members of 'the Souls', the nickname of a group whose leading members played a dominant role in British politics at the beginning of the twentieth century; they combined the traditional way of life of the landed gentry with an intellectual concern and permissive modernism[13]. As well as Julian, they had four other children: Billy, Monica, Ivo and Imogen[14]. The family seat was at Taplow Court in Buckinghamshire (near Maidenhead, Berskhire), but Ettie inherited Panshanger in 1913, on the death of her aunt by marriage, Katie Cowper, wife of the 7th Earl Cowper[15]. (See family tree).

In May 1898 Julian went to preparatory school at Summer Fields, near Oxford, where he was a good scholar and a keen sportsman; his letters from there contain details of his scholastic prowess and sporting triumphs. The school inculcated a spirit of competitiveness, into which he entered eagerly, and gained a reputation of being able to look after himself. He usually won the end-of-term prizes for English, French or Latin. He was very keen on cricket and many of the letters from Summer Fields provide details of matches in which he played.

He took the ordinary entrance exam for Eton in 1901 and did so well that he was put straight into the form usually reserved for scholars. He appears to have been happy there. He became head of his house and a member of Pop (a social club and debating society), and was one of two editors of the school magazine. Towards the end of his time at Eton he began to have battles with his mother, that were to continue on and off for the rest of his life; according to one author, he was a sensitive and somewhat serious child who found his parents' milieu artificial and hypocritical, and he grew up to distrust relationships and personal involvement. He learned at an early age to hide any worries, problems, depressions or anxieties from his mother and to bottle

---

[12] Willy and Ettie were married at St George's, Hanover Square, London, on 17 February 1887. For a brief biography, see Jane Ridley and Clayre Percy, 'Grenfell , Ethel Anne Priscilla, Lady Desborough (1867–1952)', ODNB (online edn, Oct 2006)
[13] Jeanne MacKenzie, *The Children of the* Souls (1986), p4. See also, A Lambert, *Unquiet souls: the Indian summer of the British aristocracy, 1880-1918* (1984)
[14] Both Julian and Billy were killed in Flanders in 1915, and tragically Ivo died in a car accident in 1926
[15] Francis Thomas de Grey, 7th Earl Cowper, Ettie Desborough's uncle, who had died in 1905

them up, making himself dangerously withdrawn[16]. He disliked socialising and was much happier outdoors; he became keen on various sports, especially boxing, rowing, and football, as well as the 'traditional' country pursuits of fishing, shooting and hunting.

He went up to Balliol College in the autumn of 1906, originally to take Greats, but towards the end of his time there, from late 1909 to early 1910, he suffered from a nervous breakdown, which affected his ability to study. As a result he took a pass degree, but this was sufficient to get him a commission in the army, which had long been his ambition. In the spring of 1909, before his breakdown, he began to write a collection of essays that was to be 'his true challenge to Ettie'[17]. These essays were entitled: 'On Conventionalism', 'Sport', 'On Individuality', 'On Calling Names by their Right Things', 'Divided Ideals', 'Selfishness, Service and the Single Aim', and 'Darwinism, Theism and Conventionalism'[18]. They have been described by his biographer as Julian's 'attempt to sort out for himself and others what he thought about his mother's social world of guilt, pretence and imposition, and to suggest what individuals might do about it before it carried a larger world towards perdition'[19]. The contents of the typed essays have been analysed in detail by Nicholas Mosley[20]. Ettie hated the essays, rightly perceiving them as an attack on her whole way of life, and most of his contemporaries at Oxford also disliked them[21].

On leaving Oxford Julian joined the 1st Royal Dragoons, whose colonel-in chief was, ironically, the German Kaiser[22]. In November 1910, Julian left for India with his regiment[23]. From his letters, it is clear that he loved that country and that he had settled into army life. He was able to indulge in his love of outdoor sports and particularly enjoyed 'pigsticking', which was hunting wild boar. He was a keen boxer and became president of the

---

[16] Tonie and Valmai Holt, *Poets of the Great* War (Barnsley, 1999), p26
[17] Mosley, p219
[18] Mosley, p221. The original essays are HALS: D/EX789/F7-8
[19] Mosley, pp219-20
[20] Mosley, pp 221-33
[21] Mosley, pp234-35
[22] William II (1859-1941), German emperor and grandson of Queen Victoria
[23] Letter 1, HALS: DE/Rv/C1135/513 and DE/X789/F15, 9 November 1910

regiment's boxing club[24]. He also kept himself informed of professional boxing bouts[25]. Throughout his army career, he owned various horses and dogs and frequently reported on their well-being and prowess. One of his poems was 'To a black greyhound'[26]. This was chosen by Field Marshal Wavell in his anthology, *Other Men's Flowers*, published in 1944[27]. Julian took over the editorship of *The Eagle*, the regimental magazine. In the autumn of 1911 his regiment was transferred to Roberts' Heights in South Africa, which he disliked intensely[28]. On his return from leave in 1913, the regiment was at Potchefstroom, south-west of Johannesburg, which he appears to have preferred[29]. Julian began to think about leaving the army, but by the time he had made up his mind, and had decided to stand for parliament, events had overtaken him.

The regiment left South Africa in late August 1914 and arrived in England on 19 September, going to camp on Salisbury Plain[30]. On 6 October the 1st Royal Dragoons sailed for France, forming part of the 3rd Cavalry Division of the 4th Army Corps, one of four corps comprising the British Expeditionary Force. The first battle of Ypres commenced on 19 October. Julian's division was brought in as infantry and fought near the Menin Road. He became something of a legend for his courage, as Billy's Colonel was later to write[31]. He appeared to love war and not to fear death but, according to one author, a closer study of his letters reveals solicitude for his men, for the local population whose homes and livelihoods were being shattered, and for the

---

[24] For his own boxing prowess, see, for example, letter 78, HALS: DE/Rv/C1135/577, 17 March 1912. He mentions being president of the boxing club in an undated letter to his father, written from Muttra, India (letter 42, HALS: DE/Rv/C1133/50)

[25] For the results of professional bouts, see, for example, letter 267, where he mentions 'the Moran-Wells fight', which was a match, on 29 March 1915, between the Englishman 'Bombardier' Billy Wells and the American Frank Moran, 'the fighting Dentist' (letter 267, HALS: DE/Rv/C1133/88, 2 April 1915)

[26] It is unclear which dog this referred to. Mosley (p311) says it was Toby, but both Stallworthy and Pottle state that the dog was called Slogbottom. Julian refers to the poem in letter 77, HALS: DE/Rv/C1135/576, 10 March 1912

[27] Holt & Holt, p28

[28] Letter 60, HALS: DE/Rv/C1135/558, 27 November 1911

[29] Letter 119, HALS: DE/Rv/C1135/612, 1 May 1913

[30] Letter 217, HALS: DE/Rv/C1133/72, telegram dated 19 September 1914

[31] HALS: DE/Rv/C1170/3, 30 May 1915. The Colonel wrote: 'Julian has set an example of light-hearted courage which is famous all through the Army in France'

devastated countryside[32]. On 17 November, he made a single-handed attack on a German trench to take out snipers[33]. For this he was awarded the DSO on 27 December 1914. The award was reported in the *London Gazette* on 1 January 1915: 'On the 17th November he succeeded in reaching a point behind the enemy's trenches and making an excellent reconnaissance, furnishing early information of a pending attack by the enemy'. Subsequently he was offered a staff job, but refused it, and in January 1915 was promoted to captain. His mother sent some of his letters to the editor of *The Times* in the winter of 1914-15 and these were published as an anonymous young cavalry officer's impressions of the Front[34].

During his spare time in the army, when he was not required for military duties, as well as participating in various sports, Julian read widely. Both while he was in Flanders and during his earlier postings to India and South Africa, his mother frequently sent him newspapers and books. He was clearly a voracious reader and made critical comments on much of what he read. It has been possible to establish that many of the books that he was reading had been published very recently.

In early 1915 he began to keep a diary, which details his war service, the last entry being made on 12 May 1915[35]. By this date the Allied line had withdrawn to within two miles of Ypres. The 6th Cavalry Brigade, including the 1st Royal Dragoons, was in the second line of trenches between Hooge Lake and a railway line. Early on the morning of 13 May the Germans started a heavy bombardment of the trenches and 'Railway Hill'. The Royals were told to keep a watch from Railway Hill to see if the Germans were advancing round their flank. Julian volunteered to run messages during the heavy bombardment[36]. At noon he went up the hill and was knocked down by a shell, but it only tore his coat. He returned with information that the

---

[32] Mosley, p359; Holt & Holt, p29

[33] He describes this episode to his mother in great detail in a long letter written over several days (letter 234, HALS: DE/Rv/C1135/688, 13-18 November 1914)

[34] Mosley, p367

[35] HALS: D/EX789/F23. Julian's diary, together with his mother's, has been transcribed as Appendix 1

[36] The following account of what happened on 12 and 13 May 1915 is taken from Mosley. He states that Julian's parents pieced together the events of those days from accounts given by Julian's friends (Mosley, pp388-89)

Germans were coming round the flank, then offered to take a message to the Somerset Yeomanry in the forward trenches and brought back further messages. He went up Railway Hill again, this time with the general in command, David Campbell, and both men were hit. Julian was not thought to be badly wounded and was taken to a casualty clearing station, from where he wrote his last letter to his mother, which was forwarded to her by the chaplain[37].

He was sent to hospital in Boulogne and was visited there by his sister, Monica, who was nursing in nearby Wimereux. She sent a telegram to their parents saying there was no cause for anxiety and that Julian would be sent to England to recover[38]. However, an x-ray revealed that the wound was much more serious and that a shell splinter had lodged in his skull, causing damage to his brain. He was operated on successfully, but the outcome would not be known for some days. Monica then telegrammed her parents to come out at once and they got permission from the Admiralty to cross the Channel on an ammunition boat, arriving in Boulogne at 5.00 am on 17 May[39]. They found Julian in good spirits and he seemed to be getting stronger, but on 23 May the doctors discovered more inflammation of the brain and performed a second operation. Ettie's diary gives a day-to-day account of his time in hospital and she had a bulletin typed to keep friends informed of his progress[40]. At least one member of his family remained with him until he died on the afternoon of 26 May.

On the following day news of his death appeared in *The Times*, along with his best-known poem, 'Into Battle'[41]. He was buried in the military cemetery in Boulogne, one of the smaller First World War cemeteries. No one wore mourning and Ettie covered his grave with wild flowers and oak leaves[42]. Willy and Ettie received hundreds of letters of condolence, including many from leading figures of the day[43]. Billy was killed on 30 July, leading a

---

[37] Letter 278, HALS: DE/Rv/C1135/712, 14 May 1915; Mosley, p389

[38] HALS: DE/Rv/C2303/37, 15 May 1915

[39] Mosley, p391

[40] The relevant entries in Ettie's diary have been transcribed in Appendix 1. It has not been possible to trace any copies of her bulletin

[41] Four of Julian's best-known poems are in Appendix 2

[42] Mosley, p397

[43] Mosley, pp397-98. Those sending condolences included Arthur Balfour and Winston Churchill. See Lady Desborough, *Pages from a family journal, 1888-1915* (Eton, 1916), pp561-588

charge near Hooge, within a mile of where Julian had been wounded; his name is recorded on the memorial at the Menin Gate.

In 1935, Monica published a book about her wartime nursing experiences, *Bright Armour*, which includes a number of references to Julian[44]. She recalls that: 'We were a large family and very devoted to each other. ... My brothers and their friends were clever and remarkable, and they added brilliance to an already happy throng'[45]. She described Julian just before he went to France: 'He was such an eager soldier – the tremendous activity of that time suited him, and all his vigour and the zest of his imagination seemed to spring towards the task to be undertaken'[46]. They were able to meet when they were both in France and, of course, she was the first to reach him when he was wounded[47]. She says: 'I cannot say much about the subsequent days; the anxiety was too poignant, and the sorrow too deep for expression'[48].

Julian's poems

When Julian talked about becoming a writer his family were unenthusiastic, but his poems appear to have been well regarded at the time. Julian's best-known poem is 'Into Battle', although he did write others about the war, such as 'Prayer for those on the staff'[49]. He also wrote on other subjects that were dear to his heart, such as on his animals, including 'To a Black Greyhound', and on sports, including 'Hymn to the Fighting Boar'[50]. 'Into Battle' is available in a number of anthologies. The four poems referred to here are transcribed as Appendix 2. Other poems and parts of poems, in both manuscript and typescript, can be found in HALS: DE/Rv/F120 and D/EX789/F2 and F15.

---

[44] Lady Monica Salmond, *Bright Armour. Memories of four years of war* (1935)
[45] Salmond, p17
[46] Salmond, pp65-66.
[47] They met in France in April 1915 (letter 274, HALS: DE/Rv/1135/710, 30 April 1915)
[48] Salmond, p147
[49] 'Prayer for those on the staff' has been published in full in Mosley, p372 and in Stallworthy, p28
[50] 'To a Black Greyhound' has been published in full in Mosley, pp311-12; 'Hymn to the Fighting Boar' has been published in *ibid*, p286

Julian's attitude to war and his account of the first year of the Great War

From his letters written from the Western Front, it is clear that he loved war, something that is regarded as unacceptable today. On arriving at the Front, he told his mother: 'We've got within 15 miles of them Germans now, and hope to be at them tomorrow. It's all the best fun one ever dreamed of – and up to now it has only wanted a few shells and a little noise to supply the necessary element of excitement'[51]. Somewhat curiously, on several occasions he likened going to war to going on a picnic. 'The uncertainty of it is so good, like a picnic when you don't know where you are going to'[52]. 'I adore war. It is like a big picnic without the objectlessness of a picnic. I've never been so well or so happy. Nobody grumbles at one for being dirty. I've only had my boots off once in the last ten days; and only washed twice'[53]. Mosley explains Julian's enjoyment of war, and of being dirty, thus: 'For the first time a generation brought up to be clean and bright and obedient could, without guilt, be fierce and babyish and vile. Such behaviour had been forbidden them when such attitudes might have been natural: the relief when it was allowed them later was overwhelming'[54].

From both his actions, such as his attack on German snipers mentioned above, and from his letters, it appears that he did not fear death and revelled in the comradeship enforced by war. 'It is all the most wonderful fun; better fun than one could ever imagine. I hope it goes on a nice long time: but pigsticking will be the only tolerable pursuit after this, or one will die of sheer ennui. The first time one shoots at a man one has the feeling of "never point a loaded gun, even in fun": but very soon it gets like shooting a crocodile, only more amusing, because he shoots back at you'[55]. Inactivity was particularly frustrating: 'Things are rather boring here, and we do all the regular peace-soldiering things, and grumble at the men if their spur-buckles are dirty – rather ridiculous, when the real thing is going on 15 miles away. I can't help wishing that I were fighting now with the foot-sloggers [the infantry]; especially when there is quite a chance of us [the cavalry] doing nothing more'[56].

---

[51] Letter 226, HALS: DE/Rv/C1135/681, 11 October 1914
[52] *Ibid*
[53] Letter 229, HALS: DE/Rv/C1135/684, 24 October 1914
[54] Mosley, p359
[55] Letter 227, HALS: DE/Rv/C1135/682, 15 October 1914
[56] Letter 268, HALS: DE/Rv/C1135/708, 5 April 1915

The letters give many insights into how the war was conducted and the logistics involved in moving and provisioning troops. Many of the letters include personal requests for additional clothing, such as a Burberry greatcoat and a sou-wester, and supplies, such as field glasses and batteries[57]. Others ask for items needed for the pursuit of the war. For example, in March 1915, he asked his father to send some 'Nottingham' fishing reels, to be used by snipers. He explained that 'when they go out of the trench they take the line out with them, and tie it up at a place about 50 yds out. Then when they want to come back they jerk the end of the line, and that clicks the reel and warns the sentry in the trench that they are coming back: and he tells the others not to shoot'[58]. The most frequent requests, however, are for cigarettes, not only for himself but also for his men. It appears that the family and the staff at Taplow sent out several parcels of cigarettes to Julian but many of them never reached him, presumably having been embezzled *en route*. For example, on 20 March, he wrote: 'The only thing that has not arrived is the 3,000 cigarettes. Did you send them to me? Please send on the next lot, anyhow, as the men are frightfully short. Do you think that they bag [steal] cigarettes in the post? I wonder? The other things arrived alright (pipe-lighters, electric torches, vests & pants)'[59]. Although the requests for supplies are not particularly unusual, it seems that his family were able to supply him with them fairly quickly. In the first year of the war, at least, lines of communication between the Western Front and England were wide open.

The ease with which objects and people were able to reach Flanders is most clearly demonstrated by the number of celebrities and friends of officers who 'visited' the Front to watch what was happening there. For example, on 5 April, Julian told his mother that 'Diana Wyndham & Rosemary motored up to a place quite close here last week, & Alastair & I went over and spent the day with them; it was rather amusing'[60]. Furthermore, on 4 April, he and a friend had been driven over to Dunkirk, which 'was great fun, after these very dull billets; all the picture-postcard celebrities were there – Wilding, Maurice Elliot, Bend Or, Millie, Fitzgerald, Lady D Fielding, & Col

---

[57] See, for example, letter 226, HALS: DE/Rv/C1135/681, 11 October 1914
[58] Letter 260, HALS: DE/Rv/C1133/86, 9 March 1915
[59] Letter 263: HALS: DE/Rv/C1135/705, 20 March 1915
[60] Letter 268, HALS: DE/Rv/C1135/708, 5 April 1915

Bridges'[61]. These visits also demonstrate the localised nature of the fighting.

Julian's letters as historical documents

In addition to the obvious historical value of those letters written from the Western Front, some of the ones written from India and South Africa contain reports on local events. In particular, Julian's descriptions of and comments on the strikes that occurred in South Africa in the summer of 1913 and on the army's involvement in their suppression supply first-hand information not given in other accounts[62]. The strikes were mentioned during debates in the House of Commons in July and August 1913, although technically they were not the subjects of those debates, which nominally concerned the supply and maintenance of Imperial troops in South Africa[63]. The way in which the troops were used to suppress the riots caused an outcry in the British press but Julian astutely observed that the troops were placed in a no-win situation. On Wednesday 3 July he told his mother: 'Just off to Jo'burg, on 2 hrs notice, to quell the strikers. ... I suppose they will throw bottles at us; and if we retaliate, we shall be prosecuted for murder, and if we do not, we shall be prosecuted for cowardice'[64]. As events unfolded, according to Julian, the troublemakers were not the striking miners, who had achieved their aim, namely the reinstatement of thirty-one strikers, but crowds of hooligans and 'Jo'burg roughs'[65]. Although Julian's squadron was not directly involved in the most violent incident at the Rand Club, he relates how 'After the shooting on Sat the whole thing quieted down, and nothing more happened. It was the only thing that stopped them. I believe that if they had been allowed to go on for a day longer they would have burnt the whole of the town to the ground. As it was, they did not fire until five or six of the men had been hit by bullets and slugs, and several of the horses – and the crowd were getting right on top of them'[66]. The troops remained in Johannesburg until 3 August, by which time the threat of a general strike had receded.

---

[61] Letter 268, HALS: DE/Rv/C1135/708, 5 April 1915. Some of these people have been identified in the notes to this letter

[62] Letters 131 to 136

[63] The various debates can be traced in *Parliamentary Debates*, 5th series, volume LVI, *House of Commons, 28 July 1913 – 15 August 1913* (1913)

[64] Letter 131, HALS: DE/Rv/C1135/620, 3 July 1913

[65] Letter 132, HALS: DE/Rv/C1135/621, 13 July 1913

[66] Letter 136, HALS: DE/Rv/C1135/624, 3 August 1913

In addition to commentaries on events abroad, Julian also provides various insights into the developing political situation at home when responding to the contents of the (missing) correspondence that he received, particularly from his father, and to newspaper cuttings that various people had sent him. See, for example, his remarks on Willy Grenfell's 'Declaration of London' speech in the House of Lords in March 1911[67]. He also commented on other events in parliament[68]. His letters, therefore, have a wider significance for historians of the twentieth century.

Related material

In 1916, Ettie Desborough published privately *Pages from a family journal 1888-1915*, in which she reproduced many of Julian and Billy's letters[69]. When the letters in her book are compared with the originals in the Panshanger archive, it is clear that she made alterations to their text, apparently to give the impression that the boys were extremely devoted to her. She did not always transcribe the letters accurately, changing words and phrases, and combining different letters together. The copy held by the Centre for Buckinghamshire Studies (reference D11/16/8) contains manuscript annotations about many of the individuals to whom Lady Desborough referred; they were possibly made by Mr Packe, the depositor of some of the Grenfell material in the Centre.

Lord Desborough wrote a preface: 'The following pages have been compiled by my wife from the Journal which she kept for our children from their earliest years. The book is privately printed, and is intended for Julian and Billy's brother and sisters, and for their most intimate friends. The boys wrote freely, and their letters were often of too personal a character to be printed in full, although they have not been cut down without a sense of loss. The letters were addressed to their mother where it is not otherwise stated.

---

[67] Letter 26, HALS: DE/Rv/C1135/528, 30 March 1911 and letter 28, HALS: DE/Rv/C1133/47, 11 April 1911

[68] See, for example, letter 52, HALS: DE/Rv/C1133/49, 24 August 1911, regarding the Unionist peer, the Marquess of Lansdowne; letter 62, HALS: DE/Rv/C1135/559, 4 December 1911, regarding the resignation of Arthur Balfour as Unionist leader

[69] The editor has been able to purchase a copy of this book, which will ultimately be transferred to HALS

It is hoped that the few great friends who see the book will be reminded of the happy times with which Julian and Billy will always be associated'.

Despite his preference for his own company, Julian had a wide circle of friends and appears to have had at least two serious relationships with women. He became a friend of Marjorie, Letty and Diana Manners, the daughters of the Duke and Duchess of Rutland, nicknamed the 'Hotbed' or 'Hothouse'. Marjorie was apparently the first girl whom he loved and some of his letters to her survive in private hands[70]. She married the Marquis of Anglesey in 1912, although Julian continued to write to her, his last letter being dated November 1914. In the summer of 1910 he began the one passionate love affair of his life, with Pamela Lytton (née Plowden), the wife of Victor, second Earl of Lytton[71]. There is tantalising evidence of another relationship, although we shall never know the details. Whilst editing this volume, the editor was informed of the existence of eleven letters written by Julian in the last few months of his life to a girl named Flossie Garth. She has also been identified as the subject of the photograph found on him when he was fatally wounded[72]. The letters to Flossie Garth from Julian have been transcribed in Appendix 4. There are almost certainly more letters from Julian in other collections, especially family and estate collections in various county record offices, but it has only been possible to locate those listed on the A2A (Access to Archives) website. As this database is being added to constantly, anyone interested is advised to consult that website[73].

Two of Julian's game books have survived and belong to Viscount Gage, a descendent of his sister Imogen. The second one covers the period from October 1907 until his death and includes a reference to the exploits for which he was awarded the DSO in 1914. More details can be found in Appendix 5.

---

[70] The editor has been privileged to read these letters but they all predate the events covered in this book

[71] Of Knebworth House, Hertfordshire. For a brief biography of Lord Lytton, see Jason Tomes, 'Lytton, Victor Alexander George Robert Bulwer-, second earl of Lytton (1876–1947)', ODNB, 2004. Two works on Julian's life wrongly state that Pamela's husband was the *third* earl. (Bolger, p8; Stallworthy, p24)

[72] HALS: D/EX789/F19. The present owners of the letters, the grandson and granddaughter of Flossie, did not previously know of the existence of the photograph

[73] www.a2a.org.uk

In her book *The Children of The Souls* (1986), Jeanne MacKenzie provides valuable information about the network of friends surrounding Lord and Lady Desborough and their children. She specifically considers eight men who were close friends and who were all killed in the first world war: Raymond Asquith, Ego and Yvo Charteris, Julian and Billy Grenfell, Edward Horner, Charles Lister and Patrick Shaw Stewart. Unlike Mosley, she does provide footnotes to her work but, unfortunately, neither book contains a bibliography. The curator at Taplow Court, Angela Bolger, has long had an interest in the Grenfells and in 2005 mounted an exhibition to mark the ninetieth anniversary of Julian's death. She was able to bring together some extremely valuable and interesting material, notably two commemorative cartoons which marked the graduation of many Oxbridge scholars who died in the Great War. These feature, amongst others, Raymond Asquith, Rupert Brooke, Denis Browne, Ego and Yvo Charteris, the Grenfell brothers, Charles Lister, John Manners and Patrick Shaw Stewart. They are owned by the University of Southampton and are now on loan to Taplow Court. Angela's booklet, *Julian Grenfell, Soldier-Poet (1888-1915)*, contains a useful bibliography.

People mentioned in the letters

Julian frequently refers to members of his family and friends with a variety of pet names. The most common are:

Billy (Gerald William)	Billa-boy
Monica (Monica Margaret)	Casie, Ca, Missy
Ivo (Ivo George Winfred)	Vovo, Likky, Likky Man
Imogen (Alexandra Imogen Clare)	Mogs, Moggy, Wuggins

He sometimes refers to 'the Likkies', meaning Imogen and Ivo. Julian himself was referred to as Max before he was born, and sometimes thereafter. Uncle Francis and Auntie Katie were the seventh Earl Cowper and his wife. 'Bron' was Julian's cousin, Auberon Thomas Herbert, Lord Lucas, and Charlie Meade was another cousin.

Various friends are referred to, but it has not always been possible to identify them. Those most frequently mentioned are: Guy and Rex Benson; Ego and Guy Charteris; Bim Compton; Geordie Herbert; Edward and Jack Horner;

Lawrence Jones (Jonah); Alan Lascelles; Charles, Laura and Diana Lister; Charlie Mills; Geordie and Alastair Sutherland-Leveson-Gower (Stafford). 'Miggs', or 'Migsy', was Marjorie Manners.

Various members of staff at Taplow and Panshanger are mentioned, but only a few can be identified. Lady Desborough's *Pages from a family journal* provides the best guide to their identities. Miss Poulton was the children's governess. She is probably the person Julian refers to as 'Popon' or 'Popem'. Hawa (or Wawa or Wa) was Harriet Plummer, Julian's nurserymaid. There was another nurserymaid called Ada whose surname is unknown. Mrs Matilda Wake had been Lady Desborough's nanny and also acted in that capacity for the children[74]. Barrett Good, sometimes called 'Bart', was a butler; Mrs Hurton was a housekeeper; Mrs Neave (or Near) was the cook at Taplow; Mr Joel was the boatman; Mr Williams was the groom and coachman (Julian sometimes played with his son, Alfred). Others named include Baras, Barnes, Hyams, James, Meades and Susan.

Julian had a number of horses and dogs, both in England and abroad. Many of these are mentioned frequently in his letters. His horses included: Bridegroom, Buccaneer, Caesar, Cob, Delilah, Dreadnought, Dynamite, Glory Alleluja, Goliath, John Kino, Kangaroo, Poor Denis, Puck, Rajah Robin, Ruby, Sans Peur, Schoolgirl, The Hawk, The Other Girl and Wacht Een Beetje. His dogs included: Chang, Comrade, Hammer, Mike, Sandon, Tongs and Toby.

Editorial conventions

- On the whole, Julian's handwriting is good, apart from when he was a child, and easy to read. Occasionally it has been impossible to decipher a word and this has been indicated, sometimes with a suggestion, by the use of a question mark inside square brackets.
- He sometimes used 'pet words' which have been left unchanged. Common abbreviations, such as 'esp' for 'especially', have not been extended but less obvious ones have been extended by the use of square brackets.

---

[74] She is warmly referred to by Lady Desborough in *Pages from a family journal*

- Round brackets indicate Julian's own use of parentheses, although sometimes he used square brackets.
- There are some words that he consistently spells wrongly, such as 'manoevres' instead of 'manoeuvres'; these have been left as written, but where he has clearly made a mistake the spelling has been corrected.
- Full stops after initials have been left in, as this was the style at the time.
- The letters have been transcribed in chronological order as far as possible, but difficulties have been encountered because many of them are undated. Where it has been possible to determine the date by internal evidence, this has been given in square brackets after 'nd' for 'no date'.
- He often used pet names for his family and friends and details of these are given above.
- On occasions, it has been impossible positively to identify people, books, plays or incidents that he mentioned and in such cases no footnotes have been supplied.
- In total there are 909 known surviving letters from Julian (869 in the Panshanger archive). The 11 letters to Flossie Garth are reproduced in this book and there are 29 letters to Marjorie Manners in private hands.
- All the items in the Panshanger archive relating to Julian have been recorded in a Microsoft Access database, a copy of which is available in Hertfordshire Archives and Local Studies.

Acknowledgments

The editor is most grateful to the following people for access to additional material: Nicholas Mosley, Lord Ravensdale, for the letters from Julian to Marjorie Manners; Dr Susan Sloman and Mr G Legouix for the letters to their grandmother, Flossie Garth, and related photographs; Viscount Gage for Julian's game books. She is very grateful to her former colleagues at Hertfordshire Archives and Local Studies for their help and patience, especially Susan Flood, general editor of the Hertfordshire Record Society. She also wishes to thank the Bedfordshire and Luton, Buckinghamshire, Somerset and West Sussex record offices, Eton College and Balliol College, Oxford, for access to material, and the Imperial War Museum for providing information. Thanks are also due to Jean Walker for access to Letty Green church, in which there is war memorial; and to Mrs Lapinski, head teacher of Birch Green school, which has a memorial to all those who *served* in the war, including Ivo. Heather Falvey, the secretary of the Hertfordshire Record Society, did an enormous amount of work adding footnotes, which make the text of the letters more meaningful. In addition the editor is greatly indebted both to Heather and to Christine May for their work on the index.

Kate Thompson, 2007

Abbreviations

BL British Library

FJ *Pages from a family journal, 1888-1915*, Lady Desborough (Eton, 1916)

HALS Hertfordshire Archives and Local Studies

Mosley Nicholas Mosley, *Julian Grenfell* (1976, 1999)

OCCL M C Howatson (ed), *Oxford Companion to Classical Literature* (2nd edition, Oxford, 1989)

OCEL Margaret Drabble (ed), *Oxford Companion to English Literature* (6th edition, Oxford, 2000)

ODNB *Oxford Dictionary of National Biography* (updated on-line version)

OED *Oxford English Dictionary* (on-line version)

Bibliography

Balliol College war memorial book, 1914-1919 (1924)

Angela Bolger, *Julian Grenfell, Soldier-Poet (1888-1915)* (Taplow, 2005)

Lady Desborough, *Pages from a family journal, 1888-1915* (Eton, 1916)

INTRODUCTION

A Lambert, *Unquiet souls: the Indian summer of the British aristocracy, 1880-1918* (1984)

Tonie and Valmai Holt, *Poets of the Great War* (first edition, 1996; second edition, Barnsley, 1999)

Jeanne MacKenzie, *The Children of The Souls: a tragedy of the First World War* (1986)

Nicholas Mosley, *Julian Grenfell: his life and the times of his death, 1888-1915* (first edition, 1976; second edition, 1999)

Mark Pottle, 'Grenfell, Julian Henry Francis (1888-1915), army officer and poet', *ODNB* (Oxford, 2004)

Monica Salmond, *Bright Armour. Memories of four years of war* (1935)

Jon Stallworthy, *Anthem for doomed youth. Twelve Soldier Poets of the First World War* (2002)

**Letters by Julian Grenfell
to his immediate family**

Wed – 9 Nov. 1910.

H. M. Transport "Rewa."

Dear Mother

We are off Algeria
now – we passed Gib at
5 am yesterday morning, and
so did not ~~SEE~~ it. This
letter has to be posted on the
high seas, before we get to
Malta, so it will go before
I get a letter from you.

We had a great
bucketing in the bay, rougher
they said than any passage

Extract from letter dated 9 November 1910.

1   9 Nov 1910   HM Transport "Rewa"   DE/Rv/C1135/513
                                                    DE/X789/F15

Dear Mother

We are off Algeria now – we passed Gib[raltar] at 5 am yesterday morning,
and so did not see it. This letter has to be posted on the high seas, before we
get to Malta, so it will go before I get a letter from you.
We had a great bucketing in the bay, rougher they said than any passage yet
this summer. The captain wanted to throw over my trousseau, to lighten the
vessel, but God soon sent a great calm, which has lasted ever since. To my
great surprise I found that as a sailor Cortes, Columbus & Co cannot compare
with me at all, and for two days I held the heads of my two cabin
companions without a tremor, and ministered to them. They were very bad:
one is called Sclater Booth[1], and looks it; he is <u>very</u> ugly, and very nice; he is
going with the Royals, below me. The other is called Jeffery, & is going into
the 13th Hussars – also nice. They were both at Eton, & I knew them both by
sight – also several others, so I never felt lonesome. The cabin is 5 ft by 3,
and has none of the comforts of a home. The food is all of the same taste,
size, colour, and shape, so that you never know whether it is a sausage or a
banana that you are eating; and the taste is not a very good one, as tastes go.
The family of Lieut Patch are next door (the ones we had luncheon with) and
make a noise by night like greyhounds. But it is all the very greatest fun, and
all new and exciting, and I've enjoyed every moment of it. I was inoculated
yesterday, and had some fever last night, but nothing much; today the only
trace is a headache. Never am I so ill that I do not immediately perk up at
the sight of food. The female society is nil, as far as we are concerned. I
haven't found out very many of the names yet; there is one very jolly man
called Stuart Wortley, in the Rifles, colonel. ULIA means Unattached List
India Army – all subalterns, & all nice. Some of the Glosters are very jolly.
They got up[2] < a boxing competition, & made me judge & referee. It was a
very good scene – a tiny little ring on the hatch, in one corner of which I sat,
while two people fought for their lives just over my head; and all round, on
the forecastle and cookhouses and docks and rigging a crowd of excited
yelling faces, & bodies packed like sardines. They fought rather well and
very bloodily. Then they had pillow fighting on a spur, an inferior exercise.

---

[1] 'Sclater' is a wood-louse (OED)
[2] This part between <>, separated from original letter, is from DE/X789/F15

One night I was officer of the guard, which meant that between 12 midnight and 4 am I had to go round 18 sentries once every hour. It was a glorious night with blazing stars, the Great Bear standing on its head. All the sentries slept like the 18 sleepers of Ephesus[3]. I yelled "sentry" at them 5 or 6 times – no stir. Then I kicked them gently, and with one panther bound and in one breath they were on their feet and at attention and stoutly denying that they had been asleep. This was most annoying to a lover of the truth, so eventually I lost my temper and had them hailed to prison. One wretched man, a reservist, who is going back to his home in India, was discovered on the third day in the bottom of the ship, reading the Bible. He was brought up on deck, and immediately tried to throw himself overboard. So then they put him> in a bed in the hospital, with a 19th sentry over him. I asked them if he was mad. They said 'Oh no, only religious & melancholic' – such a good description of the state of mind.

It is very very good to feel hot again, hotter than one wants to be – and sun, which one had quite forgotten. I am sure that I shall be sorely tempted to settle under the sun and the banyan tree, and never to return to the Arctic Circle. We have had the most wonderful heat and sun these days in the Mediterranean – today is hot, but no sun: and the sea like glass ever since Biscay. Cape St Vincent looked quite noble – and Africa very woild in the edlands.

Please tell Mog that I have chartered several elephants for her; and please show this to Dad & Bill. I wish I had been able to express adequately to Dad my gratitude and admiration at his wonderful generosity in paying without hesitation for all my boot-trees. He is certainly the model father. I go proudly to the hold on "change of clothing" days and say to the bystanders "Let's see, this is mine, & this, & this, & this, & this, & this, etc". They think I am the giddiest plutocrat, little realising that my brothers and sisters are now begging their bread, & that I am a devotee myself of the simple life. I shall now be unable for very shame to return to sweaters and Uncle Auberon[4] until the trousseau is worn out, which will bring me to the mature

---

[3] Actually it was the 'seven sleepers of Ephesus'. An ancient legend, probably Syrian in origin, recounted by many writers including Gregory of Tours (538-594) and the compiler of *The Golden Legend*. The reference is obviously to long and deep sleep (http://en.wikipedia.org/wiki/Seven_Sleepers accessed 26/02/07)

[4] Auberon Edward William Molyneux Herbert, Baron Lucas of Crudwell, Wiltshire (1838-1906), had married Florence Amabell daughter of the 6th Earl Cowper (d 1886), sister of Julian's grandmother (DNB)

age of 82 at least – if that is any comfort to you in your poverty. Even then I shall have to pawn Bill's watch, which is always affectionately wound about my middle. What a very very nice family I have left! Goodbye & all love from J.

2   15 Nov 1910   HM Transport "Rewa"   DE/Rv/C1135/514

Dear Mother

I got your two letters, one at Malta, one at Port Said this morning – and loved them. We got to Malta Friday at dawn – left Sat morning; got to Port Said today at 8, coaled, & left at 4. We've had simply wonderful weather all through the Mediterranean, and delicious warm sun – <u>quite</u> warm, everybody wearing drill. I'm getting sick to death of the ship, and it was heaven getting out at Malta, though the land rocks and rolls and pitches in front of me at every step – does it for you after sea? Ian[5] asked me to lunch, & I brought old toad face (Sclater + Booth) with me. Poor Jean had just arrived, & had taken to her bed with bronchitis and a temperature of 102; she could not come down, of course, but she was already better. Ian was in <u>terrific</u> form, & I had tremendous fun with him, & discussed every conceivable topic. He is a good light horseman, isn't he? After luncheon we played tennis, the frog and I completely dressed in flannels by dear Maitland and another ADC called Robbins – Rubbage – Rumpety – name gone, but he was a major, and very nice, and we had good tennis. In the evening Sclater and I went to an entertainment where the stalls cost tuppence each: a lady sang Italian songs, rather a good lady; and there was a blood and thunder play on the cinematograph, which Booth could not understand, the words being, by the very nature of the performance, left for the intelligence of the audience to supply. So I kept up a running commentary.

Booth – What <u>are</u> they doing now, Eh what?

Self – Well, you see, they are trying to kill Lewis Waller (the hero, very like LW). The cowboys are not sitting on him to try and keep him warm. The man who has just produced the pistol wants to <u>shoot</u> him – bang – dead. He does not want it to pick his teeth with.

Booth – Why have they put that rope round his neck. Eh what?

Self – They are going to <u>hang</u> him with the rope. That is why they put it round his <u>neck</u>. But I think he will escape somehow, etc etc.

---

[5] Ian Hamilton (see letter 4)

Enter the heroine & galloping cowboys, & great rescue finale and love scene. Very good tuppence-worth; and so back to the ship and bed.

I got very sick of the ship the two days between Malta and here, so I set off alone to explore Port Said in search of adventure. After rejecting several proffers of guides a charming man came up, the colour of strong coffee, and said in a mixture of English & Arab that he was a "Scotchmanne". I asked him what town he came from, and he said "town they call Dublin", with a huge grin. So I made great friends with him, and he took me off to see his "lil sister", all over the Arab quarter. But <u>God</u>, what a town. It oughtn't to be allowed to exist on the earth's face. I thought it was exaggerated in rumour, but it isn't.

We had a gorgeous Nile sunset tonight – and then dark quite quick. You said one of the people on board was called Fane; <u>all</u> the people on board are called Fane, and haven't even got the itch; and those who aren't called Fane have wives that used to be called Fane, Fanny Fane, you know, whose cousin married old Slapcabbage.

I <u>loved</u> Moggie's letter, & I've heard from Vovo and Casie. Has Alan got Buccaneer yet?[6] Oh, I'm itching to get my legs across a horse again, and looking forward to Muttra tooth and nail. But really the ship has been more fun than I thought it would, & the time has gone very quick.

I forgot to say that Malta is <u>hideous</u>, brickcolour all over, with never a leaf of green, except Ian's garden, which is lovely – and a <u>very</u> nice house.

<u>All</u> <u>all</u> love. I can't tell you what a wonderful send off you gave me – the best anyone has ever had. J.

3	17 Nov 1910	**HM Transport "Rewa"**	DE/Rv/C1137/1
		Red Sea	

Darling Likky Man

I <u>did</u> love getting your letter, which reached me at Malta. Yes, we had great fun at Boath[7], didn't we; I'm sure I shall never be as keen to get a tiger as we were to bag a snipe in the Nairn main drain; and I shall feel very frightened

---

[6] See also letter 3; Buccaneer was one of Julian's horses. Marden Hill and Warrengate Farm, Tewin, part of the Panshanger estate, were occupied by Alan C Hill in 1910 (Inland Revenue Survey HALS: IR1/300 and IR2/36/1)

[7] Seat in Nairnshire adjacent to Aldearn, Scotland, 2½ miles south east of Nairn

without Toby and you to back me. Toby has gone to Bron at Sawley[8]; and Buccaneer to Alan at Marden; and at present I have no animals at all. It is very hot here, which I love. We have gone through the Suez canal, and past where Moses and the Jew boys walked dryshod through the Red Sea, and past Sinai and the 10 commandments[9]; and now we are out of sight of land again. I am on duty tonight, which means that I have to go round all the sentries on board, 18 of them, once every hour between 12, midnight and 4 am. It is a most wonderful night, and there is a great moon so bright that one can almost write by it. I am writing this under a lamp on the top deck. It is terribly hot below, where the men sleep, and their hammocks almost touch each other; and the sentries all get very sleepy, and sometimes go right off to sleep, and I have to kick them to wake them up when I go round. Then they jump up like lightning, and pretend they were awake all the time, and say they had lain down on the deck only to look for a mouse or a pin or something. If I am in a good temper I let them off – and if I am in a bad temper I report them, and they cut off their heads next day.

SENTRY ON FORECASTLE

---

[8] Toby was one of Julian's greyhounds. 'Bron' is Auberon Thomas Herbert (1876–1916), son of Uncle Auberon (see letter 1 above) (ODNB)
[9] Both of these are Bible references (Exodus, ch 14 and ch 20)

4   18 Nov 1910   HM Transport "Rewa"   DE/Rv/C1138/9

Casie darling

I'm so sick of feet – I've got them on the brain – not even slogging over
Africa, but thrust out of deck chairs against the main-top-mizzen-halyard-
poop-rails or railings. [*sketch of a leg and foot*] Sometimes I think I have
gone mad; sometimes I know I am far from it, feet from it. There is a most
glorious sun, and wonderful heat: how you would love the heat, with your
dot-and-go-one circulation. It is life, and godliness, which comes next to
cleanliness, and <u>everything</u>. You will have to come out and settle down with
me under the banyan tree. I'm sure you're 'one of those southern women',
and you will never attain to your true greatness in the Arctic Circle. Except
for the sun, ship life is a sort of living death without funerals and champagne.
I am getting web-footed and my legs are growing together, from protracted
immobility. 2 very good letters arrived from you, to stir my soul with home
emotions – or was it 20? I've lost all sense of Space & Time. You will
probably remember. Thank you very very much, anyhow. Your student life
in Paris sounds delightful – "mosh' <u>attRAWcktive</u> fellow" as Marten the Eton
usher said about Edward Horner when he brought voluble excuses instead of
his essay, for the third time. You will be quite the newest New student-
athletic Woman when you come out this year, and you'll pull them all up by
the roots. There's one man I detest on the ship: he thinks he is Mahomet. I
foresee that I shall be pushing his face before long. [*sketch of man in
military uniform*] It is the sort of face I've <u>always</u> wanted to push. God is
very kind, and everything comes to those who wait. I've been working hard
for 13½ days now. We stopped for a day at Malta, and I saw Ian Hamilton,
and Maitland, who had taken a photograph of you at Tidworth[10], and the local
Maltese theatre, where I went with a very ugly man called Sclata Booth, who
is in the Royals, and saw a mosh attwactive play in Irish, and a lady who
sang comic songs in Arabic, and a man who killed his mother in Italian, all
for tuppence. There aren't enough stops in that sentence. I feel it. The sense
is obscure. And it's no good trying to make up with full stops now. We also
stopped at Port Said, the wickedest town in the world, Naples not excepted;
and there, oh there I made friends with a man as black as your hat, who came
up to me in the bright sunshine and said he was "Scotchmanne-boy called

---

[10] Tidworth – town in Wiltshire, where the army barracks were situated

Mackenzie", and when I asked him his clan and tartan, said he lived in "big town they calls Dublin", and also that he was very fond of me. I told him that it was nothing to my affection for him, and he took me off with him to see all his Dublin-Scottish relations in the Arab quarter. They are charming, rather like Dad's town-scoundrels in face, but with more sense of humour. McKenzie and I had one slight tiff as to money, and I had to resort to physical violence in order to persuade him. But we parted with tears and great mutual tenderness, and I'm going to spend my first leave with him. THE SUEZ CANAL IS VERY MUCH WHAT ONE EXPECTS IT TO BE. Otherwise I have no news.

I am very well.

Thank you.

Except for the fact that the members of the RAMC (the Royal Army Medical Corps) commanded by Major Stammers, insist on inoculating me for Typhoid, Measles, & Whooping Cough two or three times a week, in the right arm, or in the left arm, on the starboard side, usually about 2.57 inches from the point of the shoulder. It makes me feel very weak, but they love doing it, because they say I've got the biggest arm on board, and it's such good practise for the younger members of the RAMC (the Royal Army Medical Corps) commanded by Major Stammers. Goodbye my dear and God bless you J.

[*circle with spot in centre, and 'Watch this spot'*]

5   1 Dec [1910]   Royal Dragoons,   DE/Rv/C1135/516
**   Muttra, India**

Dear Mother

We are arrived, after perils by land and sea: and the mail is just going, so that I cannot recount them all to you! I love India and the sun and the cold (which is penetrating) and the Royal Dragoons (who are magnificent and yet friendly) and my clothes, especially my boots, and rice, and curry, and saises[11] and khitmagars[12], and the entire lack of privacy – three men as black as your hat sitting in your doorstep all day, and vultures, and those bloody little birds which look like moorhens, and are apparently doves, and the Taj which takes my breath away altogether. We are in a foreign bungalow for a

---

[11] A servant who attends to horses (syces in OED)

[12] A mail servant who waits at table (khidmutgar in OED)

fortnight, until our own is prepared for us. Sclater Booth plays the piano, but he has a brilliant brain concealed under a bushel, and a pure lily white soul concealed under a yellow hide, 'which is partially covered with hair'. We haven't started work yet properly. We arrived at Karachi on Friday, here on Monday. The Sind desert is a chirpy place, isn't it? I saw all my trousseau off the Rewa into a cart driven by Cox, Shipping agents, and pulled by two bullets; who pulled it apparently straight into the said desert, for when we came to the station the cupboard was bare, and at Muttra, when we got here, after two days stew in dust, we had nothing but what we stood in. However, everything has turned up subsequent, and we were always merry and bright. The sunsets are pretty good, aren't they? I shall never forget the first, at Karachi. I'm in the throes of horse dealing at present. I wonder if Dad could pay in half of my 1911 allowance now, as I shall have to pay money down for the horses and ponies?

O, I wish I had more time to write, but it's been the devil's own rush these days – give my best love to all the family. How I hate missing the Christmas plum pudding. <u>How are your eyes</u>? Tell Mogg I've got 8 bullets.

6   8 Dec 1910   Royal Dragoons, Muttra   DE/Rv/C1135/517
DE/Rv/C1135/567

Dear Mother

Thank you frightfully for your letter, & Mog's postcard. The exeat[13] must have been the greatest fun – how I wish I had been there – how glad I am not to be in the rain and fog! Your letter brought me all the memories of the dear old "forty foot of clay" and fourteen inches of rain and four hundred cubic feet of fog Oxford atmosphere. O, I do love this sun, and the country, and all the things, in which I move at present like a blind man in a dark room. There is so much to learn that the little one learns every day seems to make no impression at all on the bulk of the unlearnt. It is horse and saddle and boots (Field Boots, Polo Boots, Stow waxen gaiters, Wellington, undress Wellingtons, mess Wellingtons, dress Wellingtons) all day and every day, until one's poor posterior is practically non-existent, and the bones wear through the brown and shrunken skin of the face. I've bought a very good polo pony, Arab, horse, weight-carrier, very good looking, price RS 1200, £80. That is all my stud at present. I shall begin playing polo in about a

---

[13] A holiday; permission for temporary absence from an English public school (OED)

week, and pigsticking[14] directly, I hope. I've got a very good horse out of the troop which I do riding school on, and which I shall take as hired charger. I love the Royals and the rich life of the soldier. But I've had a damnable toothache which started on the ship, directly I left England, and has gone on ever since, without a break! Who told you to go to the dentist before you left, you will ask. Alright, auntie; I've been well paid out for it. Of course I could not find a dentist anywhere till I got here, so it just ached and ached, till I contemplated self self-destruction. By the grace of God I found a man at Agra, an American dentist; he is heavy of head, and very deaf, but he is a dentist. He said the nerve had been exposed for 3 weeks, & why wasn't I dead? He then tried to kill it. But I've been to him, 30 miles by train, 4 different days; and the nerve got more alive and more worse each time. But he is a dentist. It isn't aching tonight for the first time since I can remember. That is why I am so abnormally hearty.

The raquets have come, and look too wonderful. I haven't played with them yet. What fun you seem to be having & the Willoughby party sounds glorious. I am so glad that Buccaneer has gone to Alan. Do for heaven's sake tell me what is [15]<Post-Impressionism & the Post Impressionists? I see vague things about it in the papers, but never a word explaining what it is. And I feel so strongly that I am a Post Impressionist! There is really no time to draw breath here – much less to give one's first impressions of a new country. I played cricket today for B squadron v the Band; we beat the band, and won the cup. I bowled rather fast, with a long run, getting 6 wickets, the second drum on the head, and the bassoon just above his instep. Over my batting a blank is drawn. It was a very bad pitch, and the light was shocking. Tomorrow I go to riding school at 8, and then to the dental surgeon at Agra. O THE TARGE. I go straight to it from the grip of the forceps each time. Tomorrow I shall make him pull the tooth out, whether he likes it or not. I've had enough American dentistry for years.

Best best love to the family, who will be full of Christmas pudding long before this gets to them. Please thank Dad tremendously for his letter. I'll write to him next mail.

---

[14] The sport or practice of hunting wild boar on horseback using a spear. The sport is chiefly associated with India in the late 19th and early 20th centuries, where it developed as a pastime for British colonial officers (OED)

[15] The part indicated by < > was separated from the first part of the letter (HALS: DE/Rv/C1135/567)

<u>Do you think you could collect my trousseau bills and send them out as soon as poss</u>: so that I can see what has been stolen already by the dusky natives, and require it at their hands. I've got 9 servants, including a sweep, a sweeper, a bearer, a bear, and 3 dhobis[16]. J>.
[*Note in margin by underlined sentence* – Very urgent NB]

7   nd [1910]   **Royal Dragoons, Muttra**   DE/Rv/C1134/19

[*Beginning missing. ?To Lord and Lady Desborough*]
I didn't write to you any more about that in the ship – I thought our talk about it had been conclusive & I didn't want to open it up again. You know how wonderful I think you have been about it – about not worrying me. I believe so utterly and so immoderately in the complete and absolute liberty of the individual, that I know I often don't realise what the effort and the strain is to leave a person alone in what you think is wrong. But I <u>have</u> known what it cost you not to say more to me, and I am grateful to you for it. I believe you did as near exactly right as anyone can ever do. <u>Of course</u> I knew what you thought; how can you "shirk expression" when there is no need to express? And of course you knew that I knew what you thought; and there it was, black & white, with nothing more to be done – except that you might have worried me or not worried me, and you did not worry me; and for that I shall be grateful to you for ever & ever. As for the things you hear, you know that I think they are <u>pure and utter</u> inventions without the very remotest foundation of any sort, as I told you. As for me, I am utterly happy and at peace, which indeed I have been ever since I finally made up my own mind about it: I don't think you ever knew how it never bothered me after I had once decided; and the wholeness of my decision made me blunt to what must be the doubts of another mind that is undecided, or the pain of a mind that is decided another way. I miss, terribly, of course, and constantly, every day; but each time I offer up thanks for all that came to me, all the new breadth, and knowledge of tenderness, and my gratitude to be given almost kills the bitterness of separation. But to write this to you is as if you were to "worry" me: it must be a locked subject – in those two aspects, I mean. You ask me what I think, & how can I tell you? If one of us pulls & one backwaters, the boat will only go round & round; it is you who have prevented that so far, and I shall never be able to tell you, perhaps never to realise myself, how much it was to do.

---

[16] An Indian washerman (OED)

I am excited about Bill's Ireland. Of course it is over long ago now, as you read this. Damnation. It causes me the most acute annoyance, the 5 week posts; I don't know why, I feel as if it was a silly sort of make-pretend; as if one was playing at Red Indians, only doing it for years instead of ten minutes; as if one could easily get a letter through in a day if one made up one's mind.

I'm awfully glad Patrick got the Eldon; I'm awfully glad England is becoming a Republic, being a rabid democrat by nature; I'm awfully sorry to miss the Post-Impression movement – it's the right movement, got onto the wrong lines; E.G. the treeness of a tree is what you want to paint; you don't want to copy a tree, because there's no use in a worse copy of a better original; but on the other hand you don't get treeness any better by painting a pink brickbat, like the P-Is do.

Any more Dickens invitation? J.

8   14 Dec 1910   Royal Dragoons, Muttra   DE/Rv/C1135/518

Dear Mother

You will have returned from Paris ages ago by the time this gets to you, and Letty & Ego will have had babies[17], God bless them. A five-week interval is as good as a century, as far as letter writing is concerned; but I suppose one gets used to it. You must have had great fun in Paris with Ca[sie]; tell me about it, also about the Hic-Huic-Hollo balls. Yes, I got Rest Harrow[18] at Malta, and loved it, almost better than any book I've ever read; I think M H is such a good philosopher, though I know he brings tears to your eyes, and though most of it is just Plato cooked up. I haven't read a thing here; there is no spare moment, and nothing is like what it was before. We've just moved into our own bungalow, today; it lets in the rain and the rats in ceaseless volume, but there is no rain and I was always fond of ratting. O my tooth, I'd quite forgotten about it; the American-Irish dentist could not kill the nerve, so I made him pull it out all-alive-o with a corkscrew without gas.

---

[17] Hugo Francis Charteris, Lord Elcho (Ego), grandson of the Earl of Wemyss (1884-1916), contemporary of Julian at Eton and Balliol. Married 1 February 1911 Lady Violet Catherine Manners (Letty), daughter of the 8th Duke of Rutland. They had two children: Francis David born 19 January 1912 and Martin Michael Charles born 7 September 1913

[18] *Rest Harrow: a comedy of resolution* by Maurice Hewlett (BL)

He pulled them out very strongly in two pulls, the two nerves (it's a back tooth) – I squealed like a wounded hare for ten seconds, but it was all over then, and he stopped it, and it is now the hardest-biting tooth in my head – rather small, but lots of bone and very good in the deep… [*rest of letter missing*].

9   20 Dec [1910]   **Royal Dragoons, Muttra**   **DE/Rv/C1135/515**

Dear Mother

I had a bit of a fall pigsticking the other day, & they are keeping me in bed, and won't let me write much. But I'm <u>perfectly</u> well and alright, & I've got over the shaking up.
The only thing that worried the doctors is that my pulse is very slow. They want to know whether it is generally slow or not. Could you find out and <u>cable</u> to me here as soon as possible? I suppose Moore knows?[19] Because perhaps they won't let me get up until they know whether it is ordinarily slow or not. If I get very much bored I shall cable to Moore myself. But it'll probably get right long before that. It puts on about $5°$ a day already.
<u>All</u> love to everyone. J.

10   21 Dec 1910   **Royal Dragoons, Muttra**   **DE/Rv/C1133/45**

Dear Dad

I have just turned out all my trousseau, on entering our own bungalow, and I'm terribly shocked at the extent of it! It is most magnificent, and I've got everything I want; but I've also got a good deal more than I want at present in the way of socks and shirts and drawers, and I don't think there was any need for me to get a twenty-five guinea boot chest. It is very fine, and will carry my boots for me all my life; but it is just a bit too fine for me to get and you to pay for. Yes, I am filled with shame at having been a fool, and ordered so many things; and I wish you hadn't paid for them all. It was really <u>too</u> good of you; and I am tremendously grateful to you for setting me up in clothes for the rest of my natural life; and <u>such</u> good clothes! I have put away all the superfluous shirts and drawers and collars and socks and

---

[19] Dr Moore, the family doctor (see Mosley, p49)

vests and all India super-merino wool-cloth linen-cotton wear, and packed it carefully in paper, and labelled it, and sealed it, and put it in a box, so that no Indian dhobi shall ever bruise its beauty against the Jumna stones[20]; and every Sunday I open the lid and peep in at it, with great joy at possession but great shame on account of your expense. But no vest shall be wasted.

I'm enjoying all this tremendously. It's a very good life, and it's a great blessing to get one's exercise always ready-made, instead of having to think how one can get enough exercise every day. I am getting very lean and bow legged, and I have got a horrid little incipient rust-coloured moustache. I love the Royals, esp [Ernest] Makins[21]; I don't know what they think of me, but they are werry affable. There is one very dashing lady, wife of Major [George] Steel, who is pretty and amusing. Mrs Makins & Mrs Major McNeill are good riders and quite Kiplinguesce. We had one good duck-shoot, 12 guns scattered in the rushes all over an enormous jhie[22] which rose solid into the air with duck at the first shot. The other sportsmen confined themselves to the duck; but I recognised several old long-shore friends, & my bag included redshank, dunlin, greenshank, various kinds of plover, & a knot[23]; besides a vulture, a miniature stalk, and a grey green bird with absurdly long legs. I told my shikari[24] to bury them; but having no English, he laid them out proudly in a row, headed by the knot & tailing off to the vulture, to the great amusement of the company. We got 200 all told. Tomorrow we are going to stick pig; I've been out twice, but haven't had a ride yet. The country is blind, and full of the fear of God to the uninitiated. I'm riding 2 troophorses, small but very brave. I've got no horse yet, but I'm on the way to purchase two; and another polo pony, on which, when it arrives, I shall take the field in the next polo game. Our bungalow is taking shape; Sclater-Booth is very nice, but a great ass; he spends most of the riding school time on his back. His legs are admirable for a grand piano, but not for 'oss-riding.

The elections look pretty grim. I hope your orating was successful – you must have done a great deal of it? I am longing to hear all about Christmas

---

[20] Perhaps a reference to the River Jumna near the Taj Mahal where local people washed their clothes

[21] Brigadier-General Sir Ernest Makins (1869-1959)

[22] Jheel or jhil: a pool or lagoon, often of vast extent, left after an inundation (OED)

[23] A bird of the snipe family

[24] An Indian hunter or sportsman (OED)

& the family, and the Pans[hanger] pheasants, & Mr Barnes[25]: and Casie's trousseau and her coming out. Mummie & she must have had the greatest fun in Paris. Please give them, & the family, my very very best love. When exactly is Casie "shown up for good"? Does she start on the bust before that, or does she have to get that over first? And how did Bill do in the Ireland? All love Julian.

11   26 Dec 1910   Royal Dragoons, Muttra   DE/Rv/C1135/519

Darling Mother

I got your Christmas letter, but not your Christmas book; the natives apparently celebrate Christmas as a Parcel Post fast, and nothing has got through for a week. It's an awfully good present, a pocket S[hakespeare]; I haven't got one, and I've had a regular Shakespeare craze lately – I read some on that bloody ship: so you have hit the nail with your usual acumen. It is funny spending Christmas in the United Provinces; but we've had real Christmas weather, with frost, and everybody grumbling at the cold. I went to kirk with the soldier boys, which was great fun, and made one feel very military and Church Militant. I'm awfully excited about Casie, and I wish I was at home for her Forthcoming; I've bought her a very jolly Kashmir dressing-gown sort of thing, which looks as if it had been made for Gil Chesterton, but is otherwise lovely. I suppose you'll be able to get it cut down. Tell me all about Badminton and the soshals. Your Paris must have been great fun, bar the crossing; isn't it strange that I am such a good sailor? It probably comes from Uncle Charles or Great Grandfather Pascoe[26]. Sea sickness must be the worst thing in the world, worse than toothache. I'm glad Dad had such a good shoot at Welbeck, & I hope he was in good form. The elections are pretty bad, aren't they; and what a terrific muddle everything seems to be in just at present. I suppose this will get to you just when Bill & Likky are returning to Oxford; give them my blessings. I haven't heard yet how Bill did in the Ireland.
My new excitement here is Shikar[27]; I go out on a pony with Auntie

---

[25] The Panshanger gamekeeper
[26] Charles Molyneux Grenfell (1857-1915): 'Uncle Charles'; Charles Pascoe Grenfell (1790-1867) was Julian's great grandfather
[27] To hunt animals for sport (OED)

Ka[tie]'s[28] rifle and a most villainous man that I have engaged, and if the buck are out in the open we all three walk up to them pretending to be natives or turnips, and if there is any cover the man holds the horse and waits while I advance upon my stomach. The first day I got a black buck, & a chinkara, which is a little buck – both good ones. The second day I got another chinkara. It is a glorious rifle, I must write to Auntie Ka[tie] about it. I can only get away at 3.0 pm; so there's only 2½ hrs light, and I've had great luck. The country simply swarms with buck, & you may kill them anywhere over 3 miles out from cantonments.

The Crown Prince of Germany[29] arrives here on Sunday, & there is going to be no end of a tomasher for him. All the pig in the district have been herded into a great marish or marsh, into which he will go down with elephants and shawms[30] and trumpets. He stays four days, during which he is kept constantly on the gallop, polo & pigsticking; he'll be pretty sore by the time he goes.

I like India & the military life more and more. There's been no polo lately, so I haven't yet made my début. Our bungalow is charming, and we've got such a nice piano, which Sclater Booth plays incessantly. What I don't know about Schumann & Schubert and Schopin isn't worth knowing. Makins is a good man: and there's nobody in the regiment whom I dislike very much. All love to you & the family. You don't know how domestic I feel out here! J.

12   28 Dec 1910   Royal Dragoons, Muttra   DE/Rv/C1138/10

Darling Casie

Thank you so much for your Christmas letter and present, whose frame and contents are equally lovely. What fun you must have had in Paris, in spite of floods and colds; I had a screaming cold all the first bit here, and I know how miserable they make one, and how badly you get them. Your clothes must have been very exciting; I wish I was at home to see them, and to stand by and applaud at your brilliant début. When are you presented at Court? Or

---

[28] Katrine Cecilia Compton, died 1913, widow of Francis 7th Earl Cowper
[29] The Crown Prince's father, Kaiser Wilhelm II, Emperor of Germany (1859-1941) was Commander in Chief of the British Army in 1910
[30] A medieval musical instrument of the oboe family, having a double reed enclosed in a globular mouthpiece (OED)

aren't you presented at Court? Perhaps that is quite out of date by now; I feel as if the last time I was in England was when King Charles was beheaded, God bless him; and everything does change so quickly. Are you presented first, and then go to balls; or do you go to balls first, and then, if you do well, get presented? Please write and tell me all about it; also whether you have had a hunt at Badminton, or in the Aylesbury vale; also how Dynamite is; also how Alan likes Buccaneer?

I wish you Luck and God Speed and all those sort of things tremendously, my dear. I've bought you a khaki dressing gown which came from Kashmir. A man turned up with it at the bungalow the other day with it, and some other trifles, and said that he was selling them dirt cheap at a loss to himself because his mother had died in Kashmir and he wanted to go back to see her. I offered him half what he asked, and he jumped at it, and said his mother would bless me daily as long as she lived. It's rather pretty, I think; I hope you'll like it. It looks as if it had been made for Mr Joel or Mrs Joel, but they are all like that, and I suppose there is some manner of cutting them down to a normal size.

You must be frightfully excited at coming out; I suppose it's a bigger jump than going to school, or anything that we do. I hope you'll do frightfully well, and marry the Duke of Slapcabbage, who will ask me to ride his horses, when you are about 25. We're all quite "wropped up" (Mr Barnes) in horses here. The day consists in riding to riding school, riding in riding-school, riding-back from riding school, changing into very smart tight black trousers with a yellow stripe, and a very tight red tunic, riding to stables, stables, riding back from stables, riding to luncheon, riding back from luncheon, changing into riding breeches, riding to foot-drill: foot-drill on FOOT; riding back from foot-drill, polo (on horseback), or stalking (on or behind a horse). Then tea, dinner, and bed. I've got one horse at present, from the ranks, a noble animal, which looks too beautiful, but is not very swift; and a pony, a grey Arab, which plays polo very well but falls down from sheer boredom when it is not playing polo. I'm also trying to buy the horse that won the Ooty Hunt Cup, whatever that may be, last year. Pigsticking is the greatest fun; it's very like pony-hunting in the New Forest, only one goes all out the whole time, and the country is worse. You get up alongside the brute, and wait till he turns in and goes at you; then if you are lucky he runs on to the spear, and if you are unlucky he runs on to you. It is no good prodding at him; you just hold out the spear and say your prayers and gallop, and the pig does the rest with great gusto. I've only had one ride yet, and the man with me practically finished the brute first shot; he was very sick when I hit him, and after that he gave up and lay down. He was a very good one. But the country is still very thick and blind, and lots of them get away without being seen.

The sun is glorious; but we've had it cold lately – bitter wind in the day, & very cold nights, evenings, and mornings. But in a fortnight it gets blazing hot, I believe, and then goes on getting hotter. The country is glorious – the whole place is rideable, you can go in a straight line for 20, 30, 40 miles; there are no fences, & so you just go straight over railway lines & ford straight through canals. There are buck, jackal, & pig everywhere. It's very like Heaven.

Goodbye; write and tell me about your busts. All love J.

13   5 Jan 1911   Royal Dragoons, Muttra   DE/Rv/C1135/564

Darling Mother

Were the Cinderella Tableaux a succès fou?[31] How I wish I'd seen them. They're the first I've missed, aren't they? I suppose Wuggins's theatrical talent had full play, and she enjoyed herself like anything in the glare of the footlights, even dressed in rags. Was her "figger looking pretty, & had she a "good colour"? And I suppose you are at Pans[hanger] now, in bitter gloomy weather; it is hard to imagine from here. Are you doing any more Xmas holiday busts? Avon or anywhere? And is Bill going to Wigglewobble? Please give my very very very best love to all the family; how I want to write to all of them, but when we are not riding horses we are cleaning them, or else chatting to German Princes. The Crown Prince came this week, and all the best polo ponies were cleaned up for him, and all the pig in the United Provinces herded together into a swamp. He is very bad at polo, and does not gallop too hard after pig; but he seems a very good fellow. We are all quite weary with bowing and scraping; we never get to bed before 2 am: my democratic feelings arouse themselves at 11 pm, and by 12 I am a Socialist, by 1 am an anarchist. Waterhouse said wearily last night that this was the worst of living in high society.

The Royals are delightful, all of them, almost without exception. They have got a very good language, mainly Hindustani: "galloping 8 annas", of the Crown Prince; "galloping 16 annas" = going like blazes; "not worth a sick

---

[31] A 'big hit' (Harrap's *New Shorter French and English Dictionary*)

headache"; "sold him a pup"; "chello, Bags" (?). And I love the documents presented monthly by one's bearer – 1 sofoha (sofa), RS 15; 1 chare (chair) RS 5 – head coular 3/8 – coular RS 2/0; Water Bite (bit) 2/8, Brom (broom?) & Basket 0/8, Bedden (Bedding?)
0/6, Majuring Tap (Measuring Tape?) 0/6 – 4 collars stirds 0/4 – I cirsie (saucer) 0/2. Cash to Master for shuting 1/11 – etc etc.
My great difficulty at present is to get horses or ponies. I've only got the one Arab pony "Bridegroom" at present, and one troophorse – "hired charger" – on which I do riding school. The Crown Prince has interrupted all stunts for us, as only old and cunning pigstickers ride and drive the pigs back toward him, and old and cunning polo players edge the ball gently up to him. So I've had no more pigsticking and no polo yet. The great excitement has been buckstalking, which I adore. I set off in the afternoons with a villaineous shikari in an ekka[32] drawn by a diminutive pony, stalk, and get back in the dark just before mess. The shikari has no English, but we converse by signs, and generally get a buck.
I <u>do</u> love Makins; he is the best man. And the military work is great fun, and leaves little time for writing letters, and none for sleeping. I can hardly see with sleep. Goodnight & <u>all</u> love to <u>everyone</u>. J.

14   12 Jan 1911   Royal Dragoons, Muttra   DE/Rv/C1135/565

Darling Mother

This is nothing but evil news. I. About the money. I'm afraid I have already written to Dad. I thought he had not yet arranged about my allowance, owing to Manesty's illness[33]. I do not know whether he has stopped paying in my old Oxford allowance to Barclay, as I closed my account with them before I left. I hope he has? The arrangement was that I should have £600 a year starting from July last 1910. That would have given me £500 altogether last year – half of the year at £400 a year and half at £600 a year. Dad gave me more than that; and what I wanted to do was to find out exactly how much more than £500 I had last year, and to take it off from my year's allowance, so that we start fair. <u>Idiotically</u> I did not bring my Barclay (Old Bank) Pass Book with me, so that I don't know exactly how much more than

---

[32] A small one-horse vehicle used in India (OED)
[33] Nicholl Manisty & Co were the family's solicitors (HALS: DE/P/EA/77)

£500 I did have last year. <u>Dad will know how much he gave me, and then he can dock it off from this year</u>.
Then I asked him if my allowance in future could be paid in half-yearly, because of all the expenses in buying ponies & horses just at first here.
Oh, I am so sorry and grieved and heart-sick about it, because I feel fully how extravagant I was about clothes; and now that you tell me how pinched we are, I can't bear it. I wish I had not written to Dad. But now the great thing is that we should start exactly right, and that I should not have any more than £500 last year. You will be able to see to this. It would be dreadful, considering the big allowance that you give me, that I should have pinched more.
II. About your appointment![34] It really is too disgusting for words, and so ridiculous; one looks upon all those sort of things as dead and gone, like "Chop off her head", or as only belonging to pantomime. But I suppose you have simply <u>got</u> to do it, which makes it all a very grim joke. And now that Casie is coming out. It really makes things pretty impossible. Shan't you be able to resign it pretty <u>soon</u>? It does make me angry.
Here everything goes gloriously. Yes, I <u>love</u> the smell of India, and the old native towns, which round here are quite untouched; and the pigsticking, which surpasses my wildest hopes, and the buckstalking, which is good too – and the whole thing. The Royals are really extraordinarily nice. It's got much warmer – December was really very cold – and the Christmas rains and the Crown Prince are both over.
Very very best love to the family. How did the Christmas busts go? And Pans[hanger]? Julian.

15   26 Jan 1911   Royal Dragoons, Muttra   DE/Rv/C1135/566

Dear Mother

I've just had a week in bed, which has been a "dern noosince" – but I'm feeling very well, and they are letting me get up again now. I took the most imperial toss out pigsticking, and was found firmly seated upon the ground, facing my horse, also firmly seated on the ground and facing me, with the reins gripped in both hands, and using the most filthy language, in blissful unconsciousness of Major McNeile, Mrs McNeile, & Mrs McNeile's young

---

[34] Lady Desborough became a Lady of the Bedchamber to Queen Mary in January 1911

lady friend, who had appeared on the scene. The horse, who is called The
Hawk, wanted to go one side of a bush, and I wanted to go the other; we
neither of us pulled quite hard enough, and he ended by taking to his native
element and flying it. Unluckily there were two more bushes on the landing
side, and these overturned us. We were left shaken but undaunted; and after
fair hands had washed my face with soda-water, we pursued the chasse, and
had a capital ride after a pig – my first good ride. I felt quite right; I went to
bed when we got home after the day, but I got up again next day and
performed my duties. The doctor saw me that day and asked what I had done
to my face (which was mostly bush) – I told him, and he felt my pulse and
said I'd got slight concussion, and sent me to bed, since when I have used no
other, and now my pulse is going right again.

I've read lots of your Shakespeare, and Natural Law in the Physical
World, a Ecco Homo, & Mr Clutterbucks Election, and The Florentine
Frame, and the Broken Road, and Letters to My Son[35] – and now I'm pretty
keen to get up and to it again. Its almost impossible to write with a pen in
bed – I hope you can read this. I'm not really in bed now though – they let
me get up 3 or four hours a day. They are all very kind & good Samaritans,
and come in and tell me about pigsticking etc. I love the colonel; he didn't
know whether he ought to write to you, but I told him not to.

Pans[hanger] must have been great fun. Where do all Casie's stunts come
off? Have you begun your bottle washing yet? I do think it's an indignity. I
wonder if Auntie Ka[tie] was stormier than usual at Pans[hanger] this year.
Best love to the family J.

---

[35] 'Natural Law in the Physical World': possibly *Natural Law in the Spiritual World*
by Henry Drummond (1883); *Ecce Homo: a survey of the life and work of Jesus
Christ* by Sir John Robert Seeley (1st edition, London & Cambridge, 1866); *Mr
Clutterbuck's Election* by Hilaire Belloc (1908); *The Florentine Frame* by Elizabeth
Robins (1909); *The Broken Road* by Alfred Edward Woodley Mason (1907); *Letters
to my Son* by Winifred James (1901). The last was a very popular book which ran to
eighteen editions by 1919

16   2 Feb [1911]   Royal Dragoons, Muttra   DE/Rv/C1135/520

Dear Mother

How did the great party and ball go? I'm simply longing to hear about it, in
your next letter. And Pans[hanger] seems to have been splendid, although a
slight atmosphere of crise ran through a letter I had from Auntie Ka[tie]. I'm
still in my room, but longing to sally out and read the Sir A[lfred] Lyall[36]
books, and find out exactly how India is run by those who run it, and what
prospects there are of a mutiny, and the answers to all the questionings in
your letter – directly they let me. They are keeping me very close still, but
I'm a great great deal better. What about my pulse, I wonder – did anyone
know its normal condition? At present it is doing lightning-change-artist,
practical-joke changes between 50 and 80, which are amusing at first but
boring afterwards. I've read thousands of books – Cloughs poems, Ring &
the Book, all Shakespeare and Bacon, and all the novels of the last ten years;
also Ecce Homo and Indian Ducks[37], both of which are most satisfying.
I'm sending you and Dad a belated Christmas present of two rugs, which I
think are too lovely – I do hope you'll like them. And TONS of love. I'm
writing this in the verandah of our bungalow, where they let me sit every day.
I've just got to sit quiet for a few days more & then I shall be able to get
back to work again; but I'm sure it's better to wait and get quite right before
starting again: so I am possessing my soul in peace.
How are you - & your eyes – and Dad - & Ca[sie] – and did Bill do very
badly in the Ireland, that no word is said of it? J.

---

[36] Sir Alfred Comyn Lyall (1835-1911), Anglo-Indian administrator and writer.
Author of *Verses written in India* (1889), *Asiatic Studies* (1882), *Rise and Expansion
of the British Dominion in India* (1883) amongst others
[37] Arthur Hugh Clough (1819-1861). Possibly *Poems, 1862* published posthumously
with a Memoir by F T Palgrave; *Ring and the Book* by Robert Browning (1868-9);
The Indian ducks and their allies by E C Stuart Baker (1908, reprinted from the
original published by the Bombay Natural History Society)

17   9 Feb 1911   Royal Dragoons, Muttra   DE/Rv/C1135/521

Dear Mother

Casie's bust must have been the success of the centuries – it <u>does</u> all sound amusing, especially Likky's trial, and you must feel very proud as hostess and organiser. I loved hearing about it all – but I've nothing to tell you about in return, & I feel a great fraud. But I'm ever so much better, and I get up now, and drive a pony about in the afternoons. It was very good getting out of the bungalow again. With any luck I ought to be riding again in a week or so, but they won't let me do much yet. They have all been too charming to me all the time, especially the Colonel.

I've read thousands of books – Ballantrae[38] again, which I think is the best of the lot at the beginning, but tailing away after the middle, & not good at the end? He's the best fun of all to read, RLS [*Robert Louis Stevenson*]. Also "An Irish Cousin" by the authors of the RM – "A Journey in Womanland" by Max O'Rell[39] – (they've got some of the best books in the library here) – "The Ring & the Book" (not very eagerly) – Cloughs Poems, which I loved. Oh, and lots more, no good ones. One queer one, very morbid, by Machen – ("Macken" – Ronny Knox's old joke). Do you know his books at all – I <u>rather</u> like them. I read "Natural Law in the Physical World" again; it reminds me of a thing I wrote at Oxford long ago, before I read it, when I had a down about philosophy.

The Abolition of Theology

-

Law Reigns! The Universe is spanned
By Reason, swayed by Nature's rod.
Philosophy shall rule the land;
We tread where Plato never trod;
We know why sand-eels live in sand,
And why the sea produces cod.
O, we will reason, hand in hand,
From earth to fire, from flame to clod; -
And, where we cannot understand,
We'll say "It must be God".

---

[38] *The Master of Ballantrae* by Robert Louis Stevenson (1889)
[39] *An Irish Cousin* by Edith Somerville and Violet Florence Martin, (1889, new edn 1903); 'A Journey in Womanland': *Rambles in Womanland* by Max O'Rell (1903)

You see I have to fall back upon the cast-off clothes of my brain to get the wherewithal to write a letter! But the only thing to do is to keep quiet and stick it out. Apparently head is always a long job, and one has to keep very quiet. And I'm <u>so</u> much better already.

Do you know that <u>sweet</u> little sonata in D minor by Grieg? He used to play it to Beethoven when he (Beethoven) felt melancholy. Sclater Booth is playing it to me now, with equal effect.

Sclater Booth is a fat boy. He is a very good boy. He would have made his fortune with a barrel-organ.

WOY, iTs AN **ORGIN**-GRINDER ('s DOG) (Mr B)

<u>Best</u> best love to Casie, & all thanks for her letter. How many more busts has she had since her glorious opening at Tap[low][40] or Badminton? And to Dad - & you - & everyone. J.

---

[40] Taplow Court, the Grenfell family house near Maidenhead, Berkshire

18   16 Feb 1911   Royal Dragoons, Muttra   DE/Rv/C1135/522

Dear Mother

Is Mansfield House[41] a great success? I'm afraid I've never been inside it, barbarian that I am; so I can't picture you there. But you are an awful blighter not to have sent me the New Machiavelli[42] – I love anything New, and I admire all the Ann Veronicas[43] tremendously, however beastly their minds are, and however naked their bodies. Do send it, as an Easter gift. Was your Windsor party fun? And is Casie still making the running at her breakneck pace? It reads like one of the wonders of nature, her career; one of the things which one takes by faith not works, like the Grand National being run at a faster average pace than the Derby. I'm getting less wild in the ed, but I'm not allowed to do anything vigorous yet, though I expect they'll let me ride in a day or two. It's just five weeks today that I fell, so I've had a great easy. What a <u>wonderful</u> book "Jude the Obscure" is (and <u>how</u> beastly in parts and how terribly gloomy as a whole)! I'd forgotten the joy of T[homas] Hardy – I read "A Pair of Blue Eyes" too, but didn't like it much. I can't do Robert Hitchens at all ("Belladonna") – nor Robert Browning much ("Ring & the Book") – except for one or two glorious bits. Have you read "A Japanese Artist in London"[44]; there's one really marvellous bit of writing in it, when he's in the hospital: it's the most vivid thing I've ever read, but quite a fluke on his part, I think.

I simply worship all the Royal Dragoons, who have been charming to me on my bed of sickness. The colonel is the nicest man in the world – also Mrs Makins, who is plain, but very pointful and with a heart of gold. I'll write you biographies of the regiment at a later date; but the general type is marked by a quiet and gentlemanly demeanour, under which is hidden a great deal of fire. They are all tremendous friends, and there are no factions or parties. Now I've written as much as is good for me. God bless Mummie and Daddie, Brothers and Sisters, and the carriage-horse (or are they defunct), make me a good boy, I DID say A-men.

---

[41] A house in London rented only for the season

[42] *The New Machiavelli* by H G Wells (1911)

[43] This must be a reference to the novel by H G Wells, *Ann Veronica* (1909), which deals with feminist issues and caused a sensation when it was first published. Presumably Julian is referring to suffragettes in general

[44] *A Pair of Blue Eyes* by Thomas Hardy (1873); *Bella Donna: A Novel* by Robert Hichens (1911); *A Japanese Artist in London* by Yoshio Makino (1910)

19   23 Feb 1911   Royal Dragoons, Muttra   DE/Rv/C1135/523

Dearest Mother

I am so miserable for Dad & you about poor Grandmother[45]; but what a
blessing it is that she was conscious when Dad went there on the Friday, and
that she was able to talk to him. Will Connie be very miserable about it?
and poor you, and poor Casie, with all your plans shattered. I know how
good Casie must have been about it; she would be. What will you do? I
hope you'll be able to sub-let Mansfield House.
I have always thought her (Blan) such a fine serene great figure, whenever I
have seen her; she was so full of peace & dignity, and I'm sure she was great
at the end.
I'm still "invaliding" here – but they let me hack about in the evenings now,
so I'm ever so much better; and longing to be up and to it again soon. I am
glad that Casie liked my cloak. Your Windsor party must have been the very
greatest fun; but I suppose you will be able to do none of the things now for
sometime? How sorry I am for you. I wonder how long your mourning will
go on – I don't know a bit. I wish you could have done the Opening of
Parliament. And Casie's two dinners & ball, & Moggie's kindergarten – and
all the invitations gone out – oh, I am sorry for you.
About the money – I can't understand it at all, because I certainly wrote to
Dad. I would not for the world bother him now: but he's given me no
money yet for this year. What I meant about last year is that I don't
remember exactly how much I had, but I think it was more than my due; I
have written to Barclays at Oxford to find out how much. I'm very "well-
off" & I didn't want any advance – only that he should give my allowance to
Cox's, which he hasn't done yet. But I'll write to him about it soon.
I've no news at all, except struggling to get right again! The doctor, Jones,
an Irishman, is a perfect darling, and a very good man, I think, at his job. I
go hacking with him in the evenings. Aren't the sunsets marvellous – new
every evening? And I'm loving the beginning of the heat. I've got a gigantic
stud now, 3 horses and 3 ponies, including His Majesty's "hired charger",
which I take from the troop and keep. They are all good beasts, I think; but
of course I've hardly ridden most of them yet.
Best best love to all the family – I do love getting your letters. J.

---

[45] Lord Desborough's mother Georgiana Caroline Grenfell ('Blan') died 2 February
1911

20   3 Mar   Train from Meerut   DE/Rv/C1135/524
**   [1911?]   to Muttra**

Dear Mother

The Muttra doctor, who is rather an ass, would not let me go back to work without seeing the divisional doctors at Meerut. So I proceeded there yesterday, to hospital; but only stayed there a night, as they pronounced me quite well & fit for work, and said I need not stay any longer: and now I am on my way back to Muttra. I'm really feeling well again now, and I've been getting better for a long time. It's six weeks since I fell on my head now, and I'm pretty sick of doing nothing; but I expect they were quite right to give me a long rest. I hope I shall get a clear slate now.

How angelic Casie must have been. Mansfield House must be very sad, without any of the intended festivities. How do you like the waiting (it's an awfully good name - who invented it?)? How long does mourning go on? The Royals were wonderfully good to me all the time when I was ill, and I do like them. The military ladies are charming too, which I suppose is rare. Mrs Makins is very arty; but she gave up painting for the inferior art of playing the violin, which was a pity. Sclater Booth gets more hideous and more loveable every day; I'm really very fond of him, & we get on capitally. My stud now numbers 6, 3 of each size. I haven't played 2 of the ponies yet, & I'm longing to see what they are like. The horses are all good; two gigantic raw-boned Walers, which have St V[itus'] dance[46] when they stand still and run away when they gallop after pig – and a nice tame troophorse, which I do riding school on. It's getting gloriously hot – but I expect even I shall cease blessing the sun soon. I'm frightfully keen to stay at Muttra for the hot weather, and go up to the hills just before the rains; they say that nobody gets ill at Muttra in the hot weather, and everybody in the rains. Besides which it is the best time for pigsticking now; and if I went up to the hills I should have to sell all the horses and ponies without having had one proper ride on them. I think I shall stay down alright, as all the doctors here said that there is not the least reason why I should go.

The Regiment has been definitely ordered to leave Muttra for S Africa – but

---

[46] St Vitus' dance is a non-technical name for Sydenham's chorea, a neurological disorder that occurs in the course of acute rheumatic fever, involving irregular involuntary movements of the limbs and face, after Thomas Sydenham (1624-89), English physician

no time mentioned, so that it is uncertain whether we stay for the Durbah[47] or not. I hope we do; I do love society so. Why don't you bring Casie out for it, and marry her to a Rajah with tiger-shooting enough for Ribblesdale himself?[48] Can't you use your influence with the Queen while she is putting on her stays, and persuade her to let us stay? I have assured Makins that you would. We go to Pretoria when we do go to Africa, which I suppose is a terribly soshal place. You can't think what a paradise Muttra is to the unsoshal; it is an ideal place in every way, and I shall be frightfully sorry to leave it. I saw on my evening ride the other day: 2 real live crocodiles, 18 pigs, 3 blackbuck, 1 wild cat, 2 foxes, 6 jackal, and a bird of paradise: it was enough to make anyone well.

Are you going to send me the new Wells book, or rather have you sent it? I've read Emerson & Job this week – they are rather good as antidote to each other.

Its quite impossible to write in this train, it jolts so. It's a 3rd class train, but I bribed the guard, & secured a carriage for myself and my bed by ejecting a crowd of natives. They do "bweave in one's face", the natives, don't they. I love the way one carries one's bed about everywhere here; but it quite spoils the miracle of the man with the palsy for me[49]. I had always imagined him as doing Sandow feats[50] with a four-poster.

All love to the family from J.

21   6 Mar 1911   Royal Dragoons, Muttra   DE/Rv/C1133/46

Dear Dad

I hope you are all well & flourishing at Tap[low]. I was bad with my head for rather a long time here - never really bad, but it took a long time getting quite right again. However, now I am in full swing again, hard at work; and it is great fun to be out again and about, after a long lie-up in the bungalow with nothing to do. But I expect they were quite right to keep me quiet till I

---

[47] The court kept by an Indian ruler; a public audience or levee held by a native prince, or by a British governor or viceroy in India (OED)
[48] Thomas Lister, 4th Baron Ribblesdale (1854-1925), famous for his love of hunting (ODNB)
[49] Reference to a miracle performed by Jesus (Matthew, ch 9; Mark, ch 2; John, ch 5)
[50] The name of Eugen Sandow (1867-1925), Russo-German exponent of physical culture, used as a type of strong man (OED)

got quite well. It is getting gloriously hot now - but not too hot yet. The pigsticking is just beginning to be at its best; and the Kadir Cup comes off on the 20th of this month. I've got two horses in for it, both very good ones, one of them a former winner; but I'm afraid my steeds will be a great deal better at the game than their "owner up", as I've only had two days so far, and never stuck a pig myself yet! But it will be great fun all the same. A lot of the regiment are going in for it. I've not played polo lately, as all the swell players are alway competing in tournaments, & the game languishes in their absence. So I am frightfully backward at everything, owing to my bad luck in getting ill at first. But I simply love the life and the country; I don't think I shall ever get sick of horses, even living so "wrapped up" in them as we do here; and the work is very interesting; and everything is so new and queer in the way of man and beast and bird. I've shot some buck, but I have not yet mastered the new .275 rifle which Katie gave me; I shoot much too high with it, I sally out on a pony, followed by an "ekka", which Sclater-Booth and I own jointly, with the rifle in it and a most villainous-looking shikari; we scour the country and shoot whatever comes in the way. There are lots of black buck - and natives - everywhere; the bullets go for miles and miles across the plain, and the buck run one way and the natives the other, leaving their dead behind. The buck are pretty confidential, and let you walk within 150 yds of them, or nearer, if you push a pony in front of you, or black your face, or put on a turban, and pretend to be an inhabitant of the country. The great drawback of it all is that one has to pay ready money for everything. Buying the ponies and horses, and buying clothes for servants and services [?], and getting all the things one wants to start with, has proved a heavy drain on my pocket. Instead of paying the bills when my allowance comes in, like I used to in England, I have now paid all my bills without any allowance yet to pay them with; and the result is that I am £350 overdrawn. Of course when I sell my horses it will bring a lot back again. But I'm in a very bad way at present; and they charge 1% per month interest, which runs up very heavily. I'm awfully sorry to be a "bagar", especially after you have given me all my trousseau; but I wonder if you could pay in my allowance now to Cox's - so that I can get clear. You see I started here without any capital at all. If you could give me the £440 now, at Cox's (16 Charing Cross), I can manage alright; otherwise the interest will get so big that I shall be in difficulties. I thought it better to tell you at once. I do hate begging, but I think you will see that my stress is only temporary! Of course I am as rich as a duke on the big allowance you give me, and grateful according; and

I only don't want to see it all go in interest to a nigger!
The Regiment goes to Africa now for certain; but for a long time there
seemed to be a doubt whether we stayed on in India, or went to Africa, or
went home. Now it seems that we go <u>before</u> the Durbah, probably October;
to Pretoria, which will be very "soshal" after Muttra, where we are alone, and
monarchs of all we survey. I wonder what house you will have in London in
the summer? I see there have been great doings about the Port of London
Bill[51]; I hope you'll be successful. How is Mummie liking her "waiting"?
And I wonder if Billy boxed against Cambridge this year, or if he refrained,
and gave up bashing for literae humaniores?[52] Please give my very best love
to all the family, and tell Moggy that my bungalow is full of elephants and
little "bullets" for her.
All love Julian.

22   7 Mar 1911   Muttra, India   DE/Rv/C2816/23

Telegram: Perfectly well.

23   8 Mar 1911   Royal Dragoons, Muttra   DE/Rv/C1135/525

Dear Mother

I wish I could have gone to the Follies with you. I loved just the same
things, and I was just as touched by Baked Potatoes; I thought it was so odd,
in the middle of all the laughing, to come suddenly onto sadness & pathos
with a jerk. What <u>real</u> artists they are, aren't they? Don't you think that the
Pageant, too, is quite a different <u>sort</u> of fun to their old fun. I was admiring
the wonderful <u>art</u> of it, the exactness and edge of the caricatures, as often as
just laughing at it. I like the rhyme about the defunct Queen Anne, and I love
the storming of the castle at the end – but on the whole the pageant is not so
<u>funny</u> as their old things? And the cannibal supper not only funny, but also
so real that it was uncanny and almost frightening!
How do George Brod & Guy Charteris earn their living at present?[53] I loved
the photograph of Ego, but I could not help thinking that the point of your

---

[51] The Port of London Act, passed in 1908, established the Port of London Authority
[52] The humanities, ie Latin and Greek
[53] 'George Brod': Hon George St John Brodrick (later 2nd Earl of Midleton) entered
Balliol in 1907/8. He was the son of (William) St John Fremantle Brodrick, 1st Earl

sending it to me lay in the flattering likeness of the other party? Has Dad really harboured Old Old Sicky under his roof without attempting to poison him. How <u>did</u> you persuade him? Do send me the latest Margots. And Casie hunting with the Jews – how low the family honour has fallen; but what fun she must have. Things here are most flourishing now; I am back at work, (for all this last week), and frightfully well again. I sent a cable today, because I thought perhaps you would fuss, getting six weeks letters with me laid up. It was bloody enough, but I expect they were right to keep me absolutely quiet. It is pretty good getting about again – we pigstick tomorrow. I've been very lucky in my pigsticking horses; they are both capital; and the ponies are good too; but I've had none of my allowance yet, so the result is that I am heavily in debt! Of course when I sell them I shall recuperate, but everything is ready m[oney] in this country, and instead of keeping the bills against the time the money arrives, one has to have the money before the bills. So I've written to Dad to ask him if he can advance me £400 now; I hated doing it, but it is better than running up a huge interest out here. Don't you think so?

We go to Pretoria, probably in October next; I wish we were staying longer here. Work comes as a great but not unpleasant shock to me after 5 months complete idleness! We really have to do a great deal – foot drill & riding–school, and most of the ordinary regimental work as well. I'm longing for the New Machiavelli; I'm still in the callow stage of thinking that the Newest is the Best – New New Art & New New Woman -: I'm afraid you have come to the wise view that there is nothing new under the sun? I hated Letters to My Son – it's terrible ee-wee mannie, or "eye-wash", as they call it here. I can't do Mason – he is a rank materialist.

How is Moggie? She will become a little higher than the angels, or else a half-wit, if her brain goes on developing at the present rate. Give her my very very best love - & Casie, & Bill, who will have returned for "the hols" when this gets to you. I've heard nothing lately about Auntie Ka[tie] lately, or from her. Tell me the latest snippets from the Court, and all about all the former marriages and wiles of His Majesty. Are you having fun? And well? And are your eyes alright? All all love from J.

Just off pigsticking.

---

of Midleton (1856–1942), politician. His mother was Hilda Charteris (d 1901), daughter of Lord Elcho, later 8th Earl of Wemyss and 6th Earl of March (ODNB). The Brodrick family home was at Peper Harow, near Godalming, Surrey (see letters 251 and 257). The Hon Guy Lawrence Charteris (1886–1967) was cousin to George

8 pm. Just in. I slew my first pig today, at one blow, like Jack the G[iant]-K[iller]. He was a very big one, with good tuskes. I was riding the Hawk, who went like a locomotive, and knows no fear.

24   16 Mar [1911]   Royal Dragoons, Muttra   DE/Rv/C1135/526

Dear Mother

I've just got Machiavelli, and I'm in the middle of it; but I don't like it quarter as much as even Ann Veronica. This one does not even pander to the lower passions, it just catalogues dreary varieties of viciousness. I see Wells point, that if naked bodies play a large part in your own life, you ought to acknowledge it in talking or writing about your life; but I don't see why you should talk of them as scientific diagrams, numbered & classified. I don't quite agree with you that if a man talks about those things he doesn't really mean them; I rather agree with the general principle of the book, which is to keep no mental cloak whatsoever either in yourself or to other people; but I hate his method of making things ugly because he wants to make them bare; it seems so unnecessary & gratuitous. Does he (Wells) approve of the man, or disapprove of him? I haven't read enough yet to judge.
"Ecce Homo" I did <u>not</u> like; it seemed to me the old thing of starting out after Truth, only getting to Compromise & Second-Best, and then ramming that down one's throat as Truth.
I'm sorry Bill didn't come off in the Ireland; I've just had a glorious letter from him. Is he riding in the Balliol Grind? What fun you & Casie will have had there. Casie's London life sounds most happy & strenuous – also Moggy's! I love her geometry – she will knock sparks out of Euclid. Is Nan good? How is your waiting? You have given me no boudoir secrets as yet, which is most disappointing. You might as least play Harriet for your own offspring. I am very flourishing here; very much wrapped up in my horses & my work. I start tomorrow for the Kadir Cup. My two pigstickers, Caesar & the Hawk, are fit & well, & say Ha all day long.
All love to the family from J.

25   23 Mar [1911]   Train, Delhi to Muttra   DE/Rv/C1135/527

Dear Mother

We are just returning from the Kadir Cup, which was the greatest fun – four days in a very jolly camp in a spinney on a hill overlooking mile & miles of low open-country along the Ganges; about 70 people, 1 man 1 tent; & the horses in another camp next door. We got up at 7, and were out till 7 every day. It is rather a good sight, the long line of beaters, with the two heats who are going to ride in front, and a line of 40 elephants, with all the other people on them, behind. The actual pigsticking is rather poor sport, as people just race for first spear, to prick the pig, not to kill him; and of course there is a tremendous lot of luck in it, as the pig probably jinks, & the man who is first up very seldom gets first spear. The man who won this year fell in <u>two</u> of his heats, at the start; he got on again and came up behind & the pig jinked right back to him. I made a very bad miss on "Caesar", & got thrown out first round with both horses. I enjoyed the five days tremendously. Ten of the regiment went up, but nobody did any good, which was rather sad.
Bromilow won on Battleaxe (aren't they good names for man and horse?) – we are all returning tonight, and we go back to duty tomorrow.
It's a frightfully shaky train, & I'm afraid you won't read this, but it's my only chance for the mail.
<u>How is Bill</u>? I do hope he was alright for Honour Mods; but what sickening bad luck for him. However I suppose Lyne S[54] will put him alright soon.
But it was rotten luck that it should just clash with his running.
Your quiet fun in London sounds very good, & it must be great fun for Casie hunting with the Jews.
I'm absolutely <u>dog</u> tired. We don't get in till 12 tonight, & the rack w[oul]d be mild compared to this train. Everything is most flourishing at Muttra, and I believe I shall stay down there for the hot weather and the pigsticking, which is great fun. Mrs Makins goes home directly; the Colonel goes too some time this summer, I think, for a month or two. A new new subaltern arrives this week – name Hewett[55]. His father is a big-wig out here, Governor of something or other.
What a <u>rotten</u> book Machiavelli is – I utterly agree with you about it.
All all love to you & Dad from J.

---

[54] Dr Lyne Stivens, Master at Balliol
[55] Bunty Hewett, son of Sir John Prescott Hewett, (1854–1941) (ODNB). See letter 35 below

26   30 Mar 1911   Royal Dragoons, Muttra   DE/Rv/C1135/528

Darling Mother

Your wire has just come, and reminded me that it is my birthday, which I had entirely forgotten till this moment! All blessings to you, too. I'm just back from pigsticking – I didn't know I was going out today – so I've got 10 minutes to write my mail in, instead of 10 hours. So I can only send all love to the family, and congratulations to Dad on his big speech, which monopolised the Daily Mail[56]; it must have been a splendid occasion. How has Bill done in Mods? How long do you stay in London, I wonder? I suppose you go down to Tap[low] for the hols. Best love to Casie, and all thanks for her letter describing her gay life. How is Mogg? How are you? I am gloriously well again now. We had a capital day's pigsticking yesterday; I enjoy it beyond all things anywhere. Terribly busy; I've got my promotion exam for 1ˢᵗ lt [lieutenant] in a week or two – and all kinds of things.
Please thank Dad frightfully for paying me in £300. It's awfully good of him. All love Julian.
Its getting werry OK now but not too 'ot.

27   6 Apr [1911   Royal Dragoons, Muttra   DE/Rv/C1135/529

Dear Mother

I'm in bed with "a touch of fever", but not a bit bad. I hope to get about again in a day or two. It only came on yesterday. Only I can't write because it makes my head spin. And I wanted to write so much this mail. Is your fluenzy over? And Dad's? What fun he must have had fishing. All love from J. PTO. About my allowance – Dad paid me £600 last year. The arrangement was that my £600 a year should begin in July last; up to July I was on £400 a year. So that last year I got £600, and ought only to have had £500 – ie, I only get £500 this year. Is this clear?

---

[56] On the 'Declaration of London', relating to the rules of naval warfare; Lord Desborough spoke to it on 8 March 1911 and on later occasions. See HALS: DE/Rv/F13, pp35-47, for cuttings from several newspapers about the speech; it includes an illustration from the *Daily Graphic*, 28 June 1911, showing Lord Desborough presiding over a meeting of mercantile and shipping interests. See also letter 28 below

28   11 Apr 1911   Royal Dragoons, Muttra   DE/Rv/C1133/47

Dear Dad

I opened the papers the other day, and found them <u>entirely</u> taken up by your Declaration of London speech! A few paragraphs on the Lang-Langford fight was the only other matters in the Daily Mail! It must have been a very good speech; and rather fun to make? Or did you hate it? Did it take long to make up, or did you trust to the inspiration of the moment, and speak it straight off? The peroration must have been prepared, or premeditated. Please accept my "hearty congratulations".

I hope your "flue" is better now; it must have been the greatest bore and misery. Did you have fun fishing the Garry with Portland?[57] It must have been pretty cold. The sultriness here is getting quite remarkable, but they say it is nothing to what comes later! Already I am in a state of perpetual flux, like one of Heraclitus' atoms[58]. I heard from you saying that you had paid in £300 of my allowance, which is awfully good of you. Cox's wrote to me next week saying they had got £200 from you. I have looked up my old accounts ~~to make sure~~ with Barclay Oxford and I find that you paid me £600 last year. The arrangement was that my £600 allowance should begin in July only – so that by rights I should only have had £500, (being on £400 for half the year, £600 the other half).

I want to make this clear, & not pinch, <u>ie only £500 is due to me this year</u>. All love to the family, who are flourishing, I hope. I'm very well here, also my stud; polo and pigsticking hard, each 3 days a week. I've had great luck, & got two of the biggest pig of the year; I enjoy it above anything. Money is bad at present, because of buying the stud; but I shall be alright when I sell. The Colonel is going to England soon. I wonder if you'll see him.
Best love from Julian.

---

[57] William John Arthur Charles James Cavendish-Bentinck, 6th Duke of Portland (1857-1943), a great friend of Lord Desborough who wrote Portland's obituary in 1943 (HALS: DE/Rv/F132/13)

[58] Heracleitus (c540 to c480 BC) was a Greek philosopher. He argued that 'all things are in a state of flux' (*OCCL*)

29   12 Apr [1911]   Royal Dragoons, Muttra   DE/Rv/C1135/530

Dearest Mother

Thank you awfully for your letter, and all the books – and the soap, which has just this moment put in its appearance. I think the Rowton House Rhymes[59] are quite good – not better than that; and I like some of Maurice's, especially The Blue Harlequin[60]. Thank you awfully for sending them: and the soap looks too delicious.

I am sorry to hear about your "flue"; I so know all about your "symptoms", and sympathise with them. And what joy for you being well again now – your letter sounds such a "well" letter. It was "good for you" not having nerives [nerves?], wasn't it. I'm not sure that I don't agree with you about the "alternative treatments".

Pigsticking, polo, and work are going hard here, and there's really no time for anything else. We are just off pigsticking now; I've got The Hawk, Caesar, John Kino (pony), & Pompey out, and very fine they looked starting away. We take our tents & beds, and stay each night at a different dâk bungalow[61], on different canals through different jungles. It's a 3-day show today – and such fun.

I wish I ever had time to write a good letter, in reply to your glorious ones! This scrap fills me with shame, but takes you immeasurable love. Casie's bust at Oxford must have been the most dashing thing of the century. Now I've just got to go. How's that ruffian Mogg? Please thank her for her letter. All all love from Julian.

30   nd   Royal Dragoons, Muttra   DE/Rv/C1135/531
[17 Apr 1911]

Mama dear

Am not I unfortunate? For I have got jaundice. It's such a ridiculous disease to get in a country where you don't notice anything under typhoid; it's like having nettle rash, only very bloody. I was never the very least bad, and much better when I became bright yellow all over, like "God's good gift to

---

[59] *Rowton House Rhymes* by William Andrew Mackenzie (1911)
[60] Maurice Baring (1874-1945), a 'Soul' and close friend of Lady Desborough (DNB)
[61] A house for the accommodation of travellers at a station on a dâk route, a form of transport by relays of men or horses stationed at intervals

loneliness" – as I am at this minute. Thank you awfully for giving me so much news in your letter; I'm thrilled about Bill and Auntie Ca – I thought he'd try on the confidence trick once too often! I had no idea the fires were still even smouldering; but it'll soon come alright? Poor Auntie Ka[tie], she seems to have been very ill all the time in Italy?

Up till 4 every night seems a rather bad "rest cure" for you? It must make you terribly tired, and it doesn't seem like giving you a chance, after you have been so ill and miserable. But you get a long rest before the season proper, don't you? You never told me how long you stay on at Mansfield H[ou]se. I suppose Conn goes there for the summer; then where is our Town Residence? I do hope you'll be properly well and fit for the strain of that. Have you got good Easter soshals at Tap[low] – I mean have you had them – I always forget.

I wrote about a fortnight ago about last year's allowance, etc. I'm glad I wrote before you did, or you'd have thought I was trying to chisel my parents! I always knew that I'd had too much, and I'd have written before, only I never knew exactly how much I'd had, (having left my Bank Book at home!) – till I wrote to Barclay to find out. Yes, I shall do royally; I only made the mistake of thinking myself frightfully rich at first, like one always does at the beginning of a new regime, and buying very good horses and ponies at big prices (which I ought to get back alright). Yes, I think quarterly is best; I'll ask Dad.

Its fairly 'ot here now, and of course we are on all the hot weather arrangements, punkahs[62] and early hours. It's only out pigsticking when one goes on up till luncheon, and even then we don't start again till 4. I was out pigsticking when this foul disease broke upon me (1 week today); "the Major" observed me being frightfully 'ick from the impatient back of "the Hawk" as we were in ambush, and sent me home at once. On Sunday I turned quite bright yellow, and today I am quite perky again and "taking my food" – but not allowed to go out yet, of course. After this I'm going to the Hills for a fortnight, to a place called Chikrata, near Missourie; but I want to come down here again as soon as I can, for the pigsticking, which I'm quite mad about. But it's rather good fun going to quite new and cold country for a bit, and I've always wanted to see the Hills. There are a few of the regiment up there, and some of the 60th. But it's a tiny station, very dull, and I'm afraid there won't be any soshals at all!

---

[62] A portable fan or large swinging fan suspended from the ceiling worked by a cord

The Colonel has gone home; I had a yellow talk to him two days ago before he went, and loved him; I like him more & more, the more I know him. They grumble at him a good deal, and say he's inefficient; but I doubt it very much. Polo is all over now, of course; we put up a very good game against the 10th (winners) in the inter-regimental, and everyone played as they had never played before. I wish I had seen it. Lots of the regiment have gone to England – the Steeles, Major, & Mrs, who is the dasher, and was very good to me while I was ill; I wonder if you'll see her; I told her that you knew she was coming home – also Mrs Makins (a darling) – Fitzgerald – Edwardes (son of the Gaiety man, & quite charming)[63] - Tidswell (with a broken leg), etc.

Inspector of Forests in South America sounds really the ideal profession, & Guy is just their man. Please give my love to little George Brod. We have just got a very jolly new subaltern here, called Hewett, whose father was at Balliol with Dad: I like him very much indeed. I'm so glad Casie is loving her balls and things; please give her reims and reims of love from me. Also Mogg, who I'm sure is very jealous of her. I do hope you're quite well now? All love from J.

PTO It's worth writing another envelope to tell you what I'd forgotten – HOW I loved the Belloc[64] verses, even in the clutch of jaundice. What real tenderness and enthusiasm and madness they have got in them, and "char-r-m". I've never enjoyed a book so much. I like "the South Country" almost the best, and "Balliol Men", and "the Ring", and "Auverquat", & "Fille-la-Haine" – the serious ones better than the humorous ones. I think he's very nearly a great poet, if not quite.

---

[63] D'Arcy Edwardes, who had returned to England, was the son of George Edwardes (1855-1915), the musical theatre producer, who worked at both the old Gaiety Theatre in the Strand and the new Gaiety Theatre at the Aldwych (ODNB)

[64] (Joseph) Hilaire Belloc (1870-1953). Went to Balliol. Published novels, verses and travel books including *Cautionary Tales* (1907). One of his best known poems was 'To the Balliol Men Still in Africa' (ODNB)

31   20 Apr [1911]   Royal Dragoons, Muttra   DE/Rv/C1133/48

Dear Dad

Thank you very much for your letter about my allowance; and even more for £300, which Cox's have acknowledged! (They only said £200 at first, & added £100 next mail).

I had written a fortnight ago about last year's allowance; I knew you had given me too much, but not exactly how much, because I had lost my Barclay Pass Book; so I wrote to them to find out. The odd £10 was for the "Boath Shootings"! You gave me £600 instead of £500 (last year, 1910); so that £500 only is due to me this year, of which you have already paid £300. And thank-you very much. I am a very rich and lucky boy.

I have just had jaundice, which is a rather ridiculous complaint; I am as yellow as an old pea. I'm going up to the hills as soon as I get of a natural colour, just for a week or two, to a place called Chikrata, near Missourie. I'm rather glad to see the hills, but I shall be glad to get down here again for the pigsticking, which I like tremendously.

It's awfully exciting about you going to Canada; are you really starting on Aug 9th? How long shall you stay there? What fun it will be; I wish I could go with you. Mother never told me anything about it. It must be a most glorious country, to see for the first time. I hope you'll have a good time there.

The Colonel has just gone home for 3 months; I wonder if you will see him; he's a ripper. Also several more of the regiment have gone; but there's still polo 3 days a week. It's getting very OT, & I'm not sorry to be going to the cool for a little.

All love to the family. I suppose Mogg thinks herself terribly cut out by Casie now?

Best love from Julian.

P.T.O. I hope your flue got better quickly? It must have been mis for you being in London with it. Did you go on hating Mansfield House as much as ever? Do tell me all about your fishing with Portland; and all about your Canada expedition in August.

32   23 Apr 1911   Royal Dragoons, Muttra   DE/Rv/C1138/11

Casie dear I've loved your last letters, about your Oxford drag days and other
excitements; my word, what an adventurous and crowded life you lead
nowadays, and what fun it must be for you. The horse Mac supplied you
doesn't seem to have been very princely! I never rode the first Water Eaton
line – the second suited Buccaneer better – but I've watched other people
over it, and all over it. I wonder if you've had any more days with the Jews,
bath salts and chocolates and all? I forget when I wrote to you last; but
anyhow since then it has got steadily hotter, until one wonders at its sheer
perseverance. Also I've had jaundice. Also I stuck a very large pig; which
broke my spear as it were matchwood, and took to a canal, like Mac's horse;
we pursued it on foot through the waters, and an Irishman called Houstoun
pinned it to the bank, saying calmly "Gad, I thought he'd be after escapin
us"; meanwhile I beat it on the head with my broken spear, until we had the
better of it.

My stable is now full – three pigstickers & three polo ponies – "The Hawk"
& "Caesar", both big and fast, both pullers, both dancers like Mord Halling –
great ugly rawboned water horses, well-bred and common-looking like all
waters. "John Kino" – brown water pony with very large coffin-shaped head,
but a great brain; pigsticks, plays polo, & pulls a buggy (which one calls
"tumtum" here). The polo ponies are rather what one expects polo ponies to
be, or very much the revers.

I'm just off to the hills for a week or two, to get less yellow, (being at present
mustard-colour). It'll be rather good fun seeing hills, after sea & plain for
the last 6 months; and no mean hills either. But it's a rotten station (called
Chikrata) and I want to get back for the pigsticking, which is the best. We all
take the horses and tents out, dump them all down together in a wood, and
sleep there. Then next day we pigstick north and east, & the day after south
& west – a long line of natives beating, making an appalling noise with
drums and tins and guns, and several "heats" of 2 or 3 riders in front or at the
sides of the line. The country is long grass, or thorn jungle (thorn bushes
about 5 yds apart), and sometimes open fields with banks and ditches
between them. You have to go absolutely all out the whole time, & just let
the horse choose his own way – which he does a great deal better than one
would oneself. The pig goes as fast or faster than the horse for ¼ of a mile –
after that you catch him up. He jinks away from you generally once or twice,
and the third time charges in at you – that's when you spear him; so what you
have to do is just to ride on alongside him with your spear held out, gradually

edging in closer. You would love it, I think.

It is such a delicious sunny day here today; and quite warm. We get up 5.30 now, work 6 – 11, sleep 11 – 4, polo 5 – 7. In the middle of the day you shut up the bungalow, and pretend it's cool. When you wake up from restless sleep you find your head in a little pool. "This state of affairs is perfectly crool".

Where are the gay family going to live in the summer? And where have you been this Easter in the way of Statelies? Write and tell me all about your doings.

All love from Julian.

33   25 Apr 1911   Royal Dragoons, Muttra   DE/Rv/C1135/532

Dear Mother

In your last letter you were just leaving your gay life in London; you must have been rather glad of a rest; when do you start again – and where – in what glorious town residence for the summer months? It's a good thing Casie has taken so kindly to "late hours". Are you better now, or are you still at 5 st 2½ lbs? With these mails condolences for illness are always just 4½ weeks late, and arrive when the sufferer has just got a lease of new life and heartiness. I hope this one will. I'm longing for your 'poor darling' jaundice letters. I'm "nicely able to sit up and take a little arrow-root and water now"; in fact, tomorrow I start for Chakrata and the everlasting hills, half on sick-leave and half on duty. I'm still as yellow as a pea, and it's been a bore losing another fortnight; but it was only bloody at first, the first 2 days. Ave you ever ad it, as Mog would say? Sixty of our men are at Chakrata, under (Captain) Chapman, "the bo'sun", whom I've never seen; by report he is short and ugly and amorous and a valetudinarian[65]. I shall stay up there for about a fortnight, I expect, doing his dirty jobs for him, and getting white again; also working hard for "A" & "B" promotion exams (to 1st lieutenant). It's all very well talking about jaunts along the frontier, but there's enough to do and to spare for the pore Varsity man at first, when he finds himself knowing nix[66] nought nothing about soldiering, in the middle of people who

---

[65] One who is constantly or excessively concerned about the state of his health (OED)

[66] Another word for 'nothing' (OED)

have got a year's very hard work at Sandhurst[67] in their insides, and have really got the whole thing at their fingers' ends. So I've really got to know my own country first; and besides, the political views which you invest for me are certain to be better than any I could produce. What shall I do if on the strength of them the WO [*War Office*] suddenly send for me for my opinion as frontier expert?

After Chakrata I come back here again; where the heat is already very hot. About the regiment – "Mouse" Tomkinson is adjutant and very capable and very severe to the young officers; but he melts a good deal in private life. "Kid Charrington" looks just like a jockey fallen upon evil times, as a result of overindulgence in gin. Do you know the advertisement of "Flon de Dindigul" cigars? He is very gentle and quiet though, with great charm, and rather a wag. Walter Hodgson is a fine soldierly young fellah, very cheery, very good at his job, very popular; he has only just arrived, & he looks a ripper. George Steele is a cross between an ascetic and a criminal to look at; frightfully keen on the regiment and good at the books, and always poking his fun at someone in a surreptitious way. Fitzgerald I don't like so much as I used to at Eton; he has become a polo heygate[68], which is a terrific thing to be. I like D'Arcy Edwards of the Gaiety (now gone home) and Bunty Hewitt, the latest-joined, about best of the lot. I promise you that I'll get photographed soon – only there's nobody in Muttra good enough for the full-dress business, which always needs a genius.

It was really supreme that that particular letter of Bill's was put by Bart among your budget – or do you think that the bulk of Bill's correspondence is of that type. It's the most amusing thing that has ever happened. I'm glad he has been downing the Avon salmon as well; is he now alright in his innards? How are the Royal Family? Is it fun driving in processions and such like? Have you seen Charlie Lister[69] lately, & how is he? Also do you know if Tommy Lascelles[70] is abroad now, and if so when where why and how long?

---

[67] 'The Royal Military College, near Camberley, Surrey

[68] This either means 'conventional' or 'commonplace' (Mosley, pp255-6; MacKenzie, p86)

[69] Hon Charles Lister, (1888-1915) only son of the 4th Baron Ribblesdale, Julian's contemporary at both Eton and Oxford

[70] Sir Alan Frederick 'Tommy' Lascelles (1887–1981), Julian's contemporary at Oxford, later Private Secretary to King George VI and Queen Elizabeth (ODNB). Tommy wrote an entry on Julian for the *Dictionary of National Biography* which he sent to Lady Desborough for her approval in 1926 (HALS: DE/X789/C48)

Also what is Viola's address in Milan, if at all, and how long; also state
whether married or single? and if married to whom?
All all love from Julian.

34   3 May 1911   Chakrata, India   DE/Rv/C1135/533

Dear Mother

Your soap arrived last week; it is <u>too</u> delicious, and just exactly 1 shade
darker yellow than my skin which it cleanses. In use it turns mauve, and the
colour effect is simply dazzling. Also your letter was sent on up here after
me, and the Rees book, which looks awfully good and clear & concise; I've
just begun it. Your last week in London must have been the greatest fun –
and I <u>am</u> glad you've got rid of your 'flue; and done your writing pro tem![71]
I wish I could have seen the Windsor drawing, with you – and I wish I could
have come to Tap[low] for one week with the holiday family! And Likky
with his awoken intellect! What fun you will have.
The Makins address is 180 Queen's Gate; she is a <u>ripper</u>, and you'll love her.
The Steeles live at something like 160 (?) Chester (??) Square (???). I'll let
you know when I get back. I don't know what you'll think of her; she lives
in a sort of social ecstasy, but has a kind heart. All the fairies have left
Muttra now.
I came up here just a week ago – starting from Muttra Wed, & getting here
on Thursday. It was wonderful seeing hills again; and breathing air again.
Aren't they <u>wonderfully</u> beautiful, the Himalayas; it's like going into a new
world. I arrived at Dehra Dun early in the morning (Thursday), and then
drove up the 60 miles in a "tonga"[72], which took all day. I got here after
dark. It's a jolly little station, in a gorgeous place. Chapman (Capt) of the
regiment is here, and is really a great dear; a confirmed valetudinarian, and
an erotomaniac, and fat and ugly and cheerful and humorous. The 4th
Battalion of the 80th are here, & we live in their mess; they are rippers. Do
you know the colonel, A R Stuart-Wortley? My bloody jaundice returned on
me full blast the first day up here (I had not got rid of it when I started) - & I
had to take to bed again: but now I'm up again, & walking the hill with ease
and grace; and they think I'll be fit to go back in a fortnight or so. Today I'm

---

[71] For the time being
[72] A light and small two-wheeled carriage or cart used in India (OED)

going to ride up 3000 feet to the top of a hill called the Deobund (?) with
Chapman, and have luncheon on the top, wh[ich] will be good. I'm longing
in a way to get back to Muttra & my horses and the pigsticking and the heat;
but it's no good trying to hurry it and go down again into the furnace before I
get fairly fit.

Where is the "little London house" going to be; it's very sad to think I shall
never be able to make it my headquarters for the fashionable balls. All love
to the family, & you from J.

35   10 May 1911   Chakrata, India   DE/Rv/C1135/534

Dear Mother

I'm awfully glad the "Indian box" has arrived, & that you like it. I was
beginning to think that it had fallen by the way, as I sent it off some time in
Feb. I was frightfully "struck" with it when a Kashmir robber produced it at
the bungalow one day – I thought it had such a light and sheen about it. But
what to do with it is quite beyond me!

How good about Bill's first[73] – I am glad. His kidneys can hardly have
affected his great brain at all. I've just had a letter from him; he writes the
best, doesn't he – they always make me laugh for the next week. His party at
Taplow is a great improvement on yours! I see poor Patrick does not even
score a place among the commoners. When do you go back to the Queen?
And won't you have to come to the Durbah[74] on pain of being imprisoned in
the Tower? I know "since there's no help" – but do write it out for me. I'm
reading no literature now, but reading Mil[itary] Laws with both eyes: - it is
just the opposite of literature, and is expressed throughout in just the wrong
words and just the wrong way; you have to use "Cracker ducks" to get at the
meaning. Of course all the Sandhurst people had it thrust down their throats
with a bayonet & know it by heart. I sit outside in glorious sun, with the

---

[73] Billy Grenfell achieved a first in Honour Mods (*FJ*, p209); see also letter 139
[74] The coronation durbar for George V was organised by Sir John Hewett, Bunty's
father (1854–1941). 'In early 1911 Hewett was relieved from his gubernatorial
duties to arrange the coronation durbar of George V and Queen Mary at Delhi at the
end of the year. His creation of a tent city housing 200,000 people, spread over 25
square miles, was an organizational marvel and won him promotion to GCSI, but it
was not all smooth sailing and he briefly tendered his resignation when Lord
Hardinge insisted on some last-minute changes' (ODNB)

hills in front, and the snow in front of them. I'm not very yellow now, and I ride and that sort of thing, & eat eggs; and I think they'll let me go back to work in about a week now. It's a month today since I was "tuk". It's wonderful air – and everything standing on its head makes you think you've got mislaid into Mars. The 60th are very nice, but not so nice as the Royals: I'm glad I'm not a footslogger. Chapman has gone to Missourie (40 miles) for a week. I love him: he is sympathetic, & has had nerves (they go together); he is all for the "complete rest" theory, and "wait till it blows over". He's very keen about them all. We went up 3000 feet one day, & had luncheon up at the top. Today I'm off to watch them play polo, 6 miles off, on the verge of a precipice.

I'm glad you've had good "Easter hols" weather. How you must have loved getting back to the 'quiet life' at Tap[low]? Give my best love to all the family. I wish I could come for a week's "Easter hols", before going back into the burning fiery furnace.

All love J.

36   17 May [1911]   Chakrata, India   DE/Rv/C1135/535

Dear Mother

Are you installed in your London mansion now, and is it very beautiful? And are you having fun? I'm still getting well hard up here, and beginning to play polo again, and doing some work. It is too wonderful up here; I can't get accustomed to the beauty & topsiturviness of everything, but I'm no longer giddy. The first day or two I had to lie down and burrow at intervals! I don't think it was giddiness, but the effects of jaundice. I'm getting quite a nice fresh colour. Chapman has returned from his jaunt to Missourie. We have very good hard billiard fives after dinner with the Riflemen, on a table which is piebald and full of bunkers. Tonight I go to dine with the Highland Light Infantry, who live 3 miles off at a place called Kailana. I don't know when I go back to Muttra – soon, I hope.

I don't like the Max Beerbohm cartoon of Dad[75]; I thought it must be the old one, which Dad hated so much, & which I never saw – but apparently it

---

[75] Max Beerbohm (1872–1956) was a famous caricaturist (ODNB). He wrote to Ettie Desborough about his exhibition of cartoons of political figures in 1911 (Mosley, p278; HALS: DE/Rv/C191). In HALS: DE/Rv/F13 there is a cutting from the *Daily Mail*, 22 April 1911 showing the cartoon

isn't? Please give my best best love to him and the family. What divine
Easter hols you must have had. Did you go to Pans[hanger]: & have Bill &
Auntie Ka[tie] patched it up? I do hope you'll have a glorious summer.
Have you read anything jolly? I've read all the Shakespeare plays in your
little books, & loved them; I'd never read most of them before.
All all love from J.
PS I think I forgot to ask Dad if he would pay in my allowance in future
quarterly. Could you ask him for me?

37   25 May 1911   Chakrata, India   DE/Rv/C1135/536

Dear Mother

Your letter told me that Chartie[76] is dead, and I suppose as you say one can
only be thankful. Was the last time all very terrible – the last months and
weeks? I thought she had been so wonderful all through it, so brave and full
of hope? And one could hardly believe that possible in an eternal wearing
illness like hers: so that at the end even she had to go under? I feel so
miserable for the dolls; and so glad that Laura is married. I will write to dear
Charles. What a great family they are – don't you think.
Tap[low] must have been glorious (I suppose you're nearly back in London
now) – I'm glad the junior members like Burnham Beeches picnics[77]: they
will be much less trouble & expense to you than your two elder scions, who
objected to them not from dislike of Burnham Beeches but from a natural &
instinctive rebellion against all authority, especially maternal! I wish I could
have gone with you this year, to make up for past resistances! Oh, & I wish I
could have seen the Max Beerbohms: how far the greatest artist of the time
he is. And promise to send me the Belloc book directly it comes out; I'm
panting for it.
I'm frightfully well again now; and I go back to Muttra, where the sun is
very warm, on Monday next. It's been such fun up here; I worship the Bosun
(who has got dysentery, poor man), & talk to him all day. The 60th are
rippers, & I've been playing polo with them lately. And I've been working

---

[76] Charlotte, daughter of Sir Charles Tennant, sister of Margot Asquith. She married
the 4th Baron Ribblesdale in 1877, and was the mother of Charles, Diana and Laura
Lister. Laura married Simon Joseph, 14th Lord Lovat, on 15 October 1910
[77] An area of woodland between Beaconsfield and Slough freely accessible to the
public

fairly hard. And eating very hard – (I eat nothing at all for about a month, before!). Tell Bill the food is very good up here; at Muttra it is often affected by the heat.

All love to the family - & you. J.

38   2 June 1911   Royal Dragoons, Muttra   DE/Rv/C1135/537

Dearest Mother

Just back – and I missed your mail, which was sent on to Chakrata. It has been 121° in the shade here – the hottest in India anywhere & it is being a record hot year. However I'm very well, & delighted to get back; though it was like walking straight into pea soup, coming down from the hills. <u>Fearful</u> hurry. <u>All</u> love to you & the family. J.

39   7 June [1911]   Royal Dragoons, Muttra   DE/Rv/C1135/538

Dear Mother

I hear you have had a terrible and tragic heat wave in England – 85° in the shade one day. It is 117° here, and there's some fun in that. I <u>love</u> it; punkahs, & a swimming bath, and a streaming face all day; and getting up at 4; and sleeping in the middle of the day. It was such fun getting back to my horses and work and everything: I really can do a little work now, which I couldn't before. I weigh under 11 st (from 13 st 4) – in spite of eating & drinking everything I can lay hands on. I killed a pig singlehanded a week ago – my first day here; but I retired after the morning, wisely, à la M Craig. It was like galloping in a gridiron. Pigsticking again tomorrow, 4.30 am. I've a new squadron leader, Captain Hodgson, who's a <u>ripper</u>, & we get on perfectly.

What fun your gay life must be. I'm glad Dad loves the house; please give him my <u>best</u> love. You might have taken the trouble to find me out dear Viola's address: - this will delay my letter to her 5 weeks!

Yes, <u>do</u> pour the fatted calf on <u>all</u> the Royals, very much superfatted. The Steeles live at 60 Chester Square; she is an ass, but be nice to her.

All all love J.

Did Dad have a good jaunt in Buda P[est]?

40   15 June 1911   Royal Dragoons, Muttra   DE/Rv/C1135/539

Dear Mother

Your London sounds the greatest fun, and it is splendid to have got a house that even his lordship likes! I wonder if you have seen any of the Royals? Muttra is at its best; I am pigsticking three days a week, and working like blazes for my promotion exam the other four – (I take it next week); I have shot a mugger[78], to the "admiration of the Gawd-dam natives"; I have been photographed; I slew a pig on the Hawk today; I weigh about 10 stone 8, and am very well. They call me the Melon King (they <u>are</u> good), and I am editing the paper for this month. That is all my news – except that I've got a new hired charger, called Dorando, because he runs till he drops, regardless of bit and rein. Yesterday the Chok Basart, or small monsoon, caught us bending while out pig-poking, and 2 inches of rain fell in one hour, followed by a plague of flies. I'm getting quite devoted to the country, and I am going to settle at Muttra with a dusky harem when the regiment leaves for Africa. We are just back from pigsticking, & I am very very sleepy. Please give my best best love to the family. I <u>am</u> glad you're right again now, and going 14 to the dozen in defiance of Harley Street. Good night. J.

41   23 June 1911   Royal Dragoons, Muttra   DE/Rv/C1135/540

Dear Mother

I expect you'll be pretty tired today after the Coronation[79]; and I long to hear all about it, and what part you played in it! What fun the Fancy Dress balls must have been: & <u>what</u> fun Casie must be having, and how glorious for her to be so well now, just when she wants to be well. I am frightfully well now too; and so are you; the Gods are with us pro tem. I have had an awful 6 months; worse then ever before, almost, because it came just at the one time I wanted to be fit and able to render a decent account of myself. I got rotten on the voyage; then, <u>just</u> as I thought I had collared it, and was on the mend – after a month of praying for the end of each hour I was in; struggling

---

[78] A broad-nosed crocodile (OED)

[79] The coronation of King George V and Queen Mary, 22 June 1911; Lady Desborough was in the Queen's procession and Julian's brother Ivo was a page in the Prince of Wales's procession (*FJ*, p214)

through riding-school & polo & stables – I get concussion, which put me right back again. You <u>can't</u> fight nerves alone in bed in a bungalow; and of course it's the nerves that matter – I never mind the physical illness part without them. Then I started at the beginning again and just as I was coming out on top my liver went phut, & for 3 weeks I ate nothing, & then came out bright yellow with jaundice. But it's over now & I feel very fit & I've beat it.

It's very hot here, only different heat now; wet heat, like Mrs Bart's bilin ile. Everything is going splendidly. I like Bunty Hewett awfully, & he is a pretty sharp fellow – 19 with the experience of 29. We rag poor old Jack Booth; but wit is wasted on his impenetrable hide. My squadron leader, Hodgson, is the nicest fellow I've ever seen, & frightfully amusing; he rags me the whole time.

Please give oceans of love to the family; I expect Bill is leading the gay life with you now? J.

I've sent you 2 photographs   (1) self & Bridegroom[80]

(2) self & establishment

42   nd   Royal Dragoons, Muttra   DE/Rv/C1133/50

Dear Dad

Thank you very much for your letter, and the two copies of your speech. They have gone all round the regiment, and had a gigantic succès. I loved reading it, and I thought it most awfully good. Altogether you seem to have raised a good hornet's nest about the Declaration. You seem to have had great fun at the Coronation; and Casie must have had a grand year. What are your plans now? When do you go to Canada? I wonder if the family have settled yet what they are going to do? The team must have been very good this year; I wish I could have seen it.

I have passed well through all my starting work; I got 126/150 in the promotion exam for lieutenant; and I passed out of riding school yesterday, which has been very hard work all through the heat of the summer. I drive the regimental team, and I'm president of the athletic club, and the boxing club, when we have bloody fighting every month. I'm getting a bit better at polo, and I simply <u>adore</u> the pigsticking: we have had a record year at it, and

---

[80] Bridegroom was one of Julian's horses

have got 352 pig. I got the 350th, and had to stand a drink. Altogether I'm
well & flourishing, and I like the soldiering very much indeed. All love
from J.

43   28 June 1911   Royal Dragoons, Muttra   DE/Rv/C1135/541

Dear Mother

<u>Tremendous</u> congratulations on winning the tennis-tournament at
Hackwood[81]; you <u>are</u> a student-athlete mama. What fun you must have had
there, and at the balls, with your friends Miggs and Nancy! And what fun Le
Touquet[82] will be. Tell me what the Coronation looked like, & whether you
did anything big in it, and whether Likky Man looked like Adonis. Your
Oxford day must have been too divine – and the <u>weather</u>, which I resent,
coming in my only summer abroad yet! It is most exciting about your
summer plans – and Dad really going to Canada; I wonder where you'll go to
in the end. I am willing hard for Bill to win the Hertford.
Here is a photograph of self on Bridegroom, in "Review Order – White",
taken before I went to Church one Sunday. There are no proper
photographers in this jungly place, or I would have been taken in full kit
holding a tin hat and looking a BF, exactly as you approve, long ago. But
that requires a real artist behind the camera; and I must wait till I get a little
time to go to one of the centres of civilisation before it can be properly &
handsomely done. I don't know when I can get leave, as I shall be the only
officer left to command B Squadron all through the rains. I want frightfully
to get a shoot before I leave India (I <u>hate</u> going, & I long for 2 more yrs
here); and also I want to see Delhi & Simla, and the old native cities. But at
present I am working with both hands, when not eating or sticking swine! It
is still pleasantly warm & there are no signs of the rains yet, which is
glorious, as it gives us more pigsticking. I got 2 pig & 1 pig the last two
days, and a beautiful soft fall. We have got 280 pig up to date this year,
which is pretty good. Directly the rains come the grass grows as fast as a
horse galloping, & the pig rejoice secure in the cover thereof.
We leave in November. Makins returns here soon – Have you seen him.
God bless you & the family. J.

---

[81] Hackwood House near Basingstoke, Hampshire owned by George Curzon (Mosley,
p336)
[82] A coastal resort in France

44   6 July 1911   Royal Dragoons, Muttra   DE/Rv/C1135/542

Dear Mother

Are you still having wonderful weather? We are still stewing here, with no
sign of the rains yet; except that the heat is wet heat now, instead of dry. The
amount which one has to drink is perfectly incredible; when you come in you
drink 2 enormous glasses without it making the least difference! It all runs
straight out again in the sweat of one's brow, so I suppose it makes no
difference to one's inside.
Just in from pigsticking – good day; & we are all drilling hard every day. I
love some new people in the regiment – Miles, who is wild, and clever, &
rather arty. He thinks I am mad but interesting as a specimen. I'm pretty
good at the heat, but a perfect skellington.
Ascot must have been fun: yes, I love John Bigge[83], but I haven't seen him
for years. I love his deliberation. I was terribly disappointed in the Belloc
book – I don't think it's got any of the stuff of the others.
<u>All</u> love from J.

45   14 July 1911   Royal Dragoons, Muttra   DE/Rv/C1135/543

Darling Mother

It is disgusting about my letters missing. I've written every mail, and I'm
making a great row with the Post Office. I loved your Coronation letter; it
must have been gorgeous and magnificent. I wish I could have seen Vovo.
It's good about Bill and the Hertford; I'm glad he's pleased. Have you
settled any more about summer plans?
I'm frightfully well, & as strong as two lions; & having a great success with
the regiment who think I am quite mad but "good value". I got 126 out of
150 in my promotion exam for lieutenant, & was easily top of the 3 who
went up. The pigsticking is <u>beyond words</u>: I can't tell you what it means to
me: it is coursing with human greyhounds.
All all love J.

---

[83] One of Julian's greatest friends according to his sister (*Bright Armour*, p147); he
was the son of the private secretary to both Queen Victoria and George V

46   21 July 1911   Royal Dragoons, Muttra   DE/Rv/C1135/544

Darling Mother

Thank you awfully for your letter, which I loved.
Not one minute – I'm so sorry, but I mustn't be late for stables.
Polo pigsticking & work all A1 – and some new drawings in chalk, which
have had a <u>gigantic</u> success with the regiment! Yr J.

47   28 July 1911   Royal Dragoons, Muttra   DE/Rv/C1135/545

Darling Mother
<u>How</u> glorious about Bill. And what fun your Lords must have been, done in
style. I do wish I could have been with you. Do you really bear up, with bed
or India shut-eye at 4 am every morning?
The Colonel is back, and loved his luncheon with the family. He can be the
most charming man in the world, but out here he is generally pretty
cantankerous, which is probably due to ill temper or Indian liver: he is not
<u>over</u> popular with the regiment, and they think him unbusinesslike & hard to
work with.
Hodgson, my squadron leader, is <u>absolutely</u> the best man: very good-
looking, very brave, and a glorious sense of h[umour], under a sham-
pompous manner. We simply worship each other. Worse luck, he is going
home to do Adjutant of Yeomanry when we go to Africa. You <u>must</u> see him.
Everything here is perfect, and I'm frightfully well & fit, & playing polo
better (I <u>hated</u> it at first, but love it now) – and fairly downing the pig and
Sclater Booth. Passed out of riding school yesterday; it's been hard work, <u>2</u>
hrs before breakfast every morning, & very ot. Just going out for a leopard.
All all love J.

48   3 Aug 1911   Royal Dragoons, Muttra   DE/Rv/C1135/547

Dearest Mother

I'm sorry you didn't like my photographs, which I thought so particularly
handsome. I always did say that you have a degraded taste in art, and that
you mistake smartness for true & inherent beauty; now I feel certain of it.
Are you having fun in Brittany? Or did you go to Lapland with Bill? I knew
you w[oul]d like Mrs Makins – she's a topper. I like Uncle too, but he is

pretty snotty at times. Muriel Steele is desperately in humble with me, and I had to tell the bearer never to let her into the bungalow. You would (& will) <u>adore</u> some of the other people – Hodgson & Charrington (Kid) and Houstoun (Ginger).

Yes, I agree about nerves; but I think that after a certain point is passed you have <u>got</u> to slump: not on principle, but simply to get enough energy into your empty system to fight them with. At that point you are just existing, and all your energy is wanted to exist; attempting to do any more is poisoning yourself. But you can prevent ever reaching that point again, after you have once got going.

I'm going for a month's leave in Sept, to Simla and Cashmir, with the Hewetts, & to stay with the Hardings for a day or two (if brave enough). It is still 115° in the shade here, with no rain, but a glorious and inexhaustible supply of pig and buck and work J.

49   10 Aug 1911   Muttra   **DE/Rv/C1135/548**

Darling Mother

Are you in Brittany now? And is Bill in Lapland? And is Dad in Canada? And are you having fun? And aren't you rather pleased at getting away from London?

There are still no rains here, and we still stick pig most gloriously. My horses and I are like posts and rails, but full of running still. The last two nights I have been lying out on the hillside in a great ravine, in the moon, armed to the teeth, (2 rifles and a hog-spear) – waiting for four panther: but they declined combat, and I am very sleepy. We sail November 10, for Pretoria. I <u>do</u> love the people in the regiment, more than I can tell you; I really find much more in common with them than with the Oxford people – and I thought it w[oul]d be "just the revers".

God bless you J.

50   17 Aug 1911   Camp – Lalpur jungle   DE/Rv/C1135/546

Darling Mother

I hope you're having fun now with Isult of Brittany; the chateau sounds too exciting and you'll have a heavenly life there. Meanwhile what is going to happen to the British Constitution? The rains have not come here yet, and it's still warm. We camped here last night for a pigsticking meet this morning; and two of us stayed out today to shoot buck, and are just going to canter back to Muttra under the moon, 11 o'clock, 10 miles to go, and parade at 6 tomorrow. It is really a wonderful life, and I'm quite miserable at thinking of going. We never wear any clothes, and run absolutely wild, and live in the open.
The Colonel has been <u>wonderfully</u> nice ever since he came back, & I've had the greatest fun with him. He's got a sort of malevolent twinge which catches him sometimes, & makes him impossible; but when it leaves him he is very nice, & the greatest fun. He told me that I ought to be adjutant, and then go up for the Staff College.
I wish Bill was out here – of course it was out of the question, but I thought my cable might catch him in a wild moment. By the way, did he ever get the cable? All love J.

51   24 Aug 1911   Royal Dragoons, Muttra   DE/Rv/C1135/549

Dear Mother

I wonder if you are loving Brittany, and having gorgeous weather? Give my love to the Little Man, and tell him how excited I am about his swimming prize. I wish I could swim; we had a match today, and I lost my entire patrimony. I tried to give a man 2 lengths of the swimming bath here in 27 lengths, and I had my hands on the gold when I swallowed most of the bath, and sank; three times I sank, and then suddenly recovered, only to be beaten finally by ¼ length. You can imagine that the other man was not amphibious. We swim here practically all the time now, as the rains have broken – 2 months late. I hate the clammy heat; the real heat was far better. The British Constitution seems to be a thing of the past; do tell me what is going to happen. And do tell me more about Moncton-Arundell; and all about the Chateau.
I go to Simla on the 15th Sept, and then on to Cashmir, with the Hewett

family, including Miss Hewett, whom I shall steel my heart against. You cannot think how turbulent one becomes after six months in the hot wilderness, without the sight of a single fair face. We go from here on Nov 6, and sail from Bombay on Nov 10.

I read More Peers[84] again, and I liked it much better, but not like the old ones. "Picture the Viscount's great surprise" is glorious, esp the drawing. I haven't read the other two Bellocs yet. <u>All all</u> love J.

Do you like Arnold Bennett's books[85] – I do, tremendously.

52   24 Aug 1911   Royal Dragoons, Muttra   DE/Rv/C1133/49

Dear Dad

Thank you for your letter, which was written just as you were starting off for Canada. I hope you'll have a splendid trip; it will be great fun seeing the country, and the Dominion Saw-Mills. Shall you visit the future home of the family in the Lake Huron island?

The political crisis is very exciting; I don't know whether I am a Lansdowner[86] or a last-ditcher. The whole thing seems in a pretty fair mess, doesn't it? Muttra however goes on peacefully. The rains have broken, 2 months late. The Colonel is back, and <u>delightful</u>; he is much more of a rowdy when Mrs M is away. We have had the record year for pig, 386 boar up to date. I have never enjoyed anything so much as the pigsticking, and my 3 horses have stood it out wonderfully. I have put them up for sale; and I am now a perfect Croesus[87]. Thank you awfully for the £200; that puts us square according to agreement, as I shall have had £100 less this year to make up for the £100 too much which I had last year. As you say, this leaves the little trousseau out of account! Yes, and a great many other things too! You have been most awfully good to me, and I feel very grateful, and I will try and spend my riches in a fitting way!

We embark for Pretoria from Bombay on Nov 10. I am awfully sorry; I

---

[84] One of Belloc's *Cautionary Verses*, attacking and satirising Edwardian society (1911)

[85] (Enoch) Arnold Bennett (1867-1931), novelist (ODNB)

[86] The Unionist peer the Marquess of Lansdowne, Henry Fitzmaurice (1845-1927) (ODNB). The political crisis concerned the controversy over Irish Home Rule

[87] Croesus, last king of Lydia (c560-546 BC), proverbial for his great wealth (*OCCL*)

would have loved another 2 years in this country; but I love the regiment so much that it more than makes up. Before we start I am going to Simla for 10 days, to the Hardinges & the Hewetts (Sir John H., whose son is in the regiment, and a ripper); and then to shoot in Kashmir with the Hewetts for 3 weeks.

I wonder when you'll get this letter?

All love from Julian.

53   30 Aug [1911]   Unknown place [India]   DE/Rv/C1135/550

Dear Mother

I loved your letter, and I'll answer <u>all</u> the questions. The pigsticking ought to have ended 2 months ago, because the country grows up so that you can't see to ride a pig after the first rains. But there have been practically no rains. I get 6 weeks leave before we go, which I spend as follows – 10 days in Simla with the Hewetts & Hardinges – 4 weeks in Cashmir – 2 weeks in Simla? Srinagar? They have got a valley to shoot in Cashmir, bear etc, & it's very good of them to ask me. I am <u>not</u> overdoing it. There is no news in Muttra ever, so what should I want to tork about it for in long epistles? (This joke has not yet penetrated to India). The "Borneo" joke is only that they call me the Wild Man of Borneo – nothing more subtle. I heard from Dad before he went to Canada; he will have great fun. Pans[hanger] must have been delicious in the heat. What fun seeing Laura – I did not know that she had added to the dying aristocracy – I love the joke about one drunken Xtian [Christian] and 2 sober Jews.

I <u>do</u> hope you'll love Brittany, & that you'll have it hot. It is much colder here now than in the summer; and now I know that I can <u>never</u> be hot enough (in this transitory life). I do hate feeling in the <u>least</u> cold, don't you. I would so much rather 120° than 80°.

No news, except that I like some of the regiment people more and more – esp "Kid", who is the hero of India, and the most loved person there has ever been here; and absolutely un-proud.

All love J.

Do you like this, I wrote it last week, in a blasphemous form, and then bowlderised it and sent it to the Pioneer. Even then I was surprised that the theology was not too advanced for them; they are highly respectable.

54   8 Sept 1911   Unknown place [India]   DE/Rv/C1135/551

Dear Mother

What fun the Pans[hanger] party must have been, with all the bloodsome
sprigs! I had a bird letter from Auntie Ka[tie] about it. And your crossing
must have been wonderful: <u>how</u> good the sea sunrise & sunsets are, from a
Ship: it seems to make them quite different, as if you were inside them or
part of them, when you are on the waters. I remember the dawn coming over
Findhorn Bay[88], with the rush of the following tide rocking & kissing the
punt, and the widgeon whistling all round as they woke up. The King of the
Castle did you in the eye proper; but the villa with woods at the back door
and the sea at the front door sounds awfully good. You <u>will</u> have fun there.
No news here – the same animal life, at a collected gallop; but my brain is
getting rather gross from idleness, and I'm going to begin working. The
rains have come, but not real continuous rains; we go out on odd days to
stick pig, in country blind with new, bright green grass, so that you gallop
down a hidden well without any warning, and without much surprise. I'm
afraid all other sports will fall flat after this. Did you like the Fighting
Boar?![89] The polo has been great fun lately; and everyone in tremendous
form. They make me draw wild caricatures all day, and my art is suffering
according! Bunty Hewett and I go to Simla next Wed; then a three weeks
shooting trip in Cashmir; and then Simla again, and back here on 25 Oct. We
leave Muttra 6 Nov, and sail 11 Nov. All all love to you & Casie and that
preposterous Mog from Julian.
Have you read the Irish play by Synge[90]. Most <u>extraordinarily</u> good.

---

[88] Findhorn near Forres, in Moray, north-east Scotland
[89] Poem written by Julian; see Appendix 2
[90] John Millington Synge (1871-1909), playwright. The play was most likely his last
work, *Deidre of the Sorrows*, published posthumously in July 1910 (ODNB)

55   14 Sept 1911   United Service Club,   DE/Rv/C1135/552
                        Simla

Dear Mother

The frank blue Breton home sounds the <u>greatest</u> success, and what fun you
must be having there. I have just arrived here – this morning, and it seems so
strange to see names like Jakko on the signboards, which one seems to know
perfectly well already, from Kip[91]. The Hewetts' have got a very nice house.
I love Sir John, who has the <u>best</u> sense of humour. Lady H looks, and talks,
a holy terror. The beautifully Lorna is a real death trap for the young and
innocent. There's a delightful secretary man called Lindsay Gordon; and the
dear Kid is up here doing A.D.C. to Creagh; he seems to be pleasantly
enamoured of Lorna, so I shall see a lot of him. Bunty Hewett was kept at
Muttra, for a court-martial in which he is witness; so I entered the house
today alone and unknown, but unafraid! We stay here 15 days, and then we
go to Kashmir for a ten days shoot, and then some sightseeing, & then back.
I think I shall put my hunting knife below Lady H's fifth rib before that time.
I was rather glad to get away from Muttra – just beginning to get tired and
bored of the same life there day after day, through these four broiling months.
One could do nothing there all the last week, as the rains had set in proper.
Simla is not so <u>big</u> or <u>grand</u> as I had expected. I've just been playing our old
Taplow tennis; only it is ruined here by playing with brand new bouncing
balls, and a net as high as they can get it.
I've put you down as a subscriber for the "Eagle", the Regt rag[92], which I'm
doing now. Is that right?
People at Muttra were just <u>beginning</u> to get slightly short and snappy &
livery; the rains are a filthy time, and I suppose the effects of the heat come
out just when it is over. Uncle Makins, however, is still radiant, in his
bachelor existence.
All all love to Casie & Mog and the Likky Likky – and you from J.

---

[91] Joseph Rudyard Kipling (1865-1936), author of many stories about India including
Just So Stories and *Kim*
[92] Julian was editor of *The Eagle*. HALS holds one copy for 1914 (Ref:
DE/Rv/F118)

56   28 Sept [1911]   Viceregal Lodge, Simla   DE/Rv/C1135/553

Dear Mother

Brittany <u>does</u> sound divine; and how pleased you must be to go to <u>sleep</u>
again! I <u>do</u> agree with you about the Ebb Tide[93], and the absolute surrender
of oneself to it. I lent it to a man in the regiment ("that Buff"), and he said
that it was alright, but that all the people in it were exactly the same; for
which insolence he was severely punished.

This is a very gay place, and I have been living your London life for a week;
never to bed before 4.30. I loved it for 6 days, but on the 7th I began to think
of the jungles of Radhakund and Kushmoka, and to feel that there was no
place for me here. The Hewetts are <u>too</u> delicious, and amusing, and
refreshingly plain-spoken. Sir John is one of the nicest men I've ever seen;
and <u>really</u> clever. We went shooting right up into the mountains one day; we
rode out 20 miles, to a place where we thought the camp was within 3 miles:
a large meal, and off again at 4.30 pm: we walked 2 miles, and 2 more, and
2 more, 3000 feet down into a great gorge, and the dark came down. Our
guide did not know the way, and Sir John was beat out.   Then we met a
native who said the camp was 7 miles on, and brought us a torch out of a real
R[obinson] Crusoe cave. Eventually we walked 5 more miles in the dark,
3000 feet up again, over terrible ground – little paths with a sheer drop to the
river below – and got to camp at 10 o'clock! The food had arrived (thank
God), but no bedding; we rolled up in the tent flaps, and snored in 3 minutes.
Shot next day, and came back the day after.

The people of Simla are most amusing; they are immoral in speech only, and
live irreproachable lives. Do you know Bron's expression for a woman who
is a teaser; they are all classic examples of that. They are all acting the
Quaker Girl, and I live in the Green Room; there are dances every other
night, and wildly inebriate suppers, which are the best part of the show. I'm
longing for Kashmir, when we go on Saturday.

This place is quite nice, and I like the Hardinges; but they are not likely to
cause a forest fire, and not nearly such good value as the Hewetts. Dear John
Astor is here, and we play tennis a lot. Scatters Wilson is a great darling, and
I've had tremendous fun with him. He says things to dowagers which turn
their grey hairs pink. He said he would get me a job on the Chief's Staff for

---

[93] Possibly the book of that title by Robert Louis Stevenson, published in 1894

the Durbah, but I would not let him, as I haven't done enough with the regiment yet – and I should hate doing 3rd footman, I know. I have stuck "the Hawk" into John Astor, for a large sum of gold.

Give all my love to little Vovo and Mogg, and dear Casie: and thank her tremendously for her letter. Do you know a prose thing by Shelley on Love? It's the only good thing I've read for ever so long. God bless you J.

57   9 Oct [1911]   Dutchigaon Nullah, near   DE/Rv/C1135/554
**   Srinagar, Kashmir**

Dear Mother

I suppose you're just coming back from Scotland now? This is a glorious place – a camp at the bottom of a great gorge, where it takes 4 hours for the sun to get to after sunrise; and whacking great hills all round for miles & miles. We left Simla one morning, got to Amballa that night, & Rawal Pindi the next afternoon, by train; then by tonga on to Murray that night (12 midnight) – slept there, on to Kohala in the Jhelum gorge by the next night, next night Gurhi, next night Srinagar, all by tonga. We stayed 2 nights in a houseboat at Srinagar, & then rode the 18 miles out here, shooting hill partridge on the way. It was a very good journey, & the Hewetts are perfectly <u>delightful</u>. Sir J[ohn] H[ewitt] is not here, he had to go to Delhi, where he is doing the Durbah. Mrs, Miss, Bunty, & the A.D.C., Pollok, a good man, are the camp-party. Miss Lorna is nice, but puffy about the head; she is 23, which is a bad age, don't you think? Tired of doing nothing for 5 years, the pore gurls adopt a superior attitude, and are above dancing and puss-in-the-corner and such childish sports, surveying life from a giddy height. But give them another two years, when they are up against the serious business of matrimony, and they are as playful as kittens again. Simla was great fun, but a fortnight there was too long, and I longed for open country after 6 days. I never went to bed before five, and drank baddish champagne every night, up to the "Nicely, Thank you" stage. But one day on the hill got rid of all of that. You can't walk up the hills here; you have to go up on your hands & feet, and to come down on yours, in a sitting posture. I took a little tent and went up to the tops the first night – bitter cold, even under 9 blankets & my green coat. The first beast I saw was the monarch of the glen, and I got him in the heart with a long galloping shot: wasn't it absurd luck! They are "barra singh", great big red deer, just like a Scotch stag, only twice the size; and very shy and difficult. He was a royal, with a marvellous head, 43 inches from the end of the horn to the base – 2 inches short of the record for anywhere, I believe; and the first I had ever seen. I got another in a drive yesterday, & they are the only two killed by us so far. The place is full of bear, but so far they have been most churlish; I expect they'll come and join in the sport later on. It's great fun poking about in the bushes for them, not knowing where you're going to take it next.

I went to the Hardinges at Simla, but it's the gloomiest house and household in Asia. The A.D.C.s are like icebergs in appearance & conversation. It's the sort of house where you feel a gloom descending like a fog upon you, the moment that you enter the door.

They had some good names at Simla –

"Gurrum Pane" (hot water) – Mrs Coldstream

"Lalla Rookh" Mrs Crow (with red hair)

"The Universal Provider" – Mrs Whiteley

"The Flying Fox" – Miss Lake

                                            etc etc.

We all missed the mail on the journey. I can't tell you the beauty of this place, and the vale of Cashmir, & the Dhal Lake; it takes one's breath away. We've only got a week now here, worse luck; then back to Srinagar for two days. I'm dropping with sleep – we start at 5 am tomorrow.

All <u>all</u> love J.

I've had some handsome portraits taken in Simla – the Heavy Dragoon after a heavy night.

58   16 Oct [1911]   Houseboat, Jhelun river   DE/Rv/C1135/555
**   near Srinagar**

Darling Mother

Your motor drive across Brittany must have been the greatest fun; and I hope you & Casie are tossing the caber successfully. I killed 2 bears on Friday, and another stag, so I've been in luck, and left the nullah[94] without missing. We had the most delightful ten days there, in gorgeous country; and are now going to see Islamabad, and then the Woolar Lake, and then back to Delhi. The Hewetts are amusing; the girls' best friend is just engaged, & I asked her if she loved the man. "Oh yes, she loves him with a real bit of pash". We

---

[94] A river or stream, watercourse, river bed or ravine (OED)

are all terribly well & strong, with Chippendale legs, after the pahar[95] or Indian hills. I love Cashmir; fairly well; bit disappointed in the Vale, it is so terribly dirty. The floating gardens are really floating rubbish heaps. ~~You could put up "GENTLEMEN" anywhere in the lovely valley. Sorry~~. Have you read Lalla Rookh, by Thomas Moore?[96] Who is Thomas Moore? Did he write "as his corpse to the ramparts we hurried"? The beautiful dark-eyed maidens of Kashmir are a myth; they are all exactly like Auntie Mabel, only neither so tall nor so aristocratic. The ladies of Simla, upon the other hand, are like Miss Gaye, but of a stricter morality. I am reserving myself for Miss Barney Barnato of Johannesburg[97]. We get back to Muttra on the 26th; and sail on Nov 11, worse luck to it.

Give my <u>best</u> love to the scattered family as they reunite. Bless you J.

59	**25 Oct 1911**	**Flashman's Hotel, Rawal Pindi, India**	**DE/Rv/C1135/556**

Dear Mother

Our best is over now; we start from here by train this afternoon, and arrive at Muttra 4 am the day after tomorrow, in time to put on uniform and go on parade. We have about 12 hours at Delhi, which is good, as I've never seen the sights there yet. When it is a question of getting a day's leave and going to sightsee in a dusty train, or going out for a night in the jungle to shoot, how is one ever to see sights? It has been the most perfect trip: after the shooting we had about 6 days in the houseboat, going up the river, and then down to the Woolar Lake, which was gloriously beautiful. I did a lot of post impressionist works of A[rt]. The contrast is so extraordinary – the peaceful sleepy sunny misty valley, surrounded by the great grim angry blue hills, like love in the middle of war. We did the 180 odd miles down the hill, by tonga, in two days, starting at 5 each day and snatching our food by the wayside; driving over sheer rock with two little galloping ponies, and the river roaring sheer underneath us all the time. And now for a new country, and hard

---

[95] A mountain (OED)

[96] *Irish melodies. Lalla Rookh, national airs, legendary ballads, songs, &c* by Thomas Moore (1779-1852), edited and with a memoir by J F Waller (1867)

[97] Barney Barnato was a diamond merchant and financier, and colleague of Cecil Rhodes; he had a daughter, Leah, to whom Julian may be referring

soldiering; I'm going to turn professional, and become adjutant!

My last two mails have missed me, so I can answer no queries and questions. I suppose you are at Tap[low], & preparing to set out and slap pheasants in the different statelies? Have you read any good books – <u>do</u> send me one or two, if you have. I've read Lyle's "British Dominion in India"[98], but I thought it verbose and padded. And "England & the English" by Price Collier[99], very fluffy too. All all love to you & the family from Julian.

60   **27 Nov 1911**   **Royal Dragoons,**   **DE/Rv/C1135/558**
                                        Roberts' Heights

Dear Mother

We have just arrived here, and it is a filthy place; great grass downs studded with rocks, and no trees, and tin huts everywhere. It is all bleak and bare and comfortless, and the quarters are small, and horribly clean after India. But it is simply wonderful air, and I feel like a lion, even after the journey. We started from Bombay Friday 10 Nov, and got to Mauritius Sunday 19; stopped a day there; got to Durban Sat 25, and here this morning. A very good passage, and great fun; cricket and fencing and boxing & physical drill and lots of work – the only way to get through a sea-journey. Of course I've had no letter for months, but I shall find them directly we get into our own mess; at present we are at the Royal Scots Fusiliers Mess. The mail is just off: I'll tell you all about the journey next week. Now we've got to "take over" horses and saddles and mess tins for days and days. I shall hate this country.

I'm simply longing to get your letters, and to hear all about you. Give my dearest love to everyone. J.

---

[98] *The rise and expansion of the British dominion in India* by Sir Alfred Lyall, (3rd edition, 1894)

[99] *England and the English from an American point of view* by Price Collier (1909)

**61   27 Nov 1911   Roberts' Heights,   DE/Rv/C1135/557
                       Pretoria, South Africa**

Dear Mother

We don't take over saddlery till tomorrow, so there's another hour before the mail goes. But we haven't got our post yet. The mess is made of tin, and the quarters are of tin, and the stables are of tin; and everything else is grass and sky. We have one little room to live in, and a sort of box joining it where we sleep, all made of tin; and everything is numbered, F06a, and RQ21; and even the bath and chamber utensils are Army Form X something. Altogether it is all very military. Pretoria is 4½ miles away, and we are a good bit above it, with the most wonderful air you ever breathed in your dreams. It is all rolling ground, no big hills near here. I loved the country on the way up from Durban – rather like Salisbury plain on a gigantic scale, magnified to the power of 20, with no trees. Skyline after skyline, each almost exactly like the last; and clear clear air, which halves the distances to the eye. The mornings are quite cold, but there is hot sun in the middle of the day. The whole thing seems cold and clean and ordinary and ticketed after India; I am sure I like dirt and disorderliness in the long run.

We left Muttra on a hazy hot morning, and took two days to Bombay, in 2 troop trains. We were not allowed to go into the town at Bombay, but we loafed about all day on the ship, or worked like coolies stowing the heavy baggage. It was deadly hot, with the killing sea heat. We went out at night, 12 pm. The voyage was really great fun; Swedish drill for all of us at 7.30 am, cricket at 4 pm, hockey at 5.30 pm (very dangerous & the greatest fun), boxing at odd moments, parade once a day, and a lot of duty (going round sentries etc every hour). I read Kim[100] again, and loved it more than ever; and a book of M Corelli's called The Life Everlasting[101]: if it is like that, I am not going to enter. I wrote the new number of "The Eagle" (the regimental paper) – by the way, I'm sending you all the numbers since I've been Editor, and will you please send a year's subscription, 12/- post free, to the Editor The Eagle, IRD, Roberts' Heights, Transvaal; otherwise he will bear the loss.

You must see Walter Hodgson, who used to be my squadron leader (Captain)

---

[100] *Kim* by Joseph Rudyard Kipling (1901)
[101] *The Life Everlasting* by Marie Mackay Corelli (1855-1924), published 1911

– I loved him a great deal, & I think you'll like him. He went home in
September (or October) – and he is now Adjutant of the Surrey Yeomanry,
which I think is a three years job, so that he probably won't come back to the
regiment while we are out here. His address is Cavalry Club.
Are you at Tap[low] now, or in one of the other stackelies? And how is each
member of the family severally? Is it horribly cold? I wish the post had
arrived here; I feel very much in the cold about all your beings and doings.
All all love from Julian.

**62   4 Dec 1911   Roberts' Heights,   DE/Rv/C1135/559
                            Transvaal, South Africa**

Darling Mother

I've got three splendid "Pretoria" letters from you. It is the right address; at
least, it is just as good as the other and more edifying. I've also got Ethan
Frome[102], and I'm longing to have time to read it; but "settling down" means
drudgery from morning to night. You must have been torn by A.J.B's
resignation[103]. I am so glad that Bron has got his Agriculture; is he well and
happy? I am dying to see the new chow-dog; I do not envy its life under the
dictatorship of Mog. I do so agree with you about the Hardinges; they are
just like suet pudding without any treacle. What do you think of the
Gladstones?[104] I saw them at a garden party (frock-coats & spurs) the other
day, and she said quite simply that she thought it was <u>wrong</u> to have things
like garden-parties in a place where there was such a glorious peaceful
veldt[105] all round – I thought it was rather nice; and I like her glad eye; but as
her entire business here is to give garden parties, she must have mistaken her

---

[102] *Ethan Frome* by Edith Wharton (1862-1937) published 1911
[103] Arthur James Balfour, former Prime Minister, (1848-1930) formally resigned as
Unionist leader on 9 November 1911 (ODNB)
[104] Herbert John Gladstone, Viscount Gladstone (1854–1930), politician and
governor-general of the Union of South Africa (son of the Prime Minister, William
Ewart Gladstone). Soon after his arrival, the Union of South Africa was formally
constituted on 31 May 1910 and he chose Louis Botha, one of the erstwhile Boer
generals, to be first prime minister (ODNB). In 1901, aged forty-seven, Herbert
Gladstone married Dorothy Mary (*d*. 20 June 1953), youngest daughter of Sir
Richard Horner Paget; the marriage was childless.
[105] In South Africa veldt is the unenclosed country or open pasture land (OED)

profession. He is a sort of cross between Hop-o-my-thumb and a Pork Butcher. I've seen Methuen here too, and <u>loved</u> him; <u>how</u> mad, and what a good face. Mrs Steele is staying with him, more boring and more like a street-walker than ever; she ought never to be allowed about except in Piccadilly after 11 pm, on very rainy nights.

Have you seen Rivvy Grenfell lately?[106] I wrote to him some time ago, from Muttra, and asked him to get me two ponies; but I've heard nothing, so the letter can't have got to him. [Apparently none of my Muttra letters ever got to anybody]. It is too late now to get ponies from England; besides, I can't afford it. I shall get some here.

No, I did not like Fraser, not one little bit; and I'm not a whale on Lovat either, for that matter.

This is a god-forsaken country, (except for the veldt, which one never gets out into; and the stars of the night, which are wonderful against a <u>clear</u> blue, like Dulac's)[107]. I really can hardly tell you how utterly bloody it is. Semi-detached tin bungalows and colonels' wives and calling. I am going to desert, and join the Irregular Sind Horse as a Vet[108].

Please give my very best love to Dad; what does he think of England and the English just now? Have you read anything good? Have you read Helen with the High Hand and, the other book about the woman who wasn't called Janet Orgreave, I can't remember her name, by Bennett? I didn't like it nearly as much as Clayhanger, he isn't at home with a woman's character in the least, do you think?[109]

All all love J.

---

[106] Riversdale Grenfell, one of twins who were Julian's cousins. Riversdale and his twin Francis were both killed in the First World War and are commemorated in a memorial window in St George's church, Ypres, erected by their sister, Mrs L Bulteel

[107] Edmond Dulac, French illustrator (1882-1953) (ODNB)

[108] The Sind Horse was a cavalry regiment in the Indian Army but 'irregular' suggests it was not a permanent regiment

[109] *Helen with the high hand: an idyllic diversion* by Arnold Bennett (1910); *Clayhanger*, also by Bennett, first of a series of four, was published in 1910

63   9 Dec 1911   Roberts' Heights   DE/Rv/C1135/560

Dear Mother

<u>How</u> I loved Ethan Frome; isn't it a really wonderful book. Even the drive
with him at the beginning, when he says nothing, and you know nothing
about him, fills one with interest and almost horror at the hint of what is
coming; and the end, when he lives alone with the two women, makes one
shudder, it is so real. The only other good thing I've read is the Fairy Tale by
A.A.M. [110] in the Punch annual; don't you love the picture, reading left to
right, "1st son, 2nd son, 3rd son, King, dog". I like the first son best. The
book about India, that I didn't like, <u>was</u> by Sir Alfred Lyall; but I think it
<u>awful</u> stuff, and his poetry – <u>have</u> you read his poetry?
You seem to have begun the Christmas festivities very early this year. How
did Bill get back by the 23 November? Or did he only come temporarily, to
kill the Pans[hanger] pheasants. I'm sorry Dad had bad luck, and didn't get
moose or bear: please give him oceans of love from me. I will write to him
directly I get a spare moment. At present I am editing the "Eagle", running
the Reg[imenta]l Athletic Club, writing a play and lyrics for the dramatic
club, and doing the wines; I am going to strike shortly, as I want to learn
French and mule-driving and signalling and short-hand and Hegel[111]. It is a
<u>filthy</u> place, half a hill and half a hole, in a country which ought to be
inhabited only by quagga[112] and rhinoceros, instead of Jew-boys looking for
diamonds. The ugliness of the habitations of men is quite indescribable, and
the sordid regularity and cleanliness of everything. I hate it worse every day.
As for the climate being good, it is the grossest lie. It thunders every day,
and in 2 weeks I have developed a swollen liver and galloping kidney
trouble. A glass of ale costs 9½d; what does a dish of eggs and bacon cost?
A man went mad here the other day, from sheer boredom; he ran along all the
kops[113] and dorps[114] and spruits[115] and ports, simply playing with 2 infantry

---

[110] A A Milne, author (1882-1956) (ODNB)

[111] The German philosopher Georg Wilhelm Friedrich Hegel (1770-1831). Julian's
allusion is unclear

[112] A South African equine quadruped (*Equus* or *Hippotigris Quagga*), related to the
ass and zebra, but less fully striped than the latter (OED)

[113] South African word for hill (OED)

[114] In South Africa, a small town (OED)

[115] A small stream or water-course, usually almost or altogether dry except in the wet
season (OED)

regiments & 1 cavalry regiment, who were sent out to bring him in. They did not find him for two days, and eventually came upon him asleep on the high road to Johannesburg. He got up, and said good morning to them, and asked them what they wanted? And since then he has been perfectly sane.

Do you see that England has been doing very well in the Test Matches? There seems however to be great doubt as to whether the Australians are not reserving their efforts for the more important matches later on. Clem Hill[116] must have been caught on an off day; even the greatest batsmen have their "off-days", like all of us. And certainly the light was none too good when that fast ball took his leg bails from the off stump. It appears that an earthquake took place in Java at the identical moment. Clem Hill is not a Javan, but his uncle is. J.

64   17 Dec 1911   Roberts' Heights   DE/Rv/C1135/561

Dear Mother

Thank you awfully for your letter, from Pans[hanger]. I'm awfully glad that the house-party was such a tearing success. It must have been the greatest fun – also your Tap[low] Sunday. Here there is nothing new, except that we are all still hustled off our legs. The Colonel has also insisted on putting on an entertainment, tomorrow – which has not improved matters. As Chapman, who's manning it, says – a man doesn't feel like acting a "Russian Prince" when he has just finished grooming 3 horses, and has cleaned 2 saddles, and been on Coal Fatigue. I have painted 3 scenes and written 2 entire topical poems today, and I was run away with by my hitherto mouselike charger, and I took part in a motor accident. Tomorrow we have a grand tomasha[117] before Methuen – tunics and all sorts. I hate this place; it is a cross between the outer ward at Bedlam[118] and the more civilized parts of Maidenhead thicket; and an unspeakably gory climate, with Drury Lane thunderstorms in perpetual succession.

Get <u>Walter Hodgson</u> (whom I told you about before) and <u>Mouse Tomkinson</u>,

---

[116] Australian cricketer (1877-1945). He was captain of the Australian team during the Ashes Series 1911-12, when Australia lost 4-1

[117] An entertainment, show, display, public function (OED)

[118] The Hospital of St. Mary of Bethlehem, used as an asylum for the reception and cure of mentally deranged persons; originally situated in Bishopsgate, in 1676 rebuilt near London Wall, and in 1815 transferred to Lambeth (OED)

who was adjutant, and who is now adjutant of the Devon and Cumberland Yeomanry. They are both rippers – much nicer than the new people who turned up out here, & the people who came back from leave here. [Note in margin: Cavalry Club see Army List.]

	(Edwardes		Hodgson	)
all	(Fitzgerald	instead of	Tomkinson	) all
v.	(Tidswell		Miles	) v
moderate	(Leighton		Charrington	) good

Best love to the family & to you J.

65   24 Dec 1911   Carlton Hotel,   DE/Rv/C1135/562
**   Johannesburg**

Dear Mother

Thank you awfully for your letter; Pans[hanger] sounds most delightful, with Dad back. I love the idea of Evan[119] not being allowed to shoot. It is funny Christmas weather here – boiling hot, and I think one feels the heat here more than in India. But I love wallopy weather with all my soul. We have all been grinding to the bone, as the Colonel elected to startle the inhabitants of S Africa with a gala week at once, before we were anything like settled down; we had sports and a variety entertainment and a play and a ball, and now everybody is stale drunk and tired. It was all most successful. The Bosun (Chapman) & I wrote the so-called play, and I wrote 3 songs, and painted scenes and gigantic rag advertisements. 6 ft by 10 ft, red, blue, & green paints.
S C R A T C H O
for the hair and scalp

Mr Jones, before using Scratcho

Mr Jones after using Scratcho
(From a photograph)
etc etc.

---

[119] Hon Evan Charteris (1864-1940), son of 10th Earl of Wemyss. Brother of Hugo, Lord Elcho

SCRATCHO

for the hair and scalp.

Mr Jones, before using Scratcho

Mr Jones after using Scratcho
(from a photograph)

etc etc.

Sclata Booth ("that horrible Buff") got intoxicated at the Sergeants Ball, and we had a temperance orgy with him afterwards; we gave him 5 of my tabloid cascara[120], tea-spoonful castor oil, 1 glass kutnow[121], 10 grains quinine[122], 1 port-glass "Honey and Flowers" hair-oil, a sleeping draught, a small glass Kutnow & Eno[123] mixed, and some Aspirin and Phenacetin[124] – in case he got a headache. How he did not die of it I cannot guess.

Four of us are here for a beano. It is a wild place, with Jews and Boers and Africanders drinking themselves silly in bars all day long, and a lot of soldiers, and ladies of uncertain morality and gigantic hats. Everybody comes here for a fling. Its a good change for a day or two, but a week would leave you dead.

The Colonel is in terrific form: I'm sure he likes this place much better than Muttra. I do love him; he is such tremendous <u>fun</u>, isn't he. Do you know the Methuens – I rather like them?[125]

<u>All</u> <u>all</u> love to <u>all</u> the family, & you from J.

---

[120] A tablet of cascara, which was an extract of the bark of a Californian buckthorn, used as a laxative or cathartic; in full *cascara sagrada*, 'sacred bark' (OED)

[121] Kutnow's Anti-Asthmatic Powder, 'a palliative for asthmatic paroxysms'

[122] An important alkaloid found in the bark of various species of cinchona and remigia, used largely in medicine as a febrifuge, tonic, and antiperiodic, chiefly in the form of the salt, sulphate of quinine, which is popularly termed quinine (OED)

[123] A trademarked indigestion relief

[124] An analgesic and antipyretic drug administered chiefly in tablets in combination with aspirin, caffeine, or codeine (now seldom used because of toxic effects on the kidneys and red blood cells) (OED)

[125] The family of Baron Methuen (1845–1932) (ODNB). In April 1908 Methuen was appointed general officer commanding-in-chief in South Africa, a post which he held until 1912. He was popular, particularly with his former opponents, and helped to improve relations between the Boers and the British. He was governor and commander-in-chief of Natal in 1910, and promoted to field marshal in June 1911

**66   31 Dec 1911   Train, Johannesburg   DE/Rv/C1135/563
to Pretoria**

My dear Mother

Thank you awfully for your Christmas letter, which I have got – and for the
waistcoat buttons, which I expect are waiting for me at Roberts Heights.
They are a splendid present, and just exactly what I needed to complete my
disguise as a gent. I have not got any good ones at all. <u>A happy New Year to
the family</u>, and all luck to Bill in the Ireland. I have just been staying in
Johannesburg for 4 days, to buy some ponies at the tournament. I've got
three absolute smashers, and now I'm going to settle down at that disgusting
barrack, and lead the simple life, and work at polo like a nigger, and learn
some soldiering. I am <u>absolutely</u> sick of the fast life in Jo'burg. It is a sinful
and wicked town, with the most unpleasant population on earth, devoted
entirely to filthy lucre and strong liquor. I saw the Wolvertons there – what a
darling she is, isn't she? Lady Gladstone is a little stoopid. The Methuen
girl is rather nice and quite ugly, but animated. Paul Methuen[126] is coming
back in a few days, from hunting bugs in Zanzibar. There is no news – the
country is as beastly as ever. I saw David Bingham – he looks rather nice,
and is a first-rate horseman – the best out here. The regiment are in good
form; but the 4 real stars are at home or in India. I like Bunty Hewett and the
Bosun best. We have nobody who can play polo at all, which is sad.
Is there going to be a war with Germany in the spring? If there is, I shall not
be able to sell my ponies – nor to play them now, as I must devote myself to
learning the Art of War!
Have you read anything good lately? I've just finished Zuleika Dobson[127],
which I loved in parts – except all the silly end. And a <u>very</u> good poem by
Masefield[128].
<u>All</u> love, and God bless you. Tell Mog that her drawing of Coco is
magnificent; also her photograph; and that I loved her letter J.

---

[126] Paul Ayshford, 4th Baron Methuen (1886–1974), painter and landowner. From
Eton College he went to New College, Oxford, to read natural sciences (zoology) and
engineering. His father had links with South Africa, and from 1910 to 1914 he
worked as assistant at the Transvaal Museum in Pretoria. His interest in zoology was
lifelong (ODNB)

[127] *Zuleika Dobson*, or, *An Oxford love story* by Max Beerbohm (1911)

[128] The poet John Masefield (1878–1967) (ODNB)

67   7 Jan 1911   Roberts' Heights   DE/Rv/C1135/568
[1912]

Dear Mother

Thank you awfully for your letter. <u>What</u> glorious news about the Craven; the only thing that pleased me as much in my life was when that same great man knocked out the Cambridge heavy-weight. Are you really going to Cairo in the spring? I think we shall too, en route for Berlin? Really, tell me about the chances of war? Noël Mason[129] is here, and <u>very</u> nice: only he calls himself McFarlanes, for a change. I will be an awful dear little boy to the parents when they come out. I wish I had heard Dad's speech on the Naval Prize Bill[130]: it must have been splendid. I wish you didn't like Patrick S-S[131]; I have come to the conclusion that he is a really <u>nasty</u> character! Have you read "The Everlasting Mercy", by Masefield[132] – <u>much</u> the best thing for years and years. "Tante"[133] I've just begun; "The Hampdenshire Wonder"[134] I liked a little bit. Why don't you ever send me books? But the waistcoat buttons of my mother are supreme.

I've just corrected and sent in the proofs of a gigantic Special Number of the Eagle – 8 hrs solid work, and my head swims. It was great fun writing it – I love journalism. My three ponies are beyond expectation good, and I'm "wropped up" in them. We play 3 days a week: but on a horrible hard gravel ground. <u>What</u> a country! Paul Methuen has just come here, in great form; and I like the F.M.

All all love to the family. J.

---

[129] Noel Mason-MacFarlane (1889–1953), the eldest son of Dr David James Mason (1862–1930), who later added his mother's name, MacFarlane. He was posted to the Royal Artillery in 1909. War service in France, Belgium, and Mesopotamia gained him a Military Cross with two bars, two mentions in dispatches, and a Croix de Guerre (ODNB)

[130] Related to the Declaration of London (see footnote 56)

[131] Patrick Houston Shaw Stewart (1888-1917), younger son of Major General John Maxwell Shaw Stewart, contemporary of Julian's at Eton and Balliol

[132] Narrative poem by John Masefield, published in 1911

[133] *Tante* by Anne Douglas Sedgwick (1911)

[134] *The Hampdenshire Wonder* is a 1911 science fiction novel by J D Beresford

68   14 Jan 1912   Roberts' Heights   **DE/Rv/C1135/569**

Dear Mother

What fun your pantomime must have been – I wish I could have seen it, as first-night critic. Did it all go too beautifully – and did you write the songs and dances, and music of course? It is sad about Alwynne Compton[135]; I've never seen him since I was quite a likky – was he very unhappy? What do Eddy & Claude do now?[136]

Your Stanway[137] must have been perfect. Do your relations with Harry Cust[138] improve, or increase? I should simply love to see you with him. Do you know, I believe he will wear you down in the end yet! I do dislike him; he is like Patrick in many ways; but I admire the way he has stood up to you. Don't you? Have you seen <u>Edward</u> lately? What phase is he in now. I don't imagine that 23 will be a very good age for him; he is so much too old and too young for that – not wholly young, like me, or wholly old, like Bill.

I've heard from Tommy Lascelles, who sounded rather low, through a hearty letter. Paul Methuen has become a really keen scientist, and collects dead beasts' bones in Madagascar: he looks rather old and dried up himself, but still beautiful, and more aesthetic than ever. He came up to see me the other day, and the Bosun mistook him for the electric light man. He for his part mistook the Bosun for the Mess Orderly. Their interview sounded most amusing, from both sides. Billy Rawle lives in Pretoria, with his regiment; he is more amusing than ever.

We live a hard, training, life here: polo three days a week, and a lot of soldiering, and water-drinking. I <u>do</u> hate this filthy country, worse and worse. Everything is ugly and uglier. The climate up here is horrible: one feels deadly slack and half-alive. Everything and everybody is stereotyped and devitalised and flat. Red dust blows down one's throat all day, and covers one's sweating face. I am getting my room whitewashed, regardless

---

[135] Lord Alwyne Frederick Compton (1855-1911), third son of the 4th Marquess of Northampton, brother of Katie Cowper

[136] This may refer to Alwynne's two sons Edward Robert Francis (born 1891) and Claude George Vyner Compton (born 1894)

[137] The house belonging to Hugo and Mary Charteris, Earl and Countess Wemyss, situated in the Cotswolds (MacKenzie, p8; picture between pp136 and 137)

[138] Henry John Cockayne [Harry] Cust (1861–1917), politician and journalist. One of the 'Souls' (ODNB). See also Mosley, p309

of expense, to reflect the emptiness of my mind and soul. I cannot draw, or
write, or think, or breathe, and I am disgusting to my fellow-men. I am
going to buy a cat and a canary, for company, and learn to do a little knitting.
All love to the happy home J.
My ponies are <u>fizzers</u>.

69   20 Jan 1912   Roberts' Heights   DE/Rv/C1135/570

Dear Mother

Thank you for your letter, and the "Eagle" subscription, and the programme
of the Dragon of Dropmore – what fun it must have been, the Dragon – and
what a labour! I love the "Song – 'Giants'"; did you get the metre from your
own fertile brain, or from a "piece"? If so, what piece? Bill w[oul]d excel
himself as the dragon. I am longing to read the whole M.S. word for word.
It must have been good having lovely warm weather and thrushes singing. I
wonder how the glorious 29 party went off – and the Pans[hanger] second
shoot. Tell me all about them. I'm glad Bobby Astor[139] wasn't killed; did
Waldorf[140] give him the horse for a present?
The photographs arrived <u>today</u>! And I'm sending you one by this mail. They
missed me by one day at Muttra; and have taken the rest of the time to get
here. That's the worst of living in distant and inaccessible places. You will
notice the proud mien of the soldier, combined with the slightly and
gracefully bowed legs of the <u>Cavalry</u> Soldier, who cannot discard the attitude
of the pigskin even when in rest; the feet elongated by the continual pressure
of the stirrup-iron; the alert pose, with fingers resting lightly on the covered
menace of the sword; the graceful inclination of the figure, similar to that of
the Tower of Pisa and other noble pieces of architecture, but due in this case
to the photographic artist having cut out the portrait crooked. I feel sure that
you will like it. I 'ates that sort of fing, myself.
I did hear from Rivvy about the ponies, after I wrote to you. He strongly
advised me not to get out English ponies, but to buy mine here; and I can't
say how thankful I am to him now. English ponies cannot be <u>ridden at all</u> for

---

[139] Bobbie Astor was Nancy Astor's son by her first husband – an American named
Robert Gould Shaw (1871–1930). She and Shaw divorced in 1901 (ODNB)
[140] Waldorf Astor, later 2nd Viscount Astor (1879–1952), lived at Cliveden near
Taplow (ODNB); his brother, John Jacob Astor (1886-1971), is referred to in letter 56

4 months after they come here; then you have got to get them fit; then they probably break down on the cast-iron grounds. And after it all you can probably buy better S African ponies for the same money, without the risk of the passage, the cost of the passage, and the risk of break-down afterwards. I am frightfully pleased with my three new purchases. You might thank Rivvy for his good advice if you see him.

I've seen no more of the Gladstones. I like Methuen himself awfully; but I should think he was pretty wild in the 'ed; clever, but wild in the 'ed. Paul is an angel: and it's great fun having Billy Rawle here (at Pretoria). Muriel S is the worst woman, figuratively, not alas literally. Actually she is a howling bore, and <u>so</u> kind. Fancy being "kind", with a figure like a mannequin and a face and the manners of a street-walker – I mean, fancy kindness being the only positive quality attaching to qualifications like those! One would not have minded if she chewed opium, or was a baby-snatcher.

Life goes on as usual in this utterly abominable country, and the Jews and Dutch do each other in all day. We start musketry on Monday, which takes 2 or 3 weeks – getting all the squadron through. It is very dull, living in continual noise for so long; you stand at the firing-point, to see that they don't shoot each other, or you sit in the butts, to see that the markers don't cheat. We have to be on the range at 5.30 am, which means getting up before 4 am.

I've read "Tante", the "Hampdenshire Wonder", "Ralph Heathcote"[141] (biography, dull), "Zuleika Dobson" (rather stupid), the "Everlasting Mercy" (<u>good</u>, very) [three different people sent 3 copies to me by one mail!] – and I'm reading the Dop Doctor[142]. It's good, isn't it? But I hate material books, where the whole interest is centred on whether people are successful or not, successful in the most worldly sense. I like books about artists and philosophers and dreamers and anybody who is a little off his dot[143]. I can't explain to you, being in S[outh] A[frica]; and we should certainly quaddell about it, if I did explain to you. Indeed, we <u>will</u>, in the future. All love to the happy family J.

Yes, I liked "The Card" very much.

---

[141] *Letters of a young diplomatist and soldier during the time of Napoleon, giving an account of the dispute between the emperor and the elector of Hesse*, edited by Countess Gunther Groben (1907)

[142] *The dop doctor* by Richard Dehan (1911)

[143] To go off one's dot: to go out of one's senses (OED), as in 'dotty'

70   21 Jan 1912   Royal Dragoons, Roberts'   DE/Rv/C1138/12
Heights

My darling Casie

Thank-you most awfully for your letters – and for the delicious Christmas present; which is not useful, as I have nothing to put in it; but ornamental to a degree, and imposing, as I produce it from my pocket bulky with waste-papers before the impressed Africanders and Jewish Jews. What a country! It crawls with usurers, and stinks with avarice. Everything is just as good as its cash value, and no better; same with men & women. We play polo on <u>gravel,</u> and a thick spreading of it rises, and disappears down your eyes and ears and mouth, with every stride of every pony. Polo is the only amusement – you can't count cricket an amusement, can you? I've gone a bust[144], and bought three nailing[145] good ponies, which are the apple of my eye.
One can't do much soldiering, because there's no place where a single man can gallop, let alone a troop or a squadron. The ground is composed of holes and stones, thinly covered by a rough rank grass called Prativesticula[146]. Thus for the horseman two alternatives lay open. Either you fall over the stone into the hole; when all that has to be done is to roll the stone on top of you, and write the epitaph on it. Or, if you are careless enough to come down in the hole, and fall onto the stone, they have to lift your body, place it back in the hole, lift the stone, clean it, roll it on top of you, etc – which means "more work for the undertaker". I hope you follow me? So we keep our horses in the stable, and feed them on arrowroot.
Fancy the OBH[147] having bust up! I should certainly become a member of the Garth Hunt[148]. I'm so glad that Dynamite is in heavy form. I long for another day with the thrusting merchants on Maidenhead at Hawthorn Hill. There is no spot whatsoever on this blasted heath. Goodbye and best best love to you from J.

---

[144] Gone on a [spending] spree (OED)

[145] Extremely good (OED)

[146] A bundle or faggot of the grassland

[147] Old Berkshire Hunt. The 'Old Berks' dates back to 1830 in its present form but the country has been hunted since about 1760 (*The History of the Old Berks Hunt, 1760-1904* by F C Loder-Symonds and E Percy Crowdy, 1905)

[148] The Garth Hunt dates from about 1770. The hounds were kennelled near Bracknell, Berkshire. It took its name from T C Garth, master from 1852 to 1902 (Information from website of the Vale of Aylesbury with Garth and South Berks Hunt)

71   4 Feb 1912   Roberts' Heights   DE/Rv/C1135/571

Dear Mother

What a gay life you have been living at Tap[low], and Pans[hanger]! Did
Bill get blotto on the milk punch, or was it a sober affair? I wish I could
have seen the acting – you had an excellent troupe. I'm awfully glad that
Auntie Ka[tie] is well and easy – I wrote to her about Alwynne. About
Mog's "nice nature" I feel deeply sceptical; she is a poisoner at heart, and
only a fairly successful hypocrite. What are you going to do with her? I love
your lists of the Viscount parties – and oh, I do love the photographs of
Geordie[149] in the papers, like a Satyr cleaned up for the occasion, with that
monstrously sensual face, empty except for its vice and low cunning. What
is he like now? And what has Rosemary turned into?
I didn't read the Lyall poems[150] – I only saw one quoted in a newspaper,
about a Hindu prince who began to think about things, very obviously and
boringly, I thought. But do send me them, and let me learn before I criticise.
I've read the "Dop Doctor", and liked the description of the siege; but how
bad all the end is, and what poor shallow characters they all are really, not
living in the least. You feel that they might have been characters themselves,
but that he has only just touched the outsides of them in his description,
while labouring heavily and pretentiously to draw them deep. There is no
"spirit and truth" about them. Do you know some little Indian books,
translated by a man called F W Bain, called "A Heifer of the Dawn", and "A
Mine of Faults", and "In the Great Gods Hair" [151]. I think they are great fun
– and how interesting the Hindu philosophy is; I wish I knew more about it.
I wish I was in India now, O God: everything is pale & colourless after it.
I'm reading "The Gods, some mortals, & L[or]d W" [152] now; how witty she

---

[149] George Granville Sutherland-Leveson-Gower, Marquess of Stafford (1888-1963).
Following the death of his father, Cromartie, on 27 June 1913, he became 5th Duke of
Sutherland. It appears that Cromartie was affectionately known as 'Strath'. For
Julian's comments on his death and Geordie's succession, see letters 134 and 135
[150] *Poems*, by Sir Alfred C Lyall (1907). According to the jacket, 'Revised and
slightly enlarged from "Verses written in India"'
[151] *A heifer of the dawn*, translated from the original manuscript by F W Bain (1904);
Mine of faults, translated from the original manuscript by F W Bain (1909); *On the
great god's hair*, translated by F W Bain (1905)
[152] *The gods, some mortals and Lord Wickenham* by John Oliver Hobbes (1895)

must have been, Mrs C?[153] The polo here is the only real fun, in spite of the dust. We've had a tournament here, a scratched sort of affair inside the garrison; I'm in the team which has got into the final, with Uncle Makins, Leighton, & Pitt Rivers[154]. We play tomorrow, & have quite a chance of winning. Musketry is still going on; we start shooting at 6 every morning. No other excitements; indeed, everything as dull as ditchwater; polo three days a week the only saving clause, & schooling my four ponies every other day (3 private, 1 troop-horse – all real toppers).
All all love to all the family from J.

72   11 Feb 1912   Roberts' Heights   DE/Rv/C1135/572

Dear Mother

The fancy-dress ball must have been superb. I simply <u>loved</u> the picture of Bill – isn't it beautiful? And I thought your dress & Casie's awfully good. All the busts sound very good ones, and you must have been having great fun all round lately. Here there is one of the usual thunder storms going on, and my head is aching in tune to it, as usual. <u>What</u> a country. The only fun is the polo, which is better fun every day; and my ponies, which are things of beauty and joys forever. The regiment is in very low spirits and bad form – except Uncle Makins, who is supreme – and I think Mrs M[155] is a perfect darling. We play the final of the local tournament tomorrow – the Colonel, Leighton – (a grim dim fool, Captain, pompous, idiotic, and a good player), Pitt-Rivers, and me. We have just finished the musketry course (B Squadron), which is a great blessing – we had to get up at 4 every morning, parade at 5, ride out and start shooting at 6; shooting solidly from 6 – 11. It's the thing I hate much worst in soldiering.
No news otherwise – a good number of the "Eagle" this month, I think; I took a lot of trouble over it, and persuaded them to take a more arty cover.

---

[153] John Oliver Hobbes (see above) was the pseudonym of Mrs Pearl Mary Theresa Craigie (1867–1906) (ODNB)

[154] George Henry Lane Fox Pitt-Rivers (1860-1966) was educated at Eton College, and Worcester College, Oxford. He served with the Royal Dragoons in the First World War (ODNB)

[155] Presumably Mrs Maria Florence Makins, wife of Brigadier-General Sir Ernest Makins

I'm glad that Geordie has not married a mia, for the sake of the waning aristocracy. Are you at Cairo now? What fun you will have. Do write and tell me all all about it; and whether there is going to be a war with Germany. The storms are really <u>terrific</u> here, almost unbelievable. The thunder lifts you clear out of your chair. About 2 flashes a minute are going on now, all within about 200 yards.

All all love from Julian.

73   18 Feb 1912   Roberts' Heights   DE/Rv/C1135/573

Dear Mother

I loved your letter from Gis[156], and it made me long to have been with you and all the sports. I think I love that country best of all; I remember it far more vividly than any other; it is so grim and wild, and I've had more fun there than anywhere else. I'm glad you liked Peter; I suppose what you don't know now about Kerry bitches is hardly worth knowing? Grits always seemed to live in a perfect terror of somebody making love to her, in which case she would have been at an entire loss what to do, as her only directing influence in those lines is the poetry of Ella Wheeler Wilcox[157]. I don't remember Tom Garnett, except as a man with a moustache and three horses, all of which I remember exactly. The Hunt Ball must have been v[ery] amusing. I love the photographs of the Likkies; Moggie does look a "little bit of alright", doesn't she? How sad you must be at the end of the hols. There is no David Bingham here – only a Denis Bingham; but the error, which you neatly turn onto me in your best style, is yours. You wrote to me saying "Is the Bingham who is going to marry R.E. nice – find out about him". So I turned my eagle eye at once onto the Bingham of S[outh] A[frica].

No, the mistake was mine, and I can't get out of it, and we cannot even resort to Billingsgate, as in the old days. Have your Court duties really knocked your Cairo on the head? Can't you give up playing the waiting game? Say you are a Socialist!

---

[156] Gisburne Park, near Clitheroe, Lancashire was built by the Lister family in the 18th century

[157] Ella Wheeler Wilcox (1850-1919) an American poet, born in Wisconsin, whose many volumes of romantic, sentimental, and mildly erotic verse brought her a vast readership (*OCEL*)

There is nothing on here, not even soldiering. One goes out gaily to meet one's troop in the morning, and three men turn up with 4 led horses each – all the rest are painting the general's kitchen, or grooming the Brigade Major's horse, or cleaning up the canteen. All the day is taken up with messy little duties, the dirty work which our black brethren did so well in India. Our leisure hours are enlivened by the presence of Mr & Mrs McFarlane, née Mason. Don't you love the conciliatory noise which Mrs M makes between her words and sentences while she is speaking, and continuously while she is not speaking? Uncle Makins spends his time in dodging her from pillar to post. I like Noël very much; he is good at things too.

Please thank Dad very much for his letter. I love the idea of Bill training at Sandwich with a man-killer. Give my very best love to the two girls. Goodbye from Julian.

**74   19 Feb 1912   Royal Dragoons, Roberts'   DE/Rv/C1138/13
                               Heights**

Darling Casie

Thank you tremendously for your letters. What a time you have been having! I wish I could have been at Gis with you; I <u>did</u> love that country – and all the people, including the cotton merchant princes. Don't you love Saul, even apart from his name? The hunting there is the greatest joke, and the greatest fun – splashing about the river after rare and curious varieties of deer, specially imported from Japan and the West Indies, followed by hounds of every size and shape, but one plum-pudding colour. I was only once or twice brave enough to ride hirelings there, and when I did I always fetched up in the first ditch. I used to ride Peter's horses, until he caught me steeplechasing for a ½ crown bet round Bolton-by-Bolland[158] village green, over the rustic seats. After that Rib used to mount me, because the former scene tickled his humour. I wish I knew Diana Bulteel – she must go very well.

This country is undescribable, and only equalled by its inhabitants. I have bought a long-nose and a beard, and next Sunday I am going to run away to Port Elisabeth, when I shall hitch up my breeches and "go for a sailor". My mind has been perniciously influenced by cheap literature, and I think piracy

---

[158] Bolton-by-Bowland, Lancashire

is the only profession. I have got four very good ponies. One won a flat-race yesterday.

Bless you J.

| **75** | **25 Feb [1912]** | **Roberts' Heights** | **DE/Rv/C1135/574** |

Dear Mother

Thank you awfully for v good letter. I <u>am</u> sorry about your waiting knocking all your plans on the head. The skating and sun and cold rather terrify me, now that I have become one "of those nasty Southern" men. Is the flat good? Do you know I never got Chesterton's White Horse[159]; isn't it a beastly shame? Send me another copy, and I will pay for it, like you used to pay for the luncheons I gave you at Balliol. I am sure there is Jew blood in the family; ever since I've been in this "do or die" country I have been enticing my friends into wild bets, to the great advantage of my pocket and diminution of my popularity. But <u>please</u> send it me: you don't know how I love book presents now; I feel a sort of terrible emptiness and dryness inside my head, from reading so few good things. I didn't like the Masefield poem in the English Review much: not on the same plane as the Everlasting Mercy. I really <u>did</u> <u>wonder</u> at bits of that; and bits of it – <u>how</u> bad. All the tracty religious wadding at the end, the best indirect refutation of Christianity there could ever be; after the really good pagan bits at the beginning. But the "Widow"[160] poem rather shows up his desire to shock and offend at all costs, and shows one why even the other jarred a little – from pose and slight falseness. But what truth too, and the strength which cannot go without truth. Isn't he good at getting pages into one short line – "From 61 to 67 I lived in disbelief of Heaven"; it's so terribly convincing – you cannot doubt that he did! I haven't read the American book yet.

About Patrick; I don't know. But I look back with growing animosity on his memory. I hated him so when he was wallopy. I hated him in the mornings. I didn't like him much when he was drunk. I liked him very much sometimes when he was a long way off, and I liked being told the things he

---

[159] *The Ballad of the White Horse*, by G K Chesterton (1911) describes a desperate but ultimately victorious battle fought by the Christian King Alfred against the pagan Danish invaders. Its fervent English patriotism made it popular during both world wars

[160] *The widow in the bye street* by John Masefield (1912)

said. But I didn't like the way he walked, even when he was walking away. I didn't like his hands or his feet or his streaky hair, or his love of money, or his dislike of dogs. Animals always edged away from him, and the more intelligent they were the further they edged. I think there is something rather obscene about him; like the electric eel at the Zoo.

About Leave – I want to come home frightfully, in fact I'm batting for it. But with <u>any</u> luck I think I shall get home in the Autumn, after manoevres. I asked the Colonel, and he said that I should be due for it then, only that everybody would be wanting to go just at the same time. But I'm sure I <u>shall</u> get it. Write to Mrs Makins, & she will work it. It would be glorious if you came out for a jaunt in foreign climes: but <u>not</u> here – I think you w[oul]d hate it as much as I do. We will go to India or Cochin China, and Paris on the way home.

Bless you – the mail is going. All all love to the family. Are you very welly-welly? J.

76   3 Mar [1912]   Roberts' Heights   DE/Rv/C1135/575

Dear Mother

Thanks awfully for your letter. What fun the skating must have been. Don't you love the pictures of the people in the papers who win the Fen championship, held for the first time for three years? During which three years they have been cleaning their skates, and whistling for a frost, and mending the holes in their black tights. It must be such a good profession: I wish I was a Fen champion. I read the "Everlasting Mercy" and the "Widow" again: the first time I read the "Widow" I didn't like it so <u>very</u> much – I don't think the characters are frightfully good. Jim is just a clay figure; and Anna and the Widow are just <u>too</u> terrible and unrelieved to be absolutely convincing. It is as if he had worked out the drama and the situations and the complications, as though they were the inevitable result of Forces or Powers – and then put up the characters as pegs to hang up the tapestry of them. I could see and feel and understand the drunken poachers in the Everlasting Mercy much better than any of the "Widow" people: and the lesser characters in it too, like the Parson and the Squire and the man he fought and the girl in the Pub. What I thought about the "Widow" was that it was just a shade impersonal, & therefore left one colder than it should have done. Like a Greek tragedy, only the people themselves seemed to have too little share in working out their own damnation: even their characters

seemed to have too little to do with it. The Fate of it seemed above them and beyond them altogether, and does not deign to use their individuality in bringing destruction on them; which w[oul]d have been more human and moving, and at the same time just as inevitable and just as terrible. I forgot the Gipsy girl: she is a wonderful character, made vivid in four lines. I think I like the "E[verlasting] M[ercy]" best: but <u>how</u> good, both of them. And how depressing and idiotic (I suppose designedly?) the religion in them. The "Miracle" must have been great fun to see. I love Moggie's idea of Edward's face being new every morning, like the sun. No news here – except the arrival of Hardwicke and Godman, Captains, both very nice. There is only one really unutterable ass in the regiment, rank Captain, name Leighton. He is such an one. There is a new boy called Dent whom I dislike intensely by night; he came from the Varsity, and does not credit to it. A young and sharp black Jew called Swire. Another Varsity man called Leckie, nice. We start squadron training soon: regimental training in June: manoevres in July; and home, by the grace of God, in.
God bless the family. Give them all my best love. God bless you, make a good boy A Amen. Julian.

77   10 Mar 1912   Roberts' Heights   DE/Rv/C1135/576

Dear Mother

Thank you awfully for your letter: I can't make out about mine not arriving, except that they are very casual about posting them in the Mess here. I'm glad you had fun in London; but you must be glad not to be staying there right on. It must have been amusing, going to the Opening of Parliament on your ten toes, amidst the jokes of the populace. Why don't you poison Bonar Law[161] for disclaiming your acquaintance? It would liven up things to return to the times of the Borgias; and you are admirably fitted by nature for the role of a poisoner, don't you think? I suppose we aren't really going to fight Germany yet, from what Haldane[162] told you? Things here are as dull as ever, except for the arrival of a great man called Hardwick, who has been Adjutant of the Surrey Yeomanry: he is a breath of fresh air in the suburbs,

---

[161] Andrew Bonar Law, politician and later Prime Minister (ODNB)
[162] Richard Burdon Haldane, Viscount Haldane (1856–1928), politician, educationist, and Lord Chancellor (ODNB)

and makes some of the others seem greater dead-heads than ever. There's a
good new subaltern from Oxford too, called Leckie: how much nicer the
Oxford people are than the Sandhurst blood, who is put into one end of the
machine a bloody puppy, and comes out of the other end a bloody soldier.
Do you know, we have got three people in the regiment who believe in the
Apostles Creed from end to end, and most of the Nicene Creed, and the Fire
Everlasting for such as you and me. I have just seen the Colonel, and he says
that he will give me leave after manoevres – but he can't say exactly what
month – probably September. I am simply batting for home and beauty
again! We will have the greatest fun. Give my best best love to all the
family. Didn't you get those beautiful military photographs – they should
have arrived ages ago? Did you recognise drawing of "Toby" in December
"Eagle", and piece of poetry?[163] Can you read the "Eagle"? It's pretty stiff,
isn't it. The polo is going strong, and my ponies have turned out
magnificently.
All all love & blessings from J.

78   17 Mar 1912   Roberts' Heights   DE/Rv/C1135/577

Dear Mother

Thank you awfully for your letter, a very good one. How exciting about the
Silver Wedding[164]: but your pictures and Dad's in the papers look like John
Vere de Vere Coming of Age and his prospective bride from the Gaiety
Theatre, and I am sure that you signed the Attestation Papers wrong; and that
I am really about 12, and a Fraudulent Enlister: whereas Bill is like Ginger
Stott's metaphysical son, with a body developed in proportion to his mind.
Has he won the boxing – I'm simply batting to hear? Give him my love of
loves. And do send me your Articles – "The Miracle" and "Children": I
shall never forgive you if you don't. I wish I could hear Chesterton dragging
in Dickens[165], and Edmund Gosse[166] on the military covers: but that will all
come in the Autumn, and I will have a gigantic bust. I loved Tante, in spite

---

[163] Julian's poem, 'To a black greyhound', (See Appendix 2; Mosley, pp311-312)
[164] Ettie and Willy married on 17 February 1887
[165] Gilbert Keith Chesterton (1874–1936), writer. He wrote two books about Charles
Dickens. His *Charles Dickens* (1906) is a tribute to a writer for whom, like
Browning, he felt a considerable affinity (ODNB)
[166] Sir Edmund William Gosse (1849–1928), writer (ODNB)

of the length; but in a long book, which is as good & clever as that, one gets the characters soon, and then there's nothing more to find out, & one gets rather tired of them; in a less good book one would not get to know them so quickly, & the interest w[oul]d be kept up. Send me Evan on Fontenoy[167]; and Chesterton's "White Horses". About Success – I like the people best who take it as it comes, or doesn't come, and are busy about impractical and ideal things in their heart of hearts all the time. The two things really go together, I suppose; but I like the interest to be in the unsuccessful and unsuccessable more than in the successful and successable. Success is such a gross word. We start Squadron Training tomorrow – 8.30 – 1 pm every day, and 2 – 3 in the afternoons. I school my ponies 6.30 – 8 in the morning; and play polo on polo days 3.30 – 5 pm. I'm going to start boxing (for the Army Championship in May) in the evenings. But I'm drinking Stout, with nips of Sanatogen[168], and I have a good lie-down every night, with a prayer to Hickson and God and Maurice Craig[169]. My ponies are like Greek sculptures, only with a neater style of galloping: just think how tired it w[oul]d make you to play 8 chukkers on horses which always had all four legs in the air at once. Poor Mama, you are waiting now; how long does it go on for at a time? All all love to the family from J.

---

[167] The Battle of Fontenoy (11 May 1745) near Fontenoy in the Austrian Netherlands, was a French victory in the War of Austrian Succession

[168] Proprietary name for a tonic wine

[169] A doctor, later Sir Maurice (1866-1935), who wrote the standard textbook *Psychological medicine; a manual on mental diseases for practitioners and students* (1905)

79   24 Mar 1912   Roberts' Heights   DE/Rv/C1135/578

Dear Mother

It is terribly sad about the boxing; and rather bad luck. I am miserable about
it, aren't you? Thank you awfully for the Edinburgh Review, and the Lyall
poems – and the photographs of Bill & Dad. they are very good: I think
Bill's is <u>really</u> fine – I had kept the one you sent me before, out of a paper,
because I thought it so beautiful. It must have been a lovely dress. His face
is entirely Roman, I think; not Greek; too single-minded and tenacious for
Greek. I liked the Lyall poems, but not nearly so much as you do: they are
so jungly, with cheap rhythm instead of music; and I hate "easy-chair", and I
rather hate "Just for the pride of the old countree", rhyming with "me", and
recalling "Duke's son, Cook's son , etc etc". Have you finished your
"Newman". The Territorial Nursing must have been tremendous labour. I'm
glad Edith Wolverton thought I was nice and young and fresh, because I feel
so particularly nasty and old and stale just at present. The poor English
ponies out here are just getting their summer coats, and the S[outh] A[frican]
winter is just beginning, so that life is a perpetual disillusionment to them:
their state of body is exactly parallel to my state of mind. No, I'm frightfully
well, and in a vile temper at this minute. I'm going to bed; I can't write.
Best best love to the family & you from J.

80   30 Mar 1912   Roberts' Heights   DE/Rv/C1135/579

Dear Mother

Thank you awfully for your birfday presies. I simply adore the hectic
photograph of you and Moggy at the burning of Rome: and I love the
Marlowe poems[170], tremendously – especially the one when her feet look
gracious, as she goes away from him. I've only just looked at them yet – I'm
dying to read them "through & through". The "Amores" [171] are so much less
disgusting than those sort of modern things, because Ovid never tried to
make out what a fearful dog he was, like all the modern erotics do; he just
states his fun quite naturally and without surprise.

---

[170] Poetry by the Elizabethan playwright, Christopher Marlowe (1564-1593) (ODNB)
[171] Love poems written by the Roman poet Ovid

I <u>am</u> so glad Bill is better: please give him tons & tons of my love. And
thank the wicked Moggy for her letter, and isn't her complexion lovely in the
photograph. Best love to Dad, & all thanks for his letter. It is <u>terrible</u> about
the strikes[172]: and finances. I had had an idea that they had been bad lately,
although you never said a word. I <u>am</u> sorry & worried. I can easily sell two
ponies, if it is really a norful hustle. <u>Do</u> tell me: I could do it tomorrow.
<u>Please</u> tell me.

No news from here much; we are in the throes of Squadron Training, and at it
all day. I fight in the Amateur boxing in 10 days, and I'm as hard as nails, &
in full training. The polo has been v good lately. My squadron leader
(Hardwick) let me ride all the bad horses in the Squadron today, over the
jumps, for a birthday treat: and I'm black and blue, & red at the corners.
How I wish I was in England, now that the spring is here[173]. How I wish I
was 22, not 24; or 28, or 18, or 37 – no, I think 24 is a very good age, but I
wish I could see you now. This takes you tons and tons and tons of love &
blessings – and I do love getting your letters, and any little trifles in the way
of books & jewellery that come to hand. Bless you J.

81   7 Apr [1912]   Roberts' Heights   DE/Rv/C1135/580

Dear Mother

I loved your letter, and Mr Barnes' insidious flattery of my personal
appearance. Is Mr MacFarlane <u>clever</u>? <u>Surely</u> you must be thinking of some
other? What fun you and Casie must have had at the Pytcheley Races[174]:
write me long accounts of each race, à la "How we beat the Favourite". The
Methuens used to think Luke White a fool; but that was only because he was
so much cleverer than them, I think. But he is solemn & sombre. I love the
story of Bron and Old Sicky; I'm batting to see Bron again; please give him
oceans of love from me when you see him next. What was your "second
waiting" like? Everything is plodding along here as usual, as dull as ever –
the only excitement is the Jo'burg boxing, Thursday Friday and Saturday this
week. I'm taking over a dozen of the regimental pugilists to do battle, and

---

[172] A national miners' strike began in Britain on 26 February 1912
[173] Misquotation from Robert Browning, 'Home-thoughts, from Abroad', 'O, to be in
England / Now that April's there'
[174] Village near Kettering, Northamptonshire; also the name of a hunt

fighting in the Officer Heavyweights myself – but I doubt if I get an opponent. I hope I shall, because I'm very fit and full of fight. You have no idea <u>how</u> boring this place is; and dank; and dead. I love the Marlowe; what a lot of stuff there is in it, isn't there?

Bless you – and give my best best love to the family. J.

82   21 Apr 1912   Roberts' Heights   DE/Rv/C1135/581

Dear Mother

Thank you awfully for your letters: and for a beautiful new "White Horse" Ballad. I like it very much indeed; but I don't think he is anywhere near as good a poet as Belloc. He often reminds me of Belloc – a lot of his rhythms are like the Belloc ones; but they seem natural and spontaneous and true in Belloc, and in G.K.C[hesterton]. often a little forced and imitative. That is the only thing I don't like about him: I think he writes rather as if he had a set model of style before him, and was working at a true copy all the time. A very good style, but somehow not quite his own, and therefore not quite convincing: whereas in Belloc the style and matter are one and indivisible and personal. But aren't bits of the White Horse lovely? I love the men, when they are fighting for their lives, breaking out in long philosophical discourses about Christianity and Nihilism and Paradox, between the three-minute rounds. I suppose they had a system of Half-Time.

The Coal Strike must have been an agonising time for everyone. How is family finance just now? I had a Cheerful letter from Dad, saying that he thought it had muzzled the Trade Unions for the immediate future. I hope you will have the most glorious "Easter Hols". The Pytcheley Races must have been thrilling, and Casie must have had the time of her life.

About coming home – I can't get out of the Colonel anything definite as to when he will let me go. He is going on a tour of the battle-fields in October, and perhaps I shall have to stay for that. Anyhow, I should get away by the end of October; and possibly much earlier – the beginning of September. Hurrah! What tremendous fun we will have!

Everything as usual here: we have finished Squadron Training, under Hardwick (yes, Philip – charming), and passed all the tests with éclat. The Colonel said he was very pleased with me. I went to Jo'burg on the 11[th] w[i]th our boxing men, trained up to the eyes; and when I got there I found out that I was the only officer entered! So I got the promoters to give a cup for a four-round contest , and a man who was in training for the Amateur Championship said he would come and fight me. He was a fire-man, called Tye; he used to be a sailor, and he looked as hard as a hammer. I quaked in my shoes when I saw him; and quaked more when I heard he was 2-1 on favourite for the Championships; and quaked most when my trainer went to see him box, and returned with word that he had knocked out two men in ¼ of an hour. We went into the ring on the night, and he came straight for me like a tiger, and hit left and right; I stopped the left, but it knocked my guard aside, and he crashed his right clean onto the point of my jaw. I was clean knocked out; but by the fluke of God I recovered and came to and got onto my feet again by the time they had counted six. I could hardly stand, and I could only see a white blur in front of me: but I just had sense to keep my guard up, and hit hard at the blur whenever it came within range. He knocked me down twice more, but my head was clearing every moment, and I felt a strange sort of confidence that I was master of him. I put him down in the 2nd round with a right counter, which shook him; he took a count of 8. In the third round I went in to him, and beat his guard down – then crossed again with the right, and felt it go right home, with all my arm and body behind it. I knew it was the end, when I hit; and he never moved for 20 seconds. They said it was the best fight they had seen for years in Jo'burg; and my boxing men went clean off their heads with delight, and carried me twice round the hall. I was 11 st 4, & he 11 st 3; and I think it was the best fight I shall ever have.

All all love from J.

83   26 Apr 1912   Nottingham Road   DE/Rv/C1135/582
**   Station, Natal**

Dear Mother

No letter from you to answer this week, as I've just come down here for a week's holiday, to fish; and my letters haven't been forwarded yet. I hope you are having good "hols". This place is a tin hut in the wilds of Natal, near the Basutoland border[175]. Great bare hills, and a little rocky river, like a Scotch river. I came down here yesterday - 1½ days in the train, and a 20 mile drive from the station, with 4 mules and a Cape-cart[176], over a real

---

[175] Basutoland is a former name of Lesotho, in southern Africa

[176] A two-wheeled, horse-drawn hooded cart peculiar to South Africa (OED)

"dotted line" road. It is wild country, and a wild place; but oh, how I hate all this bloody South Africa. There is no warmth in it, or colour, or character: it is bare and lonely and unlovely and empty and prosaic. I can't feel comfortable or alive in it: only grumbling and malevolent and outcast. Directly I got here it began to thunder and rain; it would; and the river became pea-green with purple patches; it would: and the trout retired into their blasted holes; God damn them. Then three drunken farmers came in and wanted me to drink with them; and I told them that I took the pledge[177] in New York in '98. The Basutos are going to make war, and I don't blame them – living in a country like this. If you burnt the whole country, it would look just the same in a fortnight, houses and all, if you imported a few dozen Scotch settlers. There are no trees; think of it, no trees!

Roberts Heights is a small corrugated-iron facsimile of Purgatory. It would not be so bad, if there were some place near it where you could go from Sat – Mon and drink Veuve Cliquot[178] with glorious women in green dresses, and talk to them about art and literature & religion; or even a decent jungle with pig. But the only relaxation is to see Mrs Steele, very much overdressed, driving a lame troop-horse in a second-hand buggy.

The only good thing in the country is William Rawle, of the South Wales Borderers. He used to be a pig-head, but has now become a cynic, with an immensely powerful brain. He is the man who said to Patrick "Oh yes, I know about all you Balliol men, and Aristotle".

All all love to the family. Give them my best love, & tell them that I have fallen upon evil days. I'm longing to get your letter – I expect it will arrive tomorrow. I stay here a week – then back to Dooty[179]. I wish I were with you now. Are the Point-to-Points fun. Tell Williams to look me out a Steeplechase horse for next year. Tell Likky Man & Mog that I love them awfully J.

---

[177] A solemn undertaking to abstain from alcohol (as made by members of a temperance movement) (OED)
[178] A brand of champagne, recognized by its distinctive bright yellow bottle labels
[179] Duty

**84   26 Apr 1912   Trout Bungalow,   DE/Rv/C1138/14
                     Nottingham Road Station**

Darling Casie

Thank you for your letters. No, I don't really look like my photograph:
indeed, in this democratic country, where the lower orders are so much above
themselves, I am always mistaken for the Odd Man. So cheer up. Your
Pytchley time must have been the very greatest fun, with all the nuts – and
your hireling hoss. You are very clever to have succeeded in extricating a
water-colour from the Mad Mullah; but don't think that this establishes for
you any right of ownership therein. Or shall I have to give it you as a
birthday present when I return to the Old Country? Please give the Mullah
my best love, when you see him again. The Trout Bungalow is a small tin
hut on the Basutoland border; there are no trout, but the mutton is passable,
as it is situate in the centre of the Sheep-Farming Industry, which has made
the Empire what it is. There is one white man here, but he is deaf and dumb,
and stole £2 from me in the night; so our conversation is stilted and jerky.
The next nearest civilised habitation is 23 miles off. I have come here for a
week, to get the sound of the trumpets out of my ears. They were rather
boring at Roberts Heights when I left. There is a new man called Dent, who
is like a toothache, and was at Cambridge. We play at soldiers there all day
and all night.
I had a great fight at the Jo'burg boxing the other day, against the local
champion, a fireman by occupation and an ex-sailor by trade. In the third
round I hit him with such violence on the starboard bow that he lost
consciousness, and the fight, amid loud cat-calls and cries of Go it, Curly.
He had previously knocked me down three times in the most ungentlemanly
way. It only proves what BLUE BLOOD can do, when roused.
Goodbye God bless you J.

85   6 May 1912   Pretoria Club, Pretoria   DE/Rv/C1135/583

Dear Mother

Two letters to answer this week from you. April at Tap[low] sounds <u>too</u> delicious, and the hols, and Likkie Man playing cricket with Gibbon, and the Garth P[oin]t to Poin]t – which made me simply ache to be riding a race again. I want someone to get me two <u>nailing</u> steeplechase-hunters for next year; ask all the horsey men you see for a horse that can hunt and jump, <u>and fast enough to win races in the spring</u>. I will write to Tommy Rib[180]: tell Williams to keep his skew-eyes wide open and straight to the front. Also enlist Tricky Beaumont – I don't think I know him, unless he is <u>fat</u> and <u>curly</u>? I'm longing to get your <u>three</u> articles – how prolific you are! And Rupert Brooke[181] and Small Beer[182] – they haven't arrived yet. I read <u>all</u> the Marlowe, and loved it – esp Hero & Leander, & some lines in Dido[183]. I have been awfully good, and taken a rest-cure, instead of going in for the Amateur Championships this week at Jo'burg. I have felt very done-up all these last five months, in this disgusting climate. But I tried the cure <u>per contrarium</u>[184], driving ahead all day; it is certainly less deadly and miserable than lying up, but I suppose it means a longer "go". My weeks idling and eating and fishing in Natal just set me up, and I feel like a tiger again now; it was great fun, & the fishing good – 20 trout a day, averaging ¾lb, very small, but amusing.

Tell me all about Avon – I hope you had a glorious one. I loved Bill's wedding-garment for Geordie's nuptials; did you have a good "dress" argument with him. Did he go in his jorsey. I am buying some new open-

---

[180] Thomas Lister, 4th Baron Ribblesdale (See letter 20)

[181] Rupert Brooke, one of the major poets of the First World War (1887–1915). In September 1914 he was given a commission in the Royal Naval division; in February 1915 the division sailed for Gallipoli, but Brooke died at sea on 23 April and was buried at Skyros the same day. He is thought to have contracted septicaemia from a mosquito bite (ODNB). See also letter 274

[182] Possibly *A Chronicle of Small Beer (Sketches of Boyhood)* by John Reid (1893)

[183] *Hero and Leander. A poem begunne by Christopher Marlowe and finished by George Chapman* (Edinburgh, 1909); *The tragedy of Dido, Queen of Carthage Written by Christopher Marlowe and Thomas Nash* (republished in 1914)

[184] Latin for 'by doing the opposite', ie rather than resting Julian had been pushing himself

work jerseys for London wear next winter, and some splendid dirt-coloured shirts, so you will have great fun walking about with your two sons.

I can't yet find out anything definite about actual <u>date</u> of coming home: but it varies between August and September: the beginning of August – end of September. It <u>will</u> be fun. Do make enquiries about horses – now is the time to buy, or rather before this.

Another thing is – can you find out from the War Office or political nuts whether we are likely to stay on long in this country? Because I really <u>can't</u> face coming back here, if it is to be for long. I would sooner go and do first-footman to someone in <u>India,</u> if they would have me – or Java, or New Zealand. But I'd of course sooner stay with the regt, if they leave this place in a month or two. Advise, Mama. Do you know anyone who wants a rather untidy, unsocial, A.D.C? I could look after the dogs very well, and feeding and care of horses; don't you think I sh[oul]d do very well?

Give my best best love to the family, and all the dependents. We have got a new subaltern who has got a head like Socrates, only bigger, and took 4½ years at Oxford and ½ year at a crammer to get a pass degree: but socially he is brilliant. All love from J.

86   12 May [1912]   Roberts' Heights   DE/Rv/C1135/584

ROGATION SUNDAY

Darling Mother

How I loved the Rupert Brooke poems[185]. Who is Rupert B? Don't you like the one called "The Voice", on p 43; and the one on p 42? Who is Rupert, what is he? I like some of the Lucas[186] stories too, pretty well. It was very good of you to send me them: I <u>do</u> love getting books, better than anything. Is the new M Hewlett[187] good? And was your good quotation out of that. I will try to get it here. Your Avon must have been the greatest fun: yes, it <u>is</u> a good place for fun, and happy-go-luckiness; and <u>what</u> divine country – how

---

[185] The anthology *Poems*, by Rupert Brooke, published in 1911

[186] St John Lucas (1879-1934) mostly edited poetry. Possibly this is referring to *The last Arcadian, and other papers* (1899)

[187] Maurice Hewlett (1861-1923), novelist and poet (ODNB). The book Julian is referring to is either *The agonists: a trilogy of God and man* (1911) or *Brazenhead the Great* (1911)

one remembers it! Moggy seems to be in the greatest form; do you think she will become a sort of Messalina[188], or a saint with a halo? She has got all the elements of extreme wickedness in her; and – you say – the elements of extreme goodness. I hope the Guards Races party was a success?

I can't tell you how I hate this country; it is like being shut up in a box – a very big box, quite empty, and the emptiness exaggerated by the size of it. I saw some pictures in Jo'burg yesterday – John, Orpen, Sargent[189]: and it suddenly carried one away into a land with things in it, and warmth in it, and burning interest; out of the sordid, mercenary, ugly, inhuman sham that this country is. Did you ever see a picture by Orpen called "The Fairy Ring"? I did so like it. Aug[ustus] John must be a raving lunatic – is he dead yet, or have his habits toned down. He is the sort of man who might kill himself, or turn round and become a religious maniac. The boxing was good, very good; miners & soldiers & Jew & Dutchmen and all sorts. I love boxing more and more, to do or to watch. It is such a wonderful combination of Strength and Speed, Dash & Cunning, Steadiness & Dash: and it gives you such a good spectacle of the human body in action. They were damn good, some of them; esp a man who was disqualified for calling his opponent a bloody bastard, when the latter gripped him by the knees to escape punishment. As the man has nigger blood in him, it was only a mild statement of the truth. [Barstid is the one word which a Tommy will not let himself be called; twice a week you see men going up before the Colonel, bandaged and bloody, and the occasion is always the same]. My men did no good; they seem to be rather soft; I suppose it's the effect of India. We go down to Potchefstroom next week for the Inter-Regimental & Subaltern's Polo; I'm playing for our subalterns team. I had a dim hope of playing for the reg[imen]t, but I've been right out of form lately, and never stood a chance.

When do you go to London; and have you got a house yet? I have been having such fun with the Makins family lately: don't you think her a great dear, and amusing. They are very good together, too, which is rare. Billy Miles has just come back from India, squinting as hard as ever.

Give my best best love to the family. Goodnight I'm sleepy. Love J.

Added to first page: I want to ask for such a lot of things

---

[188] After Messalina, the wife of the emperor Claudius who was notorious for her promiscuity (*OCCL*). The word has come to mean a licentious, lascivious, or scheming woman (OED)

[189] Augustus John, artist (1878–1961); Sir William Orpen, painter (1878–1931); John Singer Sargent, portrait and landscape painter and muralist (1856–1925) (ODNB)

Faith
Hope
Charity
someone to buy my ponies
a 'grande passion' without consequences
a new face
more "loveliness"
more interest
a beautiful soul
more love of my fellow men
death of Capt Leighton I.R.D.
death of Dent I.R.D.
£250
small feet and hands
gentleness
quick repartee
less appetite
polished manners of the true gentleman
truth, sudden discovery of the
boots, polo, new
life, theory of, new
books, old
books, new
death of Capt Leighton, I.R.D.

87   20 May 1912   Potchefstroom,   DE/Rv/C1135/585
**   South Africa**

Dear Mother

You will be by now well settled down in London. What a wonderful spring
you must have had at Tap[low]. I wish I had been there; I've got a mud-
coloured sweater that would knock sparks out of Billa-boy's, and many
improved arguments on the subject of dress. The Guards Races party sounds
v good: but how terrible about poor Alistair; I <u>am</u> sorry. I suppose it will
take him an awful long time to get right again?
We are here for a fortnight, for the Inter-Regimental and Subalterns polo.
I'm not playing for the Regiment – I thought I should at one time, but I went
off in the last month. They are very bad, the Regt, as you will see from my

nearly getting in! Our subalterns are not too bad, but I don't think we shall win. This place is 4000 ft up, 2000 lower than R[oberts] Heights, and much much nicer. It is really quite <u>green</u>, and there are two or three trees to the square mile, and a river, almost as big but not so artistic as Berry Hill Brook. You really can have no idea <u>how</u> hellish is our home in the South; this place ain't no bloomin bunch of vilets [violets], but paradise in comparison. It is good to get away from it, and I think we shall have a very cheery fortnight here.

About coming home – the difficulty is to know whether I can possibly get 8 months instead of 6; you're only supposed to get 6 in this country, but I should think my clever Mama could do in the W[ar] O[ffice] alright. If I only get 6, I should like to work it Dec, Jan, Feb, March, April, May – so as to get in the races and spring fun. If I get 8, I'd come in October. I'll fix it up as soon as ever I can, definitely.

Best best love – to everyone - & you from J.

PS A harrowing account of my fight from the Transvaal Leader!

88   26 May 1912   Potchefstroom   DE/Rv/C1135/586

My dearest Mother

Thank you awfully for your letter. I hate thinking of having missed a wonderful English spring, in this pestilential upland where spring makes no difference, and comes in the Autumn. 30 Bruton Street sounds splendid, and almost barbaric. How did the Taplow bust go off? I quite agree with you about Charlie Mills – he is wonderful in every way; and <u>awfully</u> amusing? I'm glad Alastair[190] is going on well.

This is not at all a bad place, and a nice lazy life. I'm sure soldiering is the only perfect rest-cure, because it makes you take enough exercise to digest your food, and makes no call whatsoever on the brain. A lot of that nasty indigestion comes from thinking, which takes the blood away from the stomach and drives it in an ugly rush to the brain. Instead of that, the soldier sits in a large chair in the mess room, and enjoys a state which is half sleeping, a quarter reading the paper, and a quarter laughing when he hears someone else laughing, or saying "By Jove" when somebody else makes a remark. The regiment got well beaten at polo by the 15th Hussars (we're

---

[190] Alastair Sutherland-Leveson-Gower, second son of the 5th Duke of Sutherland.

living in their mess here); I occupied the glorious and vital position of 5th
man. We (the subalterns) play on Tuesday. When we are not playing polo or
practising polo, we are playing billiards or practising billiards, or playing
squash or practising squash, in the intervals between eating and sleeping. Do
you like the Eden Philpotts books?[191] I'm reading one now, called 'The
Forest on the Hill' – rather good, good about air and trees, and breezy tree-
like characters. I quite agree with you about the St John Lucas book – the
Three Grotesques are good, & the rest nowhere, except Diary of a Short
Sighted Man, which is v[ery] clever?
I've just seen the Colonel and asked him about leave. [rest of letter missing]

89   3 June 1912   IRD, Roberts' Heights   DE/Rv/C1135/587

Dear Mother

Thank you awfully for your letter. What a damned nuisance about the mails
– I always post my letters with clocklike regularity, weekly; but you have no
idea what the post office are like here – it is just a sporting chance whether
you get anything or not, about 6-4 against when there has been a holiday, and
6-4 on in ordinary weeks. I have lost at least 4 books through them.
Who is <u>John</u> Grenfell? Does he live hereabouts? I'm glad you liked the racy
account of my fight with Tyeger Tye. They made an awful fuss about it, and
men nudge each other now when I walk the streets in Johannesburg, and
mutter "E's bloody ot" – which is apparently the highest form of compliment
out here. We all got back from Potch[efstroom] at 1 am last night, after just
13 hours in the train; it should have been 8 hours; but the engine-driver had a
spite against the station-master at Pilgrim's Drift, and tried to break up the
engine, so they replaced him with an amateur Hottentot, who said he had
never driven an engine, but that he could ride a motor-bicycle. The polo
fortnight was great fun, although we got shockingly hammered both in the
Regimental (first ties) and the Subalterns (after one win). It is a far superior
place to this, and they are good people (15th Hussars and 12th Lancers). We
had two very good hunts with the Otter Hounds, and one with long dogs (bag
1 buck, 1 hare, 1 mia cat). I sold my three ponies (Rajah, Lurcher, Cigarette)

---

[191] Phillpotts' (1862–1960) best-known works are the eighteen novels and two
collections of short stories that make up his 'Dartmoor cycle.' *The Forest on the Hill*
was published in 1912

for £340, a net gain of £70 in 5 months. Wasn't that bloody ot? So I have got my polo out here for nix, and some money for hunters next year. William Rawle stood the other side at the auction, and bid away like blazes till I gave him the nod to stop. "Cigarette" (with his gammy legs) got to £85; and I had told William to stop at £80; but I knew that the £85 man wanted him badly. So I winked, and William went £90. Then there was a sickening pause, and I thought we had done it in. The auctioneer said Going . . .Going . . . Going, and at the last second the man went £95, and got him. Rajah fetched £145, which is a tremendous price out here; and Lurcher £100. There won't be much more polo here now – we start regimental training tomorrow – (we go out into camp for that) – and in the middle of July manoevres, also in camp. It will be <u>horribly</u> cold.

It's very exciting about Guy & Frances Tennant[192]. Is she nice – I don't know her. I <u>love</u> Guy – don't you? I <u>am</u> glad that Maurice's Play went well – do give him stacks of love from me when you see him. <u>Mouche</u> at the Tap[low] party sounds <u>too</u> splendid – or is she rather boring with it.

I <u>am</u> looking and longing for home. Best best love to the family from Julian.

90   9 June 1912   Roberts' Heights   DE/Rv/C1135/588

My dear Mother

Thank you awfully for your letter. It's bitterly biting cold here, freezing hard, and no fireplaces in the rooms, and only a sheet of corrugated iron between us and the great ugly empty damned forsaken wilderness. I can really hardly hold the pen. Fancy fighting for a country where it thunders all the summer and freezes all the winter, and where the hares are the size of rabbits, and can't run.

How is Tommy Rib? Is his leg well enough for him to ride; or still bad? Do ginger him up about getting swift horses for me, up to 13 st 7. I'm glad Laura is well and happy, and has found an occupation that keeps her from flopping. Give my love to Mogsy, and tell her to read her Aristotle. Here everyone is fairly cheery. I talked to the Colonel the other day about leave, and jobs etc. He said that he could not allow anyone to go on a staff job, or to the Cavalry School, until they had done 3 yrs in the regiment; and that

---

[192] The Hon Guy Lawrence Charteris (1886–1967) married as his first wife, Frances Lucy Tennant (1887–1925), granddaughter of Sir Charles Tennant (ODNB)

therefore I could not go to the Cavalry School this year, but that I must come back again after leave; and that perhaps I might go next year. The Cavalry School (Netheravon[193]) begins in February and goes on till September. So that if I went next year (I mean year after next, Feb 1914) I should come back here after leave (say May 1913) and do about 7 months more in this purgatory: but on the other hand that would probably see us over our time out here, and I should not have to come out again afterwards. If, contrariwise, I could get to the school this year (Feb 1913), I could get a job afterwards and never come here no more, O Lord, never come here no more. Thirdly and lastly, what fun is there in a job? I would liefer be a lieutenant in Africa than odd man to a general in Heaven – I think. Conclusion – I had better come out here again in May, and let things run their course. If on the other hand I go to the school next Feb, I go, and the future God will provide for. If I don't, I come back. Isn't it disappointing after a long process of thought to be left exactly where you would have been without any thought at all? Anyhow it will be good coming home – starting <u>somewhere in the middle of September</u>, and staying (if I get a 2 months extension, which sh[oul]d be done) till end of April.

Polo is rather slack here now, everyone having practised up for the Tournament, and now having no end and object to play for. I'm… [rest of letter missing].

91   16 June 1912   Roberts' Heights   DE/Rv/C1135/589

Dear Mother

Thank you awfully for your letter. I quite agree about Revolt against Environment, Injudicious. How true what you say is. How did you think of it at all? Did it come in a blinding flash, or as the result of a patient process of reasoning? The great truths that come to mankind come sometimes in the one way, sometimes in the other: and one can only pause in thankfulness, without analysing the processes. We are going to have a pretty busy month of it here; but it is nice and cold, often below freezing point, and the great

---

[193] In 1904 a Cavalry School was established at Netheravon House, Netheravon, Wiltshire, with an indoor riding school. Barracks, houses, villas for officers, and a large villa for the Commanding Officer were built in the grounds, while a War Department estate was built in the triangle of land between the High Street and the Upavon-Salisbury road. (http://www.wiltshire.gov.uk/community/getcom.php?id =166, accessed 20/06/07)

open beautiful veldt, where they have just burnt all the grass, lets the clear breezes of heaven take their way unimpeded. They whistle tunes like "Hark the h[erald] angels sing" through the aperture between one's neck and one's shirt, which is so nice for people who are musical. Today week we are going out on a regimental trek, for a week, taking our blankets and toothbrushes in our pockets. The week after that we are going to play at demoralised and defeated Boojers, retreating upon Pretoria, pursued by the 2 cavalry regiments from Potchefstroom. Then we bivouac at Hatherley for 3 weeks, and play about with livery generals.

I hope you had fun at George Curzon's?[194] I'm simply longing to see the Sargent[195] drawing of Dad – does he like it? I want awfully to see Casie managing her young men; I'm very glad that I have never fallen under thrall of one of these new strong-minded women. Please give her my best best love. How is Billa-boy? Isn't he in for Greats[196] this year – and if not, why not?

All all all love from J.

---

92   23 June 1912   Roberts' Heights   DE/Rv/C1135/590

Dear Mother

Thank you awfully for your letter. Hackwood must have been supreme. How did the fortnight's Waiting go? Promise to send me "The Charwoman's Daughter"[197].

About horses – I meant only to "look out" for some. I would sooner marry than let anyone buy me a horse. But it's always better to spy out the country beforehand, esp if there is no time to go nosing round oneself. Price £80 - £150. Up to 13st 7lbs. Must be fast enough to win a good race.

We're just this moment (9.45 pm) off for the beginning of our Regimental trek, which lasts a week. We march 20 miles tonight, to "Zilikaats Nek", which we attack at dawn. Bitter cold, and freezing hard: but, thank God, no

---

[194] George Nathaniel Curzon, Marquess Curzon of Kedleston (1859–1925), politician, traveller, and viceroy of India (ODNB)

[195] Given by Ettie to Willy for their silver wedding

[196] The final examination for the degree of BA at Oxford University (OED)

[197] *The Charwoman's Daughter* was the first novel written by James Stephens (1880–1950), published in 1912. It contained recognizable but affectionate spoof portraits of William Butler Yeats, Russell, Synge, and George Moore (ODNB)

wind. It's rather good weather in the middle of the day now; dry, and not cold, and blazing sun: but the nights and mornings and evenings bitter. We sleep on the ground, in a tiny "bivvy" tent[198], with just room inside for self and blankets (8) and karosses[199] (1) and coat, British warm, (1), and a flask. After the trek we come back here for ten days; and then off again for the manoevres, 3 weeks. I am very delicate, and I've got pink-eye[200] and a sore throat and a nasty tired feeling: but when I suggested staying here to guard the women and children, Captain Hardwicke told me that I was a young ass. Hark! I hear the trumpets sounding!

Goodbye. Please tell Moggy that I liked her "trick cyclist"[201] letter.

All all love from J.

---

[198] A temporary shelter for troops; a small tent (OED)
[199] A kaross was a mantle (or sleeveless jacket) made of the skins of animals with the hair on, used by the Hottentots and other peoples of South Africa (OED)
[200] Slang for conjunctivitis
[201] Slang for psychiatrist

93   30 June 1912   Roberts' Heights   DE/Rv/C1135/591

My dear Mother

Thank you awfully for your letter. I'm longing to see the Sargent of Dad –
you will send me a photograph as soon as you can? The "Hundred Years
Ago" Ball must have been the greatest fun. I'm glad that Edward looked
well; what a pity it is for him that a fancy-dress b[all] does not go on the
whole time! You must have been pretty full up lately, with the Derby and
waiting and reviews and Tap[low] parties. Have you read anything good?
The "Fish" poem in the R[upert] Brooke book <u>is</u> good, isn't it – the most
poetical of the whole lot, really, and metaphysical, and weird.
We're just back from the week's "trek", which started at 9.45 pm on Sunday
last. 9.45 pm – 3 am, night march, 20 miles. 3 am (Monday) rendezvous in
the valley (each squadron had come different wayses). 4 am, climb up
Zilikaats Nek, where we stopped till 8.30 am, lying behind the rocks in the
pass in a <u>bitter</u> wind, and watching the sun come up, painfully slowly. Then
breakfast. Then 7 miles on into camp, feed water, stables, luncheon, & sleep.
It's quite 'ot in the middle of the day, but cold enough getting up before
dawn, and creeping out of the bivvy (3 ft high, 3 ft wide), and breaking the
water in a bucket with a stick, for washing. Tuesday, a long trek in the dust
and heat to Hatherley, about 35 miles, with a rest and food in the middle of
the day. Wed, swimming horses at Hatherley in Piennars River, quite naked
and almost Greek, warm sun, rather fun – only the men are so dirty. They
are exactly the same colour when in khaki and when in puris naturalibus[202].
Thur & Fri, going over the Diamond Hill battle, about 25 miles each day.
Sat, march back to this worm-wood and gally hole[203].
It was really the greatest fun, cold and all; I simply loved it. Being in the
open all day <u>and all night</u>, and sitting down to eat in the bare desert, and long
drinks down a throat absolutely caked with dust, and the good heat in the
middle of the day, and the sudden cold at sunset, and the gradual return of
warmth about 1 hr after sunrise. The great empty veldt, too, has a sort of
charm, when one is living on it and in it. It is no country for horses: it is the
horses and the people and the dirty dregs of civilisation here that cry for hell-
fire. I can quite understand people getting fond of the veldt itself after

---

[202] Meaning naked

[203] 'Wormwood and gall' - an emblem or type of what is bitter and grievous to the
soul (OED)

trekking about a lot in it; by an acquired taste, like that of the King of Siam[204].

Manoevres start on the 12th of next month (July).

All all love to the family: and please thank Mogsy 1000 times for her letter. We will have some splendid cycling together when I get back.

How are you? Are you well & bright? I have been rather ill tempered of late, and I am not popular with my brother officers.

94   8 July 1912   Pretoria, South Africa   DE/Rv/C1133/51

Telegram: 'Arrive September 21st Julian

95   13 July 1912   Bivouac near   DE/Rv/C1135/592
**   Krugerdroop**

My darling Mother

Thank you awfully for your letters. I cabled last Mail to say that I arrive home Sept 21, sailing from here Sept 4, by the Great Mail Boat. It was not settled till the day I cabled. The Colonel refused to fix it up. But of course go on with the family bundobusts[205] quite irrespective, as I should hate to think I was stopping your France or anything. I hope Dad is liking his Stockholm Games[206]; he must have had tremendous work with his Commerce Delegates. You had just been for Likky's last exeat! Do give him tons and tons and tons of love from me. I am so sorry that Alastair has not done so well lately. How is he now? It is deadly cold here. I'm writing this with a candle, outside my "bivvy"; and I have to put my hands under the kaross every now and then to get my fingers warm enough to write. We are doing 20-25 miles a day, easy stages, ending up at Hatherley for manoevres in a

---

[204] Possibly a reference to the book by Anna Harriette Leonowens, *The English governess at the Siamese court; being recollections of six years in the royal palace at Bangkok*, published in 1870. The King of Siam and his entourage visited Britain in 1897 and stayed at Taplow Court

[205] An arrangement, organization; preparations (OED). The expression originated in India

[206] Lord Desborough went to the Stockholm Olympic Games of 1912. As President of the International Olympic Committee he had organised the London Olympic Games of 1908 (HALS: DE/Rv/F25)

week's time. I love it. It is the <u>one</u> life for this country. I am getting fond of it, in a way, almost against my better self. The veldt <u>grows</u> on one, when one is out in it, in spite of (or because of) its terrific greatness and greenness and dullness and bleakness. It <u>is</u> a good climate too, now in the winter, gin-clear and bracing, hot sun by day, bitter cold nights, and wonderful clear icy sunrises and sunsets. The men love this trekking. It is fun getting butter and eggs and chickens, and cooking them, when the march is done.

I'm <u>so</u> cold & sleepy. I must stop.

All all love J.

96	**19 July 1912**	**Bivouac near**	**DE/Rv/C1138/15**
		Reitfontein Police Post	

My darling Casie

How are you? I hope you've had a good London; and that you aren't yet married. But from all accounts you turn a deafish ear to your suitors at present, charm they never so wisely. I wonder where the family are going this Summer – it seems to be fairly uncertain at present. We will have tremendous fun together this winter, and we'll hunt seven days a week, fox-dogs 3 days, stag-dogs 2 days, hares on Saturday and rats on Sunday. Do you know of any good galloping horses? I arrive Sept 21; so will spend a month in horse-coping[207] before the season begins.

We are at present on trek, with 50 men and horses, and two fools, and a cook. We are supposed to be defeated and demoralised Boers, flying from the victorious British cavalry of Potchefstroom: but it is rather a farce, as the enemy (God bless them) come in to luncheon or dinner with us every other day. I'm getting a very good cook; Pancake Omelette à la Bloody Boojer is my speciality, made from Mealy Flour, tinned butter, and stale eggs. Try it in your bath. We sleep out at nights, which is very chilly in this the winter season. The horses bite each other and squeal through the night, and the Captain's temper becomes unsupportable. The country is like the inside of an enormous empty slop-basin; you can see for 70 miles all round you, and conversely there is nothing to see. The sunsets and sunrises are good: but they come at the wrong time of day, as one is then too cold to look at them. It is quite hot in the middle of the the day. Any more Dickens Invitations? You seem to have had some v[ery] good parties at Tap[low] every week.

---

[207] Horse-dealing (OED)

How is poor little Alastair now? How is your Dynamite? And is
Dreadnought still in the land of the living? I haven't heard speak of them for
years. And is Buccaneer still alive?
We start manoevres in 3 days now. Goodnight – I've got so cold writing this
by a candle outside my "bivvy".
Bless you J.

**97   21 July 1912   Standing Camp,   DE/Rv/C1135/593
                              Hathersley**

My dearest Mother

I've just got your letter about the Balliol row[208], and I've been <u>so</u> sorry for
you & Dad, knowing only too well what you must have been through during
those days. I only hope and pray that it is all blown over now, and that
nothing has happened. It does seem a little bit thick to send people down for
throwing mattresses out of window – and I can hardly believe that they could
do it: but as you say the dons must have lost their heads about it. What a
time you must have been through, though! I'm simply longing for the next
mail, to tell me that it is alright. It must have been awful for you, having a
big party at the time: and just having been to Oxford when all was peace.
I <u>am</u> sorry for you about it all.
We have just arrived here, in standing camp, after our lonely wanderings in
the wilderness. We only stay here for 14 days –
manoevres, brigade drill, field-days etc. the 12th and the Carabiniers are here
with us; the 15th, M.I. and Infantry at Bronkhorst Spruit, 50 miles E. I rather
liked our 8 days trek, all on our own and independent, open air and a free
life, and buying food on our way at the farms. Don't you think that a society
of 3 or 4 is much better fun than a society of 20?
It was grim country we went through: huge and hideously bare. A wonderful
climate now, certainly. I love the "B" Squadron hofficers – Philip Hardwick
(Captain), and one James Leckie, from Oxford, who is very sharp, and a

---

[208] At the end of the summer of 1912 Billy was sent down from Oxford for three
terms: his reputation for rowdyism had come to a head. The final incident is
described by Ettie in her *Family Journal*: 'there was a great bear-fight one evening
in Balliol Quad and all the furniture in one man's room was thrown out of the
window' (Mosley, p299-300). Billy was apologetic to his parents but refused to
take any of the consequences seriously

good sojer.

We get back on Aug 2; then in the middle of the month the Colonel takes us round the Natal battle-fields; but I don't know if I shall go with them yet. Please give all my love to Daddy, and tell him how sorry I am about it all. I've already posted my letter to him this Mail, before I got yours. Give my love to the Likkies, who are so grown up now. Bless you J.

Many many many happy returns of your birfday

98   29 July 1912   Roberts' Heights   DE/Rv/C1135/594

My darling Mother

I <u>am</u> sorry about your eyes. What a <u>horrible</u> nuisance for you. But I trust and hope that it's only from getting tired, as Lister says. You must have been doing a tremendous lot just lately: I could see from your letters that you were dead. I do hope and trust and pray that they will get alright directly, with a rest – and with the glorious news about Bill, which makes me more than glad. And you – I can imagine what you felt; and your relief after it. How <u>awfully</u> amusing about Margot's letter[209]; can't you get hold of it, to frame?

Your Brittany <u>will</u> be fun: and I'm filled with joy to think that we may be going to <u>Egypt</u> next year! Hurrah. I really dislike this country more daily. It came a bit ard to me to hear of Marjorie's[210] engagement. He is a damn lucky fellow. If I could only have got leave this year, I might have had a try to short-head him. If not, I would have done him down with a knife, or perished in the attempt. As it is, I can only bito [*sic*] here all ineffective. But I am consumed with envy and malice and all evil; and I shall die a bachelor, unless I marry a Totty Lightfoot at 55 to cheer my old age. There has never been and never will be anyone like M[arjorie] M[anners]. And he is nice, isn't he? I do hope they will be gloriously happy; I'm sure she will, as she is

---

[209] Margot Asquith, sixth daughter of Sir Charles Tennant; married Herbert Henry Asquith in 1894. Asquith was Prime Minister 1908-1916

[210] Lady Victoria Marjorie Manners (1883-1946), eldest daughter of the 8th Duke of Rutland. Julian had been in love with her and always kept her photograph and four of her paintings in his room. On 29 July 1912, Julian wrote her a letter congratulating her on her engagement to Charles Henry Alexander Paget, 6th Marquess of Anglesey (Mosley, pp314-315). Some letters from Julian to her remain in private hands

essentially domestic.

We are just back in camp from 3 days manoevres in the open. They were great fun – I liked them; and the cold had slightly abated. Another week here, & then back to the Heights; and then a week in the Natal battlefield; and then home!

I hope Dad has had fun in Stockholm. Best love to all the family. I <u>long</u> to hear that your eyes are better, and that you've done a rest cure?

All love J.

99   4 Aug [1912]   Roberts' Heights   DE/Rv/C1135/595

Dear Mother

How are your eyes? I do hope they're better. I hated getting another <u>typed</u> letter from you last mail. How glorious about Billa's tennis and tab-slogging[211] – I <u>was</u> delighted to hear about it. it must have been a wonderful game to watch, and you must nearly have died of excitement? I hope you'll have a good Brittany. We're just back from manoevres – marched home yesterday, and last night was my first night between four walls for three weeks. I loved it, the air for 24 hrs a day; but the actual manoevres were very poor, and dull. Poor old Hart, the generalissimo out here, is in his second or third childhood and is never allowed to say a word. On Wed next we set off for 8 days in Natal, going round the battlefields with the Colonel: it ought to be rather interesting.

Fancy Viola being toid up! I can't bear it. All the nice girls have gone and got married. There is a most beautiful young lady just come to Roberts Heights called Miss Hale. I think her name is Nancy. She has got chestnut hair, like Norah's in places; and she plays the piano divinely, Beethoven and all sorts. Her father is a Colonel in the Army Ordnance Department. Her mother is Irish. She has got the Celtic temperament, and thick black eyebrows, like Mr Smith the fox-hunter of Berry Hill. Her advent has set the whole garrison on fire.

I don't think I ever told you about Waterhouse, in the regiment. He is a howling bounder, but <u>nice</u>, and brave as a lion. But they all tried to get him

---

[211] Billy had obviously been winning at tennis. It is possible that 'tab-slogging' refers to him beating players from Cambridge, as 'tab' was slang for a member of the University of Cambridge (OED)

turned out, and the Colonel wrote him a bad report. He went on leave, to try and get an exchange; but that fell through, and now he has come back again. I believe his father is going to the War Office about the report – "not recommended for continuance in the service". You see, he is an <u>excellent</u> soldier; keen, capable, a beautiful rider: and they had to admit that in the report. I'm afraid there'll be a good row about it. Poor devil, I'm awfully sorry for him. I'm really the only man in the regiment who talks to him. I hope to God that they don't have a case, and pull me in for evidence. I'm not quite sure about the ethics of the case: can you say that a man is unfit for retention in the service if he is a bounder – and if there is nothing else against him, or rather everything for him, in the soldiering line?

Dad must have had great fun at Stockholm. I had a letter from him just before he went. Give him, and all the family, oceans of love. Goodnight – love – J.

**100   11 Aug 1912   Royal Hotel, Ladysmith,   DE/Rv/C1135/596
South Africa**

My darling Mother

I wonder if you are at Pans[hanger] now? And oh, I do wonder if your eyes are <u>better</u>? Still type-written letters, make me so sad about them. I do wish that you would blot out your Waiting. Your Normandy 6 weeks ought to put them right: and <u>what</u> fun it will be for you. I'm glad that Daddy is pleased about the Olympic Games. "Carnival" has not arrived yet. I'm longing for it, I've heard such a lot about it. I'm fearfully excited by the thought of sailing in three weeks now; it seems almost too good to be true.

We are staying here, 18 of us, including Makins and Gen[eral] Murray: and we go over a battlefield a day. It is really <u>very</u> interesting; and my word, what terrific fighting they had here. Buller seems to have made an almost inconceivable idiot of himself. We have done Talana Hill, Wagon Hill, Nicholson's Nek: and yesterday Colenso, Hart's Hill, Railway Hill, & Picters Hill, - all the advance when they finally got into Ladysmith. Tomorrow and Tuesday we do Spion Kop and Vael Krantz. Wed we do Elandslaagte, and Thursday we return to the Heights of Despair, for only a short time for me, thank God.

<u>How</u> anyone can call Natal beautiful beats me entirely. Hideous grey plains and hideous grey bumps; and the desolation of abomination over it all. Wagon Hill was almost the best fight, when they were at each other's throats

all night and all day, neither of them being able to move from the death-lock. At Hart's Hill, too, they got locked to a standstill; and if the Boers had made a counter-attack they would have had us beat. It is extraordinary country; those great hills standing hand-in-hand; looking north from Colenso, one wonders how anyone could even have got through. Our men must have fought like tigers. The kopjes are so steep that you can hardly walk up them, in broad daylight and with no fire.

Bless you: all all love to you and the family. I <u>am</u> glad to think of seeing you again so soon. Love from J.

101   18 Aug 1912   Roberts' Heights   DE/Rv/C1135/597

My darling Mother

Thank you awfully for your letter. How are your eyeses? Is Normandy doing them good: and are you having the greatest fun there? Your London must have been strenuous and splendid.

I got your last letter at the Royal Hotel, Ladysmith. Our battle-field tour was really tremendously interesting – and depressing. One could almost <u>see</u> the fights going on; and the unbelievable muddle and tragedy of Bullers Colenso and Vaal Krantz and Spion Kop[212]. Spion Kop itself is a fine hill; sheer and threatening and full of menace and death and disaster, even if one did not know that there <u>had</u> been disaster there. How gloriously the men and subalterns must have fought; and then twice taken off the position which they had <u>won</u>, with those losses (Spion Kop & Vaal Krantz). The Boers had <u>left</u> Spion Kop: and someone of them went up in the night to see how many of us were on the top, and found nothing!

We had a long day, the Vaal Krantz day, getting in just at dark to the farm where the food and blankets had been sent out to: then, just as we were climbing off our horses, very tired and hungry and thirsty, up came a cheerful

---

[212] The tragedy of Bullers Colenso: on 15 December 1899, General Buller's army advanced on the lines of defence that had been set up by General Louis Botha along the Thukela River. The purpose of this offensive was to relieve the besieged town of Ladysmith. The British forces advanced on three fronts. Altogether Buller lost more than 1,100 men at Colenso, while eight Boers lost their lives and thirty were wounded; the Battle of Spion Kop, 24 January 1900; the Battle of Vaal Krantz, 5 February 1900

man who told us that the wagon had broken down, and that it was 7 miles off, the other side of the huge Spion Kop ridge. But it was all the better when we did get there; and we slept like logs in a little wattle spinney afterwards.

We got back here on Thursday. All the work is over for a bit now, a rest after manoevres. Then the year begins again with musketry, in October. I sail by the "Kinfauns Castle", the Mail boat, leaving Cape Town Sept 4, and arriving Southampton Sept 21. Hurrah! I've got leave till March 3; and <u>perhaps</u> 2 months extension.

Give tons of love from me to the family, in the Norman Castle. It is almost too good to think of seeing you all again so soon. Bless you. J.

102   20 Sept 1912   Quessant Saxon Radio   DE/Rv/C1133/52

Telegram: 'Saxon Southampton daybreak Saturday'.

**103   2 Oct 1912   Parliament Street   DE/Rv/C1135/599
                              [London]**

Telegram: Arriving Maidenhead 12.43 on chance of catching you Julian.

104   11 Oct 1912   Parliament Street   DE/Rv/C1135/600

Telegram: Arriving Taplow 1.24 are you well self much battered Julian.

**105   14 Oct 1912   Knebworth Station   DE/Rv/C1135/601
                              [Hertfordshire]**

Telegram: Arriving Taplow 2.39 the end of Dauber is wonderful Julian.

**106   27 Nov 1912   Henley on Thames   DE/Rv/C1135/602
                              [Oxfordshire]**

Telegram: Coming for breakfast tomorrow morning Julian.

107   18 Dec 1912   Taplow Court   DE/Rv/C1135/603

Darling Mother

It is miserable about Billa, isn't it? For Billa more than anyone in the world.
However, perhaps he won't mind it as much as we think. I can't stop
tomorrow night – I wish I could – to see Moggy as Ballerina Prima
Assoluta[213]: but I was given a front seat at a dress rehearsal in the drawing
room tonight. And I'll see Vovo for a minute before I go hunting tomorrow.
I go to Bron on Friday 27th, for a day or two[214].
Is Grimsthorpe fun? How are you, Mumsy? I pounded the Whaddon field at
the big brook yesterday, but only by dint of a long swim in icy water! Dinner
with Bron last night – in his very best form.
All love J.
See you Friday night here, I think.

**108   1 Jan [1913]   Sawley Lodge, Clitheroe   DE/Rv/C1135/604
                               [Lancashire]**

Darling Mother

Happy New Year to you, and the Top of the Season, and Long Prices and
Lucky Doubles throughout 1913. I hope you'll have fun at Hatfield: I'm
glad that Pans[hanger] went well. Bron is in splendid form, and an ideal
person for me to live with, as we like very much the same things. In fact,
I'm getting rather sick of so much agreement, and Brethren in Unity touch.
We had a great hunt today, meeting here. Over the river about 17 times, 2
big rings of country, and a most melodramatic kill under the big rock one
mile up from here, in the water. What a lovely bit of river, isn't it.
We're just going over to Gis to dine. Rib and Charles and Dinah Do[215] are in
supreme form – all three going like Hell – Rib and Charles quite wildly, and
quite often in the opposite direction to hounds; Dinah really well, and a
lovely rider.

---

[213] The most exceptional soloist ballerina
[214] See Mosley, pp319-320 for Julian's visit
[215] Hon Charles Lister, only son of the 4th Baron Ribblesdale, contemporary of
Julian's at Eton and Balliol. Dinah Do: Hon Diana Lister, eldest daughter and sister
of Charles; Rib: Thomas Lister, 4th Baron Ribblesdale

Charles and Rib came over for a mixed coursing & shooting day yesterday at
Wiggle: Rib telling stories of Tiger-shooting all day. "Stripes".
Goodbye. Best love J.

109   18 Feb 1913   34 Dover Street, London   DE/Rv/C1135/605

Darling Mummy

I <u>am</u> sorry about Casie getting measles; and I <u>do</u> hope that she wasn't very
bad, and that she is better by now. What horrible discomfort she must have
had; and what an awful bore for you, putting out all your plans. I only heard
this morning from Wilson Taylor, who had had a letter from Daddy.
I do hope Casie is better?
Bill returned to Taplow last night from the Marshalls; or rather he said that he
was going to. Not much news here; I'm trying to cook up the wrecks of my
hunters for p[oin]t-to-p[oin]ts and Aylesbury chases. I won my fight in the
semi-final of the Belsize Boxing Club Heavyweight competition last
Thursday; and have to fight a fearful bruiser on Thursday next in the final. I
went to Picket on Sunday, and had a great colt-hunt. Bron was in the very
best form.
How are you? Taplow is very dull and miserable without you, and in the
course of spring cleaning.
Moggy however is as brisk and as completely mistress of the situation as
ever.
Bless you. I <u>do</u> want you to come back!
I have to sail April 12. War Office says "No cavalry moves for 2 yrs". Love
from J.

110   18 Feb 1913   The Bath Club, 34   DE/Rv/C1138/16
**   Dover Street, London**

My darling Casie

I <u>am</u> so sorry about your measles, my darling. What shocking bad luck for
you; and how terribly uncomfortable you must have been. But I hope and
pray that you are <u>much</u> better by the time I write this?
However, it is the devil's own bit of luck, and I'm afraid it will play havoc
with all your plans.

I saw Dynamite on Friday, looking and going the best. God, that is a good horse, isn't it? Earns his keep, and all that sort of thing.

I have got about 2 sound legs in my extensive stud at present! "Glory Allelujah" went a good gallop over Drake's fences at Shardeloes[216] on Sat last. I am running him in the Old Members Race in the Varsity Grind on the 28th.

This is to wish you a lighting recovery, and a glorious month when you <u>are</u> recovered.

Bless you J.

111   26 Feb 1913   Taplow Court   DE/Rv/C1135/606

Darling Mummy

Thank you awfully for your letter, from Alexandria, smelling of disinfectants. How lucky for you to get Casie comfortable there; the German hospital really sounds quite nice. What hell she must have had on the boat – and <u>in the train too</u>?? I've just read your letter from Cairo, to Bill-boy. It sounds the greatest fun, and I can <u>get</u> the sun and colour, from your letter, and the Arabian Nights Streets. I should <u>love</u> to see Egypt. I had a letter from Casie; she seems to be recovered wonderfully. You must <u>both</u> have been dead when you arrived at Alexandria; and one can hardly imagine what the discomfort of the ship must have been. I believe you rather liked the rest at Alexandria!? It will be fun seeing you again on March 17. I've had such shocking bad luck with my horses that really it is almost a case of the rifle for <u>all of</u> them! The judgements on Job are light, compared to the fortunes of my stud. And the odd thing is that I have been <u>resting</u> them lately. But I suppose it is the accumulated effect of hard hunting all through the middle of the worst season which there has been for horses since the memory of man.

"The Other Girl" got back here after being fired, doing very well; and I started training her for Aylesbury. Yesterday she broke away from my man at the top of the park, galloped down full split, and jumped the iron gate by the hay-rick in the corner <u>sideways</u>, landing <u>in</u> the little iron fence that runs up at right angles to the gate, and cutting herself to pieces. I don't think any <u>permanent</u> harm, but no more good for this year; just after I had got her round and doing well!

---

[216] Shardeloes, near Amersham, Buckinghamshire, the home of the Tyrwhitt Drake family

"Sans Peur" (George's horse) dead lame with a very bad leg.
"Schoolgirl" ditto.
"Glory Alleluiah" with a bad leg, but just able to pull out! I'm running him
in the Old Members Race in the Varsity Grind at Oxford on Friday, and that
will probably be the end of him!
I simply don't know what to do with them. They are unsaleable at present;
and if I keep them on, as I shall not probably get back till Jan 1914, it will be
"money from home".
So you see I'm rather on my beam ends!
I've been boxing; I won the Belsize Club Novices Competition
(heavyweights) against rather a good man, much heavier than me, after a rare
fight. I'm <u>not</u> going in for the Championships.
Bill-boy is working hard here, and <u>very</u> happy, I think. I found him and
Moggy and Hawa[217] acting a charade (Adam and Eve and the Serpent and
God) in the smoking-room when I arrived at 8.30 last night – all dressed up!
I've been down to Picket these last two Sundays, and had 2 glorious pony-
hunts with Bron.
I told you the War Office said "no cavalry moves in 1913-1914". Therefore I
sail April 12.
Goodbye. Heaps and heaps and heaps of love from J.

112   26 Feb [1913]   Taplow Court   DE/Rv/C1138/17

Casie darling

Thank you awfully for your letter. I <u>am</u> glad that you are well again, and
having fun; Cairo sounds to be the greatest thing ever known in the way of
Fun-Fun. I showed your letter to Bill-boy & Wawa. I must say, I think you
did very well to get measles over, and to get "going" again in the front of the
running, in a little over a week. Perhaps the ship doctor's treatment was of
the Kill-or-Cure variety, which produces instantaneous death or speedy
recovery – the human body thinking nothing of measles after surviving the
measles treatment! I'm sorry that your weather has not been up to sample.
But it must be very good to see the sun again, when it <u>does</u> appear.
I've had shocking luck with my horses here. "Sans Peur" lame (badly),
"Schoolgirl" ditto, "Glory Alleluiah" very dicky in his off leg, but running at

---

[217] Hawa was the Grenfell children's nurserymaid Harriet Plummer, who was also
called Wawa and Wa (*FJ*, p 13)

Oxford on Friday. "The Other Girl", (back here again last week, going sound, getting fit, and doing well), broke away while at exercise in the park, jumped the iron gate at this end into the iron fence, fell and cut herself to bits; got up again, galloped full split into the stable yard, and bashed herself against the wall. Done in for this year, but no permanent damage, I hope. What a tale of woe, isn't it? I <u>have</u> been out in my luck this year. Dynamite had a fall with Iris over a gate on Friday, but didn't hurt himself; he looks very well, & Iris said he went A1 except for that. I've had 2 grand pony-hunts with Bron in the New Forest; and I won a boxing competition in London. All all love from J.

113   3 Mar 1913   Taplow Court   DE/Rv/C1135/608

Darling Mummy

I've just got your letter, saying you hadn't heard from me; which I can't understand, because I've written to you twice – the first time about 6 days after you left. I <u>am</u> glad that you're having such fun in the heat; and it's splendid about Casie winning the prize at the Show. K[218] sounds too delightful. Bill is here, working hard, and in very good spirits; he had Patrick, Edward[219], and Duff down this Sunday, and Mrs Kilah[220], he says, rose to the occasion in the most wonderful way, and has never before attained to such heights of cooking! I was not here, as I did not know till too late that Bill intended house-warming. I stayed with Bron at Picket, and had a great pony-hunt. Poor Bron had rather a bad fall, going over some steeplechase jumps he has had put up: he ricked the muscles at the back of his neck pretty badly, but has no concussion and nothing broken. How much the bravest man in the world he is, isn't he? Riding like that, when he knows he cannot grip properly, in cold blood over fence, which very few able-bodied two-legged men would do. On Sunday morning, too, which is the most cold-blooded time! That course is really a death-trap: Flodden Field is a joke in comparison. Every Sunday we go down there in solemn procession, with

---

[218] Horatio Herbert 1st Earl Kitchener (1850-1916), Secretary of State for War, 1914-16. Ettie, Willy and Monica had gone to Egypt to stay with him (Mosley, p327)
[219] Edward Marsh (Mosley, p323)
[220] The Grenfell family cook

Nan[221]; and Nan stands there with a face growing ashier every minute, while Bron and I take fall after crashing fall! I don't know what is the matter with the place; because they're good horses, and the fences are not <u>very</u> big. But they just fall at them, and fall, and fall. Some curse must be upon it.

I've told you of the downfall of my stud. "Glory Alleluiah" alone can hobble along. I went down to Oxford with him on Friday, to ride in the Old Members Race at the Varsity Grind. I had rather good fun there, staying with John Manners[222] and Eddy Grant, at 22 Beaumont St. "Glory" really extraordinarily well; and as I had never run him before I didn't know how good he was. I lay second all the way, and he was pulling double, and jumping big – till he hit a fence, ¾ of the way round, and could not recover himself on landing. But I am tremendously pleased with him; especially as he pulled up sounder than he started.

I did not go in for the Boxing Amateur Championships, from sheer laziness. Ivo comes next Sat for his Long Leave, & Bill & I will be here to welcome him.

Hurrah for Monday the 17th! I'm just longing to see you again; because we haven't half thrashed things out yet this time, have we?

I've decided to give up my military career in favour of dentistry, and I'm just starting with a friend of mine who has a good practise in London. Bless you J.

114   25 Mar 1913   Ringwood [Hampshire]   DE/Rv/C1135/609

Telegram: Bron and I arrive 32 Old Queen Street about one o'[clo]ck unless you telephone to contrary we will come to Royal Court Julian.

---

[221] Nan Herbert (1880-1958), second daughter of Hon Auberon Herbert; sister of Bron

[222] Hon John Manners (1892-1914), eldest son of 3rd Baron Manners

115   25 Mar 1913   Taplow Court   DE/Rv/C1133/53

My dear Dad

I suppose that you will not hear the sad news of dear Auntie Katie's death[223] till you get back to Cairo. One cannot look upon it as sad for her, but only as happy, as she had been wishing for it so eagerly and for such a long time. But it is very sad for us, to think we shall never see her at Panshanger again. I saw Mother today in London, and she looked very tired and broken by it all. It is a great pity that she has to be in waiting all this time, when there is so much to do and settle. She has gone back to Windsor tonight; but I hope to go over and see her again tomorrow morning. We do not know at present when the funeral will be; because Mother has not heard yet if Auntie Minnie and Willie Northampton[224] have started from Beaulieu with the coffin. If they get home in time, it will be on Saturday; and if not, at the beginning of next week.

Bill has been away this last fortnight at Hayling Island, on a reading party with Sandy Lindsay[225]. He was working hard while he was here, and in very good spirits. Moggy has been in her best form, and has now become a hunting maniac! She makes old Williams go across Country like a flash!

I hope that you have had a good shoot, and that your trip has been a success. Mother and Casie are both full of Egypt, and say that they never had such fun in their lives! Casie seems to have made a wonderfully quick recovery from her measles.

I sail for Africa on April 12 (Saturday). So I shall see you before you start, to hear about your shoot. My poor horses have altogether given in, except "Glory Alleluiah", who is performing in point-to-points, though without success at present. I ride him in Aylesbury Steeple-chases tomorrow. Goodbye. I do hope you've had fun. All love from Julian.

---

[223] Lady Katrine Cecilia Cowper, eldest daughter of 4th Marquess of Northampton died at Cannes on 23 March 1913 (ODNB). As her marriage was childless, Panshanger passed to her niece, Lady Desborough

[224] William George Spencer Scott Compton, 5th Marquess of Northampton (1851-1913), Auntie Katie's brother; he married the Hon Mary Florence Baring

[225] Alexander Dunlop Lindsay, 1st Baron Lindsay of Birker (1879–1952), educationist. In 1906 he was elected fellow and tutor of philosophy at Balliol (ODNB)

116   27 Mar 1913   Maidenhead [Berkshire]   DE/Rv/C1135/610

Telegraph: Broke horses leg self alright Julian.

**117   28 Feb[226] [1913]   Union-Castle Line,   DE/Rv/C1135/607
                              RMS 'Saxon'**

Darling Mother

How are you? How are your eyes? Have you become a first-class horse-
coper, in addition to all your other vocations, and sold Schoolgirl? If you
have, I shall depose Hartigan, and offer you a 10% commission on the sale of
the race-horse. We arrive at dawn tomorrow morning, and I start in the train
for Potch[efstroom] at 8.30 am. It has been rather a good voyage, redeemed
for me by Peter Broughton-Adderley, an old Oxford boy, who used to know
Bill there. He is going to farm in Rhodesia, and I am going to join him at
Christmas, when we think of growing cotton together. Our great excitement
on the voyage has been the bevy of beautiful Dutch sisters in the second
class, whom you spotted with such extraordinary quietness the moment that
you came on the boat. Their chief idea in life is to have a "bit of fun". They
generally manage to get it: and it's not a bad philosophy of life. Our chief
rival has been the Canadian King, Charles James Stewart (also on the second
class); and two American rag-time dancers, who are going out to perform at
Jo'burg. I have got to be a tremendous dab at the Turkey-Trot, impelled by
envy of their happy lot. The first class, as always, consists of old gagas with
one foot in the grave, attended by physicians urging on the other foot. The
human being sitting at our table at Southampton is an entire male, which is
very disappointing. His name is Master Franke. I went to the fancy dress
ball as him, having abducted his best khaki suit and his yachting cap from his
cabin. They gave me a prize. I also won the bucket quoits, defeating Israel
in the semi final and Solomon in the final (this is true). Everyone on the boat
belongs to the chosen people – even the American Rag-Time dancers. But it
has not been nearly so bad as most ships.
It's a beastly journey to Potch[efstroom] – we get there at 5.30 on Wed night
– a day and a night and a day. I'm looking forward very much to the
regiment and work again. It will be great fun having the Tenth there, for

---

[226] This date is wrong, as Julian did not sail until 12th April

polo, and games and everything. There are also 5 trees, a pack of otter-hounds, and long dogs.

When do you go to London Town? I suppose you've been frightfully busy at Pans[hanger]; I hope Daddy will outwit Lloyd George[227]. I read all the library you bought me at Basingstoke – the Cardinal's Snuff Box, Princess Priscilla's Fortnight, and The Instrusions of Peggy[228] – how good they all are. And I've written a Short History of the Royal Dragoons – very hard work, consisting in the copying of little wads out of the big regimental history. Best best love to the family; and to you for coming down to Southampton! Goodbye J.

118   15 Apr [1913]   Roberts' Heights   DE/Rv/C1135/611

Darling Mother

How are you? I <u>do</u> hope your Neury[229] and your eyes are better? We had a very good Southampton, didn't we? The Hermaphodite sits at my table, and is one of the best doers I have ever seen; I think he must be male, and I have betted heavily on it; but he has not said a word yet, and I live in terror of his suddenly saying Good-morning one of these days in a falsetto scream, and landing me in penury. I have only made one friend yet – rather a jolly pin-head called Broughton-Adderley, an old Oxford man, Bullingdon[230] push, friend of Bill's. There are no fairies in the 1st class, as we foresay – unless the fat boy is a fairy after all.

But there are three delicious Swedes in the 2nd class, sisters; also their mother. Good old Swedish name of Bergstroom; one of the oldest families in Scandinavia, and very rich. I hope you will like them. I am engaged to the second sister, whose name is Inez. She is about 5 ft 6½ in in height, with brown hair running to gold, and a lovely complexion. She is not so pretty as

---

[227] David Lloyd George (1863-1945), chancellor of the exchequer and prime minister (from 1916 to 1922). It is unclear what this refers to

[228] *The Cardinal's Snuff Box* by Henry Harland (1900); *The Princess Priscilla's fortnight*, by the author of *Elizabeth and her German garden* (1905); *The Intrusions of Peggy* by Anthony Hope (1902)

[229] Presumably means neuralgia, an infection of one or more nerves, especially of the head or face, causing intermittent but frequently intense pain (OED)

[230] The Bullingdon Club is a socially exclusive student drinking society at Oxford University, famous for its members' wealth and destructive binges

her elder sister Seagull; but Seagull has red-hair, is very vivacious, and dances the Grizzly Bear all day – so I thought she would not make such a good wife as Inez. We are all going to bathe at Madeira, where we arrive at dawn tomorrow.

We've had a wonderfully smooth passage so far; even the dogs have not been ick, and Inez has taken her engagement quite smoothly.

Goodbye. Best love to all the family. Bless you J.

**119   1 May 1913   Royal Dragoons   DE/Rv/C1135/612
                           Potchefstroom, Transvaal**

Darling Mother

Great fun getting back here, and everyone in their best form. It's not at all a bad place, after the Heights of Despair; and our mess is a kennel for long dogs on a large scale – greyhounds eating and sleeping and fighting and playing in every corner. The first thing of the regiment which I saw was a greyhound, who attacked Misery on the railway platform, and was rescued from a bloody death by James Leckie, his master, who had come to the station to meet me. The Colonel is rather lonely, having despatched Mrs Makins and family to England; but in great fettle. Waterhouse has worked his way back into comparative favour with the regiment, if not with Makins; and I think that now he will stick it out and stay on, which will be good marks to him if he succeeds. The War Office saying that they could not do anything against him on his last report, as the only charge against him was social and not professional; and that they would wait for the next report, and see then. I believe he will get through with it now.

The officers quarters are full up, so I have been promoted to the status of a "married man with family"; and I am living in state in a large bungalow next the Colonel's, with a garden and the usual offices. There were no lights when I arrived, no water, no bed, and no furniture; and I am still camped on the floor in a corner, until the Royal Engineers with the rank and the pay of Sappers bring me a bed and lay the water on. We are doing no work at present, but start squadron training in a week. I haven't seen the Tenth yet. There are no other regiments here.

The "Saxon" was great fun, and full of adventures. I got straight into the train; with all my luggage, by the grace of God. I wish I could have had a day to see Cape Town; it is really too beautiful, sailing in to it, in the early morning, with the sun on those extraordinary great grim mountain-walls.

The Cape country is not bad – not so bare and dreary as up here.
When do you have to do waiting again? Is Bill-boy at home, or at Hayling?
Please give my best love to all the family. I'm longing to get your first letter.
Goodbye. Love from J.

120   10 May [1913]   Potchefstroom   DE/Rv/C1135/613

Darling Mother

Thank you awfully for your letter, received safe and sound. Do tell me what
you have done and settled about Pans[hanger]; how much pension Mr James
has got, and all the innermost details? How are you, and how are your eyes?
Uncle Makins has gone off on a shoot in Bechuanaland[231], for 3 weeks. We
start Squadron Training tomorrow, which will be a month's real strenuous.
The polo here is great fun – a much better ground than Roberts Heights, and
better polo, with the Tenth to liven up things. It makes a great difference to
have them here. Lady Helen is a most exciting element; do you know her?
They are a jolly regiment, full of life and buck. Polo ponies are very hard to
come by – and impossible to sell, when once you get them, as when we go
home (and the Tenth probably with us) their occupation will be gone, and the
only call for them will be to pull Jo'burg Jews in governess carts[232], at about
£15 a head. Besides, I am rather chary of investing once more in horse-flesh
after last winter's experiences. But I've got one, and I shall try and get two
more old cheap ones. The alternative amusement here is golf; so what can
do? Long dogs[233] are at present under a ban, owing to a Papal bull issued
against them by the Transvaal Government; but the General (O'Brien) is
trying to get it repealed, for the encouragement of manly sports among the
soldiery. There has been a boom of show-jumping lately in the regiment;
they take horses all round the country – Durban, Kimberley, Port Elizabeth,
Laurenço Marquez – winning competitions. No manoevres this year, or
rather shoddy trumped-up ones round the policies. It is rather good country
round here – heaven after R[oberts] Heights, but a colourless heaven.
How is Vovo? I do hope better? Please give him my best of best love. How
is Schoolgirl? I hope her leg will come right, and that you will get thousands
for her.
All love from J.

---

[231] Now Botswana
[232] A light two-wheeled vehicle with seats at the sides only, face-to-face (OED)
[233] Another word for greyhound (OED)

**121   18 May 1913   Royal Dragoons,   DE/Rv/C1133/54
                                Potchefstroom**

My dear Dad

I expect you have been tremendously busy since I left, with all the
Pans[hanger] arrangements[234]. I hope you got a good price out of Beit[235] for
the shooting: à bas les Juifs! Mr James is now once more a private
individual, I suppose? How is Schoolgirl? I expect that you will find it best
to blister her off fore, and throw her up for the summer. I hope that 47 Upper
Grosvenor Street is nice, and that you will like it better than some of our
former London houses! You will be well settled in there by now. How is
Likky-Man? I hope his German Measles left him no ill effects.
This country is as dusty as ever, but the climate is very good at this time of
the year – cold nights and hot days -; and Potchefstroom is a much better
place than Roberts Heights. It is good fun having the Tenth here, and they
are very nice; we get quite good polo with them. It's very hard to get any
ponies now, as the 12th Lancers and 15th Hussars took all their best ponies
back to England with them: and there is no traffic in ponies, as the market
will be finished directly we and the Tenth go. They seem to think that we
shall both come home the winter after next. I can't find out anything at
present as to whether they are going to send me to the Cavalry School this
next winter. Makins' time is up in January next; and he is going away about
October, so George Steele will get command then.
I hope that all the family are fit and well. Please give my best love to them
all. And I want to thank you very very very much for all the financial
assistance which you gave me, and which I have never properly thanked you
for!
Goodbye. Best love from Julian.

---

[234] On inheriting Panshanger, the Grenfell family attempted to let out the house
without success. They decided to let Taplow instead and make repairs to Panshanger
(see letter 126 etc)
[235] Otto Beit had leased Tewin Water from the Cowpers (HALS: DE/P/E288)

122   nd [18 May 1913]   Potchefstroom   DE/Rv/C1135/645

Darling Mother

Thank you awfully for your letter. Dinah's wedding must have been most
amusing; but does Percy[236] really look as fat and bloated as in the picture
papers? Or had he fortified himself with drink on the night before the
ordeal? Who is Jack Tennant? Is 47 Upper Grosvenor Street nice? Are you
waiting again? I'm so glad your eyes are better. I wonder if Likky Man
recovered soon from his German Measles? Bill will be going up for his
degree by the time you get this; I do hope he will grind the examiners to
powder. Please give him my very best love. Everything goes splendidly here;
I'm in the thick of squadron training, and polo in the afternoons. I've got
one good cheapish pony, and one very bad and very cheap one. Colonel &
Mrs Hale, parents of the young lady who was so ill at Christmas, have been
down here; the young lady herself has gone to England, and passed me in the
bay of Biscay. I had several guarded conversations with Mrs H – one of
them at a circus, where it was easily possible to divert the talk, when it
approached dangerous subjects, to the antic gestures of the clown or
performing elephant.
Makins is still away shooting, so George Steele is in command. Mrs H (who
hated Mrs Steele) said to me (in the sweetest voice) "Do you know what
somebody said to me the other day – that they were sure the Royals would
lose <u>tone</u> when Mrs Steele became the Colonel's wife!!! How ridiculous,
wasn't it?" Makins goes for good in October, which makes me very sad.
George Steele is efficient, but not stimulating or scintillating. I think Makins
is one of <u>the</u> nicest men, don't you?
I wonder if you will let Pans[hanger] this year, and become inordinately rich?
I'm sorry that Mr Barnes has become a hand-servant to the House of Israel:
he is so essentially an Anglo-Saxon. Are you having great fun in London,
and is Casie playing havoc with the coronets? She wrote me a very good
letter last mail.
I'm still reading "Tom Jones"[237] – what a good book it is, to read for 10

---

[236] Diana Lister (see letter 107) married Percy Lyulph Wyndham (1887-1914), son of
George Wyndham the politician and author (1863-1913) on 17 April 1913. George
Wyndham was one of the 'Souls'. Percy was killed in action in September 1914
(ODNB)
[237] *The history of Tom Jones, a foundling* by Henry Fielding (1749)

minutes a day. Squire Western is my favourite character in fiction. Have you
read anything good?
<u>Best</u> love to the family.
Bless you J.

123 **18 May 1913**	**Royal Dragoons,**	**DE/Rv/C1138/18**
	Potchefstroom	

My darling Casie

Thank you so much for your letter. I think it's a splendid idea that you
should have "Schoolgirl" – an idea advantageous to all parties concerned.
Dad gave me a loan of £250 last Christmas, and this is due for payment next
Christmas; so I imagine that he intends to take Schoolgirl as part value for
said loan. Of course I will not let on that you have said anything to me about
it. There is nothing that I should love better than for you to have the mare;
and I think you will find her a marvel. Of course I was too heavy for her,
hunting: I bought her for racing, and I ought not to have hunted her at all.
But the first day that I had on her was a revelation to me – I have never
ridden such a jumper; and I think she is fast enough to win a good race. I
expect she will go better for you, with your light hands, than she did for my
heavy d[itt]o: I could not get her to jump in a double bridle, but as you say
that she will do so for you, you should have an easy job with her. She
certainly used to pull very hard on a snaffle.
She is a really exceptional fencer, and will jump high and clear over
anything, going at any pace. She is inclined to rush, but I expect that you
will get her out of that.
I am sure that blistering is the best thing for her off fore; her spavin does not
affect her, and was always there; but blistering will not do it any harm at all
at all.
Dinah's wedding must have been most exciting; I wonder if Rib had out his
postilions[238] again? What is our new London abode like?
This country is as dusty as ever; but this is a much better place than Roberts
Heights, and not too bad really. It's a glorious climate now, in the winter; cold
clear nights and mornings, and quite hot in the middle of the day. We've got
masses and masses of long dogs. The Tenth are fun, and we have good polo.

---

[238] A person who rides the (leading) nearside (left-hand side) horse drawing a coach
or carriage, especially when one pair only is used and there is no coachman (OED)

Goodbye, my darling. Best of best love. I am awful fond of you. Have fun, and keep well, and God bless you. J.

124   26 May 1913   Potchefstroom   DE/Rv/C1135/614

Darling Mother

I've fallen on my silly head again – Saturday morning, when we were jumping. And I've got <u>very</u> slight concussion. I shall only have to stay in bed for a day or two.
How are you? Best of all love. I'll write a long letter next week.
Goodbye J.

125   2 June 1913   Potchefstroom   DE/Rv/C1135/615

Darling Mother

Thank you awfully for your letter. I hope you had a good party at George Nathaniel's? Did you give Bill a tremendous blowing-up for leaving Casie unprotected at the Ritz? I'm sorry that we could not let Pans[hanger] for this summer; it is most dilatory of the Jews not to have risen to the occasion. Everything goes splendidly here – my head is quite right again now, and I have "returned to duty" after a week's lie-up, which was a great bore. Uncle Makins has returned from his Bechuanaland shoot, pleased with life and in a good temper; and today we start Regimental Training. In a fortnight's time we have a Polo Week, with a tournament and all sorts; so we are very full up just now.
It's most exciting to think of Bill just going up for Schools[239] – telepathy tremendous will-power to him from me, and give him my best best love. How is the new London house? And are you having the greatest fun? And Casie? Do tell me all the matrimonial nuances!
Wasn't it rotten luck getting that smash just when I was settling down to the swing of things. However, it's only a week lost, and I'm perfectly right again now for another start. It happened when I was going round the (tiny!) squadron jumps, with my troop. My charger, who had been leaping too splendidly, suddenly and for no reason whatsoever galloped straight into the

---

[239] At Oxford, the periodical examinations for the degree of BA (OED)

bar jump, and fell like a stone; ditto me, on the bridge of my nose, which luckily broke some of the violence of the shock. If one had a Hebraic nose[240], I believe one would never get concussion: mine always does its little best, but it is too close to the inner line of defences to be of very much avail. I'm afraid your eyes don't sound <u>too</u> well? I <u>do</u> hope they are going on alright? Best of best love from J.

126   8 June 1913   Potchefstroom   DE/Rv/C1135/616

Darling Mother

Thank you awfully for your letter. Your Hackwood time must have been the greatest fun – with the unmarried remnants of the Hothouse[241]. I'm sorry you could not stay on for the arrival of the next guests! I <u>do</u> hope Bill-boy is well, and in his best train-form; but I suppose his contest is decided by now? Everything goes gloriously well here; I've taken to Bridge and Golf, and I have become a Very Old Man. Regimental Training is in full swing; but on Wed next I'm going off to live in camp with the R[oyal] E[ngineers], and look on as an intelligent observer while they build a bridge over the Vaal River at Venterstroom. It only takes three days; and after it is over I am supposed to know all about aeroplanes, demolitions, explosives, bridging, submarines, and military engineering generally. It's called a Pioneer Course. 18 of our men are going; also Brooke of the 10th,[242] and some of their men. Every sort of rumour is floating about as to our coming back; the latest is that the Tenth are going home now, and that we are returning to Roberts Heights for a year or two – but I think this is the invention of some wit endeavouring to get a rise out of us. I suppose you haven't heard anything about it at home? I asked whether they were going to send me to the Cavalry School

---

[240] Referring to the shape, ie Jewish

[241] The Manners sisters, daughters of the Duke of Rutland (Marjorie, Violet (known as Letty) and Diana); also known as the 'hotbed' (MacKenzie, p64; Mosley, p214)

[242] Basil Stanlake Brooke, 1st Viscount Brookeborough (1888–1973), prime minister of Northern Ireland. He attended Sandhurst, and then served with the 7th Royal Fusiliers (1908–11) and the 10th Hussars in India and South Africa. His military service was extended by the outbreak of the First World War. He served throughout the conflict with distinction; he rose to the rank of captain in the hussars, was mentioned in dispatches, and awarded the Military Cross in 1916 and Croix de Guerre with palm (ODNB)

next year, but I had bad luck, and caught the Adjutant at one of his bad moments; he said that I had had so much leave, and done so little work, lately, that it seemed improbable to him that I should even be allowed to go away again. However, I don't think that this means much. But I shall have to get on the right side of George Steele, who will be acting Colonel in October, and full Colonel at the beginning of next year.

Do tell me all the arrangements about Pans[hanger], and the fate of Mr James and Co[243]. I suppose you won't stay there at all this next winter. What a bore it is that we could not let it.

Very best love to Dad, and to Casie. I hope you're having the greatest fun. How are your eyes going. Goodbye and <u>bless</u> you. J.

127   16 June 1913   Potchefstroom   DE/Rv/C1135/617

Darling Mother

Thank you awfully for your letter. I was thrilled by your account of your conversation with Mama Keppel[244], fixed by her piercing eye; I know how good you were – I can see your face of earnest innocence! Have you seen Violet K's[245] evil Parisian countenance lately? Please give her my respects, when you do see her. I have behaved in the most cowardly manner about the business, and I have never communicated with her since the catastrophe, in obedience to her strict and imploring orders[246]; but I think the storm is now long enough past for me to send her a letter in disguised handwriting. Advice, not maternal. I hope the "Beauties & Nuts" party went splendidly? It is glorious that Bill-boy is happy at Oxford – and extraordinary; give him all my love. I haven't heard anything about the Alastier[247] pictures: but I <u>rather</u> like

---

[243] The staff at Panshanger

[244] Mrs Alice Keppel (1868–1947), wife of George Keppel, third son of William Coutts Keppel, 7th Earl of Albemarle and former mistress of Edward VII (ODNB)

[245] Violet Keppel, daughter of Alice and George Keppel (ODNB)

[246] According to Violet's biographer, although only briefly engaged to Lord Gerald Wellesley, Violet had 'a more serious attachment to Julian Grenfell'. Presumably this is 'the business' to which Julian was referring (ODNB). During his leave in the winter of 1912-13 it was known that he had been pursuing Violet (Mosley, p322)

[247] Alastair, pseudonym for Hans Henning Voight (1887-1969), who specialised in illustrating the plays, novels and short stories of his favourite period, the 1890s. His most celebrated author was Oscar Wilde, but he also illustrated the classic 18th century erotic novel, *Les Liaisons Dangereuses* by Choderlos de Laclos

the William Eden[248] watercolours– I love their dancing mistyness; but they don't quite come off, so I suppose the mistyness is a trick, which keeps him from getting the rest right. Do you think that Art ought to go for Truth, or that Truth is Art, in the sense of being quite different from Things as we See them? Ah! It is sad about poor A.A. – terrible. Is it the necessary result of a military life? Is there any chance of his getting better?

We are having a tremendous week here – a Waterloo festival joy-week[249], with polo and concerts and balls and all sorts. I wrote a "Bioscope Drama[250] – Without Bioscope", for the men to act. They do not talk, but act dumb show, and at the critical moments placards are exhibited conveying the sense. It is called "The Wicked Count - - - To say nothing of the Countess". It is terribly improp[er], and I shall probably lose my commission over it; but the men laugh so much while they are doing it, that I think it will have a great success. It opens with the Countess (a man 6 ft 4, with large boots) – in bed. Enter 1st lover. Business. Knock at the door. Enter second lover. First lover disappears under bed. When there are 3 lovers under the bed, enter Count, pursued by police and bloodhound. Count shoots police and bloodhound, embraces countess. Bed begins to heave gently, due to quarrel among 3 lovers underneath it.

Placard   (Count – What is it?".

(Countess – "It must be an earthquake, darling".

Count discovers lovers; shoots them. Shoots Countess. Picks up baby from bassinette[251], and compares face with faces of lovers. When he comes to 3rd lover, strikes tragic attitude. Shoots baby, & throws it out of window. Enter Orderly Officer (in uniform) and arrests Count. Placard "Barrack-room most untidy – you are a prisoner at large". Finis.

Goodbye. Best best love to the family. Bless you. How are you, and your eyeses?

Love from J.

---

[248] Sir William Eden, 7th Baronet and 5th Baronet, sportsman and artist. He was a talented artist, who exhibited at almost every exhibition of the New English Art Club between 1896 and 1909, and had work shown at the Paris Salon and at the London galleries favoured by those painters influenced by the French impressionists and post-impressionists (ODNB)

[249] Celebrations to mark the anniversary of the Battle of Waterloo on 18 June 1815

[250] An earlier form of cinematograph retained in South Africa as the usual term for a cinema or a moving film (OED)

[251] An oblong wickerwork basket, with a hood over one end, used as a cradle for babies; also, a form of child's perambulator of the same shape (OED)

128   22 June 1913   Potchefstroom   **DE/Rv/C1135/618**

Darling Mother

No letter from you this week! I'm terrified that you have broken your resolve, and have 'gone up' with Claudie Grahame White[252] after all! What fun these new aeroplanes must be, to go up in; I've had ecstatic letters about it from Casie. The Potchefstroom Season is over, having lasted just one week; a bevy of beautiful fairies was imported from Johannesburg by Waterhouse, and planted out in a spare bungalow – 6 of them. All our looking-glasses, sponges etc, were borrowed for them, and a kaffir[253] hired to cook. They must have had great fun, with the undivided attention of the male garrison. The polo was quite good – won by a team of wild farmers from Harrismith, playing on wild long-haired long-legged aboriginal ponies. They yelled weird war-cries all the time, and galloped and hit like sin.
Tomorrow we start on a "regimental trek", to the Vaal River, where we sleep out 2 nights. After that – some time – come manoevres. I'm longing to get back to polo and active life again, - because all this last bit I've been on "medicine and light duty", which has been rather dull. But I'm now much stronger in the 'ed.
How are you? I'm longing for news of Bill-boy, and how he has done. I don't know when I shall get leave this year, if any; or Cavalry School, for which I'm afraid I shall not now be qualified, as I've not been able to put in any work yet!
Very best love to Daddy. How is that Mog? Goodbye. Bless you. J.

---

[252] Claude Grahame-White, aviator and aircraft manufacturer. In late 1910, he purchased a 207 acre site at Hendon, which early in 1911 opened as the London Aerodrome. Under his dynamic management Hendon became a centre of British aviation; it included the Grahame-White Aviation company and flying school, Blériot and Farman agencies, and week-end race meetings (ODNB)
[253] One of a South African race belonging to the Bântu family (OED)

129   29 June [1913]   Potchefstroom   DE/Rv/C1135/619

Darling Mother

<u>Two</u> glorious letters from you this mail: also the English Review, which I
loved. You seem to be having the <u>greatest</u> fun, and to be very <u>welly</u>? The
Bernard Shaw play[254] is wonderfully amusing, isn't it? And I liked the
Raleigh "Boccacio". very much What did Gosse[255] say about the future of
English Poetry?
I'm glad you're getting good hot weather. It's a wonderful climate here now;
the best climate in the world, I suppose. We slept out 2 nights last week – a
regimental trek into the Free State, which is about 16 miles off from here. It
was rather good fun; bitter cold at nights, till one got into a bivouac tent and
blankets; horribly cold getting in to bed, and horribly cold getting up and
washing in frozen water; and then blazing sun, and quite hot in the middle of
the day. We did about 30 miles a day. It's rather good country just round the
Vaal River; great grey hills. No water in the river at present; great deep
puddles, with just a trickle between them. The river always seems to pick out
the largest hill in the country, and to make straight for the middle of it. when
in doubt at to its course, pick out the most unlikely place for it, and you're
right. This week we finish regimental training – and then manoevres; but
they have not got enough money to send both regiments out at once; so for 3
days we attack Potch[efstroo]m, sleeping out, and the 10th defend it, sleeping
in; and for the next 3 days the 10th attack Potch[efstroo]m, sleeping out, and
we defend it, sleeping in. Isn't it a nice simple plan! Nobody seems to know
when we are coming home, and there are no barracks at home; so we are left
in the corner, like a naughty child.
How good Scatters Wilson's Europa and the Bull parentage is![256] Don't you
love him? Has his family been added to yet? I'm simply longing to see
Pamela FitzGerald; she sounds thrilling. There are no charmers in this place,
of English extraction; but a lovely Hollander lady of the bluest blood called

---

[254] Possibly *Pygmalion*, which was written by Shaw from March to June 1912
[255] Sir Edmund William Gosse (1849-1928), writer (ODNB)
[256] Sir Matthew Wilson, soldier and MP, brother-in-law of Charles Lister
(MacKenzie, pp165, 242); 'Scatters' was his acknowledged nickname. Europa and
the Bull is a reference to the Greek myth, in which Europa, daughter of Agenor, King
of Tyre, was carried away to Crete by Zeus, who had taken the form of a handsome
bull

Miss Wessels, who lives in cantonments[257], and has a great time, the competition being extraordinary.

I'm awfully glad that Bill thinks he did well in Greats; and that Dad and Casie are having fun. Please give my best love to all the family. <u>Bless</u> you. I wish we could have some more talks; I feel I've got such oceans to say to you, which I could not say. It's there, but it's not all there. Talking to you, it would come out, because you talk for me as well as for yourself, like the Child's Guide to Knowledge[258] It would come out, absolutely and entirely different, of course, and often entirely opposite; but you would hypnotise me into thinking it and passing it as mine; which is just as satisfactory after all in the end!

Love J.

130   29 June 1913   Royal Dragoons,   DE/Rv/C1133/55
**   Potchefstroom**

My dear Dad

Thank you awfully for your 2 letters. I am glad that you are so fit and well, and it must be a great rest for you not to have to do the Olympic Games this year. The new Phaeton car sounds a great success; I wonder what you have done with the Pans[hanger] motor? I expect Mr Barnes is delighted at having a lot of birds to rear again. Are you going to stock the river again? It would be great fun to have the fishing again, and I suppose the sooner it is done the better. I hope "Schoolgirl" will prosper on her blistering. What fun you and Casie are having with your aeroplane flights; and how brave you are to go in the things at all! How did Lindsay Hogg's team, with the four-year old, go? It is glorious weather here now, and we're doing a lot of work. I had a nasty fall last month, and concussion; but now I'm much better, and back in the land of the living. We did a regimental "trek" last week into the Free State – 2 nights out. We shall do some sort of manoevres next month; but on a very small scale, as the army here now seems to be out of date – nobody wants us here, and they allow us no money. I suppose we should be sent home, only there are no barracks for us.

---

[257] The place or places of encampment formed by troops for a more permanent stay in the course of a campaign, or while in winter quarters (OED)
[258] Written by 'a lady' [Mrs R Ward]; 3rd edition published in 1830

I am sending you an application for a commission, which our Quartermaster Sergeant, D B Cronin, is applying for. He is a <u>very</u> good man in every way, and extremely able; in fact, he does pretty nearly everything in the regiment. I've had a lot to do with him, as he is Sub-Editor of the "Eagle". I think he has had very bad luck in not getting a commission before now, as he was recalled from departmental work at Simla to the regiment on the <u>promise</u> that he would be given his commission; and then another man (Jones) was put in in his place. He was very keen that I should ask you to do something for him. I told him that you had nothing to do with the army, but he said that he knew your influence would help him to get it. So I said that I would ask you. Do you think you could mention it to Seely? I'm awfully sorry to bother you about it, when you're so busy: but I like Cronin, and I'd like to help him. He is a man who could have done very well for himself at other jobs; but he stayed on simply to get his commission, and has been badly treated over it. He is getting the Colonel and the last Colonel (de Lisle) to agitate about it. Best love to the family.

Goodbye. Love from Julian.

131   3 July 1913   Roberts' Heights   DE/Rv/C1135/620

Darling Mother

Just off to Jo'burg, on 2 hrs notice, to quell the strikers[259]. Nobody seems to know why they are striking, and they are all perfectly content with their conditions; but all the mines are "out", and the railways threatening. I suppose they will throw bottles at us; and if we retaliate, we shall be prosecuted for murder, and if we do not, we shall be prosecuted for cowardice.

Makins goes to England on leave at the end of this month, sailing at the beginning of August. Mr M's address is Westnorton? Westburton? Bury. Pulborough. Sussex. Makins says he can't read the first word. But that 180 Queen's Gate always finds him. I told him that he must go to see you when he gets back.

I liked Helen Mitford – pretty well. I did not see very much of her. <u>PRO</u> – Rather good appearance, and constant cheerfulness. <u>ANTI</u> - Constant

---

[259] The army was used to maintain order during the strike. A judicial commission was appointed to inquire into the conduct of the military after a charge of unnecessary brutality was raised. See letters 132-136 below

cheerfulness and a rather aggressive garrison-queen ram-it-down-your-throat attitude.

Tremendous hustle on here. We got orders at 7 pm, and the first squadron got into the train by 10 pm. We entrain at 1 am, and start at 2 am. Goodbye. Bless you. I'll write again if I get a chance. Nobody knows a bit how long we stay, or why we were sent for in such a hurry. It looks as if they had started playing about. <u>All</u> love J.

132	**13 July 1913**	**The Country Club, Johannesburg**	**DE/Rv/C1135/621**

Darling Mother

Last time I wrote to you we were just starting off for the station at Potchefstroom – last Thursday week, July 4. We left barracks about 10 pm, and we were to entrain by 12 and start at 1. As a matter of fact, we did not get off till 8.30. They sent the whole lot of us – the 10th and us; and they had not enough trucks or engines; besides which the horses got a panic for no known reason, and we had to carry most of them into the trucks bodily. It was a lovely night – bitter cold, with great flares lit at the sidings for us to box horses by. Of course we did not know how bad things were then. We got to Jo'burg at about 2 o'clock on Friday, and got a feed – the men had had nothing since 7 the night before; and then we were hurried straight off onto the Market Square, where we met our other 2 squadrons. There were tremendous crowds, and a good deal of shouting; the Government had stopped a big meeting which was to have been held. But the actual miners seemed quite peaceable and good-natured, even when they were walking about in processions with banners. The people who looked like trouble were the real Jo'burg roughs, who are tougher and dirtier and less human than any other roughs in the world. We stayed on the Market Square till about 5 in the afternoon; and then galloped off to the big station, Park Station, which they said they were going to burn. We went through this and cleared all the people out of it, with loaded rifles and revolvers; but everyone went away at once, after a little chaff. One old lady in the Refreshment Room was perfectly terrified, and fell into my arms with about 20 brown paper parcels, imploring me to save her; which I did. She left the station, still in my arms, amid loud guffaws from the crowd.

Up to this we had come in for no unpleasantness to speak of; the policemen on Market Square had been stoned with bricks and bottles from the tops of the houses early in the afternoon, and had charged across the square once or twice to clear the people; and one of our squadrons had charged in a half-hearted sort of way, using the flat of their swords. That had been before we arrived; when we had arrived all was much quieter again, with the troops and police (our regiment and about 200 police) standing quietly at ease at the street-corners, and the crowds wandering about quietly in the middle.

When we left the station, we got into the thick of the hooligans; everyone yelling, and bottles and stones flying, and roughs upsetting the horses with whips – led by a woman who was trying to pull the men off their horses. It looked very ugly; they were the dirtiest of the crowd – not the strikers themselves – and angry. However, we did not even draw swords, but just grinned and bore it. Then they barricaded the street in front of us by jamming 2 wagons across it; and we went "sections about" and retreated ignominiously.

It's very hard to know what to do; especially when one's men are getting cut about with bottles, and one's temper getting worse every moment. As things turned out, I believe it would have been better if we <u>had</u> got off and fired. Eventually the shooting was the only thing which stopped them; and I believe that if we had shot before, they would have stopped before.

After that we went to the Nourse Mine, about 5 miles out. The next thing we heard was that they had burnt the station down; (they must have arrived there directly we left it); and also that they had burnt the "Star" (Newspaper) offices. We got to our mine at 9 o'clock, and they gave us a very good dinner there. All the striking miners were there, quite friendly and peaceable. That was the most extraordinary thing about the strike – the strikers themselves seemed to have no grievance whatsoever; and they had already <u>gained</u> the point which they struck for, ie the restoration of the 31 strikers on the New Kleinfontein Mine, which was the cause of all the trouble.

We got to the Nourse Mine at about 9 pm (Friday); and went to bed. At 12 we were called up again, as there was a rumour that the crowds were coming to blow up the mine. We "stood to" till 2 am (Sat), and then we were summoned into the town again. We arrived too late to be of any use; there had been a good deal of street-fighting, people shooting and throwing sticks of dynamite from the tops of houses etc; and 3 of our horses had been killed from the other squadrons, which had been kept in the town. We went to the main Police Station; and as we got there the police brought in 60 of the hooligans, whom they had rounded up in a pub. You never saw such brutes. They gave them scant mercy, too; banged their faces against the walls, and kicked them down 2 flights of stairs into the cells. There was one poor wretch lying there with a bullet through his stomach – and the ambulance were taking some others away. We stayed there about 2 hours, waiting in the street with the horses; then we went off (about 5.30) to the Volunteer School of Arms (where I fought Mr Tye last year). Then we lay down in our boots for about an hour, and got some coffee. On Saturday morning all the regiment concentrated at the Police Barracks; there is a courtyard where there was just room to stand the horses, and they fed the men in their mess-room. We lived then in a state of siege till Tuesday, when we moved out here, about a mile outside the town, under canvass. It was tremendously packed in the Police Barracks, as there were 200 police sleeping there as well as us.

On Sat morning, it was all pretty quiet; crowds began to collect about midday, and in the afternoon there was the shooting at Rand Club, over which they made such a fuss. Our squadron was not in it, thank God. I had to take my troop to get the arms and ammunition out of a gun shop, just after the shooting had taken place. We were shot at on the way there, and on the way back, escorting the two wagons; but nobody was hit. While we were at the place they didn't dare to touch us, because I had men lying down across the street above and below with their rifles ready.

After the shooting on Sat the whole thing quieted down, and nothing more happened. It was the only thing that stopped them. I believe that if they had been allowed to go on for a day longer they would have burnt the whole of the town to the ground. As it was, they did not fire until five or six of the men had been hit by bullets and slugs, and several of the horses – and the crowd were getting right on top of them.

We are stopping here now in case a general strike is declared, which they seem to think is quite on the cards. The men are under canvas; we are sleeping in some police barracks here, and living at the club, which is not at all bad.

I got your letter – sent on here. You <u>do</u> seem to be having fun. What plans for the Autumn? Shall you go to Scotland. Or France?

All all love from J.

133   20 July 1913   The Country Club,   DE/Rv/C1135/622
Johannesburg

Darling Mother

We're still here, loaded to the muzzle and ready to sally forth at any moment. Nobody seems to know at all what is going to happen; some bet 10-1 on a general strike, and some 10-1 against anything. The railway and the miners have both presented their grievances to the Government; but these sound quite ridiculous, as they demand a minimum wage of £1 a day, and a maximum time of 8 hrs "bank to banks", (which means about 7 hrs actual work). The Government can't give them that, without busting all the smaller mines. If there is a strike, it will knock all the mines on the head, for at least a year. The first thing they will do, if a strike is declared, will be to march all the niggers on the mines off home. They have ordered the old burgher Commandos to be ready, to do that. If they once send them away, it will take at least 12 months to get enough of them back to start the mines again. That means having all the white miners loafing about here, and starving – starving quickly too, because the railways being on strike the town will run short of food at once. I think that the miners have realised this themselves; in fact, the odd thing about the whole strike is that a vast majority of the miners are strongly against striking; but they are in such terror of the militant strikers and strike-leaders, who proclaim them as "scabs" and break up their houses, that they all come out against their will. But I think the strike-leaders will have a harder job of it this time; the shooting came just soon enough to put a wholesome fear into them. It was a pretty good thing it stopped when it did, as the 20,000 natives would have been out in another day, and there would have been fair hell to pay. It really is a shocking town to live in; Sodom and Gomorrha[260] must have been comparatively innocent. There is tremendous feeling against the licentious soldiery in the town just now, among the rabble; but everybody seems to think that we did very well. The Tenth did not have any trouble – they were just outside. Both regiments are under canvass here now. It is very good for the officers having this club here, as we can get tennis & squash; we don't sleep here, but in the old police barracks next door, ten in a dormitory, like at Summer Fields[261]. It's bad for the men, though; they have absolutely nothing to do; and we are here apparently quite indefinitely. The Government answer the strike demands on Thursday; but I don't see what is

---

[260] Two Biblical towns renowned for their wickedness and dens of iniquity (Genesis, ch 13 and 14)
[261] Summer Fields School, Oxford, founded in the 1860s, Julian's prep school

to prevent it going on like this practically for ever. All of us are longing to get it over; it's such a poor game – broken bottles if you don't shoot, and execrations if you do – heads, they win; tails, we lose.

Selfishly, I can't help hoping they <u>do</u> strike again, and get it over; it's quite exciting, anyhow, and better than sitting here doing nothing.

Of course the numbers killed were just about 3 times as many as in the papers; lots of them hit and killed by the roughs in the crowd shooting at us; and lots of them put away quietly by the police. One man, who had a shot at my troop with a pistol, hit his friend in the leg. And the police have had a high old time, because some of the real blacklegs, who have not dared to show their faces for years, came out into the streets during the strike and were immediately nobbled. The police also took the opportunity to raid some of the suburbs, which they had not dared to go near before; they just walked through them shooting people and leaving them when they fell. The strike has covered a multitude of sins.

I was going out to luncheon in the town with the Colonel yesterday, in a tram, when a former Goldilocks friend of mine came on board, and rushed up to me with open arms, saying "Dear Old Boy, how jolly to meet you again like this! How <u>are</u> you? etc etc". Tableau. What is A to do? We had a long conversation, under Uncle's flashing eye. She twigged immediately, and started talking and behaving in the most outrageous manner, until Uncle himself laughed.

Tomorrow I'm going over a mine, which ought to be rather amusing. Have you ever been down one? We see a good many of the mine managers out here, at the club. They are all terribly depressed about the situation, and think that it will take the country years to get over this blow, even if nothing more happens now.

Are you going to stay at Pans[hanger] now? I do love it so in the summer, don't you, when it is all soaked in green. Have no Jews come forward yet to hire it? I am <u>longing</u> to meet you again, face to face; but I'm rather chary of asking for leave just at present, or even for pressing about the Cavalry School; and as for the regiment coming home, I suppose that this affair has put that out of the question for years and years. Why did we ever want to meddle with this disgusting country?

Please give Dad my very best love. How did Bill do against John M[262] in the tennis?

All all love from J.

---

[262] John Manners (see letter 113). In the spring of 1911, Billy and John Manners had won the real tennis match against Cambridge. A real tennis court still exists at Taplow Court (Mosley, p298)

134   27 July 1913   The Country Club,   DE/Rv/C1135/623
Johannesburg

Darling Mother

Thank you for your awfully good letter, which I <u>did</u> love; it was as exciting to read as the Thaw case, and full of lurid details. <u>Poor</u> Bim! Do tell me whether they are still fond of each other? It would be a great triumph for love if it transcended £50,000! I just know the woman – only just: I always thought that she looked rather nice. The Sackville-West case[263] is exciting too; I'm sure Violet Keppel[264] must have got some good new imitations of Little Vita" from it. I've got the Mrs Meynell poems[265], but I haven't read them yet. Thank you awfully for sending them. Did you ever read a book called "One of Us", by Gilbert Frankau; a "Novel in Verse", in the Don Juan metre?[266] A lot of it is awful, but bits are very good; some good lines, and a really wonderful character sketch of a Chorus Girl. I don't know Laurence Binyon's[267] things; is he any good?

---

[263] There were two very public lawsuits that threatened the security and reputation of Vita Sackville-West's family. Firstly, in 1910, her mother's relatives tried to prevent her father's inheritance of Knole, Kent. Secondly, the relatives of Sir John Murray Scott (*d* January 1912) tried to overturn his large bequest to Lady Sackville on grounds of undue influence. Vita gave evidence in court. Both were successfully overcome (ODNB)

[264] (See also letter 127). Vita Sackville-West became engaged to Harold Nicolson in August 1913. Violet Keppell married Denys Trefusis in June 1919 but the two women were having an affair which continued during both marriages (ODNB)

[265] Alice Christiana Gertrude Meynell [*née* Thompson] (1847–1922), poet and journalist. She published many articles, essays and poems. The poems that Julian is referring to may be the anthology simply entitled *Poems* published in 1913 (ODNB)

[266] Gilbert Frankau, novelist and poet. In 1912 he published *One of Us*, a novel in *ottava rima* as used by Byron in Don Juan (ODNB)

[267] (Robert) Laurence Binyon, (1869–1943), poet and art historian. He wrote a number of poems and, with his friends W B Yeats and Thomas Sturge Moore, worked towards the revival of poetic drama on the London stage. In 1913, he published several books, so it is not possible to identify the work referred to here. On 21 September 1914, less than seven weeks into the First World War, *The Times* published what would become Binyon's most famous poem, the remarkably prescient elegy 'For the Fallen'. This contains the now famous lines: 'They shall grow not old, as we that are left grow old: / Age shall not weary them, nor the years condemn. / At the going down of the sun and in the morning / We will remember them'

I <u>am</u> sorry about poor Bill-boy losing to John. What a tremendous game it must have been. I hope he is well and flourishing.

<u>Brooke</u>, Basil, Sir, 10th Hussars, is one of the nicest fellows I've ever seen. You don't know <u>how</u> nice the Tenth are. We have had the greatest fun here together all this time, living in the little club here, 2 miles out of Jo'burg; and sleeping on the dormitory system in the police barracks, next door: the men under canvass. The strike trouble is still dragging on, apparently quite indefinitely. The Government cannot possibly grant the men's demands; and the men cannot possibly declare a general strike, as they would starve. So things are at a deadlock, and nobody knows when we shall get back to Potch[efstroom]. Things look rather worse today; but I think that there will be no more trouble, for the present, say 4 months, as all the troops are here, and they have a wholesome fear of them now. I don't know what effect it will have on our coming home. All of our people are in great form, but languishing at present from want of occupation . Clem Mitford[268] in the Tenth is charming – do you know him? Also, especially, Brocklehurst, lieutenant – a great hearty boxing man, tremendous hard rider, with a v[ery] good sense of humour. I am enjoying life tremendously just now; having bottles flung at my head cleared it wonderfully. I'm having my usual temptation, to plunge straight into La Vie Orageuse[269], for which Jo'burg offers ample opportunity, with the added excitement at present of being a marked man among the roughs; and the added stimulus of the brisk competition of the officer-boys of 4 regiments.

How I wish I could come to Pans[hanger] in Sept, to shoot the partridges with the Likky Man; please give him tons of love from me; and that Mog too. I'm so awfully sorry about Strath dying; but I really think Geordie is <u>nice</u> now, and that he will do well. Don't you? Bless you. Are you <u>well</u>? Love from J.

Stop press News

The Federation of Trades Unions have just declared, after a meeting, that they will declare a general strike unless the Government accept all their demands.

---

[268] Clement Mitford, eldest son of Algernon Bertram Freeman-Mitford, 1st Baron Redesdale, diplomatist and author (ODNB)
[269] An outrageous life

**135   27 July [1913]   Country Club,   DE/Rv/C1133/56
Johannesburg**

My dear Dad

Thank you very much for your letter. I am so sorry to hear that Strath is dead. I wonder if Geordie will do well; I should think he might do very well, he is so much more responsible than he used to be.

Bill must have had a tremendous game with John Manners in the tennis singles. I only wish that he had won. I hope that he defeated the examiners alright. I'm glad that the Likky Man is so well and happy; it would be wonderful to be so unconscious of outside opinion as he is.

Things are very bad here. We and the 10th are under canvas here, waiting for contingencies. We have been here a fortnight now, and it has been great fun having them. They are an extraordinarily nice lot of fellows, and we are all bosom friends and brothers-in-arms. The strike has been dragging on; the Federation of Trades Unions presented quite impossible demands to the Government last week, and the Government granted a few of the requests, and said that they would see about the rest. Just this minute (Sunday 10 pm) we have heard that the Trades Unions, after a meeting, have issued an ultimatum to the Government, proclaiming general strike unless all their demands are granted. A general strike means starvation to the people, in a very short time. The first thing they will do is to march off all the 20,000 natives working on the mines – straight off to their homes. That will mean no work on the mines for at least a year – and all the miners out of employment. That will ruin the country; and will mean a crowd of roughs starving and looking for trouble. It is a pretty black outlook.

The Royals got great kudos for the last business; and the men certainly stood the shooting and bottle-throwing with marvellous patience. If there is a strike this week – that is, if the Trades Unions do not give in, because the Government can't give in – it will mean a lot of trouble; but I can't help thinking that the miners will see that they are cutting their own throats, and refuse to come out. The whole strike is being run by the socialist agitators, largely against the will of the men themselves.

I'm feeling very fit again now, and my head has stopped buzzing after my bang. I hope that you are fit. Mum tells me that Likkie is having a battle of the Panshanger partridges in the Autumn. What about putting some trout in the river?

Goodbye. Very best love from Julian.

136   3 Aug 1913   Potchefstroom   DE/Rv/C1135/624

Darling Mother

We are just this moment (7 pm) back from Jo'burg, by train, starting at 9 am
this morning. The strike is finally bust up – for the present; although I
believe it was the nearest thing in the world at the Trades Hall meeting last
Thursday, whether they would declare a general strike or not. If they had
declared it, we should have had a pretty thin time, as they had all got
dynamite, made up into bombs in bicycle pumps, which they were going to
throw from the housetops onto our devoted heads. It is just a month today
when we got orders to entrain for Jo'burg.
I am awfully sorry that Bill got beaten in the tennis by Westmacott: it is an
awful blow: - and that poor Likky has had measles; I hope he hasn't been
bad, but it seems to have been going on for a long time. Please thank Dad
very much for his cable, which I got today.
The only lasting impression left by the strike is that utter beastliness of both
sides – the Jews at the Rand Club, who loaf about and drink all day; and the
Dutch and Dagos who curse and shoot in the streets. I suppose that they are
only the worst of each lot but one sees most of; that there must be some
decent mine-owners, and that the body of the miners are not so bad. But
from walking the streets one really wonders why fire and brimstone is
withheld from Jo'burg. The ladies, on the other hand, are rather pleasant, and
interesting. They all dress like chorus-girls on a holiday, and behave with
much less hypocrisy. It is a very good town in which to see life for a little,
with a smile on one's face and a revolver in one's pocket. I had great fun
going round some of the suburbs with the detective fellows. The opium dens
are extraordinary; and I actually saw men playing poker with their pistols
loaded on the table, which I thought only occurred in a wild west novel.
Jews and Dutch and Indians and Greeks and Russians and Chinamen, and
white women and black women, all chock-a-block. It must be the most
cosmopolitan town in the world.
I've just bought two new ponies; so that I've got four good ones now, and am
well equipped. A lot of our people are going for leave – this is the end of the
so-called Drill Season, and a very amusing one it has been. We are a very
happy family in the regiment just now, and live in peace and amity with one
another and the Royal Hussars. My dogs are very well, and my affairs in
good order. I shall take my promotion exam for Capen [Captain] this year.
Goodbye. Give my love to all the family. Bless you. J.

137   11 Aug 1913   Potchefstroom   DE/Rv/C1135/625

Darling Mother

Thank you awfully for your letter. I am so sorry that Mrs Good has been so
ill – I hope she is better now. I wrote to Mr Bart[270]. I'm glad that the Likky
Man is over his measles. Thank you for sending me the Spectator obituary
on Alfred Lyttelton[271], which I thought excellent – and strangely <u>truthful</u> for
an obituary. Please give my love to K of K [*Kitchener of Khartoum*]: I hope
Hatfield was fun? It was very good to get back here again, to home and
horses and hunting, after wild life in Jo'burg – although we had a great time
there at the last. I went up again yesterday, to pick up the threads.
Everybody here is preparing to go on leaves; Uncle Makins goes home on
this mail, and I have told him that he is to go to see you. Waterhouse and Pitt
Rivers and self will be about the only subalterns left here this autumn.
Waterhouse got great kudos in the strike, and is now Uncle's bosom friend!
My stud and kennel are now the best here, and are great fun – the red dog is
a wonder – do you remember him, the one with the big stifle? [272] (of course
you do, with your lightning sporting instinct). I've got the "Eagle" again
now, and the Athletic Club. Some of us are taking a lot of horses down to
Laurenço Marques[273] next month for the horse-show and the jumping; I think
I shall go down there for it.
I wonder if you are at Pans[hanger] now? In lovely summer weather? It is a
bore not having been able to let Pans[hanger] or Tap[low]: and a bore for
you not being able to go to France. Please give Dad my best love. What is
Bill-boy going to do this autumn?
Have you read a book by Winston Churchill about Christianity called "The
Inside of the Cup"[274] – stiff, but not bad. <u>Do</u> send me some jolly books.
Have you read anything good lately?
Best love from J.

---

[270] Mrs Good was the wife of Barrett Good, the family's butler. 'Mr Bart': in this
context is probably the family name for Mr Good
[271] Hon Alfred Lyttleton, eighth son of the 4th Lord Lyttleton and a friend of Ettie. In
1885, he had married Laura, daughter of Sir Charles Tennant (Mosley, p408)
[272] The joint at the junction of the hind leg and body (between the femur and tibia) in
a horse or other quadruped: corresponding anatomically to the knee in man (OED)
[273] Port in Mozambique, now known as Maputo
[274] *The Inside of the Cup* by Winston Churchill (1913)

138   16 Aug 1913   Potchefstroom   DE/Rv/C1135/626

Darling Mother

Yours to hand, of July 28; with 2 very good jokes, the "Quidlet" and "Four Wo-man", which were greatly appreciated in the mess here – a great tribute to any non-Essex jibe! I hope Esher was fun? And that the Pans[hanger] H.Ds[275] are smoothing out – the heavy responsibilities of the Very Rich. But what I complain about is that you are so apathetic about the strike at Jo'burg; I was longing for letters full of anxiety, sympathy, and admiration for the little 'eros facing undaunted the bullets of the fierce alien mob; and all you ask is "How did the strike strike you"? I do call it a bit hard; and I always thought you disliked puns? You don't know what dangers and discomforts we went through, with the complete Sang Froid of the Anglo-Saxon. And what is the good of Sang Froid if you do not get the full kudos for it?

We are here again, living the simple (and idle) life; in depleted numbers, as everyone has gone on leave. The polo is great fun; and all the fairies of Johannesburg have followed us to Potch[efstroom], which makes life most exciting, as you never know round which corner you are going to run into the General, Mrs General, and Miss General, with one of the sane fairies upon your arm. We are hunting a lot, with the long dogs too, and life is very pleasant.

How is Billa-boy? I hope he's recovered from his Greats? Please give Dad and the Family my best love. How are your eyeses? And are you really welly? I do want to see you again: more now than ever before. Every time I go away I curse myself for not having made the most of you and your fun! Bless you. Love from J.

---

[275] Heating and drains: many repairs to Panshanger were found to be necessary after the property was inherited by the Grenfells

139   24 Aug 1913   Potchefstroom   DE/Rv/C1135/627

Darling Mother

I'm so <u>awfully</u> sad about poor Bill-boy. It is a terrible blow; but I know he'll
be wonderfully good about it, as he would be about any <u>big</u> thing. I had such
a funny premonition about it, in the form of a curious anxiety to hear about
his Greats – a frightened feeling which one dismissed before it became more
than an anxiety. He had almost too much insolence and confidence about it
before; and indeed one could not let oneself think of the possibility of failure,
after what he has done[276]. But I expect it will collect him and pull his hocks
under him tremendously: and I hope and believe that the luck will turn for
him now. What is he going to do? Will he go up for All Souls, or not?[277]
Did you have any feeling about it before, with your uncanny prophetic sense?
How is he? I do hope that he is better now, and that he'll have a good
holiday.
How are you? I'm glad that you've got a step up in Court circles! Have you
been having fun with Kinkie? I told Makins to go to see you directly he got
back. I'm glad that your letters show more interest in the strike! Sclater
Booth was not hit at all by anything, but just fell off onto his head from
nervous agitation. He has gone home, for good, as we hope and expect: it
will be for his own good if he stays there.
I think that the oddest thing of the strike was the entire unconcern of quite
half the crowd, who were casually looking on in the streets while their
friends were shot down next them. A lot of people came out of a matinee
while the firing was going strong, looked on for a bit, and then walked back
into the theatre again and finished their play. Think what would happen if
you fired a few shots down a street in London!
Very few of us here now, doing musketry and odd jobs. I'm training my
ponies and running my dogs, and running the Eagle and the Athletic Club and
the Boxing Club, and starting to work for my promotion exam – and enjoying
myself and the work and the people better than ever before.
Best of best love to the family.
And you you from J.

---

[276] Billy had achieved only a Second in Greats (Mosley, p333)
[277] All Souls College, Oxford, a post-graduate college

140   3 Sept 1913   Royal Dragoons,   DE/Rv/C1133/57
                              Potchefstroom

My dear Dad

I'm so glad that you've managed to let Taplow to the Hebrews[278]; and I hope
that all the Panshanger arrangements are smoothing out. <u>Do</u> write and tell
me what you have done there? I hear that "Schoolgirl II" has become the
property of Miss Monica; I think shat she ought to carry her very well, as she
is really a most wonderful fencer, and has got a light mouth and a nervous
temperament, which will probably go better with a woman's hands than with
my fist! What about your £250 loan to me? You (very kindly!) said that you
would continue Auntie Ka[tie]'s £100 a year to me. If you stop that for this
year, and if you have given "Schoolgirl" (for whom I paid £150) to Casie,
that will make up the £250; and I think that this will be a very good way out
of it, if you are agreeable. The time the loan started at Cox's (16 Charing
Cross) was Jan 1913; and it was for a year, renewable after that. Will you
please write and tell me what you think about it? I ought to pay Schoolgirl's
keep for the six months, whatever that comes to? Then shall we be quits? I
haven't seen the £100 yet; but perhaps you have paid it in to Cox's? If you
have, I can pay it back to you now.
I hope that you are fit and well. It is very sad about poor Billy-boy, and I
hope that he is not very much cut up about it. Please give him my best love;
and also to Casie and the Likky Man. I'm quite fit again now after my
concussion, and enjoying myself tremendously. They have given me the
Regimental Scouts, which is most interesting work. The polo is great fun,
and I've got 5 good ponies. The long dogs are great from here, too, after
hares and buck; but the going is very rough. Most of our people are away on
leave now.
Best love from Julian.

---

[278] It has proved impossible to identify the lessee of Taplow Court; the 1915 trade
directory (the nearest to 1913) shows Lord Desborough as the owner and there is no
mention of a tenant. It was at this date that Lord and Lady Desborough made
Panshanger their home rather than Taplow

141   3 Sept 1913   Potchefstroom   DE/Rv/C1135/598

Darling Mother

Thank you awfully for your letter. I'm so glad that you've got some Jews for Tap[low], and it must be a great relief to you. I'm glad Esher was fun; what was Lord Milner's[279] like, and Rudyard Kipling's ball?[280] I hope Likkie Man will enjoy his Panshanger partridge shooting. How I wish that I had had the same opportunities at his age! I'm thrilled about Rock and Sybil Sass[oon]: but how I should hate to be married to her![281] Please give Billa-boy my best love: he is much too big to be depressed by things like that, isn't he? I'm writing to Dad today to discuss our financial position. I hear that "Schoolgirl" is now the property of my dashing sister. She is a marvel, though of course I made a mistake in buying her. I think Casie will ride her quietly, as she ought to be ridden; and well, as she ought to be ridden. I hope the Panshanger H.D.s all go smoothly – please tell me about them. Our mail from here is altered now – Thursday instead of Monday, ie Thursday morning from here instead of Monday morning from here; which makes it as bad as poss[ible] for our letters, as your's arrive here Thursday midday. When do mine arrive? Yours leave on Friday, don't they?

Great fun here, although almost everyone is on leave. They wouldn't let me go to Laurenço Marques, because of the chance of my falling on my head again. In a way, I'm very glad; because that trick jumping is dangerous, without being very exciting. Waterhouse and Pitt-Rivers have gone; and some NCOs. I should have liked to see Marques, which they say is as good as Port Said, from the independent observer's point-of-view. We still get our 3 days a week polo; isn't it lucky to be in a country where you can play polo all the year round? It's just beginning to get hot – the rains will start in about a month. The climate is wonderful now – just right. I've got 5 real smashing ponies; and four good greyhounds. I've had a lot of trouble with the dogs I brought out; their feet get cut so badly, on the rocks: but they're alright now. We get good coursing; a lot of the 10th are very keen on it. We've just started a new sport – riding down buck. We killed two last week. It's almost as good as pigsticking, only terrible for the horses, over the rocks. You just ride

---

[279] Alfred Milner, Viscount Milner, public servant and politician (ODNB). Milner's house was at Sturry Court, near Canterbury, Kent

[280] At Kipling's house, Batemans, Burwash, Sussex

[281] In 1913, Sybil Sassoon, sister of Sir Philip Sassoon, married the Earl of Rocksavage, heir of the Marquess of Cholmondeley (ODNB)

the buck to a standstill, and then shoot him with a revolver. For about two
miles he goes right away from you; then he begins to "come back", if you
can keep pressing him. Of course the going is awful, rocks and holes; and
the pace, top pace: but we take King George's horses, so he pays the piper!
I've just got our regimental scouts, which I've been trying to get for years
and years. It's interesting, wild work; and you get the jolliest and keenest
men on it. It's the first soldiering I've been keen on.
I haven't asked yet about the Cavalry School. I don't much mind whether I
get it or not, except for you, and seeing the family again: because I'm liking
my work here now very much. And I think I do much better in the wilds
than in England, where there are so many more conventions to gird against. I
mean, everything is so old and settled in England, that if one girds against
settled things, we gird there all the time. And girding is so bad.
Goodbye, & bless you, darling. J.

142   4 Sept 1913   Royal Dragoons,   DE/Rv/C1138/19
**   Potchefstroom**

Casie darling

Yours to hand, with many thanks. Your Sussex time must have been great
fun; but I'm sorry you're having beastly weather at Pans[hanger]. It's a good
thing that Tap[low] is let to the aliens. Poor Bill-boy: give him all my love.
I'm tremendously excited about you and Schoolgirl; I love your description
of her shoeing, with Dyna[mite]. I think you will love her beyond words; her
jumping is like an aeroplane, it's so quick and smooth. Did you have fun this
summer, my dear? Are you getting "toid up"? [282] This place is good fun.
I've got our Scouts now, and we spend day and night in the wilds, visiting
little Boer farms, and making love to the farmers' daughters. They are jolly
nice wild men, the Scouts. Then there is the polo; I've got 5 good ponies.
And the long dogs, who pursue hares and buck over the wild dry veldt. I
love the Tenth; there is one perfect darling, called Basil Brooke. We galloped
down a buck last week – 4 miles full split over rocks and holes and all sorts.
Goodbye and bless you, dear.
I'm engaged to such a nice girl in Jo'burg[283], so I shall beat you yet, unless
you gallop. J.

---

[282] Engaged or married
[283] It seems that Julian did have a steady girl-friend at this time but is unlikely to
have been engaged (Mosley, p335)

143   11 Sept 1913   Potchefstroom   DE/Rv/C1135/628

Darling Mother

Thank you awfully for two very good letters. I didn't find out last week that
by leaving it to the last minute, one gets the English Mail letters on Thursday
morning early enough to answer them by the same mail. Now of course I've
left it <u>too</u> late, this week. You must have had a terribly busy time at
Pans[hanger]; poor darling, what a holiday for you! I'm glad that it's all
smoothing out now. But I can hardly imagine <u>what</u> an undertaking it must
have been. Did you ever get the misgiving that big houses are a thing of the
past? I wonder. But how right you are to pitch clean in to the thing of the
moment. Excessive idealism is not only stupid, but so <u>lazy</u>; because if you
decide only to do the thing perfectly "worth while", you do nothing; there
being nothing <u>perfectly</u> worth while (or very little, and that little comes after
you have started something imperfect). I can't express myself – the mail is
going or gone.
I'm <u>so</u> sorry you had a bit of a slump: although you don't call it a slump,
and I'm sure it was less of a slump even than you call it. Are you getting any
rest now?
I'm so happy here; having decided, at last, that my job is the Profession of
Arms. I love my fellow officers now: and my dogs; and my horses. Isn't it
funny that the more one loves one's fellow officers, the more one loves one's
dogs; instead of the less!
Please thank Casie & Dad for delicious letters. I'll write to them next week.
Tell Dad to cancel my letter of last week, re settlement: as I thought
Schoolgirl's leg w[oul]d be quite well. As it is not, she is not worth what I
gave for her.
Bless you J.

144   17 Sept 1913   Roberts' Heights   DE/Rv/C1135/629

Darling Mother

I hope the Pans[hanger] estate is now straightened out into beautiful working
order; or anyhow, that the worst is over? It must have been a terrific grind.
How are you going to divide up the time between Pans[hanger] and
Tap[low]? Or are you going to cleave to the one, and leave the other? I can
so understand all the ghosts Panshanger must hold for you. Life is a good
rush here too nowadays, as there are so few of us, and one man doing the

work of five – that is, a great rush for anyone so unsuccessful to toil as I am! Of course it is light work, and a lot of it very jolly bashing work[284]; but now that I have made up my so-called brain that it is <u>my</u> work, I can pitch into it without misgiving. While before, it seemed to matter so little whether one did it or not, that one naturally didn't: and it is so deadly easy to get through with ease and grace, and a certain amount of credit, without doing a hand's-turn, by the aid of a little cheap swank and invention! The Scouts are the greatest fun, and they are all very keen. We live all day and all night out of doors, on and off and under horses, sketching and watching and swimming: and doing wild west shows, like vaulting and riding back to front and riding double, and picking up handkerchiefs at a gallop, and making the horses lie down, and that sort of thing. Next month we go down to Basutoland (great mountains) for a month, on a scheme.

I'm not coming to the Cavalry School: I didn't at all want to, latterly, as I want to work at these things out here. And after all, the Cavalry School only means learning to ride under a teacher and in a manège[285], what one can teach oneself as well and with much more fun in the open.

I hear that Billa-boy has gone to Venice. Give my best love to the family. I loved the photograph Casie sent me, with the Tango neck-twist! How are you. No more nonsense about failure of course, please! J.

145   25 Sept 1913   Potchefstroom   DE/Rv/C1135/630

Darling Mother

Thank you awfully for your letter. I'm so glad that Dad and the Likkie Man are having fun with the partridges. I'm simply longing for the Miss Belloc[286] book. I wish I knew Brocket[287]: you must have had such wonderful fun there. Please give the Likkie Man my best love, and a kick for luck for his birthday. How sad it must be for you going through all the old papers! I should like <u>very</u> much to have Uncle Francis'[288] dressing case. I'm glad

---

[284] Services' slang denoting any arduous task (OED)

[285] An enclosed space for the training of horses and the practice of horsemanship; a riding school (OED)

[286] Marie Belloc Lowndes, sister of Hilaire Belloc. Over a period of fifty years, she published at least 70 books of various kinds, including biographies of royal persons, but more usually romances or crime novels. It was the last genre with which she came to be most associated, especially through her novels *The Chink in the Armour*

you've got through most of the other H.D.s': how true it is, what you say
about the necessity of Compromise! What grief one comes to, through trying
to get things straight and exact and altogether! But how rotten one would be,
if one didn't start by trying that way!

I'm just going up to Jo'burg to get my nose cut. There's a really clever man
up there, a Scotchman, McNab, a specialist at that sort of thing. He says it
will make the whole difference to my health, and hearing: and that the dust
out here always makes that sort of thing ten times worse.

Our Scout jaunt to Basutoland is put off a month. We're doing sports and
Skill-at-Arms and Mounted Combat now, having just finished Musketry: I
missed "Marksman" by 1 p[oin]t, 129 instead of 130; but I was the best in
my Troop. I'm doing a lot of night-work with the Boy Scouts, which is fun.
We've just had a very good Garrison Boxing Tournament, 3 nights: I do hate
doing accounts!

Oh, when you see Makins, tell that I asked you <u>long ago</u> to try to get out of
<u>Lord Delware</u> a "Diary of Col Johnstone, Col of the Royal Dragoons during
the 7 years war". Col Ainslie had it when he wrote the Regimental History:
and it went on to Delware. Makins is always bothering me about it, and I
promised him that I would ask you to try to get it for him. Do you know
Delware? He takes after the King of Siam, celebrated in rhyme, so I believe.
Can you get it. Send Duff Cooper[289] along to him.

Goodbye, and <u>bless</u> you. I do hope that you are <u>welly</u>, & <u>happy</u>? I do want
to see your face again. J.

(1912) and most of all *The Lodger*, published in 1913, a story of a London couple in
the 1880s who suspected that their lodger was Jack the Ripper. This is probably the
book that Julian is referring to and was a best-seller in its day (ODNB)

[287] Brocket Hall, Lemsford, Hertfordshire, a former Cowper property

[288] Francis Thomas de Grey Cowper, 7th Earl Cowper (1834-1905), husband of Lady
Katrine Cowper. Panshanger had been their home

[289] Alfred Duff Cooper, born in 1890, the son of a doctor. Went to Eton and New
College, Oxford; joined the Foreign Office. Married Lady Diana Manners in 1919
(MacKenzie, pp133, 262)

**146   25 Sept 1913   Royal Dragoons,   DE/Rv/C1138/20
                          Potchefstroom**

My darling Girlie Gurl

Yrs to hand, and many thanks. I'm glad you're so well, and that the family
are having fun. Cultivate Will Coggin; he is a great character, and a genius
about horses; but not a patch in either respect on his father, Will Coggin
Senior, who is usually blotto, and can give points, when in that condition, to
any other two men sober. Look here, darling, I'll give you "The Other Girl"
for a gift, Raca (or Coran, I forget which). I think she will stand. Either take
her away from Coggin, and "take her up" steadily; or tell him to do so. (But
he does it very slowly and lazily.) I have written, advising him on the matter.
Let him know <u>at once</u>.
Then, if her leg does not look like standing, put her to a <u>real</u> <u>good</u> horse, an
expensive thorobred, a <u>big</u> horse, with big bone, (steeplechasing blood). She
comes of a really wonderful staying strain, and ought to breed smashing
chasers. Send her to Coggin to foal.
If she stands, she is the best hunter you'll ever have. She will jump any
dammed thing: and she will win any p[oin]t to p[oin]t, and most Hunt
Chases. Ride her in a snaffle, if you can; she hates a double bit.
Bless you, my dear. Be happy. I'm having the time of my life here, with my
Scouts, and 6 long dogs, and 5 ponies! J.
[Written on outside of envelope (part missing): 'Dar[ling?] write me out …
family birthdays; with dates, and photographs if pos[sible]']

147   30 Sept 1913   Potchefstroom   DE/Rv/C1135/631

Darling Mother

Tomorrow I start at crack of dawn with the Scouts for the Orange Free State;
we shall cross the Vaal soon after dawn; and then a free week in the
wilderness. So I have to write tonight, before your letter arrives. Are you
well, & happy? Are you still at Pans[hanger], downing the partridges. Have
you read anything new and jolly? Do you like Belloc's "This & That"
Essays?[290] I'd never read them before; I loved some of them. But how badly

---

[290] *This and that and the other* by Hilaire Belloc (1912), a collection of 40 essays on
miscellaneous subjects

all the journalists write, when you can see that they're writing because they've got to. I read "New Arabian Nights" [291] again, too. I went to Jo'burg on Thursday nights, and Dr McNab, on Friday morning, cut and banged and hammered at my nose for <u>1 hr 5 min</u>, without chloroform[292]. He took out stacks of bones and heaps of gristle: and said it was the best thing he had ever done. He said that the inside of my nose was a perfect maze of shattered stuff: and that I shall feel quite different now. He's such a good clever little canny evil-minded Scot; with perfect hands, like a jockey. On Sat morning the nurse (in hospital) flouted me, and said that I should be there for another week. So I packed my bag, and shouted out of the window to stop a taxi, and offed it, all incontinent. Jo'burg was in great fettle; and I had the succès of my life with the Gaiety Company, in spite of a bloody nose. I always bear a grudge against ladies of the Profession: they are the fairest of game, on the rare occasions when one can get home at them. I got back here this morning.

Goodbye, darling. Give my best love to all the family. I shall get your letter sent on to the Free State, and work the scout scheme according! J.

148   9 Oct 1913   Potchefstroom   DE/Rv/C1135/632

Darling Mother

I had such a good letter from Bill-boy this week, just returned from his lurid Venice tour. He must have been splendid about it all; and I expect it will give him exactly the right stiffening. I'm glad that he is with Douglas Radcliffe, who is one of the real 20th Century Saints, and at the same time full of bite. My <u>dear</u>, what a terrible go you must have had at Pans[hanger]! Are you really out of the Slough now? It's too bad that you should have two houses; but O gracious Lord, what about me, who every year have an increasing desire to live in a blanket under a bush; and will soon get bored with the bush and the blanket! I'm glad that the Tobacco King[293] has come to the rescue. I'm so glad, too, that you have decided to sell the little

---

[291] *New Arabian Nights* by Robert Louis Stevenson (1st edition c 1880)
[292] The common name for a thin colourless liquid, having a pleasant ethereal odour and pungent sweetish taste, the vapour of which when inhaled produces insensibility; hence it is much used as an anaesthetic in surgical and obstetrical operations (OED)
[293] See letter 140 above

Raphael[294]; of course, you <u>must</u> have done something, and it is good to have come to a decision. I think the "Panshanger Fund" is a very good idea. What is Lloyd George doing meanwhile: and what will the next minute bring forth? How far do you agree, in <u>general</u> <u>theory</u>, with the Lloyd George schemes? Write me an arch-baker. I have never quite known, exactly, and how little, and how far.

Mummy darling, will you please give these two intensely and immensely important messages to Dad, as I forgot them in my letter to him.

Can he do anything about <u>Cronin</u>, about whom I wrote to him 2 months ago?[295]

About my thorobred "Poor Denis" – I have handed him over to Waterhouse, who goes home next month – to train and race. W is in with all the racing stiffs, and a good business man. If he does no good with him, and cannot sell him or win some races, I told him to hand him over to Dad (provided he is agreeable): the horse is a good hack, and should make a good hunter (light-weight). But with any luck he should win a race or two, and fetch a price. The rains have started here, a leaden downpour, with intervals of thunder and waterspout. I had a real good week with the boy-scouts on the Vaal River before they started. They are very good fun. One of them got stranded in a field with three horses all one night; and in the morning asked me for extra pay, because last night he had done 5 men's work – the Orderly Officer's, the Orderly Sergeant Major's, the Orderly Sergeant's, the Orderly Corporal's, & the Night Guard's. Another stole a dog, and said "What shall I call this little barstid?" "Oh, knock one of his eyes out, and call him <u>Napoleon</u> (!)".

Best love to all the family.

Bless you. I'm so glad you're going up, up, up. How are your eyes? J.

---

[294] The Madonna and Child by Raphael was sold by Lord Desborough in November 1913 for £70,000. The painting is now in the National Gallery, Washington DC, USA (HALS: DE/Rv/F1 refers to the sale)

[295] See letter 130 dated 29 June 1913 in which Julian asks his father to acquire a commission for Quartermaster D B Cronin

149   15 Oct 1913   Potchefstroom   DE/Rv/C1135/633

Darling Mother

No letter of yours to answer this week, as I've got to write tonight, before the mail comes in. I hope you and Casie had fun at Gosford[296]. Are you back at Tap[low] now? When are you on waiting again? I hope Daddy had some good stalking. Bosun (Captain Chapman) returns to us tomorrow, having been home for five months. He brings with him a new boy for the regiment, Watkin Wynn. Bosun has spent his leave seeing French doctors in Switzerland. He is the most awful valetudinarian in the world; he thinks that Rest is the sovereign cure for all ailments, and consequently has been resting hard for 5 years, ever since he had a bad go of Enteric[297] in India. He does absolutely Damn All, except running the regimental gaff (concerts & acting) – which he does extraordinarily well.   It's such a pity: he used to be a real tiger: and still he has got a wonderfully good sense of h[umour] about other people, but absolutely none about himself. he is a great dear, though; and so serious about himself that everybody else takes him seriously until they are with him, and then dashes to somebody else to laugh about him. I'm very glad that he's coming back, as we've only had five in the mess lately – Philip Hardwick (rich and rare), Parker Leighton (poor and common), Waterhouse, Pitt-Rivers, & self.

A nasty thing happened last Monday. I sent a man to fetch my sergeant-major (Reserve Troop) to Orderly Room; and as the orderly arrived at his bunk, the sergeant-major shot himself. The orderly rushed back, & told me. I went and found him lying huddled in a corner, with the revolver still in his hand. He had put it into his mouth, and shot himself dead. He was such a jolly man, from Princes Risboro'[298]. He had got into trouble over his accounts; but thank God, I had never blamed him at all about them – I just left him to fight it out with the Pay Office, saying that I trusted him absolutely, and that it was all their fault. There are awful rows going on now about the accounts. The poor man left a wife & child. He had been 21 yrs in the regiment.

Goodnight, Mummy darling. Give my best love to the family.

Bless you J.

---

[296] Gosford House, the family seat of the Charteris family, situated near Longniddry in East Lothian, Scotland

[297] Typhoid fever

[298] Princes Risborough, Buckinghamshire

150   23 Oct 1913   Carlton Hotel,   DE/Rv/C1135/634
Johannesburg

Darling Mother

Thank you awfully for y[ou]rs rec[eive]d last Thursday, and the two books,
Wells & Maxwell[299]. I started the Wells one when it came out in the
magazines, and I've read some more of it; I think it will be a very good one –
with perfectly intolerable bits about powdered footmen and gold plate and
luscious peaches. He has apparently returned to High Life: I think he is
better at Medicine[300] to Low to Very Low – truer, and very little more
unpleasant. But <u>how</u> <u>how</u> <u>how</u> subtle and minute and clever and <u>exact</u> he is,
in analysis; and how much more <u>constructive,</u> in a very vague way, he is now
than he used to be! Is the Maxwell good? I haven't read any of him before.
I hope your Scotland has been fun? It must have been a good and hardly-
needed and well-earned rest for you. When did you go? Gosford & Whitte?
I hope Daddy got some good stalking.
I have got lots to tell you. First, and most important. I. A. I killed a fox
with my greyhounds at 5.30 am on Erste Ranges North on Sunday last: very
rare in this country, most of our chaps wouldn't believe it till I showed it to
them. My little black puppy killed it – broke its back in one snap, going at
full speed. It was much bigger than she is. I've never had such good long
dogs as now; 4 great big lashing dogs, and this little bitch, who is the best of
the lot. I do think that greyhounds are the most beautiful things on earth;
they have got all the <u>really</u> jolly things – affection, and courage unspeakable,
and speed like nothing else, and sensitiveness and dash and grace and
gentleness, and enthusiasm.
There have been terrific rows about Fordom, the Quarter Master Sergeant
who shot himself. He had got into trouble with his books; drank; forged and
erased and cheated for 6 months to get right; failed; and dared not face the
music. Poor Devil. He was £240 out. Lechie (rich) and The Buck
(Waterhouse, dirt poor) have to pay the piper – or they may get out of it, as
you cannot really hold an officer responsible if the Sergeant forges his name

---

[299] *The Passionate Friends* by H G Wells (1913) and *The Devil's Garden*, by William
Babbington Maxwell (1913)
[300] A reference to Wells' book *Tono-Bungay* (1909) in which one of the characters,
Uncle Ponderevo, is an entrepreneur intent on peddling a worthless patent medicine

and cooks his figures. You have no idea how intensely complicated Army accounts are. We have all spent the last fortnight trying to unravel these books, under Boards of Officers: but the Boards, who come fresh to it, while we have spent weeks in trying to twist it out, - understand damn all about it, and send in the most ridiculous statements, which are immediately quashed by Headquarters, who then appoint a new Board; and ditto occurs. Luckily Fordom did not cheat at all during the month he was under me; isn't that odd; he and I were great friends, and I suppose he didn't want to do me down. The Regimental Scouts are composed of 16 "squadron" scouts, who work with their squadrons on service; and 8 "regimental" scouts, who work for the whole show. Their job in war is to find out all they can without being seen – right ahead of the regiment. In peace you train them by keeping them out in the open all the time, to teach them country, and how to use their eyes, and how to work alone, and how to keep themselves and their horses "on the country", with nothing supplied. It's a very interesting job. Vide[301] the Boy Scout Manuals, and Mr Ivo G W Grenfell.

My <u>nose</u> is now working like a motor with the throttle open, and is of a fine Grecian symmetry. I can blow through it like a Sperm Whale (or is it a Cachalot? [302]). But there is no solid bone backing to it; in fact, it is like the Pharisees and Sadducees[303]; and the next punch I receive thereon will flatten it out like butter in the summer months.

Miss Babs Hale (late of Roberts Heights) is engaged to be married, God bless her. She is really a very nice girl, and I wish I had married her.

I got one day's leave up here yesterday for the Rag-Time Ball[304], last night, at this place. It was really wonderful – everyone out for blood, and the time spent in lightning changes from the ball-room to the bed-room. I always

---

[301] See, refer to, consult; a direction to the reader to refer to some other heading, passage, or work (or to a table, diagram, etc) for fuller or futher information (OED)

[302] A genus of whales, belonging to the family Catodontidae, distinguished by the presence of teeth in the lower jaw (OED)

[303] The Jewish party of the Pharisees first appeared in Judea in the reign of John Hyracanus I (135-104 BC). They had a profound influence on the development of orthodox Judaism. The Sadducees opposed the Pharisees. The only thing that united them was their opposition to Christ and his disciples (*Brewer's Dictionary of Phrase and Fable*, 2000 edition)

[304] Rag-time was musical rhythm characterized by a syncopated melodic line and regularly-accented accompaniment, evolved among American Negro musicians in the 1890s; hence, music (especially for the banjo and piano) of this character, the immediate precursor of jazz (OED)

expect an immediate visitation of fire and brimstone[305], when living in Johannesburg. Just off back to Potch[efstroo]m.
Goodbye, Mummy darling J.
Can you do the Tango?[306] We are all tigers at it now.

151   30 Oct 1913   Potchefstroom   DE/Rv/C1135/635

Darling Mother

Thank you for your letter. I'm <u>so</u> glad you're better, after your Scotland time: it sounds the very greatest fun. But it's hateful to think of your having returned to W[indsor]C[astle] work again! <u>Poor</u> Mummy! How about the little Raphael? Is it sold yet? I had a letter from Moggy today, with a picture of herself shrimping, in a Botticelli sea[307]. She started by saying that she was so sorry she hadn't written to me for such a long time, but that she had really had <u>so</u> little time. I heard from Casie-girl too. Had Dad had good stalking? I start on Sat for a 3 week trek with my 24 Scouts, down to Basutoland, fighting the Tenth Scouts under Basil Brooke. We take a waggon, which they try to capture: so we shall lie up in the rocks all day, and march all night. My long dogs go with us, and we practically live on what they kill. The camps are just like gypsy camps; all the men round the fire, watching the dinner being cooked – and all the horses round outside, watching too. They are jolly men, all the wild spirits, and they love being out. One gets to know them very well, too, living with them – more than one would in years of barrack life. I think they have rather melted towards me, living with them and sleeping with them and eating their food. It rains now most nights, and we all sleep under a big tarpaulin hung onto two trees. We've got a horse, who always breaks his shackle, and tries to get under the tarpaulin about 3 times a night. He charges down at it with his head down, at a good trot; and the shower of profanity which meets his entering head really almost raises the tarpaulin.

---

[305] Reference to Biblical displays of the wrath of God on sinners
[306] A syncopated ballroom dance in 2/4 or 4/4 time introduced into Europe and North America from Argentina, related to the Cuban Habanera but probably of African origin, characterized by a slow gliding movement broken up by pointing positions. (First date of this useage in OED is 1913)
[307] A reference to the artistic style of Sandro Botticelli, the Italian Early Renaissance artist (c1445-1510)

I've had to take my name out of my promotion exam, because I have not had time to do my regimental work, much less extra work. But isn't it extraordinary how much better and how much more one does, when one is doing four things in the time of one. I've had the "Eagle", Boxing Club, Athletic Club, Cricket Club, Reserve Squadron, Scouts, Boxing Competition, and my troop on Troop Training all this month – and they are all "one man" jobs. And I've been frightfully happy.

Goodbye, Mummy darling. Mail just off. Give my best best love to all the family. J.

152   5 Nov 1913   Union Hotel, Vrede   DE/Rv/C1135/636

Darling Mother

This place is in the NE of the Free State. We trained to Standerton on the 2nd, and got here in two marches. Tomorrow our scheme starts; we have got to get our waggon past Bethlehem & Harrismith to Basutoland, and the 10th have got to try and capture it, starting from Potchefstroom. I've got 27 men, 37 horses, and 10 mules in the wagon. We live on the country, buying our rations and forage at the farms as we go; doing about 24 miles a day, a nice comfortable march for men & horses. The men are the most wonderful thieves; whenever we go past a pond, two of them ask leave to fall out for a minute (with a broad wink) and return shortly afterwards with 2 or 3 ducks, a chicken, and probably a dog. We have got every kind of Napoleonic scheme to outwit Basil Brooke and the Tenth Scouts; 2 of our men dressed up as Boers, with beards and little hired pones, to follow them up and wire to me every day: a patrol with orders written by me, carefully describing an entirely different route for our wagon, which is to blunder into their route, get captured, and have the orders found sewn into their helmets: and a hired false wagon going along this route, to draw them away safely.

It's a very jolly bit of country here – the High Veldt, quite green now, great rolling waves of ground like a heavy swell, so that you can only see to the next skyline, and anything beyond is completely hidden. It's different to Potch[efstroom] – not so many little hills – and entirely different to Jo'burg & Pretoria, with none of their bleakness, and still greater spaces. We ran into tremendous hills further down South. We've escaped the rain so far, but I expect we'll catch it soon.

I shall get your letters in a fortnight, at Harrismith. I wonder if you are at Tap[low] now? I am loving the Wells book: I love the vague swank about

not going in for politics or anything, because the larger interests of the
Universe are so much more important. I've got about half way through it.
Don't you love the man who got his colours at Eton for diving, and the man
who was clawed out of a tree by a panther? Are you well, after Scotland?
And are you doing the drains marvellously?[308]
Waterhouse has gone home: I've told him to pull out my horse "Poor Denis"
and run him in some chases: but as W has not got a bean to his name I don't
see how he can do it. Henry Jump, "the biggest liarr in Asiar", who went
into the wilds to shoot lions and tigers for three months, was discovered in
the Carlton Hotel Jo'burg 10 days after he had bade us a sad farewell; and a
month afterwards at the Victoria Falls Hotel, Zambesi; but he returned with
terrific stories of the prowess of his rifle, and of frantic deeds by field and
flood.
Goodbye – best best love to the family. I must return to camp and <u>lonely</u>
bed. That's why this letter is so long, boring, and ill-natured. J.
[Note at top of 1st page, next to name of proprietor of hotel: Observe the face
of William Jackson. How typical an Anglo-Saxon!

153   13 Nov 1913   Royal Hotel, Harrismith   DE/Rv/C1135/637

Darling Mother

I got your letter, forwarded here, yesterday. I can't understand you not
getting my letter, because I buzzed it off alright. I'm so glad that Netherly &
Drummond Castle and Holker were such fun[309]. Dad seems to have had a
bloody time with the monarchs of the glen[310]. Are you all at Tap[low] now?
Yes, I'm <u>now</u> very glad that we had such a good fight (although I feel that it
has taken years off my life). But I wish that I had been a little older: I
should have put up such a much better game for you in my maturer age. And
I'm afraid I shall never have another chance, because we shall always laugh
too soon in any future conflicts.
What good things letters are, for keeping touch; in one way they bring us
almost closer than talking, because they stir the imagination more. When one

---

[308] A reference to the refurbishment work being undertaken at Panshanger
[309] Netherley, Aberdeenshire; Drummond Castle, Muthill, Crieff; Holker Hall, Cark-
in-Cartmel, near Grange-over-Sands, Cumbria
[310] Deer

talks, there is no need or use for imagination in that way. When one writes, the whole thing depends on imagination. But I do want to see you again. I loved the Wells book; we must have read it at exactly the same time. I don't think it's a failure. I think his books are so good just for that reason, that they are so inconclusive, and therefore so true. How can anything be true that is worked out to a black and white conclusion? What thing has ever worked out to a black and white conclusion?

I read it in little bits on the trek down here, lying on the veldt, near the waggon, by the light of the camp fire. Such a funny contrast – the absolutely primitive conditions against the subtle hyper-modern hyper-civilised intricacies of the book. I don't like the man, or believe in him much. His passion is so unctuous and conscious and Made in Germany. I like the woman, except when she talks about her poor courtesy title. What terrible little gentilities there are in it.

We did our 150 miles to Kestell very comfortably, and utterly confounded the bloody uzzars. Basil will hardly speak to me. I sent two men to get captured, with messages hidden in their putties[311], written by me to patrols "Concentrate at once on waggon at Cornelis River Bridge". Basil got them, and drew in his patrols to C River Br, from over 100 miles of country. Meanwhile I walked into Kestell from the other side. I got great kudos for this simple manoevre.

Such a good life, and wonderful wild country, with little tracks running over the little deep rivers; and hills like bastions & battlements. We're all resting here for 3 days; off back to Potch[efstroom] tomorrow, 200 miles, 7 days. This is a good place, a little town under a huge mountain wall. The population comprises many faeries. I always think the biggest nonsense in the world is when people (like Wells) talk about women tempting men & leading them on to destruction, poor fellows. When the poor fellows are using whatever brains God has given them in a fervid gallop for the one end. What harm, when the women are as independent, and as anxious, as the men? Discuss this.

Mail going. I meant to write to Dad, but no time. Love to him, and thank him for his letter. Love to you. J.

---

[311] A long strip of cloth wound spirally round the leg from the ankle to the knee, worn as a protection and support to the leg by sportsmen, soldiers, etc (OED)

154   18 Nov 1913   Greenplatz, Orange   DE/Rv/C1135/638
Free State

Darling Mother

This is a little lonely store, with a little lonely railway coming from nowhere
and going to nowhere; and you can see 50 miles each way, and about 3 tin
huts. We are 3 days march from Potch[efstroom], where I shall get two of
your letters. Did you ever get my missing letter? Are you at Tap[low] now?
Are you well? How are your eyes? Are you having fun? I have loved this
trek more than almost anything ever; I'm really only happy and quoiet when
I am eating with my hands and sleeping on the ground with dogs all round
me. They are so far more trustworthy as companions than the fickle fair.
The tenth are camping next door to us tonight, and the men are all round the
fire, singing. Horse-show in Jo'burg next week, and I move my stable up
there.
Such wonderful clear nights here, with blazing stars; and a great loneliness.
I wish you could see the Basutoland hills: there is very little to beat them.
Goodnight, Mummy darling, and bless you. Give my love to the family.
Have you seen Waterhouse, who is now at home. I think you'd like him; he
has a great heart.
All all love from J.

155   18 Nov 1913   Greenplatz, nr Heilbron   DE/Rv/C1133/58
0.75, South Africa

My darling Dad

I got a letter from you last week, forwarded to me at Harrismith. I'm so glad
that you had good stalking: you must have done very well indeed. I hope
the pedigree cattle will be a success at Panshanger[312]. All the Panshanger
arrangements seem to be pretty well smoothing out now? I'm writing this
from a little store in the High Veldt here. It's a wonderful great rolling lonely
country, the Free State, and I believe it has a great farming future. It is much

---

[312] Lord Desborough established a pedigree herd of shorthorn cattle at Panshanger in
1913 by purchasing a herd at the sale of the late Sir Richard Cooper of Ashlyns,
Berkhamsted in Hertfordshire. He was already breeding pedigree Jersey cattle at
Taplow (HALS: DE/P/E13-16)

more pleasant, and much less barren, than the Transvaal; and of all places in the Transvaal Pretoria is the worst, so that we got all the beastliest side of S. Africa to start off with. One gets very fond of the veldt after trekking about in it. I've got 27 men here (Scouts) and 37 horses, and a back-waggon with ten mules for the kettles and blankets: no tents, and no food – we just buy forage and bread and meat as we go along, and peg the horses down wherever we fetch up in the afternoons, generally doing 24-30 miles a day. We had a scheme against the Scouts of the 10th, under Basil Brooke. They had to catch our wagon on the way to the Basuto border. I sent out two men to get captured, with false messages calling in my men to a big bridge; Basil got these messages, and concentrated on the bridge, while we slipped past 50 miles East. He was very sore about it. We have been on trek 3 weeks now; we get back to Potch[efstroom] in 3 days, and then I go up to Jo'burg for the Horse Show, where I've got my ponies showing, & 3 jumping horses.
My greyhounds have been great fun on the trek; we have got a hare or two or three each day, and a couple of buck.
About my finances; I have written to Cox asking him when the year is up, as I've forgotten exactly the time when the £250 loan is up. I haven't got much actual specie[313] at present but a lot of valuable horseflesh!
Goodbye. Please give my best best love to the family. The store pen is very bad, so please don't scream at my writing! I hope you are fit and well. I am very fit, but I should not care to walk against you over the Scotch hills! Best love from Julian.

156 **27 Nov 1913**	**Carlton Hotel,** **Johannesburg**	**DE/Rv/C1135/639**

Darling Mother

I got your two letters last Saturday, when I got back from trek. I <u>am</u> glad that you had such fun in the ancestrals, and that you're well. When do you start waiting again? Did you see Makins, & Mrs M, at all? He comes back here for a bit, at the end of December, to hand over to George Steele. G.S. is much nicer than one would think at first sight: when he does say anything, he is always amusing; but if you press him, he dies away altogether. The Boy (Pitt Rivers) and I have just been up for the horse-show here (2 days). We had all our ponies up, and five jumping troophorses. Of course show-

---

[313] In actual coin, in money (OED)

jumping is <u>the</u> thing you <u>must</u> have practise for; and I had never ridden any of the horses before. We got second in the pair jumping, going round at racing pace (the Boy is as wild as wild horses!). Then at the last minutes we got up a section, the Boy, me, & 2 gunners, for the big thing – the Open Section Jumping – for which everyone had been practising for months. AND WE WON IT!! to the concern of the military and the astonishment of the goddam natives!! going round at a tearing gallop, and doing a clear round: nobody more surprised than the winning section!

The Boy got a first in the polo class, and 3rd in the open jumping. I got 3rd in the officers jumping, and 2 seconds and three thirds with my ponies. I had rather expected my ponies to win hands down; but the judges seemed to go for the fleshy light thorobreds.

The Military Steeplechase in on here Dec 10th, also 2 hunt races, so I'm training a bit. This town is really a great place for 3 days; it must be the hottest place in the inhabited world. However, this leaves me more or less untouched now, as I am completely settled in regular habits at my own ancestral villa on the outskirts of <u>P[otchef]stroom</u>.

Nothing much doing just now in the soldiering line, until we get the new rifle, and start musketry. I got great shabash[314] over the Scout Trek. I am frightfully complacent and happy just now. Only I want to see you again dreadfully. We <u>might</u> come home February. I should <u>think</u> we would come home November 1914.

Bless you.

---

[314] 'Well done': a phrase from Northern India (OED)

157   4 Dec 1913   Potchefstroom   DE/Rv/C1135/640

Darling Mother

I hope that you have not been corrupted from normal and ancient English habits by the Russian royalties. The Taplow party sounds full of lovelies – Rosemary & Bridget: but my word, you should see some of the S[outh]A[frican] stars! I'm <u>awfully</u> glad your eyes are <u>really</u> better? I've just started Ronald's books; isn't it flashing every sentence of it. Yes, Cavalry School is right off for me this next year. I've relevéd "Passionate Friends". I liked "The Devils Garden" – fairly – only fairly. It's a bit stodgy: but I suppose everything is a bit stodgier in life than it is made out in novels. But the characters didn't quite <u>live</u>, did they?

Mummy, get hold of the Buck (A W Waterhouse c/o Messrs Cox & Co 16 Charing Cross SW) – he is at home to marry his sister. You will like him; he is pure gold and steel underneath, and cute without any cleverness; loyal as death, & capable. Also Bunty Hewett (same address) who goes home this week – a good beery-face. I'm <u>very</u> fond of both of them – esp the Blackbuck. You know his regimental history. Well, this year he got <u>perfect</u> reports, and did wonderfully in the strike. So he has conquered the powers & principalities, which always means good staffing.

In the Jo'burg Horse Show the Boy (Pitt Rivers) & I, and two Gunners, got up a section at the last <u>instant</u> for the jumping, went round at full <u>bat</u>, did a <u>clear</u> round, & won it! One of the extraordinary surprises. When one practises & thinks of nothing else for years, one is whacked. When one rushes in at the last moment with a yell and a grin, one wins. Boy & I were second in the Half-Section Jumping. Boy was 3rd in the Open Jumping – I was 3rd in the Pony Jumping. And we got 1 first, 2 seconds, and 8 thirds with our ponies. Not too bad, considering that we had none of the best jumping horses up. And great fun. Show the photographs to Casie, and bid her remark that I ride with my knees up to my nose in the real show-jump style! Uncomfortable, inelegant, and unsafe, but I think it helps the horse.

Quiet life here now, till we get the new rifle. I am <u>frightfully</u> happy, and have become the typical Colonial, with a racy twang.

Bless you, dear. Please give my best love to the family; and thank Casie for her letter. She is <u>not</u> to marry Hamel[315], or any blue-blooded idiot. Goodbye. Love J.

---

[315] Gustav Wilhelm Hamel, (1889–1914), aviator. His father was German and his mother from Schleswig-Holstein. He trained with French aviators and made his first

158   18 Dec 1913   Potchefstroom   DE/Rv/C1135/641

Darling Mother

Thank you awfully for your letter. How lovely your October must have
been! I <u>did</u> enjoy the Wells book; and I'm loving Ronny's, for writing and
wit and cut, although I so disagree with his attitude, that I often can't see the
importance – one way or the other – of the things he is talking about. I liked
the Devils Garden. The only one I <u>could</u> not read was the Belloc sister! Did
you really like it, or did you only read the reviews of it? <u>Do</u> send me Sinister
Street; I liked Carnival, didn't you[316]. I'm glad Bill is having fun, and liking
Paris. It's very good getting such a lot for the Raphael and it ought to make
things easier oughtn't it? I'm glad that the noise in the water-pipes at
Pans[hanger] is getting less. And the New Old Smoking Room sounds as if it
would be awfully nice. I <u>do</u> hope that Schoolgirl is better. Yes, isn't she a
perfect little thing – and a <u>real</u> galloper and sticker. She should win a good
race, if properly trained, by a very <u>quiet</u> man. I'm glad some good is coming
of some of my horses, after that terrible year. What fun Mr Kipling's party
must have been; I wish I knew him. I'm glad Willie Good and Irby are doing
their duty, and increasing God's people. When shall I bring home my
colonial-born family. My girl is very well, and sends you and Poppa her best
respects. We are to be married in February. She is the loveliest, gentlest,
best, and most loving little darling I have ever met. Gee, but I am happy.
I had a day in the country at Jo'burg last week. They only have the one day's
steeplechasing in the year – and only three races. I rode a mare belonging to
a fellow called Lees-Smith in the first race – the Bedford Steeplechase. She

flight to Brighton in April 1911, landing on the lawns beside the seafront at Hove.
From then until his untimely death, his flights were extensively reported in the
national press. At Hendon on 11 May 1911 he was invited to demonstrate the
military potential of aircraft in time of war before the parliamentary committee
concerned with aerial defence. According to his biographer, 'he was extremely good-
looking and debonair, and he possessed an engaging personality. To him flocked not
only society's young ladies, but many of their mothers also'. His plane crashed in
the Channel on 23 May 1914. Duff Cooper penned a poem 'In Memoriam' and sent
it to Lady Diana Manners (later his wife, but then a very close friend of Hamel) and
a slightly altered version was published in *The Times* on 29 May (ODNB). There are
four letters from him to Monica Grenfell in DE/Rv/C1212, relating to visits he was
making to Taplow. The earliest, dated 14 July 1913, asks for a sheet to be put down
on the landing place!

[316] *Sinister Street* (1913) and *Carnival* (1912) by Compton Mackenzie

pulls like old boots, and they had a double Crocker with nose-plugs, and a twisted snaffle[317], on her. I had been going to ride her all along, but Lees Smith got a professional jock[ey] at the last minute, & put me in the sack. However, this boy lost his nerve at the 11th hour, so I rode her – in a plain racing-snaffle. She went off like a cannon-ball: so instead of hauling her about I let her go, and sat still, for ½ a mile, and then steadied her. She jumped like a hurdler, and had the rest stiff at the 2nd mile. No money in it: they betted 8-5 on, when I got up. Sir George Farrar[318] gave a very big cup for a military race, and I trained "Delilah" very carefully. Her distance is about 2 m, and this was 3½ m. but she gained 2 lengths at each fence, and cracked the others in the second mile; so that though she was stony beat, we struggled home out of harm's way. We got an even tenner on her, and the boxing boys watched the man carefully; so all was well.

I put out for my Promotion Exam because they told me to; I was doing half the work of the regt for 2 months. Kid is back now, & Leger Atkinson, and two new boys – one of them a topper, Percy Browne. Just starting musketry with the new rifle. I've got leave Jan & Feb, and don't know where to go, as it's close season for shooting. I think I shall take my family for a trip to the sunny south-coast seaside. Cape Town or Durban. I think they would enjoy that more than anything!

Goodbye Mummy darling. Are you welly? And your eyeses?

Had such a good letter from William Rawle in China. He is fairly filching the Heathen Chineses at Poker & Racing.

All all love J.

---

[317] Type of bridle and bit for a horse

[318] Sir George Herbert Farrar, baronet, mine owner and politician in South Africa. In 1911 he was created a baronet for his work in helping to create the Union of South Africa, but towards the end of the year serious difficulties in the East Rand Proprietary Mine forced him to retire from politics and devote all his energies to restructuring the company. In 1913 he successfully sued for libel when accused of ordering troops to fire on striking miners. He was a very successful racehorse owner (ODNB). See letters 130-138 above

159[319] **nd**   **Unknown place**   **DE/Rv/C1135/644**
                     [in England?]

Darling Mummy

I called here tonight, but you hadn't arrived. Do you go down to Tap[low] tomorrow? Telephone to me at Bron's what time I can see you: or we might go down together, if you're going.
I do want to see you. <u>All</u> love J.

160   **18 Dec 1913**   **Royal Dragoons,**   **DE/Rv/C1133/59**
                              Potchefstroom

My dear Dad

Thank you very much for your letter. Can't you hire some bravo to give David [*Lloyd*] George a nasty right uppercut? Or why not come and live in Sunny and Salubrious South Africa. I hope the drains at Pans[hanger] are running with greater freedom and accuracy now? It must have been a great help selling the little Raphael so well. The new smoking-room sounds delightful. I'm so glad that Schoolgirl has been doing Casie well. She is the most brilliant hunter I've ever ridden, and ought to win a good Hunt Chase. Everything going very well here. We've just got the new rifle, and am starting to shoot with it. Makins comes back about Christmas. My kennel and stable are a pride and glory – I suppose as a recompense for last year. I've got some of the best polo-ponies in Africa, which is a good investment, as they are fetching such terrific prices in England. The 12th & 15th did so well last year, they said entirely through the ponies they brought from S. Africa. But I'm afraid I've got no surplus cash at present: so what are we going to do about the £250 loan?
You'll like Waterhouse, who has gone home. He's a roughish diamond, but of the best water. If the Other Girl is anything like fit, he would be a very good man to sell her for me. I've told him about her.
Goodbye, and the best of luck. I hope you're fit, and having fun. Bill seems to be enjoying Paris. All love from J.
PS I won 2 races at Jo'burg last week: but no money in it!

---

[319] This letter has been misplaced; it probably belongs with letters written while Julian was on leave in England from October 1912 to March 1913 (see letters 103-116)

161   25 Dec 1913   Royal Dragoons,   DE/Rv/C1133/60
Potchefstroom

My darling Dad

A <u>very</u> <u>very</u> happy Christmas and new year to you. Thank you awfully for
your cable, which arrived today. It's very good of you to give me a tenner
for Christmas: I shall spend it on drink. You say "will pay bank" in your
wire; but I think that's a great shame, as I have got a lot of money in horses
now, and shall be like Croesus when I sell them! I hope you had a good
shoot at Grimsthorpe[320]. I've got leave for Jan & Feb, and I shall endeavour
to slay the King of Beasts[321]; though it's very hard to find a place at this time
of year, rains being on, and grass high.
Makins is just back from England, to hand over the regiment to George
Steele.
Goodbye, and all love from Julian.
Pitt-Rivers of the reg[imen]t is going home, & wants a horse to race. He will
write to you, and wants to come down to see The Other Girl. Can you tell
Williams to bring her on as fast as he can. He will probably buy her, if she is
still alive!

162   25 Dec 1913   Potchefstroom   DE/Rv/C1135/642

Darling Mother

Thanks awfully for your cable: and a very very happy Christmas to you, and
the family – and a wonderful 1914! I hope Grimsthorpe was fun, and that
Dad had a good shoot. Was our Ball splendid?
Makins is back today, to hand over the regt to George Steele. I wonder if
you saw him.
I'm on duty today – a terrible day – I must gallop now. <u>All</u> <u>all</u> <u>all</u> love. I've
got leave Jan & Feb; I think I shall hunt the King of Beasts!
Bless you J.

---

[320] Grimsthorpe Castle, near Bourne, Lincolnshire, home of the de Eresby family
since 1516
[321] A lion

163   8 Jan 1914   Carlton Hotel,   DE/Rv/C1135/646
**   Johannesburg**

My darling Mother

How terribly overworked your poor letter sounds! It is really too bad if you
have to do other people's work as well as your own. It really sounds almost
impossible, even to try it: but I suppose you'll measure it up and see the
exact amount of possibility. Grimsthorpe must have been fun. Thank you a
million times for the <u>very</u> good useful letter case, which I shall always take
with me on my wanderings: and for the delicious cigarette-holder. I do love
them: and you! Yes, I've read some of the occult books – those books which
range from ultra-mystical descriptions of the Spiritual World to exactly
detailed regulations for getting up early in the morning and not eating too
much! They always have the effect of making me get up at 12.30 pm and
order champagne and oysters in bed.

I missed last mail: I <u>am</u> sorry. I was in the throes of a matrimonial crisis.
We've been up here a week now, playing polo etc; mostly etc. The 2nd
leiut[enant]s 10th Hussars won the Rhodes Cup. We played them in the first
round. We were just a scratch team – 2 Royal and 2 bad Tenth. We couldn't
send a proper team, as we were all on musketry. We had a terrific galloping
game, and tied – 4 goals all. It was rather good, as we'd never played before
together, and then bad for 3 months. We played extra time, & they got a very
lucky winning goal, cannoned off one of our ponies. They won it easily
afterwards.

A railway strike was declared yesterday: and this morning they said that
everyone was coming out again. Now, however, they say peace is declared
again. I'm going straight back to Potch[efstroom], by motor if they don't run
the trains. Isn't it an awful country? Yesterday I was going to Cape Town, to
ride a horse called "Video" in the National here, for one of the racing swine.
Rather bad luck – he was favourite, and had a big chance. But they may call
us out any minute, so I'm answering the stern call of D[uty].

Nobody seems to know when we are coming back home – October, for a
guess – or October year – or October 1916, or 2016.

Are you welly, Mummie? Or really doing too much? Don't do too much.
About "The Other Girl" – Pitt-Rivers, who arrives home about Feb 10, will
buy her if she is sound. Tell Williams to get her fit steadily, and just <u>take her</u>
<u>to the meets</u> to get her qualified. P.R. will give me a good price. God, I wish
I was at home to ride her in a race. She's far the best horse I've ever had:

and I believe she'll stand this year.

Please give my best best love to Dad; and to Casie & Mog – thanking them tremendously for their jolly presents to me.

Lionel & Loughborough & Johnny Douglas are staying here: Lionel <u>the Knut</u> of the centuries. I took £37 off them at poker last night. We play till 8 am, after dancing. Bless you J.

Loughborough really rather a <u>nice</u> ass. I like him. Do you know the Dale Laces?

164	**15 Jan 1914**	**Royal Dragoons, Potchefstroom**	**DE/Rv/C1133/61**

My dear Dad

Thank you very much for your letter. I hope that all the Pans[hanger] arrangements are working well; and I'm so glad that Beit[322] got his 4000 pheasants – how many did Barnes rear? Hurrah for the trout again: they ought to do well. I'm longing to see the prize short-horns.

About horses – I've got a horse "Poor Denis" ch. q. 6 yrs, by "Tredennis", dam by "Poor Fur", by "St Gris". He was blistered in the shoulder as a 3 yr old; and when I bought him he was passed <u>Absolutely Sound</u> by Clancy, the Irish Vet. He went lame in the shoulder soon after I bought him, and I only rode him in 3 gallops, and he ran once (over hurdles). He was <u>very fast</u>, and promising.

When he went lame, <u>Pat Hartigan</u>, Bonita, Marlborough, Wilts[323], took him and turned him out for the summer (1913). Last Autumn he wrote to me saying that the horse had summered badly, and was still lame. He then sent him over to Ireland, where he is at the present.

I asked Waterhouse to get hold of him for me, and run him, if he was sound. Hartigan told Waterhouse that he was not fit to bring over.

I don't trust Hartigan much. Why did he go to the expense of sending the horse back to Ireland, if he was no good, and unsound? <u>Do you think you could find out from Hartigan where the horse is, and get him over again, and see what he is like?</u> If you tell Hartigan, he will get him sent over, and send

---

[322] Otto Beit, the financier, philanthropist, and art connoisseur, lived at Tewin Water

[323] The Bonita Racing Stables are situated in Ogbourne Maisey, Marlborough, Wiltshire

the bill to me. I've written to him, and told him to do so. The horse has cost me a lot, one way & another, and I know I'll never see the colour of my money if he stays over there.

I've got some real good heavyweight thorobred polo-ponies here, and they ought to make a good price at home. People seem to think we're coming home in October next: but it's all most uncertain. A General Strike is declared in Jo'burg now: and the place is full of Defence Force, mostly Dutch; 20,000 of them. The trains are still running, which is odd, considering the railways being declared "out". Martial Law is declared. It's a funny situation; each side waiting to see what the other will do; and no violence as yet. But I don't see how violence can be avoided, once they get hungry, which they will get at once. Then they must give in, or fight. If they fight, up we go.

Makins is just finishing here – I'm so sorry: he's worth 40 of Steele.

I'm so glad that you, and all the family, are fit and well. Please give them all my best love.

Goodbye & bless you Julian.

165   15 Jan 1914   Potchefstroom   DE/Rv/C1135/647

Darling Mother

Thank you awfully for your letter, and the Programme, which brings back so many of our happy Christmases under your stage-management. I'm so glad that little Moggy was happy; give her all my love; and Bill – but he is gone [back to Paris], I suppose. It's hot out here: I don't think anyone outside realises how hot. One feels it more than in India, as there are not heat-protectors here. Thunder hovering about all the time; but, thank God, it no longer makes me feel wild in the head, like it used to. How is darling Mr Barnes? How are the Pans[hanger] drains? And the death-duties? And Schoolgirl and the Other Girl. Don't forget to get the Other Girl as fit as you can, for Pitt Rivers.

There is a fair muddle here. General Strike Declared, Martial Law Proclaimed, and Jo'burg stiff with Dutch Defence-Force-men, 20,000 of them. And then – the absolutely extraordinary thing – practically no violence, and trains running almost as usual. Each side waiting on the other. Two possibilities; (1) they go back to work when they begin to starve; (2) they fight when they begin to starve: (1) we stay here living the peaceful country life; (2) we gallop up, loaded to the muzzle. Betting about evens.

The Government has done really <u>well</u> this time, taking a dead firm stand. You should have seen all the back-veldters going up by train – in cattle trucks. Buffalo Bill's Wild West w[oul]d have taken a stone and a beating. Tall grim Boers with long hair and short stubby beards, only opening their mouths to spit, slung with rifle & cartridges and span boots and socks and bread and biltong[324]. You could see what a tough lot they must have been to fight. And with them the new Dutch generation – the "jongs" – weedy, fleshy, pale faced, chattering wasters, mostly drunk.

Goodbye, Mummy, & bless you. The last rumour (official) is that another cavalry reg[imen]t relieves us in October next. Makins goes in a fortnight, worse luck. Just starting work for promotion exam.

Best best love. I <u>do</u> hope you are welly; and I <u>do</u> want to see you. Julian.

166	**15 Jan 1914**	**Royal Dragoons,**	**DE/Rv/C1138/21**
		Potchefstroom	

Casie darling

How are (1) you (2) Schoolgirl (3) The Other Girl (4) the aeronauts.
I am very well, thank you.
All all all love from J.
Will write next mail.
Like Waterhouse; no intellect, but the cunning of a monkey, & the heart of a lion.

167	**22 Jan 1914**	**Potchefstroom**	**DE/Rv/C1135/648**

Darling Mother

Thank you awfully for your letter. <u>What</u> a good party it sounds; did Mog leap well from her basket? I'm so glad that Bill-boy is happier. How are you? How are all the clars?[325] How are your eyeses? Have you seen Our Alf (Waterhouse), and what did you think of him? Please give my love to Violet K[eppel], and tell her that Absence makes my Heart grow Fonder, making sleep of a night-time a complete impossibility. Please give my best love to Daddy, and tell him how tremendously grateful I am to him for

---

[324] Strips of lean meat (of antelope, buffalo, etc.) dried in the sun (OED)

[325] Privies – a reference to the Panshanger drains

paying the £250 to Messrs Cox, and that I'll try to pay him back when I sell my stud.

It's been a very interesting week out here – an absolute fizzle-out of the strike, after everything had looked as black as ink. The Government really did extremely well this time; they filled Jo'burg cram full of burghers, and enforced Martial Law (unlike last time, when they proclaimed it and didn't enforce it). They also nobbled all the strike leaders, and shut them up; the whole thing collapsed automatically; and they are all back at work now. Of course this utter failure knocks strikes on the head for some time in this country. But considering the extraordinary bitter feeling, and the great number of criminals, one can't help thinking that the violent section will refuse to take it lying down; and that, next time they do anything, they will start straight away by blowing things up, before the burghers arrive. But they won't get the body of the workers to back them for a long time to come, as they are pretty well fed up with the agitators just now. Besides, the main agitators are off for a trip to the Andaman islands[326].

Everybody says now that we are going home in October, for a cert.

I'm training our Scouts now: we do rather jolly things – vaulting, picking up handkerchiefs at a gallop, bare-back riding, tracking, raft-building, shoeing, steering by the stars, etc: in fact, they're supposed to be able to do anything. Show-jumping is the great thing here now: and we're all starting to practise for the big Agricultural Show in the spring. It's a poor game, compared to riding fast over fences; as any "trick" thing is, compared to any real thing. Tell Alf this: and see him smile with rage.

Army & Navy Boxing here next week; I'm taking our men up for it. I won't box myself, because my nose is really too beautiful to spoil now. It is thin delicate and aesthetic: the wind whistles through it like a cyclone, with perfect freedom, and the nostrils open and quiver and close like 'Ascetic Silvers', or Guy Benson's[327]. I am sometimes quite amazed at its beauty. I'll wait till I get home and you see it, before I start bashing it again.

I thought you w[oul]d like to hear about my nose.

Goodbye, Mummy darling. Bless you J.

---

[326] A group of islands in the Bay of Bengal. There was a penal colony at Port Blair

[327] A friend of Ego and Guy Charteris; he later married Ego's widow, Letty Manners (MacKenzie, p228)

**168　22 Jan 1914　　Royal Dragoons,　　DE/Rv/C1138/22
　　　　　　　　　　　Potchefstroom**

Casie darling

I hope your party was fun: it <u>does</u> sound a good lot of people. Was Bill-boy
in good form? Are you in good form? How are your prancing palfreys, and
have you had good hunting? Give my love to Arthur and Iris and the nuts.
Does Gertie Millas grace the meets now; if she does, give my love to her too.
I do hope Schoolgirl is right again: you must run her in the p[oin]ts to
p[oin]ts, and at Aylesbury. Pitt Rivers is going home by this mail, and he will
buy Schoolgirl. The Other Girl if she is right. The regiment comes home in
October – everybody seems to think.
We're starting a Race Club here, called "Grenfells Benefit", which ought to
be rather fun; and profitable for me, as I've got the only 4 racing ponies.
Hurdles and flat, handicap weights from 12 – 7 downwards.
I bought a pony for £30 the other day, which I saw standing in a field in the
Free State: He had got strangles[328], and was all skin & bone: but <u>such</u> a
shape. He is big & well now, and <u>far</u> the fastest thing I've ever ridden. He's
by Irish Lad, dam by Storm King: bred out here. He's going to make my
fortune, over hurdles.
Goodbye, & bless you Julian.

**169　29 Jan 1914　　Carlton Hotel,　　DE/Rv/C1135/649
　　　　　　　　　　　Johannesburg**

Darling Mother

No letter yet to answer: I'll get it tomorrow, sent on here. No news in
particular. I came up here yesterday, and I'm just going on to Pretoria, with
all our boxing boys, for the Army & Navy Championships. I think they
ought to do pretty well. I've tried to get them to box on the New American-
French methods, the Ugly Useful style. Nobody entered for the officers
show, so I shan't get a fight unless I pick up someone at the last moment.
Makins leaves Potch[efstroom] today, amid great sadness. I think people are
just beginning to realise, now that he is going, what a very good colonel he

---

[328] A disease in horses and other animals, characterized by inflamed swellings in the
throat (OED)

was. I'm afraid Steele won't be nearly so good: but safe and steady.
This town is very quiet, after the fizzle-out of the strike. They have just
deported the leaders; in fact, they've acted in a pretty high-handed way all
through, and I expect there'll be a pretty good hullabaloo about it.
Do you know Mr & Mrs Dale Lace? She is really rather good fun, and
doesn't care a d[amn] what she says, to the intense dismay of all the other
Jo'burg Smart Setters. Lionel Tennyson and Johnny Douglas are both back
here again, with their cricket nuts. Loughborough has disappeared, nobody
seems to know where.
Have you read Sinister Street? I'm reading it now, but I don't think it's very
good. All the tiny intricate personal-history details seems like a crib of
Wells, whom nobody could ever possibly crib. I've not read the
Dostoevsky[329] yet; is it good?
Are you welly & happy? How is Billa-boy? When does he go up for his All
Souls? Please give my <u>best</u> <u>best</u> love to all the family, and ask Mogsy what I
shall bring home for her.
Goodbye, & bless you, and tons & tons of love. J.

170   5 Feb 1914   Royal Dragoons,   DE/Rv/C1133/62
**   Potchefstroom**

My darling Dad

About my horses – of course whatever I get for them goes to you to repay the
£250; that was always the arrangement. But I have given the First Refusal of
the "Other Girl" to Pitt-Rivers of the regiment, who will be at home before
this arrives. Price £40 down, and another £40 if her leg stands the rest of the
season. So will you please keep her till he has a look at her.
The steeple-chaser "Poor Denis" is apparently in very bad condition now, so
that it is no good thinking of running him, or of selling him, this year. But if
you could turn him out this Summer at Tap[low] or Pans[hanger], and pick
him up in <u>August,</u> and get him fit gradually, I ought to get a really good price
for him at the beginning of next chasing season. Could you do this for me?
I'm sure it's no good trying to sell him now: and I'm sure its no good
leaving him where he is, and that it's worth the money to get him over from
Ireland. I wrote to you about him some time ago. Did you get it?

---

[329] Fyodor Dostoyevsky, the Russian writer. Two of his novels, *The Idiot* and *The
Possessed*, were translated into English by Constance Garnett and published in 1913

Pans[hanger] must be an extraordinary sight, with all the "improvements" going in. I hope they are successful. It's very good about the pheasants; and the shorthorn heard sounds magnificent! What an awful shame, having to pay the Government £6180! on the Raphael[330]. What sharks they are. Things are very flourishing here. I've got some rather good ponies. I'm reading for my promotion exam, in April. I shall soon be a Spring Captain! I think we really <u>shall</u> come home in October next: I'm longing to see you again!

Best love from Julian.

171   5 Feb 1914   Potchefstroom   DE/Rv/C1135/643

Darling Mother

I can't understand <u>two</u> of my mails missing. I did miss one, as I told you, but one only: and I always post them <u>myself</u>. But you've no idea of the utter carelessness of all the officials out here; they simply don't care a damn whether they do things or not. How good the Forest sounds; I <u>do</u> love it, don't you? You must have had the greatest fun at Avon. I wish I could have seen Mog on "Wild Tom". It's a pity that Betty is getting so much like Francis: and that James is dead. I hope the Hochgeboreners will dance well at Tap[low]. What did Venetia reply to Margot, when M said that she was sick of seeing V's face?

Peace here again. The Army & Navy Boxing at Pretoria last week was great fun. Titmas won the Middles, and Double fractured his thumb when in the final of the Welters[331] – so we did pretty well, and I got some satisfaction in return for all the bits T and D have knocked out of my face at different times. I could not get a fight myself. It is extraordinary how Roberts Heights <u>kills</u> me, directly I get into the five mile radius. As the motor or train passes in, my heart gradually sinks into my boots, and my temper gradually rises into my throat! It really is <u>Hell</u>. I had thought that perhaps I had hated it out of prejudice; but going back there on holiday, only intensified my detestation of

---

[330] Estate and legacy duty paid by Lord Desborough on inheriting the Panshanger Estate amounted to £6,183 8s 6d. He appealed against this judgement but had to settle (HALS: DE/Rv/F1)

[331] Welterweights: a boxer or wrestler whose weight is between that of a light-weight and a middle-weight (OED)

it. I met my old love at Pretoria, after two years complete silence; isn't it good how one goes in a straight flash to the <u>status quo ante</u>[332], even when one has quite forgotten what <u>status</u> it was.

The old life here – Training – Training the Scouts, Training the Troop, Training the Horse and Man, Training Polo Ponies, and Training One-self. How terribly hard the latter is: I never get any forrader. But I like trying to do the others. It's getting a little cooler here: no one knows how hot this country is at Xmas.

Goodbye, Mummy darling. It <u>will</u> be fun seeing you again in October: and I believe we really <u>do</u> come home then. We will fairly knock them in the Old Kent Road, won't we? Please give my best best love to the family. Are you <u>welly</u>? Bless you J.

172   5 Feb 1914   Royal Dragoons,   DE/Rv/C1138/23
**   Potchefstroom**

Casie darling

Thank you so much for your letter. I'm glad you liked Buck, alias Alf, alias Methusaleh. You must have had the greatest fun in the shires; also at the Tap[low] party. How is Schoolgirl? You didn't tell me, blast you. I hope you'll have fun with Vi de T. Don't sell The Other Girl till Pitt Rivers has a look at her, as I gave him 1st refusal.

Greatest fun here – I've never had such a good lot of ponies, and I'm awfully happy. I wish I had time to write to you properly. The worst of this life is the swift transition of the wheels of time, and the evanesce of realities. <u>Bless</u> you J.

---

[332] The state of affairs previously existing (OED)

173   12 Feb 1914   Potchefstroom   DE/Rv/C1135/650

Darling Mother

Thank you awfully for your letter. It must have been very sad to get to the end of the hols. Have you managed to lead John Manners and Jack Althorp[333] to the altar yet, or have you had to resort to locking them up in the Tennis Court in the early hours of the morning? I always thought your choice of the Tennis Court Gallery so odd; it seems to me a place calculated to damp the most ardent lover, with its vault-like atmosphere and acid smell, and the scattered symbolic remnants of the dry wings of dead moths. I hope that better provision has been made in the new En Tout Cas court?[334] I hope darling Casie will have wonderful hunting in Leicestershire. I'm so glad that Mrs Bart can swallow; I've written to Mr Bart congratulating him. I hope that Pat will surprise the Americans; you must be very sad at losing him. Please give my best love to Daddy. How funny that Polly should have a baby; one w[oul]d have betted on a frog, like the Glamis offspring[335]. Do send me new, Poetry books; and any books. Are you still reading Psychology and Psychotherapy and Autotherapy? Do you know that wonderful series "What a Young Man/Woman of 1/5/15/35/55/85/105 Should Know". They are awfully good, and much easier to understand than the brainy ones. Did you read Sinister Street? I got to like it at the end. I rather like the boy's character; but it was a pity that he chucked Rugby Football for Roman Catholicism? Or not? I wish I wasn't so terribly normal; just think of the fun one misses, by having no sympathy with the King of Siam – or at any rate, by not talking consistently about one's decadent desires. The most brilliant and original conversation about Adam & Eve is bound to be boring; while the slightest hint at a more civilised affection has everybody on the jump immediately.
Are you waiting now? Oh, have you read another book translated from the German, The Song of Songs, by Sudderman?[336] Pretty gross, but pretty true.

---

[333] Albert Edward John Spencer, 7th Earl Spencer (1892-1975), known formally as The Hon Albert Spencer until 1910 and from then until 1922 as Viscount Althorp, and less formally as "Jack" Spencer

[334] Manufacturers of non-grass tennis courts, still in business

[335] The Bowes-Lyon family, Earls of Strathmore; Julian's allusion is unclear

[336] *The Song of Songs* (Das hohe Lied), written by Hermann Sudermann and translated by Thomas Seltzer (1910)

All goes very well here. I'm reading hard for my promotion exam in April, and spending my spare time in buying horses and selling them to the unsuspecting at varying profits. It's very amusing, but tends to unpopularity. Scout-training in the mornings. Lovely soft weather now, just the right heat. Buck comes back this mail, which is fun – I mean he leaves England this mail. I've done chalk drawings of all the most beautiful women in the world, all round the walls of my room, which have had a great success.

Please give Moggy a slap from me, and tell her to amend her morality. Goodbye Mummy darling from J.

174   19 Feb 1914   Potchefstroom   DE/Rv/C1135/651

Darling Mother

Thank you awfully for your letter. Are you waiting now? Are you going abroad later on? I hope you had a good Hackwood? I had such a happy letter from Casie, from the Shires, this week; she really does seem to <u>love</u> Schoolgirl, doesn't she? I'm so glad that the mare is alright again; she must have got over her leg very quickly. Who is Mrs Hart Davis?[337] I've never heard tell of her; but from your charitable appreciation of her, she must be a credit to her sex. Oh, Mrs Dale Lace is really far far better than any stories of her could possibly be. She gave a "moonlight-romp" at her farm outside Jo'burg the other day, with Chinese lanterns & bottles of fizz under every bush. In the middle of it she came up and drew me aside, and said "Look here, old <u>chap</u>, if you want a bed, it's the first room round on the right, and as safe as houses". At cricket, or at the play, she suddenly stands up, and screws her eye-glass well in, and fixes some neighbouring fairy with a glassy stare; and then proceeds, at the <u>top</u> of her voice, to discuss her figure, complexion, dress, character, ancestry, and personal habits.

No news much here. Everybody seems to have quite forgotten already about the strikes and the Labour Leaders; everyone in Jo'burg is always so frightfully keen on their own immediate pursuit of cash or pleasures, that they don't take much notice of anything even while it is going on; and directly it is over, it is bus nogia [*sic*]. In that first strike, when the air was simply sticky with pistol-bullets, they were all walking to the pub or the

---

[337] Sybil Mary (1886–1927), daughter of Sir Alfred Cooper FRCS and Lady Agnes Duff; she married Richard Vaughan Hart-Davis (*d* 1964), a stockbroker (ODNB)

Cinema with their best girls, hardly taking notice.

I'm reading the Brothers Kamaravitchskof ponpskinremya[338]. It is good, isn't it? I love it. I got muddled up between the names of the brothers and uncles and lady friends at first; so I made a list. Then they all have three names, used alternately, so I made a new list, at greater length, with imaginary sketches. Then he began calling them by pet names, so I made a glossary, with numbers. And now, (about p 30), he has started trying all the possible permutations and combinations of the fifteen names, and varying the characters slightly for each new combination.

Please thank Wuggins tremendously for her letter, although the tone of it is slightly insolent! Give her my best love.

All all love from J.

175   25 Feb 1914   Roberts' Heights   DE/Rv/C1135/652

Darling Mother

Thank you awfully for your letter. Hackwood must have been great fun. Isn't it funny how drunk all the savants[339] get? I believe that this is the real distinction between the brain and the body – if you want to have a brain, you must get drunk, the oftener the better. If, on the other hand, you want to have a body, you must not get drunk more than, say, twice a week. I'm glad that Pans[hanger] is getting forrader. Will that be our ancestral home, when I return in the Autumn? Or shall we be living in Windsor Castle, with nice private flats in Buckingham Palace for fiery nights in the metropolis? How is waiting? I'm so glad that Billa-boy is at joy with himself; and Daddy; and Casie; and Mog, who is much too clever to be ever anything else. Daddy has stiffed me over money; he said that he had given me a Christmas present of £10, and also that he had continued my £100 a year, which Auntie Ka[tie] used to give me: but advice from Messrs Cox & Co, 16 Charing Cross, does not confirm these excellent paternal intentions. Moreover and furthermore, I believe that the Raphael was entailed, and I am getting up a law suit against

---

[338] *The brothers Karamazov* by Fyodor Dostoevsky, translated from the Russian by Constance Garnett (first published in English in 1912)

[339] A person with generally impaired intellectual and social functions who is extremely gifted in a particular way, frequently as a musician or in the performance of rapid and complex mental arithmetic. Hence in a weakened sense: a naive or simple person who displays natural wisdom or insight (OED)

him; and I am also meditating a libel case, founded on the evidence of the
man who wrote the You Panther You Jaguar letter. Please advise my father of
these facts.

You don't know how the universal atmosphere of "stiffing" in this country
affects one – the perpetual feeling of Do or You Will be Done In. I measure
and weigh every sack of oats and lucerne[340], pound for pound, as it comes in.
I'm almost (not quite, but it's a matter of time) as bad as you with the house-
books, browbeating Mrs Neve-Kylah[341].

There is a queer reaction going on here now, against Botha[342] and his Boer-
log; the feeling that the last show has made S Africa more Dutch than ever.
It was a funny time; we were on the brink of (I) Revolution (II) Civil War
between Dutch & English.

Everything very good here. I'm working for my promotion, working the
jumping horses for all the big shows, which come off now – working polo
ponies, and working the Scouts. I've given up your sex; they would come
down here and make scenes on the platform, which is undignified and
degrading for a gentleman and an officer; besides, you see, when you are in
command of men, you <u>must</u> consider what they are thinking; you can't think
only of yourself; it is the Responsibility that is so sacred. Your loving son
Julian.

176   5 Mar 1914   Roberts' Heights   DE/Rv/C1135/653

Darling Mother

Many thanks for horsey letter. What a wonderful Mamma you are, aren't
you?

I <u>did</u> write to Dad, some time ago, asking him to give the Refusal of the
"Other Girl" to Pitt Rivers, as I had promised this to him. I wonder if Dad
ever got the letter? I also told Dad that Pitt Rivers was coming by that mail.
But it was stupid of P.R. not to write to Dad directly he arrived.

As it is, I am quite contented with the £35; especially as there is some
question about her soundness behind. I only wanted to sell her to Pitt-Rivers,
so that I could buy her back next year. Because she really is a <u>wonderful</u>

---

[340] The leguminous plant *Medicago sativa*, resembling clover, cultivated for fodder;
purple medick (OED)
[341] Mrs Neave was the housekeeper at Taplow
[342] Louis Botha (1862-1919), first president of South Africa (1910)

mare – a strong man's horse, and as hot as hell. But she has never been tried out in her life, and has beaten some good horses by <u>fields</u>. She is the only one of my horses that never put me down once last year: and I gave her every chance. When she broke her leg down, at an unjumpable place, she did not fall; and tried to go on galloping on 3 legs. She is really one of the best things God ever made.

Perhaps it's a good thing that she did not go to Pitt Rivers, as he is not strong enough for her.

As to "Poor Denis", I wrote to Dad a long time ago and asked him if he would arrange with Hartigan for Hartigan to send her over from Ireland. I wrote at the same time to Hartigan telling him to arrange with Dad, and send her over as soon as possible. But it is alright, now that he has arrived. Will you please ask Dad if he will turn him out for the summer, and take him up in <u>August</u>, early in August, and get him into work gradually. He is as well-bred for a chaser as you can get, and has proved his pace; so that if his shoulder does not interfere with him he will be worth £500 - £1000 next year. It would be simply chucking money away to sell him now, at a shortish price. If Dad will keep him for this summer, I will place him myself next year. I shall be home in September-October anyhow: if the regt does not come home, I shall come back for a musketry course, before Cavalry School.

But I can't understand you saying that you had never heard about him, because I wrote twice, or three times, to Dad, giving fullest details! Also exactly what I wanted done with him, if Dad would be good enough to do it for me. Didn't the letters arrive? It is really time to make a fuss, if they didn't. But the P.O. here is beyond belief. <u>Please</u> let me know if Dad did not get it?

I'm glad that Schoolgirl is doing Casie so well. Is she going to put her in the races? She ought to win a good race.

I'm glad that Pans[hanger] is going well. Are we going to live there next year? You seem to have had some divine February weather. Waterhouse has just arrived here today: it is great fun having him back here. I'm working hard now for my Promotion Exam, which comes off in a month's time. Everyone here very fit. I <u>do</u> like this life – I'm quite "wrapped up" in it now, and I don't care much if there are two other subconscious hyper-physical worlds, or only one, or none at all.

I'm longing to see the Likky Man again – has he changed? Or is he as sublime and unchangeable as ever? He is entirely beyond my feeble comprehension.

Are you well, Mummy darling? And happy? Have you read anything good.

Oh, I do love the Brothers Pavvalofitchkop. More and more, every page that
I read. It makes me love the Russians, too. I believe they really are like
that, aren't they?
Goodbye & bless you. All all love from J.

177   12 Mar 1914   Royal Dragoons,   DE/Rv/C1133/63
**   Potchefstroom**

My dear Dad

I am glad to see that Du Pree got in so well for South Bucks and Scatters![343];
Please give him my very best love.
I hope that you are fit and well. I suppose that you're doing a tremendous lot
of work, as usual? I am so sorry that there was a muddle about my horse
"Poor Denis"; but it was entirely due to the S. African postal arrangements,
as I wrote you a long letter about him, at the same time as I wrote to
Hartigan, telling him to send the horse over.
Anyhow, I'm very sorry, as it must have been a great shock to you to find the
horse arriving suddenly like that without warning! Could you please summer
him for me somewhere, and get him taken up in August, & put into slow
work, so as to get him fit for the chasing season? I think he ought to fetch a
good price, as he is a fast horse, and very well bred.
St Gris
|
Tredennis = Poor Fur
|
Poor Denis
It was good work getting £35 for "The Other Girl", as she seems to have
been very unsound.
About money, I now owe you the £250, minus School Girl and the £35 for
the "Other Girl". I ought to be able to pay that next year, when I sell Poor
Denis. I shall be home in the Autumn, whether the reg[imen]t comes or not.
Money's a bit tight with me now, but I've got a lot of good heavy w[eigh]t
thorobred polo-ponies, which ought to sell in England like anything.
You said you w[oul]d pay me the £100 a year Auntie Ka[tie] used to give me.
I only say this because Cox have not acknowledged it – nor the £10

---

[343] William Baring Du Pre was elected as MP for South Bucks and Sir Mathew
Henry Wilson for SW Bethnal Green, both in February 1914

Christmas present – and I thought perhaps there was some mistake. Everything going very well here. Best love from Julian.

178   12 Mar 1914   Potchefstroom   DE/Rv/C1135/654

Darling Mother

Thank you awfully for your letter. God, just think of those letters about Poor Denis and The Other Girl never having arrived! It does make one absolutely despair of writing letters at all. However, all is well now; as I'm sure you've kept Poor Denis till you get my letter about him, written last week.
I ought to get a good price for him at the beginning of next chasing season, if he summers reasonably well. And as for the "Other Girl", it seems I am well out of her for £35. So all is not so black – nothing like so black as I have made the eye of our Post-Corporal.
I'm so glad you're welly and happy, and dross-earning. Do send me some dross, or I shall get into a horsecoping scandal here, or plunge on the Turf, or start financing a House of Ill-repute. I bought a pony for £25 last week, and sold him for £50 today, but that is only a temporary respite. How splendid about South Bucks – and <u>Scatters</u>! Tell him that it only confirms my ancient conviction that Napoleon is nothing in comparison to him: and give him my best love. The Keppels Fancy Dress Ball must have been great fun. Casie seems bird. I'm so glad you like Bunty; but he's no patch on Waterhouse really.
Very strenuous here again now, with Musketry, and imminent Promotion Exam (April 21). I'm riding over hurdles next Sat in Jo'burg, and I think I've got a chance.
Kid Charrington has got "B" Sqdn now, and he's the most delightful man to work with in the world. You <u>would</u> love him. The Buck is in great form. I think George Steele will make a good Colonel, but he has got none of the glamour of Makins.
Goodbye, Mummy darling: think of us quarrelling again as soon as next Autumn!
Bless you Julian.

**179   12 Mar 1914   "The Eagle", Royal   DE/Rv/C1138/24
                        Dragoons**

Darling Casie

Thank you for y[ou]rs of Feb 20, rec[eive]d today. I'm so glad you're well
and happy, my darling; and I'm <u>so</u> glad that Schoolgirl had proved her metal.
I wish you'd put her into a race; I'm sure she's a winner. Perhaps it's as well
that the Other Girl is sold; I didn't know her spavins[344] had got worse. Try to
find out what happens to her, and if she runs in anything this year.
Isn't it a gime, writing letters from here. The PO officials read them, and if
they are uninteresting, send them off, perhaps a week late: if interesting, they
stick them into their albums: if very interesting, they blackmail you on them.
I wrote you four (or was it 14) letters during Dec & Jan, which never reached
you. The least you can do is thank me for them now.
Daddy must have smoiled when "Poor Denis" turned up all of a sudden loike
(the warning letter having been promoted to the album). Do you like him?
He goes like the wings of the wind.
I'm so glad you mashed Bunty. Give him my best love.
I'm riding over hurdles in Jo'burg day after tomorrow. Might win. On the
other hand may not win, unless the reins break, as I am too high in the
handicap just now. Bless you dear.
See you next Autumn J.

180   19 Mar [1914]   Potchefstroom   DE/Rv/C1135/655

Darling Mother

Thank you very much for your letter. You must have had fun, alone in
London, with time to do things and to see people. I envy you your Sergeants
and Max Beerbohms and Milners. What a pity that Gladys dances the Tango!
Can't you dissuade her? Isn't it a beastly dance – inconclusive, without
being in the least strong or restrained; like a Platonic friendship, a sort of
dreary negation of <u>joie-de-vivre</u>.

---

[344] A spavin is a hard bony tumour or excrescence formed at the union of the splint-
bone and the shank in a horse's leg, and produced by inflammation of the cartilage
uniting those bones; a similar tumour caused by inflammation of the small hock
bones (OED)

You never told me about going to Apopokatapetal[345]. <u>What</u> fun.
Constantinople never seems a real place at all to me. I could never believe in
it, till I saw it. I wish I were going with you. How do you and Helen hit it?
Does the atmosphere turn blue and purple?

There is such a good horsey man in Jo'burg called Deacon. He was trying to
sell me a pony – a fat beast with a tail like a dabchick[346]. He said "It's clean
thorobred, by Galloping Lad – Malagas. It used to have a long tail, but the
bloody fool of a boy shut the stable door on it one day – they <u>are</u> so
careless". Selling a horse to a mug, he took the tape to measure its bone. He
put it round the outer edge of a gigantic splint, and said "There you are – 9
inches – look!" I said to him "What do you do with the lame ones?" He said
"Oh let them get dirty, and they forget about it". I was talking to Scottie
Duff, a trainer, v hot – and Deacon stopped us, and said "One day, when you
two are talking, you will suddenly disappear, and all that will be left will be a
grease-spot on the ground".

I sold a pony at 50% profit to the Queen's yesterday. But against this comes
an awful disaster. I rode Midnight Sun in the Nigel Hurdle Handicap on
Saturday. I fancied him, so I went round the town borrowing money, and
backed him for £ s d. They gave me an awful weight – 13 st 7 lbs. Then it
rained all night, and was deep in mud. But still I thought he must win. We
rode in a hail-storm. It was only 1½ miles, and we went hell for blast all the
way. At 8 furlongs I was in front, going strong. I thought I had it stiff; but I
looked round and saw a horse called "Old Soldier", who was only carrying
11 st, beginning to come. He passed me like a streak, and got a length ahead.
We raced under whip over the last hurdle, and I gained at the jump.
Midnight Sun is the gamest horse that ever ran, and he kept coming and
coming, under that fearful weight, and in the mud. But the other beat me ½ a
length.

I'd have beat him on dry going, or in another 2 furlongs; but there it was.
The ride was worth the money, almost: and I'll get down in the weights for
next time.

I'm working hard all for my promotion exam now. My <u>leave</u> was postponed,
because we had too few officers here then. But I don't mind much, and I
shan't take it now, because I'm really happier here, with my haarses and
dawgs; and I've got to get through the books. Besides, if I don't take long

---

[345] Popokatapetal, the second highest peak in Mexico
[346] The little grebe, a small water-bird, found in rivers and other fresh waters, and
noted for its diving (OED)

leave, they let me away often for 2 days, to ride races and to see the fairies. But how much better than anything in the way of sensation (except perhaps knocking a man out) is racing over jumps!

Mumsy darling, I hope you have <u>gigantic</u> fun in Apopokatapetel. I <u>do</u> want to see you again. I'm sorry for writing you such a horsey letter; but the society here is really hardly worth writing home about. Oh, young Joel is out here now, in Jo'burg; also young Alan, who wants to marry the Miss Mosenthal.

Goodbye, and bless you J.

181   26 Mar 1914   Potchefstroom   DE/Rv/C1135/656

Darling Mother

No letter from you this mail. Jolly old posts, I suppose. How are you? Are you well? What are your plans for the Summer Months? Are you waiting now? Are you reading anything jolly? Thank you so much for all the books you keep sending me. How do you find time to send them?

Fearful hustle on here now, with musketry and the beginning of the Training Season. But surely the happiest life is to have too much to do. The worst of this is that one has too <u>many</u> things to do – all different, & all wanting time. Musketry – Scouts – Troop Tra[ining] – Promotion Exam – training polo-ponies – training race-horses – training show-jump horses – cricket, etc etc etc. I'm not sure that's not a good thing too, doing a little of everything, because doing everything badly is better for the soul than being mediocre and conceited at one thing.

Goodbye, darling. I <u>am</u> looking to seeing you in the Autumn; and I do hate a break in our letters. I must <u>dash</u> to play final Squadron Cricket Cup. <u>Bless</u> and <u>keep</u> you J.

182   26 Mar 1914   Royal Dragoons,   DE/Rv/C1133/64
**   Potchefstroom**

My dear Dad

Thank you very much indeed for your letters - & I got this mail. I'm so sorry
about the muddle about "poor Denis"; but I've written to you about that
already. It is very good of you to turn him out at Panshanger; I'm sure that's
the best thing. Do you think he could be taken up, and put into slow work,
early in the Autumn?
I wrote 2 letters to you about him; they must both have been appropriated by
the P.O. here!
I'm so glad that Pans[hanger] is let for the Summer, and that the drains are
now like whirlpools! It is very good hearing that you have got the trout in.
How are the fat kine doing?
I love the Westminster verses about the Covenanters; and it makes me
prouder than ever of having you for my father. But it always makes me
terribly jealous and envious too; and it is strictly contrary to the Christian
Religion to be jealous of ones Father.
We're all very busy here, with the training season just coming on; and I'm
working hard for my promotion exam, next month. I can hardly contemplate
becoming a Spring Captain! I like the life here enormously. I've got some
A.1. ponies, and I get a ride over hurdles at Jo'burg about once a month.
I hope Likky Man had a good exeat. Please give him, and the family, my
very best love.
It will be fun seeing you again in the Autumn.
Goodbye and best love from your degenerate and inferior son Julian.

183   2 Apr 1914   Potchefstroom   DE/Rv/C1135/657

Darling Mother

You'll just be back from Constantinople, today. I wonder if you've had
tremendous fun? Do tell me all & everything about it. I'm glad the Likky
Man is so well; and how is Billa-boy? No, I don't agree with you about the
"cloudless happiness of Eton-at-fifteen". I think each year is a step forrad, in
the happiness way. Fifteen, for instance, is so damned inconclusive. Not that
one gets any more "conclusive" with age, but only more reconciled to the
inconclusiveness: and therefore slightly more certain of the ground. At

fifteen it is so empty: at 25 and 35 45 55 65 75 – 125, all that has happened to one for good or bad is "all there", anyhow. And don't you think that happiness counts rather by fullness?

Thank you awfully for the new "Wells" book[347] – just arrived. Did you send it? It looks v[ery] good & Wellsey.

The English politics must have been <u>thrilling</u> all this time. I love the poem and the picture of Dad & Niagara[348]. I can't quite make out exactly what part <u>Winston</u> is playing now? Please write short appreciation on his situation. Musketry and polo and promotion work here. It's hard to fit it all in, for anyone with such stupendous natural and acquired and cultivated laziness as myself! Lots & lots of different <u>little</u> duties, all day; and it's cruel ard to sit down to work for 12½ minutes, before you start off, instead of sitting down & smoking a cigarette because there's not really time to start working. But I'm frightfully well & happy, and I'm in my "misogynist 3-months" period, which is most convenient.

<u>All</u> all love from J.

184   9 Apr 1914   Potchefstroom   DE/Rv/C1135/658

Darling Mother

Have you loved Constantinople? <u>Do</u> tell me all your thoughts of it. How is Chawlie Lester now, and what is he like? He is one of the people I want most to see again. Who is he in love with? Is Pamela Fitzgerald as divine as her photographs? Has she got the entrée to Taplow Court and Panshanger? Oh, I must show you the <u>most</u> priceless Heygate that ever anyone could have imagined in their wildest dreams. It's a pamphlet of advice to young officers by George Steele. I found it in M.S. in the Orderly Room, and read it, as there was nobody there. It begins

<u>Don't</u> ever forget that you are a "Royal".
"   dress too well. Remember that you are a gentleman.
"   dress too badly. Remember that you are a gentleman.
"   mix the demi-monde with the monde.
"   forget to say "Good Morning" to your superior officers.

---

[347] H G Wells published several books in 1914
[348] Lord Desborough swam across Niagara Falls twice (ODNB); there is a cartoon from the *Westminster Gazette*, 5 March 1914, which refers to it (HALS: DE/Rv/F14, p12). See also letters 182 and 185

and so on, better & better. I am drawing up a rival one, on the lines of Development of Individuality.

<u>Don't</u> ever forget that you are an INDIVIDUAL.

      "   dress if you feel more <u>natural</u> naked.

      "   go naked if it's cold. Wear a bathing dress.

      "   draw class distinctions. It's against the spirit of the Age and the Spirit of the New Testament: besides, it's almost impossible to draw the line.

Don't salute your superior officers, if you feel that your Individuality is on a higher grade than theirs.

Everything is going well here. We finished our Musketry Course today, and did well – best squadron. I got "<u>Marksman</u>" alright this year. We won the Squadron Cricket yesterday, after a terrific game. The big S.A. horse-show next week – I've got 2 jumpers in. The next week, Promotion Exam. The next week 2 Hurdle Races at Jo'burg. Then Squadron Training & Regtl Training & Manoevres, and perhaps a Polo Tournament here.

I don't like the new Wells book, do you? I suppose the Theoretics are only good when they stick to Theory. Because when he says that a small mobile adventurous army will beat an army three times its size, because it can move quicker.

X   X   X

We're bound to come home this year, I believe. Hurrah! I <u>am</u> longing to see you again. Are you happy and welly?

<u>All</u> <u>all</u> love from Julian.

185   9 Apr 1914   Royal Dragoons,   DE/Rv/C1133/65
**   Potchefstroom**

My dearest Dad

I got your cable yesterday, saying that you had paid £110 into Cox's for me. Thank you awfully. It is very good of you. I'm afraid it is more than I really should have; because the first quarter of poor Auntie Ka[tie]'s allowance (£25) <u>was</u> paid in to me last year.

Everything is going very well with me here. We ("B") Sqdn have just finished our yearly Musketry Course, and we passed out the best Squadron. I got "Marksman", but only by the skin of my teeth. Then yesterday we won the Squadron Cricket Cup, beating the favourites on the post. It was an extraordinary game; we went in first & made 299, then they made 371, then we made 384, and then they cracked up – 70!! Never has the like of it been heard of before, because 120 is a big score for Squadron Cricket! I got 89 (3 sixes) and 36 (2 sixes), which was also almost unbelievable!

Next week is the big S.A. horse show at Jo'burg; I've got two horses jumping. There are four jumping competitions each day, so they get pretty well fed up with it by the end. The week after next I'm in for my promotion exam.

I <u>loved</u> the F.C.G. cartoon in the Westminster, of you encouraging the Covenanters to swim Niagara. There has been a pretty good mess about the Home Rule bill[349], hasn't there? It looks more like a settlement now.

I hope that you are fit and well. It will be great fun seeing you again this Autumn. I wonder if Mummy will have fun in Constantinople! How is the egregious Mog?

Best love, and many grateful thanks from Julian.

186	**16 Apr 1914**	**Carlton Hotel, Johannesburg**	**DE/Rv/C1135/659**

Darling Mother

Whereabouts in the world are you now? I haven't had letters for two weeks, because your this mail letter is not forwarded up from Potch[efstroom] yet. I suppose you are back in the Old Country again now? <u>Do</u> tell me all about Constantinople. Was it the <u>greatest</u> fun?

The big Rand Show is here now – it started yesterday. Waterhouse and I have fairly cut it up between us. There have been 4 competitions up to now (Jumping) – Waterhouse won the first, and I was third; after a dead heat first round, 3 horses doing faultless rounds, and running off afterwards. I won the second competition; 4 horses did faultless rounds, and when we ran off, I did another faultless, & the others all <u>fell</u>! That was yesterday. There were two more today. I won the first, with two faultless rounds; Waterhouse second, with 1 fault. Then Waterhouse won the last, and me second.

So out of 4 competitions W & I have each won 2! Rather a triumph. There

---

[349] Home Rule for Ireland. The movement for Irish independence led to a number of bills from the late 19th century; the 1914 one referred to was suspended for the duration of the war and the whole issue of Home Rule ultimately failed (*The Oxford Companion to British History*)

are two more days, and we're both all out to beat the other. Probably we shall neither of us get a place in the next two days!

But it's fun, because they have brought horses here from all round the country – Durban, Cape Town, Bulawayo, Gwelo, Maritzburg, and the Free State. It's the Olympia of S Africa. We get 30 – 50 horses running in each competition. One fault does you in: one little rap on the wall, without moving a brick! It's a funny thing, my champion horse, Kangaroo, who used to jump at Olympia, has done no good so far. He always makes one fault – just tips something. And yet he is probably twice the jumper anything else here is. I've won on an old broken-down troop; and on a runaway Jo'burg mare, which nobody up here would ride!

Promotion exam next week: and I'm trying to work up here, which is d[amne]d hard.

We start away on Squadron and Regimental Training when we get back – and maneovres: but I don't expect there'll be much maoevres this year.

Were you very glad to get back to the family? How are they? <u>What</u> fun seeing you all again in the Autumn.

Goodbye, Mummy – are your eyeses alright?

Bless you J.

187   23 Apr 1914   Potchefstroom   DE/Rv/C1135/660[a]

Darling Mother

I got two glorious letters from you last week, at Jo'burg. Constantinople <u>does</u> sound good value; and Chawlie Lester. Did you say he is in love? Why and with whom? What are you doing now, in the Spring weather? Or is it snowing? It generally has a good snow in England about April 20, unless my memory fails me.

I am in the deadly throes of Promotion Exam, so please excuse brief letter due to pressure of book on the brain. I am writing this before the mail has arrived. This is the last day, thank God. We started on Monday. Two 3-hr papers a day. I've done <u>well</u>. I can always work best cramming by myself. I suppose that the abnormally lazy can only work by sitting down in misery and irons and coffee and wet-towels for a short space, under the whips and scorpions of fear.

"Kangaroo" came off, after all, at the 11th hour. I won the High Jump (over wall with bricks piled on top). He cleared <u>6 foot 5 inches</u>, a record for S Africa, previous record being 6 ft 1 in. Rather a performance for a heavy boy like me. I should think it is a world's record for a horse with over 13 st up. It felt like (I imagine) one of those new Hairyplanes must feel. I said the collect for the day each time before descending to Terra Firma. You know the feeling of being under gas? Like that. I'll send you pictures. Why do I always fascinate the press so. I fear it's a family failing. Buck & I won 6 out of 9 jumping events. 3 each.

Please give my <u>best</u> love to the family. I do want to see you again. Goodbye J.

188   30 Apr 1914   Royal Dragoons,   DE/Rv/C1133/66
**   Potchefstroom**

My dearest Dad

How are you? I hope fit and well. What is going to happen over the Ulster business now?

Thank you awfully for the £110 which you paid to Cox's. I did well with my horses at the big show at Jo'burg. I won three jumping Competitions, which made me very happy, as there were 30-40 entries for each of them, and all the best horses from all over the country. My "Kangaroo" cleared 6ft 5 in the high jump, over a brick wall; which is the record for this country (previous record 6ft 1 in). I should think it is the world's record for a horse with over 13 stone up?

We are just starting Squadron & Regimental Training now; and it's getting very cold. Mummy seems to have had great adventures by road and rail in the Balkans! How is Billa-boy? How are the new prize cattle doing at Pans[hanger]? I hear that Poor Denis is looking well. Are the trout in yet? Everything most flourishing here. I've just finished my Promotion Exam. Goodbye. Best love from Julian.

189   30 Apr 1914   Potchefstroom   DE/Rv/C1135/660[b]

Darling Mother

What fearful adventures you had in the Balkans! Maur[ice][350] seems to have been splendid – and how <u>amusing</u> it all must have been, through the fog of travelling-tiredness! But <u>how</u> tired you must have been! What explanations did Maur[ice] give of your companionship?

I'm so sorry Likky Man has had Mumps. How is Bill-boy? When does he go up for his All Souls? Casie seems to have had the greatest fun at Belvoir[351]. Have you read any jolly <u>books</u>? Is it still raining and snowing? Last time I wrote to you I was in the middle of Promotion Exam. I had a <u>ghastly</u> cold – you know, one of my real blasting-powder colds – right through it. But I think it made me do better; because I had to shake off laziness, and concentrate, before each paper, in order to do anything at all but sneeze. On Saturday Kid & I went down to race at Nigel. I had an awful day – "Midnight Sun" broke down (hopelessly) in the Hurdle Race, when leading, and winning easily. "Wach'n Beetjie" (Wait a bit) was only out for a gallop. I didn't want him to win, because I want to get him down in the weights for a £125 hurdle race at Pretoria next month: but he ran away with me, and ran away from his field, for 1½ miles, when he cracked up. Which means they will put him right up in the weights! Curse him. Then "Mallingham" got beaten <u>½ a head</u> in the flat races. Luckily I wasn't betting. Kid rode like an angel, & won two races.

Yes, why do you understand so much about horses? Do you read McCall and Rough's Guide in the early hours of the morning? It isn't fair. It's like Mr Barnes hen "wot crowed loike a cock", which he shot for being "unnatural-loike".

Nothing much on here just now. My best girl has thrown me over for a stock-broker, and is more determined than ever in her decision, since I wrote to her (in a stupid mood of desperation) saying that I had only got to wait until the glamour of filthy lucre wore off, when she would return swiftly to the arms of True Love.

Do send me books.

Good-bye, & <u>bless</u> you Julian.

---

[350] Hon Maurice Baring (1874-1945), the fourth son of the 1st Lord Revelstoke (Mosley, p403)

[351] Belvoir Castle, Rutland, ancestral home of the Dukes of Rutland. Members of the Manners family were friends with the Grenfells

**190   30 Apr 1914   Royal Dragoons,   DE/Rv/C1138/25
Potchefstroom**

My darling Casie

Thank you awfully for your letter. Belvoir <u>does</u> sound fun. Do you like
Marjorie now? I love Michael's Penny Novelette wit; but I would not have
felt quite certain about it going down with the Dook & Duchess. Isn't it an
absurd thing, really, that there should still be places like Belvoir? It's just
like a pantomime scene. And even the owners cannot quite take it seriously,
hard as they try. Your day's hunting in the borrowed hat, etc, must have been
amusing. I'm glad you're soppy about George Paynter, because I am: I
think he's the nicest thing there ever was. I admire his gentleness and
quietness so tremendously.
How do you like that Diana?
Give George P my love when you see him next.
I'm so glad Denis is well. Yes, I think he might do something next year, with
any luck.
We did awfully well in the big Show at Jo'burg, Waterhouse & me. We won
6 out of the 9 jumping competitions, 3 each. There were generally 30 or 40
entries in each one, so if one touched one jump one was out of it. The Buck
won on his own horses (ie troop-horses he had trained himself). I won two
things on a runaway Jo'burg mare called Molly O'Connor. She always went
round hell-for-blast, which surprised the orthodox show-jumpers. When I
was schooling her, I tried the show-seat (sitting on the ears); but she shot me
neatly into an ant-heap about 10 yds half-left! She jumps like the spring of
an air-gun let off. My own "Kangaroo" won the High Jump (over the wall)
with <u>6 ft 5 in</u>, which is a record for this country (previous record 6 ft 1 in),
and I should think a world's record for a horse carrying over 13 st.
What are your plans for the Summer Months, Darling? Please God I shall
see your face again in the Autumn.
Goodbye & bless you Julian.

191   7 May 1914   Potchefstroom   DE/Rv/C1135/661

Darling Mother

Thank you awfully for your letter. Welbeck[352] seems to have been the
greatest fun: and how exciting Paris sounds! Although I suppose you can't
take the King to Maxims[353] & Montmartre? Or do you, on the quiet? Where
is the new London house, where I suppose you are now safely ensconced? Is
it nice? It is very exciting to think of staying at Panshanger for six months in
October. Are we going to keep the shooting this year?
I'm sorry "The Other Girl" did not win in the Hertfordshire Races. I wonder
who rode her? Who is Mr Lofts? I'm glad that Poor Denis seems to be
getting on well. Thank you awfully for sending the books; they have not
arrived yet but the P.O. will probably send them on after they and their
friends have read them. Poor Belloc! He was devoted to his wife[354], wasn't
he?
I hear that you and that Diarna are absolutely inseparable now. Is it true?
Philip Hardwick and the Boy Pitt Rivers have come back by this mail; Philip
as hard-headed and the Boy as woild in the ed as ever. The Buck is going to
the West African M.I.; at least, he has put in for it. Bad climate, good sport,
big pay, and always a chance of a scrap. Isn't it good, the complete way in
which he has broken down opposition in the regt. He now gets "model
cavalry officer" reports.
I am going to the Flying School this year. My girl is marrying her
stockbroker.
Mrs Steele is going to have a brand new baberoon, which will keep her
quoiet for a bit, poor dear.
We've got a little polo tournament next week; also squadron training. We go
out on the Veldt for a bit in July, which will be cold, but good fun. They've
got a big Hurdle Race (£125 on £25 Cup) at Pretoria on June 1st.
Here are some jumping photographs. They say that one ought to get all the
weight off the horse's back in high-jumping, and consequently all one's

---

[352] Welbeck Abbey, Nottinghamshire, the home of the Dukes of Portland
[353] A high class restaurant in Paris
[354] Elodie, the wife of Hilaire Belloc died in early 1914. According to his biographer,
'Belloc was shattered when Elodie died (probably of cancer) ... He treasured her
memory for the rest of his life, turning her room at King's Land into a shrine which
was never opened, and always wearing black' (ODNB)

posterior up from the saddle: which is most uncomfortable and inelegant. But it certainly seems to help the horse. The Buck sits right up on the ears, like a monkey on it too, Hawa. And HE ought to know, like Bobby Johnson. Goodbye, Mummy darling. The family sound awfully well & happy. I <u>am</u> longing to see you all again.

My pets is all well, and sends you their best love. My bl[ac]k & wh[ite] greyhound dog "Night" has had a touch of mange, but he is better now. Tell Moggie that I'm bringing her home a meer-cat[355], which is the most disreputable of animals, as its name implies. It ought to get on very well with her.

Bless you J.

192   14 May 1914   Unknown place   DE/Rv/C1135/664

Darling Mother

Thank you awfully for your letter. <u>What</u> fun your Paris sounds: and how <u>beautiful</u> it must all have been, with the pageants and the spring sun. Your big room with the windows into the garden sounds heavenly. The Vincennes review must have been good to see. How did the Diana Manners – Beauties – Rowdies party go. Ivo's Young Generation party must have been amusing. I know that you meant the 15-yr-old happiness <u>before</u> problems begin; but don't you think the problems <u>are</u> there before 15, undeveloped and unformulated and almost unrecognised, but really all the worse and all the more uncomfortable for that very reason? Or is that arguing from my own case only? Or is it posthumous imagination even in my own case?

You <u>do</u> sound fit and well and busy and happy; and I <u>do</u> want to see you. I get more & more astounded at the extraordinary variability of my luck (?) – skill and the want of it – coolness and loss of head-steadiness and utter lunacy! Look at this for a day's racing.

Spring Meeting, May 13 1914

–

Spring's & District Handicap – 6 furlongs
                    My "Wach'n Beetje" – Cochrane up – 1

---

[355] Meerkat: generic word covering any of several small, agile mammals found in southern Africa, such as mongoose, African ground squirrel and zorilla (OED)

Stewards Handicap – 7 furlongs

                  Gordon Wright's "Found Out" – self up – 1

Hurdle Handicap - 1½ miles

                  My "Delilah" – Cochrane up – 1

Hunt Hurdle Handicap - 1½ miles

                  My "Wach'n Beetje" – self up – 1

Four races out of a total of six! Isn't it an unbelievable day! I made £87
betting, besides stake money. It was high time – the fat boys owed me a bit.
The Stewards Handicap was a great race. I got shut in, and was a length to
the bad a furlong from home; then I got through on the rails with an 11th hr
rush, and won ½ a length.

No news much here: everyone pretty contented, and everyone grumbling,
which is always a good sign. I got back last night, and am terribly overeaten,
to make up for 2 days starving before the races. I rode 11 st 10, which is the
highest I've ever done. After the first race I ate a banana, and went up <u>2 lbs</u>!!
Goodbye Mummy darling & bless you J.

Did I ever thank you for the <u>darling</u> little knife?

193   14 May 1914   Royal Dragoons,   DE/Rv/C1133/67
**   Potchefstroom**

My darling Dad

Thank you awfully for your letter. I am glad that Panshanger is getting
straight now: I hope the trout will not get disease. The Tap[low] garden
sounds <u>lovely</u>: but it's a great pity about the Cedar. Mummy seems to have
had a bit of a tomasha in Paris.

Everything is going well here, and we are just starting our training. I had a
great day at Spring's Gymkana Races yesterday, and won four races out of
six. Everything came off right: I rode 2 winners, and had a real good man
riding for me when I couldn't do the weight. I did 11st 10 (in a 2lb saddle),
by dint of a days starving! I got £87 out of the books, besides the stake
money. It was almost too good to be true!

The mail is going, so I must stop. Goodbye, Daddy; it <u>will</u> be fun seeing you
again soon.

Best love from Julian.

194   20 May 1914   Potchefstroom   DE/Rv/C1135/665

Darling Mother

Writing before the mail this week, as we are out at cock crow tomorrow
morning; so I can't catch your letter before writing. I suppose you are at the
grand new house in London Town? Are you having fun? And are you
welly? I <u>loved</u> the Belloc "Tristan & Iseult" book[356]; I love the way they
shift the onus of blame – when they say, after having employed the most
flagrant deceit for years and years, that <u>nobody</u> can accuse them of not
having behaved most honourably, considering how much they were in love
with each other, and how deeply they had fallen under the spell. It would be
so easy that way. "Her hair was so lovely, and I had had Burgundy for dinner
that night".
I haven't read the Connie Lytton book on prisons yet[357]. Is it good? Have
you been reading anything good, or have you been too busy? Have you been
doing any jolly things since Paris? I've heard from Daddy and Casie, who
both seem frightfully happy. No news here much. I did my "C" exam,
promotion, practical tactics on the ground, on Monday. I did best of all, and
got "Distinguished". The Captains do the same exam for promotion to major,
and I beat all them too! But it wasn't much, because I knew the country like
the back of my hand, every bush and every fence (having poached hares on
each acre of it!). We've got a polo tournament on, squadron teams. We
played the ante-final today, and won after a fearful game, in choking dust, 3-
2. We play the final on Friday, and stand a chance.

---

[356] *The romance of Tristan & Iseult drawn from the best French sources and re-told
by J Bedier*; rendered into English by H Belloc (1913)
[357] *Prisons & prisoners: some personal experiences*, by Constance Lytton and Jane
Warton (1914). Lady Constance Lytton was a suffragette. Her protest activities led
to her being imprisoned in Holloway in early 1909, but she was treated leniently on
the grounds of having heart trouble, after the authorities became aware of her
powerful connections. Later in the year she was again arrested for throwing stones at
a ministerial car during a political meeting in Newcastle, and again released quickly.
In early 1910 she decided to test the existence of class differences in the treatment of
suffragist prisoners, and assumed the dress and name of a working woman, Miss Jane
Warton, for a further protest in Liverpool. She was imprisoned in Walton gaol, went
on hunger strike, and was this time force-fed eight times before her release, with no
medical examination. The book *Prisons and Prisoners* is an account of her
imprisonment (ODNB)

Goodbye, darling. It's very strenuous here now; every minute occupied, which I suppose is the happiest way really. All all love to the family, and you from J.

195   28 May 1914   Potchefstroom   DE/Rv/C1135/666

Darling Mother

Thanks awfully for your letter. London sounds fun, and the new little house. I heard from Dad too, and he seems v happy. When does Billa go up for his All Souls? He seems to have been a long time in training; but I expect I have forgotten, and everyone goes up 2 or 3 yrs after going down? Are you very well & happy? Have you read anything, or does your practical life crowd out your theoretical? It does with me now; every day is 12 hrs to[o] short to 'get through'; and I never know whether it really is so, or only appears so through excessive laziness. Of course half the ploys are play; but playing with horses is after all my business in that state of life into which it has pleased God to call me.

We've just finished Squadron Training, today. Yesterday the cable came that we go home this trooping season – Oct – March. Our polo final is still unplayed – it rained all last week. My polo ponies are really things of wonder; they play in tournaments 2 days a week, and turn out and win a race on the third day! They are racehorses in the morning, and do their gallops; in the afternoon they become polo ponies, and play their 2 chukkers!

"Mallingham" won the Pony & Galloway Handicap at Ventersdorp last week, with one of our sergeants (an ex-jockey) up.

The big hurdle race at Pretoria on Monday - £150 & cup. I'm afraid that all the best horses in Africa will be having a cut; so, unless they fall, my two won't stand much chance.

We've got 3 new boys this yr, all toppers. All at Eton, & 1 from Cambridge. Henderson, Browne, & Watkin Wynn.

No more new, Mummy darling; but a very happy life. I've never felt so well – thankful & propitiating towards the Gods before.

I loved Diana Manners' letter of thanks & praise to you. Yes, <u>why</u> is she not more attractive. <u>No</u> charm. And no very tangible reason for its absence. I mean, the only reason one can give is only amounts to saying that she has not got it.

<u>All</u> love. I <u>am</u> looking to seeing you again. <u>Bless</u> you J.

196   4 June 1914   Potchefstroom   DE/Rv/C1135/667

Darling Mother

Are you razzle-dazzling with Vovo today? Thank you awfully for your letter.
Is Tommy Rib[358] <u>really</u> going to marry Vera Arkwright? Poor Nan; I'm sorry
about her arm. Will Bron be able to let Wrest now?[359] I hope Chawlie
L[ister] will not marry the Tango Tea; because he could get just the same,
only rather prettier, from any musical comedy, at a low price and without any
bother. You seem to be having <u>great</u> fun? It's very sad about Hamel[360].
What a tiger he must have been? Did you like him? I'm sorry little Marjorie
is looking ill[361]. Yes, <u>what</u> a gutless swine that man must be?
No news much out here. I'm getting a lot of riding over hurdles, which, as
you know, I adore. Whenever I get up, the papers call attention to "perfect
horsemanship", which is unfortunate, as I'm always falling out of the horrible
little saddles which I have to ride in, (to do the weight). You should see them
– a small bit of rag, a paper girth, and two stirrups, loosely tied together.
Why didn't you think to make me a nice likka boy, when I could have
reflected some credit on you?
We got disgracefully whacked in the final of the polo yesterday: everything
went wrong. We go out into camp in a fortnight, for about 10 days. It's
<u>bitter</u> cold here now; but gorgeous hot sun in the middle of the day. George
Steele a fair colonel; but I don't love him like Ernest Makins? Have you
seen Makins? I don't know when we come home – probably not until
Christmas, but I'll try to get leave August or September.
Give my best love to the family. When do you move to the Ancestral Home
in Herts? Is Tap[low] looking lovely? Goodbye. Best best best love from J.

---

[358] Thomas Lister, 4th Baron Riblesdale (see letter 20). His first wife was Charlotte
(Charty) Monckton Tennant (1858–1911), a member of the 'Souls' whom he married
on 7 April 1877. They had two boys and three girls. She died after a three-year fight
against tuberculosis in 1911. In 1919 Lister married an American, Ava, the widow of
John Jacob Astor (ODNB)
[359] Auberon Herbert, Baron Lucas (Bron) inherited Wrest Park, near Ampthill,
Bedfordshire in 1905 from his uncle, Francis Thomas De Grey Cowper (Julian's
Uncle Francis)
[360] Gustav Hamel, the aviator was killed on 23 May 1914 (see letter 157)
[361] Presumably a reference to Marjorie's marital problems (see letters 200-202)

197   4 June 1914   Royal Dragoons,   DE/Rv/C1138/26
Potchefstroom

Casie darling

I suppose you're at Eton[362] today with all the nuts. The Hawthorn Hill party
must have been v good. It's <u>terribly</u> sad about poor Hamel, isn't it? He was
a tiger, from all a/cs.
I gave your message to Our Alf. He is in great form. No news from here
much, except that we come home this next trooping season for sartin sure.
We've all been agitating to get hurdle racing started here by the big clubs.
Pretoria gave a race on June 1st, £125 and £25 Cup. We had 18 starters - 2¼
miles; it was a great success. I ran my two horses, Delilah & Wacht Een
Beetjie. Won't the bookies make a mess up of the latter's name, if I bring
him home! He was carrying 9 st, and I had a real good boy to ride him; but
just as I was weighing him out, a furious bookies lout dashed in, followed by
3 of the stewards, who pulled my brave boy out of the chair and hustled him
out for a "blacklister". He owed the books £20. Catastrophe. I had to ride
myself, 2½ stone overweight!
The next thing was that I found Delilah doped and half-alive. They had got
at her in the train. What a life! What a country!
Give my love to everyone. It will be fun seeing you again. You seem to
have had a great year.
Bless you Julian.

198   11 June 1914   Potchefstroom   DE/Rv/C1135/668

My darling Mother

Thank you awfully for your letter. You must have had a wonderful May in
England. You are the greatest weather-worshipper in the world, aren't you?
And it is, after all, the nearest manifestation of God. Milner's place sounds
lovely; and I adore his Tua Domus Mea môt![363] I don't know Basil B well,
but I think his quietness and gentleness has extraordinary charm. He is
coming out here on some job, isn't he? I had the <u>most</u> amusing letter from
Bill in Paris. Nobody can write letters like him; such terrible concentration

---

[362] She was at Eton to collect Ivo on the day when the Long Summer Leave begins
[363] 'Your house is my house' or 'my house is your house'

of wit and venom & irony.

The weather out here is like iced champagne. Next week is our big festival – Waterloo week – frock coasts and ceremonial parades in the morning, and assault at arms and polo in the afternoons; and a bevy of fairies from Johannesburg town, staying in the bungalows here. Such fairies, too! So genteel! They would not allow me to compete, with my friends, in a rival bungalow, because forsooth they were not genteel enough. In fact I am under a slight (but silver-edged) cloud at present, and was warned by the Powers that be (Cap-off in Orderly Room on Friday morning) that further leave would not be granted me unless I confined myself to a World of Men. But I think it will blow over, if I lie doggo for a bit, and if Mrs George adds successfully to the race.

No more news about going home: I should think it would be November or December. But I don't know whether they will not send me back sooner, for a course or something. Everything is unsettled just at present. O Mummy, I can't tell you the daily joy of my glorious thorobred polo-ponies – new every morning, like the sun. They <u>are</u> fit and fierce and beautiful. I let them out loose in the mornings, and they gallop and play about with the greyhounds in the sun. Sorry for being a bore.

How is the Likky Man? And Mogsy? Give them all my love. Tell Moggy that I am bringing her a tiger and three diamond bracelets, if Dancing Wave wins the Handicap tomorrow.

I <u>do</u> want to see you again J.

199   18 June 1914   Potchefstroom   DE/Rv/C1135/669

Darling Mother

No time to write this week, except to send you oceans of love & blessings, and to thank you <u>tremendously</u> for your letter. We've just had our "Waterloo Day" parade, with all the geegaws[364]; and the German Consul presenting a wreath from the German Emperor, etc etc. Of course the awful thing happened, and the horse with the man carrying the standard kicked, bucked, & bolted! Awful scene. The standard had to be handed over to another man! All this week is a glorified show, parades & balls & polo & all sorts. I wish I had been born in the Fiji islands, with a nice brown stomach cloth, & nothing

---

[364] A gaudy trifle, plaything, or ornament, a pretty thing of little value, toy or bauble (OED)

else.

You seem to be aving the greatest fun, in the ight of the season; and you <u>do</u> sound welly.

I <u>am</u> sorry about poor Hamel.

We come home <u>November</u>, by the latest rumour. I'm going to have a shoot in Rhodesia before that.

I'm awfully well, Mummy; and I <u>do</u> want to see you. J.

**200   25 June 1914   Camp, Mooi River,   DE/Rv/C1135/670
                           South Africa**

My darling Mother

Thank you <u>awfully</u> for your letter. Your Hackwood must have been the most glorious fun: and Likkie's Fourth of June. I thought of you at Eton that day. I'm glad that Moggie's pets is all well: please give her my very very best love.

We are out in camp here, squadron camp, 5 officers and 100 men. Rather a jolly place, by a tiny little reedy river, like a drain, very narrow and very deep. We are not roughing it by any means, having an enormous marquee, besides ordinary tents – and seas of drink. It is much too grand; I had much rather be out with my Scouts, and no tents nor nuffink. No exact news about when we come home; betting on November. I don't think I shall get leave home before that, so I shall go lion-hunting out here for a bit. They won't give me leave for the Durban Show, next month, because we shall be on regimental training: which is a pity, because the Buck & I might have done some good there.

When does Billa-boy go up for his All Souls exam? I hope he is welly? Please give him my very best love. I <u>am</u> sorry about poor little Miggy [*Marjorie Manners*]: yes, I'll write to her. How is Bron? Have you seen anything of him?

I <u>am</u> longing to see you again, Mummy!

Goodbye – all all love J.

201   2 July 1914   Potchefstroom   DE/Rv/C1135/671

Darling Mother

I loved your letter, and I'm thrilled by the scandals in high life. What a far
far better thing it is not to get married! Marriage is such a short odds
gamble; and the funny thing is that the real gamblers and chancers have the
sense to leave it alone, knowing that it is a bad bet; while the careful ones,
who know neither the form nor the odds, plunge and go down. That doesn't
apply to Bend Or, does it? But no rules or exceptions apply to him. And I
think it's right as a general rule? Poor little Migs – I <u>am</u> sorry for her. I
wonder what will happen about it? Will they get a separation? Jezebel in the
witness-box trying to prove O.W. on Anglesey would be the end of the
British aristocracy.
The Horse Show must have been good fun. I'm frightfully keen to have a cut
there next year, if all goes well. The Buck is going to the West African
Rifles, so he won't be able to go; which is a pity, because he's about the best
show-jump rider we've got, I should think. I've never seen the criss-cross
jumping. I'm glad you like Scatters; he's <u>great</u> fun , isn't he?
Not much on here; we came in on Sunday from our week's camp, and we
start regimental drill tomorrow; in the middle of the month the foot-sloggers
come down from Pretoria, and we play about with them for a bit. At the end
of the month I am going off with Kid Charrington to British East [Africa],
with Billy Miles' brother, who farms up there. I think it will be great fun.
Kid and little Miles are both absolutely wild in the ed, beneath a gentle and
almost stolid outward appearance & demeanour. We're taking the
greyhounds up to hunt the wily lion, and some hog-spears and Ghurka knives
for close quarters. Kid said the other day "We've forgotten something".
"What?" "Pocket pistols for the husbands". No.
I'm not allowed to go to Johannesburg city now, nor to have any friends
visiting at Potchefstroom. This is a great mistake.
Mrs Steele has just got a very fine boy, and both are doing well.
Please give my very very best love to Dad & Bill-boy & Casie & Vovo and
Mog. Hurrah for the hols – I mean next Christmas.
Have you been working any big ramps[365] lately, Mummy? You never tell me
about your secret doings, while I am always most open to you about what I
do. This isn't fair. <u>Bless</u> you J.

---

[365] Swindles (OED)

202   9 July 1914   Potchefstroom   DE/Rv/C1135/672

Darling Mother

Writing this week before your mail arrives, because we are going out
soldiering tomorrow. Are you waiting now? Or have you finished? Are you
going abroad this year? Or only Scotland? When do we take up residence in
Hertfordshire? When does Billa-boy go up for his All Souls? That is what
you will never tell me. How are Marjorie's affairs progressing? How is
Bron? Have you seen him lately? Have you read anything good? Thank
you awfully for all the books you've sent me. I liked the new one, by the
post-impressionist man, very much indeed: especially the bit when the
woman looks at the running water, and says sadly "Nothing Nothing!"
Everything goes well here, but it gets a bit monotonous; I've been here for 15
months solid now, without a week at a stretch away; and I'm looking forward
tremendously to my shoot next month. I haven't yet settled where to go –
Rhodesia or British East; but I've got a fellow in each place ready to fix up at
a moment's notice. It depends on whether they will give me leave to come
home before the regiment goes. I don't think they will go much before
January, and I'm frightfully keen to get back sooner than that. If I can get
leave for home, I shall go to Rhodesia, which is nearer, quicker & cheaper. If
not, I shall go to British East. Denis Finch Hatton[366] lives in B.E., or rather
he lives there more than he lives anywhere. At present he is away on a real
Denis expedition; he went 7 months ago to Further Arabia to buy a million
head of cattle (where they cost 2/6 a head), with the idea of driving them
back across the desert to B.E., where they cost £150 or 150 guineas a head.
He is expected back daily, unless he is dead, or has become King of Further
Arabia. He is a great man in British East, they say. He made a lot of money
by shipping timber out there from his place in Norway, and bought a palace
there from an American millionaire, where he entertains the country-side on
champagne & caviar. They are very amusing about him. I'm longing to see
him again; he's such a tonic after all the dead-beats. If he's there when I go
up, I've often thought of growing a little cotton out there with him. Don't
you think it would be great fun? They have never grown any cotton there
yet, and the soil is most unfavourable to the growth of the same; but that

---

[366] Hon Denys Finch-Hatton (1887-1931), second son of the 13th Earl of Winchelsea.
(Mosley, p405). He was a big-game hunter, the lover of Karen Blixen, who wrote
about him in her autobiographical book *Out of Africa*, first published in 1937

really only makes the experiment more interesting.

Now I've got to walk round the horses, being orderly officer. It's bitter cold, it's bitter cold, the Sergeant-Major always says when we walk round.

I <u>am</u> looking to coming home & seeing you again, Mummy. Are you welly? Are you good-tempered? I'm in a terribly bad temper tonight. It's all so silly. Goodbye.

<u>Bless</u> you Julian.

203   15 July 1914   Potchefstroom   DE/Rv/C1135/673

Darling Mother

Thank you awfully for your "Ascot" letter. It must have been good for you, getting a bit of sun again. Yes, the American polo <u>was</u> good, wasn't it; and <u>what</u> good reading the accounts were, especially the "Times" one; that last chukker must have been one of the most exciting things that ever were. Mouse must have played quite brilliantly; I suppose he was the best man they could ever have got, for that game, as No 1 – with his wonderful strength on a horse, and his dash and bitterness. I've seen him come into a man and knock him clean over, pony & all. How is Billa-boy? How pleased you must be that Ivo has not been sacked from Eton! Don't you think that it is nearly a record, to have 3 sons at Eton without even a hint of expulsion? Have you read anything good. I've read General John Regan and an awful book called "The World & Mr Freyne" and a bloody awful book called "The Valley of the Moon" by Jack London (<u>the</u> worst man)[367]. I've quite settled up about my leave now; I'm going to hunt lions in Rhodesia (<u>not</u> British East) in August, very soon; and then I'm coming home (in October or January) by British East and the Red Sea. Then I'm going to the Flying School at Netheravon; and up for the Staff College exam in June 1914. In March I am going to the Polo at the Panama Exhibition; and next year I will stand for Parliament.

Goodbye, Mummy darling. It <u>will</u> be fun seeing you again.

<u>All</u> <u>all</u> love J.

---

[367] The novel *General John Regan* was written by James Owen Hannay and published under the pseudonym George A Birmingham (1913); *The World and Mr Freyne: A fantastic romance* by Beryl Tucker (1913); *The Valley of the Moon*, by Jack London (1914). London was an American writer; his 1908 novel *The Iron Heel* is about class struggle, which prophesies a Fascist revolution. *The Valley of the Moon* advocates a return to the land in an ideal community (OCEL)

204 15 July 1914   **Royal Dragoons,**   **DE/Rv/C1133/68**
                                       Potchefstroom

My dear Dad

Thank you very much for your letter. It must have been an envious task, judging the teams after the Coaching Marathon. Did you have fun at Ascot? The family sound most flourishing. It will be great fun to see you all again. I have got 6 months' leave from August 1st, and I am going for a shoot in Rhodesia, and then coming home, in October or November. I am sending four polo ponies home next month, with a man. Do you think you could keep them for me, till I come home? They will arrive in September; and I should think that they will soon get their winter coats, so that they can turn out to grass all the winter, if there is some shed or place where they can turn in and keep warm for the nights. Could they be turned out at Panshanger, do you think? I ought to have written to you earlier about this, but do you think you could manage to fix them up somewhere till I arrive? I would be awfully obliged if you could. I will let you know later when they are due to arrive; and I will tell the man to wire to you, when he arrives in England, for directions where to take them. They are good ponies, heavyweight and thorobred, and I think they ought to fetch good money in England.

Everything goes very well here; but after 15 months solid I shall be glad of a change! We are doing "regimental training" & manoevres now, and the "feet" come down for their manoevres here next week. It's a wonderful climate here now; cold nights and hot sunny days. I think the regiment is very flourishing; but Steele is not so good a colonel as Makins.

I hope you are fit, Daddy, and having fun. It will be good to see you again soon. But I have aged terribly!

Goodbye love from Julian.

205   22 July 1914   Potchefstroom   DE/Rv/C1135/674

Darling Mother

Thank you awfully for your last week's letter, after Welbeck. Writing again before your mail arrives this week, as we are out for a big field day with the "feet" tomorrow. Your Welbeck sounds fun. What is going to happen about Ulster? Poor little Marjorie; I do think she has been hardly treated by life; because she is simply artist, compelled by force of fate not to be artist. I suppose she is absolutely under the bludgeoning of Fate now? But she must always by nature have a more exciting life than Laura[368], whose most ambitious action would be falling off a log. Billa-boy sounds well & happy? And Casie? Hamel really must have been (and be) a most wonderful person: I wish I had known him; I like so tremendously everything that I've heard about him. He sounded so "outstanding", without trying in the least for that effect. Yes, Longmore[369] <u>does</u> sound a drear place, doesn't it? But then there are so many alternatives for me – Cavalry School – Staff College, for which the Colonel says I may go up next year, if I promise to work – Somaliland, fighting the inky cannibals – East Coast of Africa – West Coast of Africa – polito-militario job in the further forests of India; I <u>wish</u> you could get me that! What's the good of your being in with the Heads, if you can't get that sort of thing for a deserving son? – ranching in Texas – ranching in Bucks – ranching in Herts – and cotton growing in British East!! I have at last settled

---

[368] Possibly Laura Lister, second daughter of the 4th Baron Ribblesdale. In 1910 she had married the 16th Baron Lovat (Mosley, p408)

[369] Army camp near Liss, Hampshire

my plans, pro tem, for the remainder of the year. In a week's time I go to Southern Rhodesia, to hunt the wily lion (as I've said before). As a matter of fact, that will probably mean living a riotous life in some small Rhodesian town, and riding in 3rd rate steeplechases; for the thought of a lion fills me with dread untold. Then in October I return to England and the Old Country via the East Coast or the West Coast and British New Guinea: arriving before Christmas, if possible. It <u>will</u> be fun seeing you again.

Are you welly, Mummy? Do you think we shall get on this time, or shall I still be frightened of your watchfulness, craftiness, and intellectual activity? Goodbye. <u>Bless</u> you. Julian.

**206   22 July 1914   Royal Dragoons,   DE/Rv/C1138/27
                         Potchefstroom**

My darling Casie

Thank you awfully for your letter. Your Ascot must have been great fun; but it was wise and pusillanimous of you not to bet. I bet in thousands now every week; and invariably lose. That is what makes life so monotonous. It must have been fun for you to see dear John Bigge again; please give him my very best love. No, you're quite wrong about the seasons here; it is <u>not</u> boiling hot now. You are a most unthoughtful girl. Also a grossly uneducated girl, considering that you were for some time under one of the best governesses in the South of England. I call it a pure waste of money. In the Sub Tropical regions of the Southern Hemisphere, at this season of the year, the sun sometimes rises at 12 midnight, and sometimes not at all; especially when there is a fog. It is bitterly cold, whether the sun rises or not, and when one wakes up, one's beard is always frozen into the collar of one's pyjamas: so that even if one does not have to shave one's beard off one's face, one has to shave one's pyjamas off one's beard. And that means a lot of money spent per annum in razors.

How is Mrs Dale Lace? If you do not kiss her on the carmine bull's-eye[370] on her right cheek, she is always very angry with you. Please do this, and give her my best love.

Next week I go off to hunt lions in Rhodesia with a hog-spear. And so home, probably about October or February. It will be great fun seeing you again. I'm sending four of the most delicious polo-ponies home next month; will

---

[370] Heavily rouged cheek

you order a railway box to carry them from the Port of London to wherever Papa thinks fit that they shall spend the winter? I will let you know the time of their arrival later. Don't forget this, as the whole of my financial future depends thereupon.

Goodbye & bless you Julian.

207   28 July 1914   Potchefstroom   DE/Rv/C1135/675

Darling Mother

Thank you awfully for your last week's letter. Also for your kind cable re lions – pore little barstids, as my troop-sergeant would say. We are most terribly overworked and underpaid here just now – out from dawn till dusk, doing manoevres with the foot-sloggers from Pretoria and Pietermaritzburg. We start before daylight tomorrow, and sleep on the bare ground tomorrow night. Oh, we are 'ard chaps. So I've got to write tonight.

On Friday that ever is I start off for my shoot. I'm going to Gwelo, Southern Rhodesia. Everybody always produce with unction the names of the desert places to which they are going to venture, knowing perfectly well that their friends and relations are no whit the wiser. It "delights the ladies, but does not deceive the roaring men", as Jonah used to say about people who groaned and rolled about and fainted in the boat after rowing a course.

Oh Mummy, it <u>will</u> be fun seeing you again; in October or November. You had great fun this year? Isn't it an exciting age, with Ireland and Austria and the Servs and Serbs and Slabs [sic][371]. What is going to happen?

Please give my very best love to all the family. <u>All</u> <u>all</u> love from J.

---

[371] Presumably a reference to unrest in the Balkans, which was an important catalyst for the First World War

208   6 Aug 1914   Royal Dragoons,   DE/Rv/C1133/69
**   Potchefstroom**

My darling Dad

Thank you very much for your letter. You must be having an exciting time at
home now, with the war! We get very little news here; rumours arriving now
of a sea fight going on off Flamborough Head[372]. I wonder if this letter will
ever reach you? We do not know in the least what they are going to do with
us. People seem to think today, now that the Turks have joined Germany,
that we shall be sent to Egypt. It is hateful being away in a corner here, at
this time. I suppose that the whole thing will be over in a very short time. I
only hope that they will move us quickly, and that we get somewhere in time
for something!
It was very sad that all the English crews got beaten at Henley. You must
have had great fun with the Likky Man at Lords. Did you go with K to see
the Carpentier-Bell fight? [373]
Goodbye, Daddy; and very best love. I am quite flourishing here: but I wish
we were in England. It must be an extraordinary time to live through, at
home now!
Julian.
I shall get a man to keep my 4 ponies in Jo'burg, if we move off suddenly.
Of course it is no good thinking of sending them home at present.

209   6 Aug 1914   Potchefstroom   DE/Rv/C1135/676

Darling Mother

Things have gone pretty quickly this last week, haven't they? There was
hardly a breath of war here when I wrote last week. Then the next day
(Thursday) we were called back in the middle of a big manoevre battle post-
haste, and told that we must be ready to start at any minute. It is horrible
being tucked away here at a time like this. We only get the merest driblets of

---

[372] Flamborough Head, just north of Bridlington, Yorkshire
[373] A boxing match. Julian seems to have got the name of the second boxer (Bell)
wrong as Georges Carpentier, a French boxer, does not appear to have fought anyone
of that name. He did, however, beat Billy *Wells* in June 1913, to win the European
heavyweight title

news, and can only wait, knowing that the biggest battles of the world are going on at every and any moment; and without any word of what they are going to do with us – Europe, Egypt, India, or just stopping here!

It must be wonderful in England now! I suppose the excitement is beyond all words? Didn't you think that it was a <u>wonderful</u> speech of Grey's?[374] Of course when this letter gets to you, (if it ever does, which seems doubtful), all these things will be swallowed up in bigger things, and forgotten. And don't you think it has been a wonderful, and almost incredible, rally to the Empire; with Redmond[375] and the Hindus and Will Crooks[376] and the Boers and the South Fiji Islanders all aching to come and throw stones at the Germans. It reinforces one's failing belief in the Old Flag and the Mother Country and the Heavy Brigade and the Thin Red Line and all the Imperial Idea, which gets rather shadowy in peace time, don't you think? But this has proved it to be a real enough thing.

Today came the news that the Turks have joined the Germans. Philip Hardwick said "I wonder if my servant has packed my tin-lined drawers. You know what the Turks do if they capture anyone – especially a good-looking chap like me".

I wonder how long it will last? Isn't it bad luck, that it should come when we are at Potchefstroom? Or do you think that they will fetch us over in

---

[374] In December 1905, Viscount Grey of Fallodon (1862–1933) became Foreign Secretary. On 3 August 1914 he spoke in the Commons, one of the most important speeches ever made by a British foreign secretary; he repeated that Britain still had freedom to decide and was not committed by treaty, and referred to 'obligations of honour and interest' which were at stake and which would compel Britain to take a stand. The speech convinced many waverers in his own party and produced near unity in the country. An ultimatum was sent to Berlin, but there was no reply. Few people grasped the enormity of going to war, except, perhaps, Grey himself who remarked, according to an (unidentified) friend, 'The lamps are going out all over Europe; we shall not see them lit again in our life-time' (ODNB)

[375] John Edward Redmond, Irish nationalist politician. In exchange for Prime Minister H H Asquith's commitment to place the Home Rule Bill on the statute book (and to make some later provision for Ulster), he supported the British war effort (ODNB)

[376] William (Will) Crooks, politician. In 1903, as the Labour Representation Committee candidate, he won a sensational by-election at Woolwich, a Tory constituency. Although he had been a vigorous opponent of the South African war, the patriotic Crooks greeted British entry into the First World War by leading the singing of the National Anthem in the House of Commons (ODNB)

time? One thing is, that there is absolutely nothing for us to do here.

We heard about the French airman and the Zeppelin; the best thing ever done in the world, wasn't it?

They seem to think there that the Turks having joined in will make it more likely for us to go to Egypt.

Your Lords week must have been great fun, and very strenuous. I <u>am</u> glad that you are so <u>welly</u>, eyes and all. Who is Frank Tinney? I've never heard tell of him. It was awful about poor Denny Anson[377]; and it read so terribly the "Idle Rich" in the papers, didn't it? It's such a <u>waste</u>: a man like that, who was just the man for doing a big dash, or leading a forlorn hope, chucked away because he could find nothing exciting enough to do in the ordinary things. Those fellows ought all to be sent out into the wilds, and not allowed near London.

I wonder if they have mobilised the army yet in England; and where they are going to send it? You must be living a stirring life now, Mummy! I wonder where we shall meet next!

Goodbye, & <u>bless</u> you. I <u>do</u> want to see you again <u>soon</u>.

<u>All</u> love from Julian.

210	**6 Aug [1914]**	**Royal Dragoons, Potchefstroom**	**DE/Rv/C1138/28**

My darling Casie

Thank you awfully for your letter. It was <u>terrible</u> about poor Denny Anson, wasn't it. I liked him awfully; what a real Berserk wasted! Your nerve must be almost broken – those two accidents one after the other. Oh, I wish we were in England now; just think of being here, when the biggest thing in the world is going on. We get no news here, practically: and we do not in the very least know what they are going to do with us. Now that the Turks have joined in with Germany, I should think that it would be most likely that we should go to Egypt.

Wasn't it the best thing you have ever heard, that French airman and the

---

[377] Denis Anson was known for his bravado. In the summer of 1914, during a party on a boat on the Thames, he jumped over the side. He got into difficulties and two men, a musician and the son of the Russian Ambassador, jumped in to try to save him; only the Russian survived. The next day, and following the inquest, the popular press blamed the tragedy on an irresponsible smart set (MacKenzie, p134)

Zeppelin? Aren't you all almost wild with excitement at home?
We don't even know here whether they have mobilised the army at home yet.
Vague news coming in about a sea-fight off Flamborough Head.
I wonder if this letter will ever get to you? It is just to take you <u>all</u> my love.
Did you have fun at Lords? And are you welly?
Bless you Julian.

211   13 Aug 1914   Potchefstroom   DE/Rv/C1135/677

My darling Mother

Thank you awfully for your letter, with no breath of war in it! I suppose your
next letter will be the war one. Aren't you mad with excitement about it?
What are you going to do about plans now? Are you going to take up
residence at Panshanger just the same? And going to Scotland? Is Billa-boy
going to fight? Have they taken Poor Dennis & Dynamite and Schoolgirl to
be pore troop-horses? Don't let them take Poor Dennis, because he is a
steeplechase 'oss, and would be no good as a fighting 'oss. The midnight
water-party at Tap[low] sounds the greatest fun; and all the end of the season
bust-ups. I never knew that Bron had entered the lists with Magog Duff. I
love Belloc's "Ivor Guest" poem. I wonder what news you've got in England
now? We heard that the Germans had been defeated and driven back at
Liege with 25,000 loss, and at Mulhausen with 30,000 loss; but today again
comes the news that they have got past both Liege and Mulhausen. We heard
that the German fleet had been wiped out in the North Sea; and today they
say that it has not put out of harbour yet!
We have been "standing to" now for a week, with all our baggage down at
the station. They seem to think now that we shall go straight to England; but
nobody seems really to know. Do you think this war is going to be a long
thing, or very short? We have no news at all yet of any movement of our
troops from England. Anyhow, every day that we wait here is a day to the
bad. I don't know why they have not sent us sooner; whether they have not
got the transport ready, or whether they are waiting until something happens
at sea. It is horrible to have to wait here, with nothing to do, except just wait.
If we come to England we shall have to stay there for a day or two, anyhow;
because our horses will be fit for nothing, after 3 weeks sea, and we shall
probably pick up a fresh lot, which will take time. So I shall probably see
you again soon, which will be great and good. Goodbye, Mummy, & bless
you. Julian.

212   13 Aug 1914   Royal Dragoons,   DE/Rv/C1133/70
Potchefstroom

My dear Dad

I got your cable about not sending my ponies home, and stopped them at
once. I'm going to leave them with a Dutch farmer out here. The worst of it
is that I do not know if they will not commandeer all the horse in this country
too!
I wonder if you have got more news at home than we have out here; because
we are absolutely in the dark. We heard of the German Navy crushed in the
North Sea; 25,000 German casualties at Liege, and 30,000 at Malhausen.
But today all that is denied again.
We are waiting here, all packed up and ready to start. They seem to think for
England, in which case I shall see you; as they will have to keep us for a day
or two till our horses get fit again, or till they give us a fresh lot.
No news here of any movement of troops from England; I do not know why
they are keeping us, from lack of transport, or until something happens at sea,
or what. But I hope, and really believe, that they will move in any day now.
I wonder if Poor Dennis and Dynamite & Schoolgirl have been taken yet?
Goodbye, Daddy, and all love from Julian.

213   nd   Potechefstroom   D/EX789/F15
[part of letters only]

…He says that you can only get 6 months in this country; but I'm sure we
can work 8, and anyhow I'll chance it and come in the middle of September,
or a little later, to arrive somewhere at the beginning of October. I can't bear
to think of coming back to Roberts Heights; besides being the dullest place
this side Heaven, it is horribly unhealthy, and simply poisons the springs of
energy, so that you go to sleep directly you sit down to work or write.
Everybody is the same here, - half-dead. Directly you get away from it, as
here, you wake up; directly you return, you sink deeper than before. We start
regimental training when we get back, and then manoevres, sleeping on the
naked earth, like Adam without Eve, and bitterly cold. Ain't this a nice
cheerful little letter?

Can you get me a job? Black Rod, or Minister of Agriculture, or Envoy
Plenipotentiary to the King of Barbados?
Give my love to the family. I'm sorry about Bill & Casie being so cold of
'eart; I feel that I shall fall an easy prey to the first little thing I meet, from
sheer boredom with myself. Goodbye, all all love J.

'Champion Boxer of the 15th Hussars. He has got indomitable courage and
no neck'

…horse-coping hard, buying young or badly broken ponies, to train for these
three months and then sell at a profit. Regimental Training in full swing,
8.30 am – 2 pm everyday: then polo in the afternoon, with a bite of luncheon
in between. We go out on trek for a week at the end of this month, rolling up
in a blanket on the hard ground of a night. Then manoevres, ditto of a night.
Its cruel ard on a pore young chap, when others are riding in their own
kerridges at home. I wish I hadn't sold my ponies – Rajah, who used to

come out for walks with me, loose, and rub my hat off with his nose when he wanted sugar. He walked up the steps into the verandah one day, when it was raining, and he got tired of waiting outside. And when the saddle slipped round at polo one day, he came back to pick me up. I've got 2 troop-horses that play now – and a £20 pounder – and a pony I'm breaking for another man; but they are all fools, and one of them has got a very nasty nature.

All all love to the family. J.

214   19 Aug 1914   Potchefstroom   DE/Rv/C1135/678

Darling Mother

At last we have got orders. We go to Cape Town the day after tomorrow, and sail on the Dunluce Castle on the 24th. For England? For German West Africa? Nobody seems to have the least idea. It is good to get some definite news, after waiting here for a week with none at all. But they change the orders every day, so that there is no betting on it even now.

This evening the news came about the English expeditionary force having landed at Boulogne. I suppose that is right. But all the news about the thousands of Germans killed in Alsace and at Liege was so vague and so often contradicted that it looked like pure invention or exaggeration? I don't think they <u>can</u> keep us out here, do you think? Provided, of course, that the sea is safe. German South West makes so little difference to anyone; if we win, we shall walk in and take it; and if we lose, we shall not have it. And the country here seems pretty quiet – the blacks fairly peaceful, and the Boers wonderfully loyal, and dying to have a slap at someone. So there does not seem to be much occupation for us out here.

It's extraordinary to think that I may see you almost as soon as this letter arrives – I can't believe it, though. It is fatal to believe anything, in this state of affairs. I'm writing this before your letter arrives – the first war letter from you: so I'll leave it open till tomorrow.

Aug 20th. Your letter arrived, with all the exciting doubts & probabilities just before war. Yes, how good Grey was. But why haven't they sent the English force straight to Belgium, instead of to Boulogne? It looks rather as if the Germans had got Belgium by now? Don't you hate the hysteria of the newspapers? It drives me mad to read them.

I wonder if they will let me cable to you when we get to Cape Town, or if the Censors will stop it? I'll try, anyhow. But I'm not in the least sanguine yet that we will start!

I <u>am</u> sorry about poor Bron, and I hope it won't be bad[378]. Isn't he the most gallant thing there ever was? I love little Bab's little letter: but "Niece" is such a distant and uninteresting relationship for <u>her</u>, of all the firebrands on the earth, to choose. I will tell you all about it later; it's all too complicated to write. You will like her <u>awfully</u>.

Goodbye Mummy. All all love Julian.

---

[378] Bron Herbert, Baron Lucas, a Liberal peer; in 1914 he became president of the Board of Agriculture and Fisheries, though without a seat in the cabinet

**215   20 Aug [1914]   Royal Dragoons,   DE/Rv/C1133/71
                            Potchefstroom**

My dear Dad

Thank you very much for your letter. We are starting for Cape Town
tomorrow, with orders to sail by the Dunluce Castle on the 25th; but where we
are going nobody seems to know. There is a lot of talk about German West
Africa; but I don't see that it would be much good to us to take that now; and
it can't do any harm to us out here. I suppose that there is a chance of Egypt:
but I think that most likely we shall go home, to be a sort of stuffing for the
Second Army. Anyhow it is good news to get <u>some</u> orders, after a week of
nothing at all. But every thing is so uncertain that we are expecting to get the
"Stand To" again at any moment. I'm leaving my ponies out here, at a farm,
when I hope that they will not be commandeered.
I'm so glad that you've done great things with the Panshanger Shorthorns. It
is wonderful, for so short a time.
Goodbye, Daddy. Here's hoping to see you in a month!
All love from Julian.

**216   Thursday [nd]   Royal Dragoons,   DE/Rv/C1142/1
                            Potchefstroom**

Sgt Morgan

Can you come to Ventorsdoup with me on Monday, starting from here by
motor at about 12.30 midday, to ride my pony?
Julian Grenfell.
The pony is carrying 8 st 7 lbs, so if you come, do as light as you can. I will
bring a light saddle. JG.

**217   19 Sept 1914   Southampton   DE/Rv/CC1133/72
                            [Hampshire]**

Telegram: Regiment arrived today going Ludgershall[379] tonight Julian.

---

[379] Ludgershall, Wiltshire

218   30 [Sept 1914]   Windmill Hill Camp DE/Rv/C1135/679

Telegram: Cannot get leave but don't think starting immediately Julian

219   2 Oct 1914   Windmill Hill Camp   DE/Rv/C1133/73

Telegram: Could you send me revolver service bore and £25 gold by messenger or by mother if coming tomorrow Julian.

220   5 Oct 1914   Windmill Hill Camp   DE/Rv/C1133/74

Telegram: Send things here today and early tomorrow morning Julian.

**221   Monday [nd,   Western Front   DE/Rv/C1135/685
        5 Oct 1914]**

Darling Mother

Thank you for your letter. We got orders to leave at 10 tonight, and entrain at Amesbury (10 miles) at 1.30 am tomorrow. That was at 5 pm. Now, at 5.15 pm, it's cancelled. So my wire to you this morning was right.
Mr Bart will tell you that my bags were <u>not</u> ordered at Sowter!! But by God's fluke I bought a pair from a man at Tidworth today. So tell Sowter <u>not</u> to send the others. I also bought a revolver. And I expect my Burberry coat will arrive tomorrow. So I'm <u>alright</u> & complete now. Send me an <u>aircushion</u> as soon as you can. I expect we'll go tomorrow anyway.
Goodbye & <u>bless</u> you. J.
6th Cavalry Brigade
3rd Cavalry Division
Expeditionary Force.
Also find out from Burberry whether my coat has arrived, & if not send after me (abroad).

222   6 Oct 1914   Southampton   DE/Rv/C1135/680

Darling Mother

We left Ludgershall at about 1 am this morning, and went 12 miles to
Amesbury, where we entrained at about 4.30 am. Lovely night with blazing
moon, which was very lucky. We got here at 7.30 am, & embarked. <u>Awful</u>
ship for horses, with steep ramps & low ceiling. However they rose to the
occasion and went in like lambs. They say we are going to outside Dover, to
await orders there. I wonder if this will pass the Censor.
We first got orders to entrain yesterday afternoon, & we all packed up. Then
it was all cancelled, & we seemed no nearer than ever. Then at 10.30 pm we
got orders to start at 12.30 pm.
It seems <u>too</u> good to be off at last. Everyone is perfectly bird about it. On
this boat are 2 sqdns of the 2 LGs [Life Guards], & 2 of us. Now we're off.
Bless you J.
Try to get my Burberry cloak. Tell Sowter to stop the saddle bags, as I've
raised a pair.

223   6 Oct 1914   Southampton   DE/Rv/C1133/75

Telegram: At last please recover coat from Burberry and forward tell Sowter
I don't want saddle bags now all love I am glad Julian.

224   Monday   [Windmill Hill Camp]   DE/Rv/C1133/77
**   [5 Oct 1914]**

My dearest Dad

I got a little cavalry revolver (by a <u>great</u> fluke) today, from a man at
Tidworth. So I've taken it, as it's easier to carry mounted: and I've sent
yours back by Mr Bart. It was <u>awfully</u> good of you to take all that trouble
about getting it, and it would have been my salvation if I had not had the luck
to get a service one.
Goodbye Daddy. I expect we'll go tomorrow.
<u>Bless</u> you Julian.

225   6 Oct 1914   Southampton   DE/Rv/C1133/76

Telegram: Embarked here 5 this morning please try to get hold of my coat from Burberry and forward tell Sowter I do not want saddlebags now all love Julian.

226   11 Oct 1914   Western Front   DE/Rv/C1135/681

Darling Mother

I've just been censoring all the men's letters, which are the best things ever. They are all on the one formula
Dear Mary
Hoping this finds you as well as it leaves me
I remain
Your affectionate husband
J. Smith
It is really just as satisfying as a proper letter, and much more restrained and dignified.
We've got within 15 miles of them Germans now, and hope to be at them tomorrow. It's all the best fun one ever dreamed of – and up to now it has only wanted a few shells and a little noise to supply the necessary element of excitement. The uncertainty of it is so good, like a picnic when you don't know where you are going to; and the rush and hustle of trying to settle things in the whole confusion, unpacking & packing up again, and dumping down men and horses in strange fields or houses or towns, and fighting to get water & food and beds for the horses and water and food and beds for the men and oneself, when one knows that probably another start will be made long before anything is got. There are really so many different things to do at the same moment that one does not bother about things one has forgotten or not done, because there is only time to go on with the actual thing of the moment. And the extraordinary thing is that everything does seem to get done, somehow.
We have had great luck with the weather. It has been warm ever since we landed, & bright sun; except one night, when I was of course on "inlying picket", and I had to stay outside all night. We bivouac generally, and billet when we can. The people are quite frantic about us, and they line the roads giving beer and fruit and cakes to us as we ride by. They shout "IP IP

WHERRAY"[380], and "OLAPP" (hold up?) when a horse stumbles. They have got some of the London motor buses out here, carting about supplies and wounded; a great fat red London driver passed us the other day, and shouted at us "Oxford Street, Bank". The buses have still got all the London play bills and advertisements on them. The roads are chock a block with troops and guns and supplies and transport and wounded; and aeroplanes always in the air. It is a wonderfully peaceful looking country here; [*rest of sentence taken out by censor?*]

Here is a list of things in addition to the things you said you would send every week.

Goodbye, Mummy. Give Dad my best love – I am frightfully fit and well, and just exactly where I want to be. Are you welly?

Bless you. J.

We finally left Windmill at about 12.30 am on Tuesday 6th morning, rode to Amesbury and entrained there at 4 am (it was a wonderful night & blazing moon); embarked at Southampton from 7 am, and sailed in the dark early next morning (7th).

Wasn't it luck for me to get saddle bags like that, at the last min[ute].

List of things I want.

X Burberry – the coat I ordered. It did not come in time.

X Map Case, with sling. The folding sort which shut up, because the light catches the open one I got.

X Matches – plenty.

A pipe-lighter, with tinder. You know the sort you light by striking a spark.

A Sou-Wester hat, warm lined, rather big for me. You will get the size from my hats at home.

X my prismatic Compass, which I gave to Steward Strand, and told him to send to Luggershall, or if lost, a new one.

X 3 Battery refills for Stewards (same shop 406 Strand) "Orillux" electric torch[381].

Field glasses, because mine werry out of focus, when I got them cleaned up in London, and are not too good now.

Holdall – a good strong one (not filled), waterproof, leather fittings, to hold hair-brush, razor, knife, fork, spoon, soap, nailbrush, shaving brush, toothbrush.

---

[380] The Belgians' rendering of 'Hip, Hip, Hooray'

[381] Orilux trench torch; it was not standard issue but purchased privately by officers

<u>Toothpaste</u> – one or two tubes.
X <u>Daily Paper</u>
X <u>Candles</u> – 1 doz[en] hard lamp candles, the thick ones.
X Methylated spirits – a <u>tiny</u> tin.

227   15 Oct [1914]   Western Front   DE/Rv/C1135/682

Darling Mother I've just got your letter of Oct 8. I hope the Burberry will
arrive soon, because it rains like cats and dogs every day, and an ordinary
coat just gets and remains sodden. But wet doesn't matter when it is
constant; it's only harmful when it comes as a shock to the system. And we
get indoors every night, in every kind of nook & corner. The inhabitants are
really <u>wonderful</u>, and take trouble no end. You can imagine the fun it is
trying to get a cavalry division, man and horse, into a strange town in the
dark.
Just got your "start of war" letter from Africa.
We've been fighting the German cavalry patrols for the last day or two, but
not much damage to either side. We downed one of their aeroplanes
yesterday, which was good; and exciting – a sudden tremendous burst of fire,
maxims and all. What has done best for us so far is the armoured
mitrailleuse motors[382]. <You can't possibly hit a man in them, from in front
or from behind. So the only thing to do is to get off and into the ditch the
quickest the best.> God help a patrol if one of them comes round the corner.
Luckily we have not seen one of theirs yet. The guns go on all day, & most
of the night. Of course it's very very hard to follow what is going on; even
the squadron leaders know nothing; and one marches and countermarches
without end, backwards & forwards, nearer & further, apparently without
object. Only the Christian virtue of Faith emerges triumphant. It is all the
most <u>wonderful</u> fun; better fun than one could ever imagine. I hope it goes
on a nice long time: but pigsticking will be the only tolerable pursuit after
this, or one will die of sheer ennui. The first time one shoots at a man one
has the feeling of "never point a loaded gun, even in fun": but very soon it
gets like shooting a crocodile, only more amusing, because he shoots back at
you. Our horses have stuck it well so far; of course it was bad to start with
unfit horses, but I suppose the same for everyone, as all the cavalry get unfit
horses after they lose their first lot of fit ones.
I loved one day on the top of Windmillhill: it was too good. You & Daddy

---

[382] Armoured cars

were wonderful at getting me my things. My equipment was <u>splendid</u>, bar the coat. I think we shall hammer these Germans now. But their men and horses, which we have taken, are fat and will-liking, which is a disappointment: I've seen hundreds of old friends; it's good to spot one suddenly in the confusion along the roads.

Tell Moggy I loved her letter to Luggershall. And give all my love to all the family.

I started this letter thinking I wouldn't have time to write more than 3 words. But as we haven't gone yet I've written a book.

I wrote for things 3 days ago, so I won't give a list again. Remember that Mr Bart took back some things from Luggershall, which are in the list.

Goodbye & bless you. How are you? I am <u>extraordinarily</u> fit, and grossly fat still, and I eat everything I lay hands on, and it generally agrees with me. Now they've started chucking some shells this way, so I expect we'll be shifting. J.

The man who has my 4 ponies is Johann Grimbeek – Elandsheurch – Potchefstroom. The man who promised to see them shipped is Mr Quinlan – Experimental Farm – Potchefstroom.

228   17 Oct 1914   Western Front   DE/Rv/C1135/683

Darling Mother

We've left the big fight, which we just got into the edge of, and have gone off against another German army. But it's still marching and countermarching, with everything in the entirely vague and noncommittal stage of the start. Only patrol and outpost fighting. We've knocked up one or two of their patrols. <Only 2 horses & 1 man of ours wounded.> None of us know anything. The Germans seem to be all over the place; and our different allied armies all mixed up. We are going to clear up a forest tomorrow, where there are Germans and three different varieties of allies; so we hope for a fair mixed bag. The worst of this is that when one is coming in or going out on advance patrols, into fog <u>and</u> rain, one is just as likely to get shot by the allied forces as by the Huns. That has happened rather too often.

We've had 2 days complete rest now – today and the day before yesterday – with only advanced troops and patrols fighting. I haven't been on, worse luck. Yesterday they only marched us up a hill, and then marched us a little further back again. We've had two nights in the open, but not really <u>too</u> cold yet. Fog and rain every day. It's always amusing in the morning to see the place one came into in the dark the night before – sometimes a village, sometimes a little outlying field with a cottage or farm. I hope and believe that they have got us ready for our dart now: but each day one says "Tomorrow".

Our horses are <u>well</u>, and getting better every day. But the German horses we have taken look <u>damn</u> well too.

I got today my BURBERRY, posted from Basingstoke to Ludgershall dated 5/10/14. Thank God it has come. It is a topper. Also an air-cushion. Also my compass (sent to Ludgershall). Also some very good waterproof loose leggings. Thank you <u>awfully</u>, Mummy. I am now the world's completest campaigner. I got no letters today, but I expect they have gone wrong and will turn up. No cigarettes or chocolate yet. Will you please send me a tin of Benson & Hedges smoking mixture once a fortnight. I forgot to ask for it. And 100 cigarettes a week will be ample, not 200. If you would like to give me a real treat send me Robert Lewis's cigarettes Balkan Sobranies, small size. I love them better than heaven, but they are v expy [*expensive*]. Tell him to pack them in proper boxes for travelling.

I like the Savoy & Moon peptonised chocolate best, although I know you tried to make me say I didn't. Please send me also woolen <u>mittens</u>, with the fingers open. Also a pair of putties from Thresher & Glennie, the sort that fix with a clip. Also one of <u>LETTS'S Diaries</u> for 1915, bound in limp leather, with 7 days on the 2 pages, very thin. Also a waterproof sleeping bag; the best is the big wooly bag with a loop to pull up over the shoulders, buttoning at the neck. It is made at 115 Fore Street London EC, and I think they make the thin waterproof covering too. Remember the battery refills for the Orilux Lamp (Steward Strand). Send one a week[x]. That lamp has been the salvation of the British Army. My little medicine case has also been so far wasted on my rude health. Hawa's stocking cap is absolutely <u>THE</u> thing, like all Hawa's things! [x There were 2 or 3 in the things Mr Bart took.]

We got a paper today (this morning's London paper, of all extraordinary things) and saw that the Germans have got Ostend. I wonder what troops we have got up there by the sea? It's a great war whatever. Isn't it luck for me to have been born so as to be just the right age and just in the right place – not too high up to be worried – to enjoy it most?

18th. We are living like fighting cocks. The Maconochie tin ration[383] (meat

---

[383] Meat stewed with vegetables and tinned, supplied to British soldiers on active service, originally produced by Messrs Maconochie of Aberdeen (OED)

& vegetables) is delicious when you heat it up. And they give us very good
bread & butter in the houses, and also their beds and everything, without
worrying much whether they get paid or not. The only thing is that we are
eating & resting too much, and doing too little, just at present. It has been
the same lately with all the other cavalry fellows, who have been out here all
the time. Most of them have got very fat and lazy of late. Isn't that unlike
one's ideas of war? But the all-pervading thrill of interest makes even
bivouacking in a field interesting.

Rumours today (18th) of four German destroyers sunk off Ostend, I hope it is
right. But how did they get to Ostend?

Best best love to everyone.

My corporal said today (he's an atheist), as he looked at one of the little
shrines – "what tires me in this bloody country is Jesus Christ and all his
relations in glass cases at every bloody corner".

Goodbye, & bless you J.

PS Could you also get me a service jacket from <u>Daniels</u> Bury Street, the
same exactly as the one he made for me this month (lined), only made of
<u>riding-breeches material</u>. I also enclose stuma[384] cheque from Loughborough
in S Africa. You might keep it safe. I expect the African bank will try to get
the money from me soon.

229   24 Oct 1914   Western Front   DE/Rv/C1135/684

Darling Mother

I got your letter of the 17th two days ago: and also one of yours from South
Africa! And today one of Dad's of the 22nd, brought by Charlie Burn. Also
two boxes of cigarettes, which was heaven, after Belgian cigarettes or
nothing.

<u>Oct 27</u> – we've been in the trenches for 2 days and nights since I started this;
but no excitements, except a good dose of shrapnel 3 times a day, which does
one no harm, and rather relieves the monotony. I've got ½ my troop, 12
men, in this trench, in a root field; with the rest of the sqdn about 100 yards
each side of us, and a farm, half knocked down by shells, just behind us. We
get our rations sent up once a day in the dark, and two men creep out to cook
us tea in the quiet intervals. Tea is the great mainstay on service, as it was in

---

[384] A forged or dishonoured cheque (OED)

manoevres and treks. The men are <u>splendid</u>, and as happy as schoolboys. We've got plenty of straw at the bottom of the trench, which is better than any feather-bed. We only had one bad night, when it pelted rain for 6 hrs. It's not <u>very</u> cold yet: and we've had 2 or 3 fine days.

They have just sent up our mail to us – a letter from you, & one from Dad, & one from Casie, dated 11th and 12th. Also some chocolate. I expect you don't know where we are now? I tried to keep as far as I could from the boundary line of censorship. I wonder if we have brought down many of their <u>aeroplanes</u> by rifle fire? They are a constant source of annoyance to us.

We have not seen any of the German infantry from this trench – only one patrol and a sniper or two. Their guns too are out of sight; but only about a mile off; hardly that, I believe. The country is so fearfully enclosed.

I suppose if any "relations" knew of our whereabouts, it would be <u>instantly</u> traced back to the writer? Which would be a terrible thing indeed.

Our first day's real close-up fighting was Monday 19th. We cavalry went on about a day and ½ in front of the infantry. We got into a village, and our advanced patrols started fighting hard, with a certain amount of fire from everywhere in front of us. Our advanced patrols gained the first groups of houses, and we joined them. Firing came from a farm in front of us, & then a man came out of it and waved a white flag. I yelled "200 – white flag – rapid fire"; but Hardwick stopped me shooting. Then the squadron advanced across the root fields towards the farm (dismounted, in open order) – and they opened a sharp fire on us from the farm and the next fields. We took 3 prisoners in the roots, and retired to the horses again. That was our first experience of them – the white flag dodge. We lost 2, and 1 wounded. Then I got leave to make a dash across a field for another farm, where they were sniping at us. I could only get half way. My sergeant was killed, & my corporal hit. We lay down; luckily it was high roots, & we were out of sight. But they had fairly got our range, and the bullets kept knocking up the dirt into one's face and all round. We just lay doggo[385] for about ½ hr, and then the firing slackened, and we crawled back, to the houses and the rest of the sq[ua]d[ro]n.

I <u>was</u> pleased with my troop, under bad fire; they used the most filthy language, talking quite quietly, and laughing, all the time; even after the men were knocked over within a yard of them. I longed to be able to say that I liked it, after all one has heard of being under fire the first time. But it's bloody. I pretended to myself for a bit that I liked it; but it was no good; it

---

[385] To lie quiet, to remain hidden (OED)

only made one careless and unwatchful and self-absorbed. But when one acknowledged to oneself that it <u>was</u> bloody, one became alright again, and cool.

After the firing had slackened, we advanced again a bit, into the next group of houses, which were the edge of the village proper. I can't tell you how <u>muddling</u> it is. We did not know whether our own troops had come round us, on the flanks, or whether they had stopped behind and were firing into us. And besides, a lot of German snipers were left in the houses we had come through, and every now and then bullets came singing by, from God knows where. Four of us were talking and laughing in the road, when about a dozen bullets came with a whistle. We all dived for the nearest door, which happened to be a clar, and fell over each other, yelling with laughter. It was a very dirty clar. James Lechie, the Old Old Man, said "I have a bullet through the seat of my best Sandon twilette breeches"[386]. We looked, and he had; it had gone clean through. He did not tell us till two days afterwards that it had gone through one of his buttocks too! None of us knew, till he went up to the doctor on Wednesday, and said "Please will you wash my bottom; a bullet went through it". We still laughed; but there it was, like the holes you make in an egg to blow it, only about 4 inches apart.

We stopped about 2 hrs. Then the cav[alry] regt on our right retired. Then we saw a lot of Germans among the fires they had lit (they set the houses on fire to mark their line of advance). They were running from house to house. We were told not to fire, for fear of our own people on the other side. I was furthest troop out, in a house at the edge of the main village. Then came a lot of them, shouting and singing and advancing down the street, through the burning houses. One felt a peculiar hatred for them. I sent back word that I could not stay there and the sq[ua]d[ro]n retired, without losing much. We heard afterwards that there had been a division of their infantry in front of us. At first we thought there were only one or two patrols of them.

We retired about 2 miles, & dismounted for action. Soon they began to come up from 3 sides of us, and we retired again. They were pretty close, advancing higgledy-piggledy across the field, & firing. They shot <u>abominably</u> (nothing like the morning, from the houses, when they had all the ranges marked to a yard) – we lost only about 20 horses. No men killed. Watkin Wynn (do you remember Hell-Fire Herbert in my story) had his horse shot under him, when they were within about 200 yds. He was next troop in

---

[386] Sandon were breeches-makers, based in Bond Street, London

front of me. He suddenly got complete <u>fou rire</u>[387], when he saw me. I got him a spare horse, and he was still laughing, and saying over and over again with a sort of triumph "Look at the bastards". We only trotted away. A man in my troop kept raising his cap to the Germans, saying "3rd class shots, 3rd class shots". We retired behind our guns that night, and the infantry came up next day, and took up their positions.

The next day we went forward to another place and entrenched ourselves against a very big German force, with orders to hold out as long as we could. But they took a long time deploying for attack, and we only had to face their guns. Poor Kid Charrington was killed. They pushed us pretty hard back to our infantry. We were supposed to have done well.

Since that we have been doing infantry work in the trenches. We have been out of work in our trenches: only shrapnel & snipers. Someone described this war as "Months of boredom punctuated by moments of terror". It is sad that it is such an impossible place for cavalry. Cavalry work against far superior forces of infantry, like we had the other day, is not good enough. The Germans are damn good at that house to house fighting business. It is <u>horrible</u> having to leave one's horses; it feels like leaving half oneself behind, and one feels the dual responsibility all the time; besides which it depletes our already small numbers, for horse-holders. I hope we get them on the run soon; then will come our chance. They have been having terrific fighting in the line on each side of us, and it has gone well.

I <u>adore</u> war. It is like a big picnic without the objectlessness of a picnic. I've never been so well or so happy. Nobody grumbles at one for being dirty. I've only had my boots off once in the last ten days; and only washed twice. We are up and standing to our rifles by 5 am when doing this infantry work; and saddled up by 4.30 am when with our horses. Our poor horses don't get their saddles off when we are in trenches.

The wretched inhabitants here have got practically no food left. It is miserable to see them leaving their houses and trekking away with great bundles and children in their hands. And the dogs and cats left in the deserted villages are piteous.

---

[387] Laughed madly

9/ It is sad that it is such an impossible place for cavalry. Cavalry work against far superior forces of infantry, like we had the other day, is not good enough. The Germans are Damn good at that house to house fighting business. It is horrible having to leave ones horses; it feels like leaving half oneself behind, and one feels the dual responsibility all the time; besides which it depletes our already small numbers, for horse-holders. I hope we get them on the run soon; then will come our chance. They have been having terrific fighting on the line on each side of us, and it has gone well.

I adore war. It is like a big picnic without the objectlessness of a picnic. I've never been so well or so happy. Nobody grumbles at one for being dirty. I've only had

Extract from letter from Western Front, 24 October 1914

Oct 28. We were relieved after dark last night. Althorp, of the 1st LG [Life Guards] relieved me with his troop. We're back here in our old bivouac, where we were shelled out by Jack Johnsons[388] the other night, for a day's

---

[388] Large guns, from the name of a noted American Negro boxer, whose nickname was 'The Big Smoke' (OED)

rest. I got today, your letter of the 23rd, also Dad's & Casie's. Yes, you are a really great War Mother. All emotion is fatal now. Today arrived

Tooth Paste
Daily Mails (2)
Candles
Chocolate
Sou Wester (a <u>topper</u>) [just the thing]
Mittens (d[itt]o)

What I want most now is

<u>Sleeping cap</u> (Hawa's pattern with ear holes – I lost mine – Have already written for this)
<u>Writing paper</u>, & <u>small</u> writing case.

What the men want most (I asked them) is

Cigarettes
Mufflers
Mittens
Note paper, and esp <u>envelopes</u>.

They only got 8 cigarettes a man out of the last dole, which is miserable.
Most of them like cigarettes far better than tobacco.
I expect the other things you mentioned in your letter to me will arrive in due course.
What I am most undecided about is underclothes etc. I'll try to get them washed; but we've had no chance yet. If not, I'll try to send the dirty ones home in a parcel. Anyhow, could you send out one <u>big</u> coloured handkerchief a week? And one of my khaki shirts, when you get this; and one suit thick underclothing, if Mr Bart took one from Luggershall.
It's not much good sending little tins of cocoa or coffee. If one gets warm things, one gets them cooked all together with the officers mess (sqdn) or the men (troop).
I can't make out what has happened to the Battle of the Aisne³⁸⁹. It seems to have got tired and died?
I wish our Royals had had more fighting. We've been unlucky about trenches; we've always had the quiet ones, so far.
Mummy, will you <u>promise</u> on your <u>honour</u>, to show my letters to Bron?
Because short letters are no good, and I can't write Times Histories, like this,

---

³⁸⁹ The First Battle of the Aisne, 13-28 September 1914. See, for example, M M Evans, *Battles of World War I* (2004)

to my numerous clientele of friends. The plan I am working on at present is to write one (long) to the monde, and one (shortish and highly coloured) to the demi-monde, whenever occasion arises.

If you only knew what fun it is out here!

Please give Dad my best love, and thank him <u>awfully</u> for his letters;

My dear Dad

I am only writing one letter for you and Mummy and all the respectables, because the A.S.C.[390] do not supply enough paper for two of this sort.

Yr ever affectionate Julian.

Good stories.

'The Indians had 2 men killed direct'.

"All wars are good, but this is a bot' atcha war. Now we advance".

Colonel of French regt on our flank the other day at -. When the Germans were coming round that flank, sitting in a pub in the village. They started firing their maxim gun. Colonel and his orderly rushed into the street and each discharged 10 rounds quick out of their rifles, then returned to their drinks.

If you could sent one bottle whisky and one bottle brandy for our little squadron mess, we should be thankful to you for evermore.

Best of best love.

I hope they will hurry up the big guns at Woolwich. It's horrible when they put Jack Johnsons into one's bivouac at night from about 12 miles off. You can hear them coming for about 30 seconds, and judge whether they are coming straight for you, or a little to one side.

Goodbye & bless you J.

230   24 Oct 1914   Western Front   DE/Rv/C1134/20

My darling Mother & Dad

Charlie Burn has just arrived here, so I've got 5 minutes to write one line for him to take before he goes again. He brought Dad's letter with him. We've had it pretty hot this last day or two: in the <u>trenches,</u> we take to it like ducks to water and dig much better trenches than the infantry, and <u>far</u> quicker. We're all awfully well, except those who have stopped something. We've been fighting night and day; first rest today, for about 4 days. The worst of it is <u>no</u> sleep, practically. I can't tell you how wonderful our men were, going

---

[390] Army Service Corps, responsible for transport and supplies

straight for the first time into a fierce fire. They surpassed my utmost expectations. I've never been so fit or nearly so happy in my life before; I adore the fighting and the continual interest which compensates for every disadvantage. We've only had cavalry these days in this part of the line, and I imagine it has been rather critical; but all goes well. Horses are not much good in this country and in this fighting. The German guns are terribly good, they have spies everywhere, signalling to them by night and day; and they pick you up wherever you go.

No time for more now. I've written to you about things I want. I had 2 battery refills in the things Bart took from Luggershall. I want another of Hawa's sleeping caps, with holes for the ears.

I am awfully glad you're so well: you must be <u>frightfully</u> busy, with all your things. How is the big commerce scheme going.

All love from J.

231   2 Nov 1914   Western Front   DE/Rv/C1134/21

Darling Mother & Dad

Here we are, in the burning centre of it; and I would not be anywhere else for a million pounds and the Queen of Sheeba included. The only thing is that there's no job for cavalry. So we are just become infantry, and man the trenches. I believe we're getting entrenching tools, which is good hearing, we want them. Col Burn is taking this, so I've only time to write one word of love.

He's off.

He tells me I was reported dead. But there's life in the old dog yet.

Bless you both Julian.

Things arriving splendidly from you. Are you both well? Thank you for your letters today.

Arrived today

> Tobacco
> Socks
> Woolen band

232   3 Nov 1914   Western Front   DE/Rv/C1135/686

Darling Mother

I sent you a scrap of a letter yesterday by Col Burn. Wasn't it sad about his
son – his first days soldiering! My things are arriving splendidly. Yesterday
came (in addition to what I've already acknowledged)

> Holdall (capital)
> Lamp refills
> Pipe lighter (beauty)
> Tobacco
> Woolen belt
> Socks.   Methylated spirit (thank God)
>   Daily Mails

What I want most now is

> Sleeping cap (Hawa's earhole pattern)
> Handkerchiefs (1 a week)
> Brandy – a bottle w[oul]d be <u>ripping</u> now & then
> Writing papers & envelopes
> A few <u>hard</u> pencils
> Methylated Spirit once a week

Some of these I have already written to you for.

I asked you to stop the tins of café au lait. But please <u>send</u> them. They have
been very useful just lately. Two a week. They <u>are</u> good, and such a fall-
back when one sleeps away from the wagons. Stop sending pipe tobacco.
I've got plenty.

And I am now the most completely outfitted soldier of the Expeditionary
Force. I have everything I want. You have been too <u>wonderful</u> at sending
the right things.

No matter about putties. The sleeping bag as per picture is just what I
wanted. It hasn't arrived yet. Nor has the map-case.

How splendid about Casie coming out here – and you coming with her!
Please thank her awfully for her darling letters. I wish I had time to write to
her; but there really isn't. Also Daddee. Can you show her my letters? The
recruiting in England seems to be going splendidly: it will be necessary too,
from what one can see.

To carry on my history of my personal exploits in the war – I got in my last
letter to our first days in the trenches. The next day we had a real hot time,
in a sort of small salient in the line. "A" Sqdn was holding it – held it for 5

days and nights, unrelieved. On the 6th day I took my troop up to reinforce; and 2 more troops came up afterwards. The shrapnel was coming about 2 shells a minute; you could not hear yourself speak. But we were well dug in, and we only got hit when a shell burst absolutely in the trench. It was almost all gun fire; the Germans don't use their infantry most days; they are getting tired of that attack in massed battalions. We held on till latish in the afternoon, when our ammunition was almost out, and the German infantry began to mass in front. Then we retired. That was when Burn was killed. We took position again in a wood about ¼ mile behind. The Germans did not come on that night. I believe we got great kudos. The Toe Guards relieved us at 1.30 that night and we got back to our poor horses, who had been standing, saddled up, all the time – as they do now every day, and all day, and most of the night. There is no work for cavalry; so we are just mobile infantry, without entrenching tools. We form the Corps Reserve. "Oh yes, bloody Knight Errants" said one of our men. "No, night and day bloody errants" said another. Little Watkin Wynn said (re having no spades) "Foxes have holes and the birds of the air have nests[391], but the bloody Dragoons have not [sic] where to lay their heads".

I have not washed for a week, or had my boots off for a fortnight. But we cook good hot food in the dark in the morning before we start, and in the night when we get back to the horses, and we take our good cold rations with us in the daytime. It is all the best fun; I've never felt so well or happy, or enjoyed anything so much. It just suits my stolid health and stolid nerves and barbaric disposition. The fighting excitement vitalises everything – every sight and word and action. One loves one's fellow man so much more when one is bent on killing him. And picknicking in the open day and night (we never see a roof now) is the only real method of existence. There is loads of straw to bed down on, and one sleeps like a log, and wakes up with the dew on one's face. The stolidity of my nerves surprises myself: I went to sleep the other day when we were lying low in the trenches, with the shrapnel bursting within 50 yds all the time, and a din like nothing on earth! The noise is continual and indescribable. The Germans shell the trenches with shrapnel all day and all night, and the reserves and ground in rear with Jack Johnsons, which last one gets to love as old friends. You hear them coming for miles, and everyone imitates the noise; then they burst with a plump, and make a great hole in the ground, doing no damage unless they fall into your

---

[391] Quotation from Luke ch 9 verse 58

237

trench or onto your hat. They burst pretty nearly straight upwards. One landed within 10 yds of me the other day, and only knocked me over, and my horse; we both got up and looked at each other and laughed. It didn't even knock my cigarette out of my mouth.

We are all waiting in a wood with our horse – (as we do every day, till we are called for somewhere). Yesterday we only went out as supports. The day before we relieved a regiment in the firing line. They had been under shrapnel & JJs for 2 days. One will never forget the look on those men's faces: utter weariness and numbness and carelessness.

Our men are splendid – really splendid. One marvels at them. We shall beat these bloody German swine by sticking it out – the old "Bull-dog breed" joke. We shall muddle through somehow.

Alastair had a great story yesterday – a real Alastair[392]. He was told to rally some men and take up position, by a windy general. He said "Right you are, general" – and to the men – all of different regiments "Follow me, you men". When he got to the crest he looked round, and found one Scotchman behind him. They waited for some time, discussing together their chances of escape. Suddenly the Germans came in sight, and the man said quietly "Thatt changes ma doubt to a certainty – we're doon forr".

We took a German officer and some men prisoners in a wood the other day. I felt hatred for them, after our dead, and as the officer came by me I scowled at him – and the men were cursing at them. The officer looked me in the face and saluted me as he passed; and I've never seen a man look so proud and resolute and smart and confident – in his hour of bitterness. He made me feel terribly ashamed of myself.

How are your work-parties going? I told you the men wanted mittens, gloves, mufflers, stocking caps, cigarettes, and writing paper and envelopes most. They have not got much yet – and very small doles of cigarettes. But I expect the thing has not really got working yet. And their own things have lasted them so far. And the real cold has not set in yet.

How is your Red X [Cross] going?

I wonder if we shall be able to let the Pans[hanger] shooting.

All all love to you & Daddee and Bill, Mogsy & Casie. I think of you always J.

We have not been called on today yet (12 noon).

Nov 4th. We did nothing yesterday – stayed in reserve all day, which is a

---

[392] Presumably Alastair Sutherland-Leveson-Gower who was known for his stories. Also, this refers to a real person, rather than to 'Alastair' the illustrator (see letter 127)

good general sign, I suppose, but damned boring for us. Never mind. I feel in my heart that the time will come when we get right into those grey-blue coats; with our swords and horses. I think every man in the regiment is praying for that day.

Arrived today

> 6 Daily Mails
> Cigarettes, beautiful Balkans, from R Lewis
> Chocolate
> Lamp refills.

The cigarettes arrived in a <u>china</u> box! Tell Mr Lewis from me that the Lord did not allot a fair share of intelligence to him or to his forefathers in the Creation. Also tell him to get a tin box next time, as china almost invariably breaks.

I got a letter from Casie, dated Oct 27. Please thank her <u>awfully</u>.

We sallied out at 2 o'clock this morning under a blazing moon – all the division (cav[alry]), each from his fold or wood, to a hole made in the line. But it was patched up before we got there, so back we came again for another hour's sleep.

Did I tell you the good description of the war from a cavalry p[oin]t of view? "Months of boredom punctuated by moments of terror".

I think our papers lie more about the war than the Germans. Anyhow, it's a great war whatever. It's very interesting to hear about South Africa. This morning is the first I've heard about De Wet and Beyers. It was good that they fixed Delarey in time. Botha is some man, isn't he? I told you when I came home that they would fight us: but nobody would believe me. Thank heaven we got out of the country first, or we should have missed this.

Please send

> 1 stick Williams' Shaving Soap
> 1 piece Coal Tar Soap
> 1 hand towel
> 1 large enamelled mug cup with handle

Post just going now.

What are the <u>Canadians</u> like?

Our 3rd K.D.G.s [King's Dragoon Guards?] are not here yet, but we expect them every day.

Goodbye & bless you all J.

We are off saddled now, for the first time since I don't know when. I feel terribly clean and uncomfortable, after shaving & washing my tooties.

How is Mogsy. I hope she has not relapsed from rheumatism into chronic gout. It's the worst of belonging to one of these old <u>port</u>-drinking families. It is extraordinary the different rumours one gets about the war. One day utter despair, and the next hour triumphant optimism.

233   6 Nov [1914]   Western Front   DE/Rv/C1135/687

Darling Mother

Another day's rest since I wrote to you last; and last night the regiment left the horses here, at a little farm, in the fields, and went out into trenches, to relieve the infantry for six hours. They are due back tonight. I was left to look after the horses, which I <u>hated</u>. We've heard that the regiment came under very heavy shell fire, but lost only 1 man hit. The whole cav[alry] division went to the trenches. The 3rd K.D.G.s [King's Dragoon Guards?] have arrived, and went out too. So now our brigade is full strength (3 regts). When we go out like this we leave the horses saddled up, and 1 officer & 8 men per sqdn with them. It is a hopeless position, because one had not enough men to move the horses if one comes under shell fire. We all sleep out with the horses. The 10th officers and our lot have meals in the farm, leaving only 1 room to the poor inmates; who are lucky, however, not to have been eaten up by Germans or shelled down and burnt by either side, up to the present.
I sleep like a log of a night time – hundreds of blankets, and Daddie's Canadian coat, and 2 waterproof sheets. The wet is the worst; everything is sodden, although we've had 2 fine days today & yesterday. I'm longing for my waterproof sleeping bag. Could you send me another Woolen stomach-belt because I gave mine to one of my men, who had bad flue. Also another Souwester hat like the last, which I left hurriedly in a very hot trench. Also another (not so large) Flask which I left my old one hurriedly ditto. I'm afraid the blasted Germans have got them now.
They seem to think it's going <u>well</u> now, after a shaky bit. But one gets terribly little information here; and what one gets is always contradicted the next day. One hears that the Germans are retiring in train loads: and the next minute there is a vicious night attack.
I'm in such a bad temper I can't write any more. Its horrible to think that one might just as well be in Piccadilly Circus for all the good one is doing; and much better, for all the pleasure one is getting.
Are you welly, Mummy?

Is it true the Canadians are absolutely untrained?
The French troops here say that "les Hindus" [393] cannot stand shell-fire; but that is probably pure invention, like everything else.
Goodbye – all all love from J.

234   13 Nov 1914   Western Front   DE/Rv/C1135/688

Darling Mother

Thank you awfully for your letters – 2, I think, since I wrote last; and a lot of things.
<u>In a house!! Nov 15 1914</u>
I've made a list of all the things that have arrived, as far as I can remember them – and of the things I want. You don't know how <u>wonderful</u> the whisky was – in this cold. If you could have seen the look on the faces of "B" Sqdn mess when I said I had got some, you would feel as 10:1 compared with the Good Samaritan! But it only lasted 2 hours. I think that the others are getting some sent out now. And I've made endeavours to get some sent out with our monthly food-boxes. I gave the cigarettes to the men, also, the writing-paper. They are getting plenty of smokeables now; and there was a dole of woolen things to them the other day. Mufflers, gloves, and wooly waistcoats are the things they want most. I like getting the things for my own troop <u>myself</u>; as it is nice to be able to give them things oneself, and it makes sure of them getting them. My goodness, they will want warm things now!
It's our first morning of snow today. It's been raining a lot lately, and the roads and fields and even the insides of the houses are two inches deep in slush; while the trenches of course are just muck-pits. We've been doing all shelled trench work lately, and it's horrible. You just lie there, hunched up; and all day long the shells burst – just outside the trench, if you're lucky, and just inside, if you're unlucky. Anyhow the noise is appalling, and one's head is rocking with it by the end of the day. They generally start about 8, and go on till 4.30 pm.
<u>Nov 18. In the same house</u>. They had us out again for 48 hrs trenches while I was writing the above. I can't write with a pencil. About the shells – after a day of them one's nerves are really absolutely beaten down. I can understand now why our infantry <u>have</u> to retreat sometimes; a sight which

---

[393] Presumably members of the Gurkha regiments fighting in France

came as a shock to one at first, after having been brought up in the belief that the English infantry cannot retreat.

But these last two days we had quite a different kind of trench – in a dripping sodden wood, with the German trench in some places 40 yds ahead. Too close for them to shell us. Dead Germans lying all along in front. Most of the trees, (fir trees) cut down by bullets and shrapnel and piled along the ground, with the branches sticking up over the ground.

We had been awfully worried by their snipers, all along; and I had always been asking for leave to go out and have a try myself. Well on Tuesday 16th, day before yesterday, they gave me leave. [Note I carried this letter and paper in my pocket all through my crawls. Hence the artistic edges]. Only after great difficulty. They told me to take a section with me; and I said I would sooner cut my throat and have done with it. So they let me go alone. Off I crawled, through the sodden clay and branches, going about a yard a minute, and listening & looking as I thought it was not possible to look & listen. I went out to the right of our lines, where the 10th were, & where the Germans were nearest. I took about 30 minutes to do 30 yds. Then I saw the Hun trench, and I waited for a long time, but could see or hear nothing. It was about 10 yds from me. Then I heard some Germans talking, and saw one put his head up over some bushes about 10 yds behind the trench. I could not get a shot at him; I was too low down; and of course I couldn't get up. So I crawled on again very slowly to the parapet of their trench. It was very exciting. I was not sure that there might not have been someone there – or a little further along the trench. I peered through their loophole, and saw nobody in the trench. Then the German behind put his head up again. He was laughing and talking. I saw his teeth glisten against my foresight, and I pulled the trigger very steady. He just gave a grunt and crumpled up. The others got up and whispered to each other. I don't know which were the most frightened, they or me. I think there were 4 or 5 of them. They couldn't place the shot. I was flat behind their parapet and hidden. I just had the nerve not to move a muscle and stay there. My heart was fairly hammering. They did not come forward; and I could not see them, as they were behind some bushes and trees. So I crept back, inch by inch.

I went out again in the afternoon, in front of our bit of the line. About 60 yds off I found their trench again – empty again. I waited there for an hour, but saw nobody. Then I went back, because I did not want to get inside some of their patrols, who might have been placed forward. I reported the trench empty.

The next day just before dawn I crawled out there again, and found it empty again. Then a single German came through the wood towards the trench. I saw him 50 yds off. He was coming along upright quite carelessly, making a great noise. I heard him before I saw him. I let him get within 25 yds, and shot him in the heart. He never made a sound. Nothing for 10 minutes; then there was noise and talking, and a lot of them came along through the wood behind the trench, about 40 yds from me. I counted about 20, and there were more coming. They halted in front, and I picked out the one I thought was the officer or sergeant. He stood facing the other way, and I had a steady shot at him behind the shoulders. He went down, and that was all I saw – I went back at a sort of galloping crawl to our lines, and sent a message to the 10th that the Germans were moving up their way in some numbers. Half an hour afterwards they attacked the 10th and our right in massed formation, advancing slowly to within 10 yds of the trenches. We simply <u>mowed</u> them down; it was rather horrible. I was too far to the left – they did not attack our part of the line; but the 10th told me in the evening. They counted 200 dead in a little bit of the line. <The 10th and us only lost 10!!> They have made quite a ridiculous fuss about my stalking, and getting the message through; I believe they are going to send me up to our general and all sorts. It was only up to someone to do it – instead of leaving it all to the Germans, and losing 2 officers a day through snipers. All our men have started it now. It's the popular amusement.

We were relieved by Territorials last night at 9 pm, and got back here at 2 am this morning, to food and bed – tired out. The men sleep in a barn; the poor horses outside still, in a pitiless frost. The reliefs in the dark are rather wonderful; the new line creeping up, and popping in to the trenches, as the old lot pop out; with the snipers shooting away at you all the time, and probably the German trenches too.

I got your letters of the 10th yesterday; and your's and Dad's & Moggie's (by messenger) of the 14th today. Please thank them and you frightfully. The fleecy waterproof helmet from Cording is the best rain-proof and mud-proof you ever saw – I love it.

<u>How</u> <u>awfully</u> good of Putty[394]. I will write to him tomorrow. Of course it is the best <u>kind</u> of staff job that I could possibly get. But (A) I feel I am doing far more good as a fighting-line soldier than I ever would on the staff: (B) I should not like it nearly so well as roughing it out with my own friends and my own men: (C) even if I wanted to go, the Colonel would never let me,

---

[394] General Sir William Pulteney (1861-1941). Julian had been offered the job of his aide-de-camp (Mosley, p368)

because we are now so woefully short of officers – I asked him tonight, just as a matter of curiosity: (D) I should have to be clean and well-mannered, which has now become a matter of impossibility to me. But I <u>do</u> think that it is good of him. I'll write to him, saying that you have told me of the <u>chance</u>. I believe that we have really worn most of the heart out of these Huns now; and that sooner or later, perhaps sooner, we will have our slap back at them, and work after our own hearts.

I never know how much I can say, because of the Censor. I expect I keep far <u>too</u> wide of the dividing line.

Mummy darling, <u>don't</u> publish my letters; because I think that things which one can write in a letter look somehow vainglorious and swaggery when they are in print.

They are talking of taking us back a bit for a week to rest and refit; and of not putting us in the trenches any more. We've certainly had a hardish go. <u>Best best</u> love to the family. How is Billa-boy? It is <u>too angelic</u> of Wa and the servants to send things for my men. Please thank them tremendously from me, and the men. (I have 35 in my troop). (There are 150 in the sqdn). Send them to <u>me</u>. A <u>lot</u> of clothes arrived for the regt today. Put your card in saying who they are from, so that the Colonel can acknowledge receipt. I will write to the Editor of the Maidenhead Advertiser, and enclose here. I do think it <u>good</u> of them all to have made the things; and never were things of greater use & blessing.

Goodbye & <u>bless</u> you J.

<u>Things wanted (A), Nov 12</u>
<u>Cording's waterproof leggings</u> – the pair you sent were not long enough – the strap would not come up high enough to fix on. I have torn them badly. They are <u>most</u> useful things.
<u>Waterproof bed</u> roll – ~~none has arrived yet~~. Yes, arrived today (15)
<u>Billy (portable kettle)</u>, with spirit lamp inside, in leather case to go on saddle
<u>Methylated spirit</u> – 1 a week – only 1 can arrived yet.
<u>Silk socks</u> – 2 pr, to wear under other socks
<u>Handkerchiefs</u> – 2 a week, for love of God. Only 1 arrived up to now.
<u>Envelopes & writing paper</u>.
<u>Small towel</u> – could you send one a fortnight?
"<u>Times</u>" instead of "Daily Mail", which is hateful.
<u>A leather waistcoat</u> – <u>with leather sleeves</u> – Daniels in Bury St have got my measures, but please tell them to make it <u>well on the big side</u>.
My <u>hunting spurs</u> (with very short necks & blunted rowels) if Mr Bart can

find them, and their straps.) [I think] they are in boot box
<u>Whisky & Brandy</u> (esp Brandy) is of course above rubies.
<u>Knife</u> – strong field knife with tin-opener. Mine was blown away by a shell.
<u>Novel</u> – is there a good Chesterton after the Flying Inn[395] – or a good late
Wells? I <u>might</u> have time now, and one <u>does</u> want a switch-off for the mind!
<u>Wrist-compass</u>, luminous. They have got them at the A & NSC[396]

<u>Things arrived (B), Nov 13</u>
Map case – I think I acknowledged before
Cigarettes for men
Writing paper & envelopes, for men
Underclothing, for me
Stocking cap, & letter from Hawa – please thank her awfully. It's a topping
cap. Also another, which I gave to the men.
Woolen belts
Holdall – a beauty. Did I thank you for it?
Chocolate
<u>Nov 15</u>
Sleeping bag & waterproof cover – ideal
1 bott Whisky – alright
1 bott Brandy – broken
<u>Nov 18</u>
New <u>sleeping cap & Balaclava cap</u> combined, which is the ideal.
5 Handkerchiefs – hurrah – I've been blowing me nose on me ands till today.
1 Towel – hurrah
writing case – just the right size and shape. You are a <u>genius</u> at getting the
<u>right</u> things.
Chocolate
Methylated spirits
1 pr Socks
I lovely big Mug with handle
The things for my soldier servant; he <u>loves</u> them.
Woolen belts.

---

[395] *The Flying Inn* by G K Chesterton (1914)
[396] Army & Navy Stores Co-operative, Victoria Street, London

235   22 Nov 1914   Western Front   DE/Rv/C1133/78

My darling Dad

Thank you so much for all your letters. You have been very good in writing so many, and I have loved getting them. I expect you are most frightfully busy too. It was good getting 1500 at Pans[hanger], after the preserves had been disturbed by the army! I hope that Germany is getting no more copper. I wrote Mother a long letter 2 days ago, when we came out of the trenches. Our last day then was really most exciting. Now we have come back 20 miles to rest and refit – for a week, they say, or 10 days. There is about an inch of snow, and hard frost every night; but sun in the daytime, and altogether much better weather than the rain and slush which we had before. I think our men are very fit; our losses in officers have been very heavy, as you will have seen. I would not think of the staff, when the regt wants officers so badly: but it was very kind of Putty to suggest it. Our horses have stuck it wonderfully; just think what it means for them to stand out all night now, with only one very small blanket. There does not seem to be much prospect of cavalry work for us just at present.

From what one can see of it, the German heavy guns are excellent, and their spying system very thorough. Their Jack Johnsons just follow you about, even when you are two or three miles behind the firing line. But their infantry tactics are extraordinary. I think we must have rather knocked the heart out of them here now. The Tenth, who were next to us in the trenches the other day, were standing on the top of their parapet yelling for them to come on, just before their infantry attacked. Then they simply <u>mowed</u> them down. They were all big men – I think it must have been their Guards. (I saw them within 40 yds when I was out sniping, just before they attacked). We are living in a farm-house now, very comfortable; with the men sleeping in barns. I have never felt so fit in my life: but I like the fighting part better than the resting part. Your Canadian coat is the admiration of all beholders, and does me very well. I hope you are fit and well, and that all the family is flourishing. It was great fun for me to see you all again for a little before coming out.

Goodbye. Very best love from Julian.

How is the prize herd of kine?

Who were the guns when you shot at Pans[hanger]?

236   28 Nov 1914   Folkestone [Kent]   DE/Rv/C1133/79

Telegram: Arriving Victoria 3.15 this afternoon will come Taplow tonight are you at home wire Bath Club Julian.

237   4 Dec 1914   Western Front   DE/Rv/C1135/689

Darling Mother

Weren't our 3 days awful fun? I've never loved 3 days better. It was absolutely perfect, and better from being so unexpected. What news have you got? Everyone here seems to think that we are going to wait here till the spring, as the French have no intention of moving one inch forwards (or backwards). If this is so, I quite agree with you that the ratepayers ought to raise tallywhack and tandem. And think of the awful boredom of it for us! Meanwhile great fittings-up and reorganisation are going on here – we are being taught new ways of digging trenches, and of taking trenches, and of retaking trenches. The Scouts now lead everything, under the newest regime. Hurrah! I am now the second most important person in England to K[itchener] and Lord French[397]. Next in magnitude to the Scouts come the Snipers; and I have been made Organiser and General-in-Chief of the Regimental Corps of Snipers. So I am working day and night, making men crawl through the mud steering by the stars! The new idea is that the Scouts lead night attacks, right in front so that unless shot by the blasted Huns, we get bayoneted (with much cheering) by the Sons of the Empire.
Which will all be great fun, and God damn all Little Englanders!
I thought (no I didn't) –
A stove has arrived, a most glorious thing. If I ever get it into the trenches I will use it as a mortar for night attacks. Also a pair of hawking gauntlets. I retract everything I said against them. They are perfect. Beautiful and useful – and never to be taken off. They are really the best things ever. Why doesn't everyone wear them. They are warm, and you can slip them off directly. Also a letter, grumbling about nothing from me. Also inc – 1 pr gloves & 1 cummerbund.
Your cake will be glorious for the mess. And remember how fond we are of whisky and brandy (labelled "Medical Comforts"). The cake will be glorious

---

[397] Sir John French, commander of the first and second armies of the British Expeditionary Force in France in December 1914 (ODNB)

for our mess.

Could you send me 100 Benson & Hedges cigarettes (as well as the Robert Lewis) every week. I like his mild ones, Egyptian I think. I am rather short. I'm sending this by James Lechie, who is going on leave.

Fearful rush.

All all love, & bless you. I did love seeing you, as indeed you know. J.

Writing paper & envelopes. Candles.

238   5 Dec 1914   Western Front   DE/Rv/C1135/690

Darling Mother

Re letter written yesterday, can you send me also these things

    A thick Cording waterproof (absolutely) coat, warm lined.

My burberry lets through the rain, if it really rains, as it did today.

    Some writing paper & envelopes.

    Did you get the compass?

    Candles.

    Towel (only one has arrived yet)

    Soap.

    Anything you can send to the Mess is most acceptable, eg whisky, brandy, sloe gin, cakes, pheasants. Label them "Medical Comforts", as indeed they are.

Could you get me the waterproof leggings from Cording?

All all love from Julian.

239   8 Dec 1914   Western Front   DE/Rv/C1135/691

Darling Mother

Two letters from you today, one in parcel of wrist compass from Dixie (for which many thanks) – dated Dec 2nd, and one by Evan dated Dec 5. I was wrong about my wooly waistcoat – I'd never brought it home. Your new one hasn't arrived yet. I have got the 1915 Diary, the towels & pants (fancy you using the military term) – not the new pants, and not the Haseldon. What is a Haseldon? The Christmas numbers arrived alright, & were given to the Sergeants. A splendid cake arrived. Also Marquis chocolate from Casie, with a letter written before I got home. Also today [Wed Dec 9th] a pair of waterproof overalls, long ones, but not quite the right kind, because they do not reach down to strap under the ankles, to keep your feet warm. Also cigarettes, which were glorious, as I've only had Players Navy Cut to smoke these last 5 days. Can you please send 200 a week, 100 from Robert Lewis as before, and 100 <u>Benson & Hedges</u> in addition? Arrived also today a splendid Folding Kettle from Barrett, Piccadilly. By the way, Barrett, Taplow, has send no more <u>methylated spirit</u> lately – which is always useful here. Please also send 1 Orilux Lamp refill from Steward Strand, <u>weekly</u>; please tell him to send. The glorious silk socks with red clocks arrived with the pants, and created quite a furore: also 2 handkerchiefs. And today the beautiful new waistcoat (wooly) which I will give with your love to my Scout Sergeant.

Do you think you could possibly get me the following Scout articles – a <u>Map Measurer</u>, one of the little machines with a wheel at the end, which you run along the map, and it marks the distance on the indicator (like a pedometer); (I have one or two in my things at home, but I don't expect you'll ever find them) – a little metal <u>inch and centimetre rule</u> – a small <u>magnifying glass</u> (for maps) – & some <u>magnesium wire</u>[398].

What a terrible begging and thanking letter!

The Russian victory wasn't much?! Here we are doing damn well. We are absolutely refitted now, and our horses are pretty well fit again. We are practising different things, like Scouts and Retaking Trenches and Remaking Trenches. But it's all terribly dull. I'm trying to organise a Brigade Steeplechase (on H.M.'s poor horses). Rex came over to see me yesterday; <u>what</u> a darling he is. He brought his mouth organ with him, but I couldn't get him to play it. He is doing just the same as us (damn all). Can't you get the British Ratepayers to revolt against paying for an idle army? There seems to be no prospect of us moving till May or June 1915 or 1916. I know we could hammer these Germans now.

Give my <u>best</u> love to Daddy, Casie, Billboy, Mog, & Vovo.

When is Casie coming out?

Philip Hardwick was awfully pleased with Dad's letter.

I <u>did</u> love seeing you. You know how much J.

---

[398] A thin strip or wire of magnesium prepared for burning (OED)

240   13 – 17 Dec 1914 Western Front   DE/Rv/C1135/692

Darling Mother [*repeated with different date*]

Thank you awfully for 2 letters, one written Dec 7, and another which I got today. I got compass, underclothes, towel; and waterproof cording leggings – all glorious: also cigarettes, candles, writing paper & envelopes, towel & soap. I can't understand about Cording saying that they have got no lined waterproof coats – because they have made such a lot of splendid ones for three fellows out here. But I shall be able to manage beautifully (even better, I think) with the unlined Cording over my lined Burberry.
[17 Dec 1914]. Darling Mother
also recd your letters of 10th & 11th. It's a wonderful list of things which you've sent for the regt; I love the 1 vest. I hope I shall be able to snaffle some of the Cherry Jam for our own mess; we are so sick of the eternal rational Plum & Apple! I think it's a <u>glorious</u> list, with all the right things. <u>How</u> exciting that you are all in this Country now! I long to hear what sort of a time you have there. What a hustle you must have had, your last day or two before you left. Where are you going to live? What an interesting experience it will be.
Here <u>we</u> are still stuck in the mud, very comfortable and excessively dull. We had an excitement on Sunday (13th) when we were told to be ready to turn out (of all our different farms & cottages) at a moment's notice. We turned out in the dark hours of Monday morning, and marched (the whole division of cavalry) through to within sight of the good old shells again. But we only stayed there for four hours, and then came back three miles to the town, where we put the horses out in fields, and slept ourselves in some enormous glass grape greenhouses – dry, but coldish! We stopped two nights in the greenhouses: - - and then - - returned here to our farms and mud! It is a beastly existence here; you know how I hate it. it feels so wrong to be comfortable when others are in the trenches. One got the "right" feeling again when we moved out; and we all thought it was, at last, the Grande Attaque³⁹⁹. But now people are beginning to talk about leave home again, and about our settling down here for the winter! Which I simply cannot believe, can you? We are absolutely fitted out now, and ready to move; and the horses are fit.
It was good to have got those Pacific German ships wiped out, wasn't it?

---

³⁹⁹ Great onslaught

I'm writing this to the address Casie gave me at Boulogne. Do write and tell me all about it there. Are you all welly? There was a rumour of Dad coming up here last Saturday, (from Glynn in the regt. I got Casie's letter, written just before you started. How is little Mogsy? I hate being a Captain; I would like to be either God or a General or a Lieutenant. I've had <u>such</u> fun as a Lieutenant. I wonder if we <u>shall</u> get leave? it would be very good to see you again.

All love Mummy darling J.

PS Horrible "Daily Mail" still arriving for me instead of "Times".

241   19 Dec 1914   **Western Front**   DE/Rv/C1138/29

My darling Casie

It is fearfully exciting to think of you next door to us at Boulogne-Sur-Mer! Are you having fun? Do write me a long letter, and tell me all about it. I got a letter from you, written just before you started. Are you starting nursing[400] straight off? Or are you just living the life of the idle rich for a little before starting away? Have you seen Angela Forbes and Ruby Peto and all the other crowd of lovelies and unlovelies who inhabit there? We had a brisk game of footer with them on the quai, on our return from leave. I expect that you are working like blazes, really.

I thought it was such a funny scene when all us boys came back to the wars, when we boarded the train at Victoria – all the relations who were seeing off (except you) in copious tears; and all the being-seen-off soljier-boys playing a game of romps! As a matter of fact, we have done absolutely Damn All since we came back, except to sit in ease and comfort in farms 10 miles distant from the firing line. Who would be cavalry in the bloody war? Their occupation is gone, like Othello's[401]. That is, unless we get these Huns on the run. And as they have got separate lines of trenches every ½ mile between here and the Rhine, it will not be much better then! Today I went to

---

[400] Monica (Casie) became a nurse during the war; she was offered the chance of nursing in France and in December 1914 went to Wimereux near Boulogne. She became an expert and much-loved nurse, as letters to her from patients testify (Mosley, p366). She wrote a book about her experiences, *Bright Armour*, published in 1935

[401] *Othello* by William Shakespeare, Act III, Scene III, line 357: 'Othello's occupation's gone!'

the Flying Corps, and asked if they would take me as observer. The man looked askance at my increasing corporation[402], and asked How much did I weigh? I replied (with singular cunning, I thought) "9 st 6, sir". But when I found out that they would only take observers who would leave their regiments & go to them for good, I cried off.

We sleep in beds now; and eat in a room in a Farm-house; and the horses are under cover by sections in different barns and shanties; and the men sleeping in rooms and barns, section by section.

Goodbye darling. It <u>was</u> fun seeing you for a bit at home. I wish I could get to Boulogne. Bless you J.

[*Stain on page 3, with note:* This bit has been unlucky with the mutton-fat]

242   24 Dec 1914   Western Front   DE/Rv/C1135/693

Darling Mother

Thank you awfully for your letter (Dec 17), which I got yesterday. Your Boulogne time must have been <u>most</u> interesting. I heard of your arrival from Glynn in the regt; but I always rather doubted whether the Fates would let you come up here. I could have got to your luncheon in ½ hour. What fun it would have been!

However, I get leave again (things being <u>in status quo</u>) on Tuesday next, Dec 30th – and a <u>week</u> this time; which we don't deserve in the very least, having done nothing quite persistently ever since I can remember.

Post off – have just caught it with this one line.

Please give Dad my love, and thank him for his letter. Also Mogsie. All love J.

243   30 Dec 1914   Folkestone   DE/Rv/C1133/80

Telegram: Will arrive Taplow Station 8.30 tonight if you are at home wire Bath Club Julian.

---

[402] The body; the abdomen; especially when large and prominent (OED)

244   30 Dec 1914   Taplow Court   DE/Rv/C1146/1

Dear Mr [*Blank*]

I want to thank you very much indeed for the most generous contribution
which you, and others connected with the Panshanger Estate, have made
towards providing comforts for the troop which I command in the Royal
Dragoons.
First, I would like to tell you how very much pleased I am myself at the
interest which you have thus shown in thinking of me. And secondly, I can
assure you that the liberal sum which you have provided will surely keep my
troop well supplied with much appreciated comforts for a long time to come
– until such time, I hope, as we have thoroughly demolished the Germans!
I think that money spent on providing comforts for the fighting man is
always money well spent; and I am sure that you have put the selection of
these comforts into good hands; as my mother has already had considerable
experience in this matter.
I need hardly say how much touched my parents were by your kindness in
thinking of me and my men. I only wish that I could see you to thank you
personally. But unfortunately Lord Kitchener does not allow extra leave for
these matters.
Yrs faithfully Julian Grenfell Capt The Royal Dragoons.
[*Note in different hand: 'Most treasured letters – about 2 to Julian & Billy –
and one poem of Julian's. Written on voyage home f[rom] South Africa'*].

245   10 Jan 1915   Western Front   DE/Rv/C1133/81

My dear Dad

I hope that you are well & flourishing. Little Watkin Wynn of the regiment is
very keen to get into the Bath Club, and I told him that you would probably
be able to get him in quicker. I asked him to write down his full name and
description, his father's name, and his address. (He can hardly write!) He
handed me the enclosed screed. I like "C of E <u>Christian</u>"! It is at least an
exaggeration, as is also the following statement. The address seems to be
Wynnstay
Ruabon
North Wales.
The boy was educated at Eton and Trinity, Cambridge. He is a good boy.

I forgot to ask you before I left, but my old friend Mr Currell wants to know
if he can have a day's pike-fishing at Panshanger. I told him that I would ask
you, & that I was sure that you would give him a day. I wish you could tell
Turner to give him a permit? He has been awfully good to me always in
getting me dogs. H.A. Currell, The Chaplains, Ware Road, Hertford.

I hope that your One Million Army are going strong, and that they will make
good shooting with the .470 rifles! The heads here seem to think that the war
will be over by May or June, but I don't see how that can happen, do you?

I met today the man on whose parents Billy is billeted![403] He is attached to
the 10th Hussars. He is an ugly and boring little devil. He is just going
home. I expect he will be surprised when he sees Bill.

The dogs are all well, and have killed, up to date,

    1 white leghorn chicken (cock)

    1 Royston crow (winged)

    1 hare.

Basil Brooke in the 10th has got a lurcher, and we went out today and killed a
hare, after much walking over ploughed fields, which was good exercise
anyhow. But the country is terribly wet here – mostly under water, in fact.

I hope that Moggie is better from her gout, and that Ben is alright. I'm glad
that Casie is not bad. Please give them both my best love.

I did enjoy my days last week.

Best love from Julian.

246   17 Jan 1915   Western Front   DE/Rv/C1135/694

Darling Mother

Thank you awfully for your two letters. I am sorry not to have written
before, but I've only had one eye this last week, having stopped a good stiff
punch with the other; and it's an awful nuisance to write with one eye.

I am so glad that Casie's hand is not really bad. Please thank her very much
indeed for her letter. It was bad luck, us two just missing like that. You must
have been delighted when you saw her, not bad.

I loved your Gazette letter of the Sayings of the Great. It's the first time that
I've actually seen it stated, that it was going to be a terrible long war. I had
always wondered, myself, with a great wonder, at the people who said (and

---

[403] Billy had enlisted on 7 August 1914. Within a week, he was a second lieutenant
in the 8th Battalion of the Royal Rifle Brigade (MacKenzie, p148)

are saying) that it will end in May June July; because it was impossible to imagine what <u>could</u> make it end then. I believe that they really thought on the Stock Exchange that it would end this summer? And think so now? It's very interesting <u>but not convincing</u> that they say there will be lots of work for the miserable over-fed Cavalry. I am applying for an A.S.C. job, myself, because I am so interested in food.

The life here gets worse as it goes on (although the long dogs have been a real saving clause). One would not mind "waiting" in the least, if only one could feel sure that there would be a good <u>fat</u> piece of work at the end of the wait. But what I feel about it is that we shall have to wait <u>years,</u> and then (possibly) get a thin piece of work. If the Germans do have to go a long way back to their next line, then we should probably get some good cavalry work – for a little. But otherwise our job will only be to do dirty little bits of infantry work, if they are hustled again, and are forced to put us in the trenches. I wish I was in the Grenadier Guards with the young lords and dukes!

They had a boxing show at the other night, in the town hall. Feeling warlike, I got them to issue a challenge (anonymous) to anyone in the room. The boxers had not been very good, and I hoped for a soft job. But a <u>very</u> large private in the A.S.C. immediately put up his gigantic hand, and said he was only too ready to fight! Imagine my chagrin and horror! Especially when I was told that the man was a boxing pro, who had joined for the war! He closed my left eye right up in the first round, and they wanted to stop the fight, because it was bad. But I told them I was right; and in the second round, I caught him a beauty, and they had to carry him out to hospital. It was a terrific fight while it lasted. I <u>had</u> to make the pace, because I was so unfit. My eye is alright now, and a glorious colour – purple, shot with green; and the man is alright too.

The dogs have been the greatest fun. Basil Brooke has got a very good dog, & plenty of hares at his place. Hugo Baring[404], who used to be in that squadron of the 10th, has gone to the Intelligence Corps (the corps who buy the eggs and ducks and copy out the orders); they did not like him at all in the 10th.

All your things arrived while I was at home, and I found them waiting for me here when I got back – the <u>very</u> good map-measurer & magnifying glass, and the inch-rule, and the sponges from Ivo and the lovely handkerchiefs from

---

[404] The Hon Hugo Baring (1876-1949), youngest surviving brother of John and Maurice Baring (*Burke's Peerage*, 107th edition, vol 3, p3324)

Moggie. Please thank them both tremendously: also for their letters (2 from Moggie and one from Ivo).

Please tell Dad that I saw Alan & Rex[405] yesterday, and that they were still talking about how much they had enjoyed their shoot at Panshanger.

What we would simply <u>love</u> for our mess here is

> A big <u>cake</u> once a week.
>
> Some home-made <u>jam</u> every week.
>
> A bottle of <u>port</u> every week.

Pack the jam and the port in good stout wooden boxes, or they will get crushed in the post.

Can you send me a good <u>big</u> block of writing papers. These bits are fiddling work.

I do <u>not</u> want any more towels now; but I'm frightfully short of <u>handkerchiefs</u>.

Goodbye, Mummy, & <u>bless</u> you. Leave again soon, hooray. How are you? Are you welly?   Julian.

247   25 Jan 1915   Folkestone   DE/Rv/C1133/82

Telegram: Leave will come Taplow dinner tonight if you are at home wire Bath Club Julian.

248   15 Feb 1915   Western Front   DE/Rv/C1135/695

Darling Mother

I could not write before, because directly I came back we went up for 5 days, and then 5 days in the trenches. We're just back and I'm writing this one line in a fearful hurry to catch James Leckie, who goes on leave tonight, and will take it. We had an easy time – only 1 man killed in the regt, (& he was in my troop, poor fellow, & <u>such</u> a good man). We were in the same wood

---

[405] Sir Reginald Lindsay Benson (Rex), army officer and merchant banker. In August 1914 he joined his regiment, the 9th Queen's Royal Lancers, which formed part of the 2nd cavalry brigade, in France, and survived the battle of the Aisne. After serving at Ypres and then Messines, he was awarded one of the first Military Crosses. In May 1915, during the second battle of Ypres, he was severely gassed and wounded by a bullet that destroyed the brachial artery and the nerves of his right arm (ODNB). 'Alan' is probably Alan (Tommy) Lascelles

where I used to crawl about before, only further to the left. Germans 30 yds off. I will write today to tell you all about it.

Best best love. I do hope you are all well. Is Moggie better. Give my love to Daddy, & thank him <u>awfully</u> for his present. J.

249   15 Feb 1915   Western Front   DE/Rv/C1135/696

Darling Mother

I wrote you just one line today, for James Leckie to take, to get to you quicker; because I haven't been able to write since I saw you last. I forget whether I told you that Philip had heard that the regiment had moved probably up to the trenches; and that he said that he and the others were going back by the early morning train on Tuesday – no, I didn't tell you, because I didn't know myself till Tuesday morning, when I found his letter. Well, I was left on Tuesday morning, too late for the early train, not knowing when to go or how to go, when I arrived in France, and only knowing that Charlie Burn had been out for 2 days the week before, and had neither been able to find the regiment nor to discover where they were! A cheerful look-out. If Burn could not find them with a motor in two days, how could I with no motor in 5 hrs? However, Rex & Alan came over with me to Boulogne, and Rex of course had got a motor waiting for him. We went to GHQ at St Omer and then I bearded GHQ, and found out that the regt had moved back a bit, but were going up into trenches early next day. Rex & Alan angelically took me on, out of their way, to our place, and when we got there (11 pm) everyone was in bed and nobody knew where the Royals were billeted! After wandering about with the motor for about 2 hrs; knocking up sleeping French in the farms, I gave it up, and sent them on in the motor, poor dears. A kind but sleepy Frenchwoman at a farm gave me a bed, coffee at 5 am, and a cart to take me on, when it was light on my explorations. Luckily I found the regt at 8 am; and, still more lucky, found out that we were not leaving till 1 pm that day.

We all went up the 30 odd miles in London motor buses, 22 to a bus, and arrived at our new billets, in the town where the young lady was riddled by snipers, after dark, at about 11 pm. We went into good billets in the town for 5 days. Every other house has a shell through it; and they put about 20 shells in every night while we were there. It was <u>the</u> most lovely town in the world, before they battered it. I had not seen it since it was badly knocked about. It was very sad to see it in its present state. But the people, the townspeople, were as happy as grigs[406], charging 500% for everything, and enjoying themselves hugely. Many of them had stopped in the town the whole time. The girls – some of them really lovely – were splendid about it. One of them said to me "Oui, c'est terrible, la guerre. Maar ek bet ne jamais en autant de plaisir que pendant cette guerre"[407].

Then we went into trenches for 5 days, in our same old wood where I got into the Boches. Very good trenches, with the German trenches 15 yds off at one or two places, and generally about 50 yds. The drawback to our trenches was that in odd places in the parapet there were buried very shallow, poor dead Huns and French & English, whose bodies were periodically resurrected by the rain and bombs and bullets. We took over at dead of night, as usual. We had a quiet time; but every night the Germans dug and dug, and every morning one saw a new German trench a little nearer our own. We did nothing: but I will reserve criticisms till I see you again. One afternoon they fired 5 bombs at us, out of a trench mortar. I was off duty, and asleep, when they first arrived. I did not know what in Hell it was. I rushed out with your macintosh bed-roll round my feet, like a man in a sack race, and found the men all roaring with laughter, because the bomb had landed near old Sammy Smith's dug-out, and had pretty near buried Old Sammy. Old Sammy was pulled out from the debris by the feet, uninjured except in self-respect. Then they all shouted "Look out, boys", and we looked up and saw the next bomb coming; that just missed the trench too. Then I got our rifle bombs, and starting shooting back at them. They sent 3 more, close to the trench but not into it. I shot 3 at them, and I must have been on my lucky day, because I burst all three <u>slap</u> into their trench; and then they stopped, and left us in peace ever afterwards. The Somerset Yeomanry, who were opposite where they fired the mortar, told us afterwards that all our 3 landed absolutely plum into their trench. The nights were the best – flares going up from each side all the time, and lighting up the pines like a wood in a pantomime; and intermittent rifle firing the whole time, right along the line. We were relieved about 12 o'clock, marched back our 4½ miles laden with all our stuff, and got into our motor-buses again, getting back here at 7.30 am. They were good trenches, with dug-outs all along, and wood in the bottom. Ours were dry, but "C" Sqdn had one 2 ft deep in water. It rained, and snowed, and

---

[406] An extravagantly lively person, one who is full of frolic and jest. Also in phrase 'as merry (or lively) as a grig' (OED)

[407] 'Yes, war is awful. [But I have] never had as much enjoyment as [I have had] during this war'

froze. But we had whale-oil for our feet, which is a great thing. It was very good to get an experience of this sedentary non-aggressive fighting; but what nonsense it is. I want to talk lots about it to you.

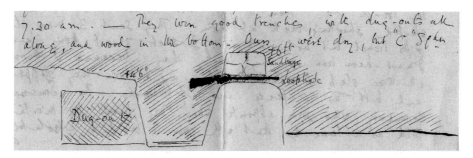

I've got one letter from you, a very good one; also the glorious handkerchiefs, which have been a great godsend. No more <u>cakes</u> arrived, and no more <u>cherry jam</u>. The cakes were <u>awfully</u> good – the richest one the best. Please tell Mr Bart to send me a can of methylated spirits every fortnight – I had told him to stop it. The Billy was a godsend; I made hot cocoa for myself and Philip at all hours of the night & small morning.
I <u>did</u> love my last leave; it was absolutely perfect. Have you got over your Flue? The Russian news sounds not too good? Do write and tell me what people are thinking about things. How is Daddy? And how is darling Casie; give her my best best love.
I'm sending you a photograph, done in London. How I wish I looked like that. The man who did it should have painted sunsets; it's such a pity to waste creative genius of that calibre upon photography.
Goodbye & all love J.
You should have seen our men setting out from here for the trenches – absolutely radiant with excitement and joy to be getting back to fight again. I <u>do</u> love fighting – even sedentary fighting. I wish I was a footslogger[408] now.
[Please send <u>envelopes</u> *written on outside of envelope*]

---

[408] A foot-soldier, infantryman (OED)

250   19 Feb 1915   Western Front   DE/Rv/C1138/30

My darling Casie

Thank you awfully for your letter. I wonder if you are back at Wimereux now, or just going? Are you quite right again? It was a proper dose of flue that you had. Are you really selling Dynamite to <u>Charlie Meade</u>, or do you use the name as a mere type of the idle (and horse-ignorant) rich? You will like getting back to work again.

Spring weather – real spring weather – at last, and isn't it wonderful! We came back here from the trenches to our first spring day. It's rather a good billet, and on a hill, for which thank God. The water no longer ooses into the collar and into the rare wines of the country. I told Mother about my eventful drive all over France with Rex & Alan in their motor, on the night when I came back from leave.

We had 5 days in the trenches, and only lost one man. We were within 30 yds of the Boches in one place. They started firing silly little sticks of nitro-picric-high-explosive-fire-and-brimstone-glycerine[409] at us out of a trench gun. I was asleep, when suddenly there was a deafening crash, and half of the dug-out roof fell onto my face. I rushed out, and found all the men roaring with laughter, because Old Sammy had been buried in his dug-out. Old Sammy was pulled out by the legs, amid yells of ribald laughter. Then someone said "Look out". and another blasted stick came over, like a rocketing pheasant. After that I started rapid fire with our rifle grenades; and by great luck I pitched the first three plum into their trench. Then they stopped – by a sort of mutual agreement on both sides to remain inactive and comfortable, so long as each knew that the other side was able to retaliate if provoked. Oh, it's a funny game!

It was fun to get onto a horse again – even after 5 days sitting in trenches, I felt as if I hadn't ridden for years. I ride bare-back always. I'm going to see Hubert Hartigan tomorrow, & I'll give him your love.

Goodbye, darling, J.

---

[409] A combination of lethal weapons. Picric acid is a yellow crystalline acid with a very bitter taste, obtained by nitrating phenol and used in the manufacture of explosives; nitro-glycerine is an explosive oily liquid, which is obtained by treating glycerol with a mixture of nitric and sulphuric acids, and is used in the manufacture of dynamite (OED); fire and brimstone was a punishment sent by God to obliterate sinners (eg Genesis, ch 19, v 24, where fire and brimstone was rained on the cities of Sodom and Gomorrah)

251   20 Feb 1915   Western Front   DE/Rv/C1135/697

Darling Mother

Thank you awfully for your letter of the 17th inst. How quick letters are now! I got another one from you two days ago. <u>Do</u> send me the novel, I'm longing for stuff to read. Yes, isn't the Russian news terrifying? But of course, it's only a feint, like that very good early feint of theirs up there, when they lost 3 army corps. What did they say about things at Peperharow? I'm so glad that Casie is quite right again now. How good that you heard direct from the heads good cavalry news; and that they said we had done well in the trenches.

All goes well here – and <u>real</u> spring weather, which is wonderful. I had forgotten that it <u>could</u> be warmer than it has been this winter, in non-sun countries. We've got <u>good</u> billets, up on the hill, about 6 miles further back from our last ones. I was inoculated today, the second time (1st time was at Luggershall). It always gives me gyp[410].

Now about things for the men. They are frightfully short of <u>cigarettes</u>; in fact, they have none, and have had none for the last month. I think that this is a great shame, considering the money that has been given. Could you send me some cigarettes for my troop, out of the Panshanger money? I expect Daddy will be able to send them out of bond[411]. The great thing is that they shall have a fairly continuous supply – not spasmodic. If ever the Taplow people want to send anything more, the thing to send is <u>cigarettes</u>.

The thing they want next worst is underclothes – vests and pants. They have only had one Government issue of these since they came out, and their things are practically worn away. From what I can gather, there is no probability of another Govt issue now. Six dozen pairs were received for the regt this month or late in last month. I don't know if they came from you. But anyhow it was not enough to go round, by a long way. Could you send out 3 doz <u>pants and drawers</u>.

Could you also send a doz <u>electric torches</u>. I believe you can get them now quite cheap, 2/6 or 3/6. Some of them have been a government issue. Please send an extra refill for each, and another refill for each every fortnight. Please send also a doz <u>cheap pipe-lighters</u>, with plenty of tinder.

   Also a good supply of matches.

---

[410] Pain (OED)
[411] Free of duty (OED)

Also some "bivouac cocoa".

For our mess, cakes and cherry jam always most acceptable. <u>Did you ever discover what happened to the letter to Diana Wyndham[412] which I sent to Taplow</u>?

I haven't seen anyone "outside" lately, since we came back from trenches. How nice Stanley in the 1LG [*Life Guards*] looks? I saw Titchfield up at Ypres, and have heard afterwards that he made the most appalling floater[413] about me to Byng[414]. I will tear his eyes out when next I see him. I'm going off tomorrow for ten days, with 2 more of our officers and 100 men, to look after the Cav[alry] Brigade horses, while they are in the trenches.

Goodbye Mummy darling. I <u>am</u> looking forward to seeing you again; perhaps in 3 weeks time, as leave still seems to be going on. Best love to Daddy & Moggy. <u>All</u> love J.

I've got a real "Spring Running" on me. I wish they'd let me go and fight the Boches on my own.

252   24 Feb 1915   Western Front   DE/Rv/C1133/83

My dear Dad

I hope that you are well and flourishing. I am over here in the next billets to Rex, looking after some horses for a regiment that has gone into trenches. I had dinner with Rex two nights ago, and he was in great form, with his Military Cross and his mouth organ. They are in trenches now.

I have put in my name today for Foot Guards, during the war. They sent round to the cavalry for names of cavalry officers willing to serve. I don't see how cavalry can get much work in this country, and it is a wonderful chance of getting into a good infantry regiment. I hate leaving the regiment, but I am sure that it is the right thing to do, and there should be great chances of doing well and of getting on, with the Toe-Guards. But I had never regarded myself as a possible Guardee! Neither do I know how many men are in a platoon! However, I shall perhaps learn that in the first week or two. Or perhaps they will make me a general straight off, and I shall not have to worry about platoons! The only thing I know about platoons is from the

---

[412] Diana Lister, who had married Percy Wyndham in 1913

[413] A mistake, a 'bloomer' (slang) (OED)

[414] Julian Hedworth George Byng, Viscount Byng of Vimy (1862-1935), commanded the 3rd cavalry division at the beginning of the war

poets –

> "Then down from off the mountain came the squadrons and platoons
> with twenty thousand fighting men, and a thousand bold

dragoons".[415]

Anyhow, I'll write to tell you all about platoons in a short time. Do write and tell me what you think of this scheme? And tell me any news you have got at home.

I hope Moggy has recovered from her gout? Casie, I suppose, has gone back? I had a letter from her some time ago, saying that she was going back the next day.

Goodbye & best love from Julian.

253   25 Feb 1915   Western Front   DE/Rv/C1135/698

Darling Mother

We are here for 10 days (100 men and 3 officers) looking after the 11th Hussar horses, while their men are in trenches. They took all their men up, and only left 1 officer a Squadron; each of us takes over a squadron's horses – about 4 horses to 1 of our men, so they exercise and groom all day, while we walk about and smoke cigarettes and whistle just to cheer them up.

An order has come round the cavalry asking for volunteer officers for the Foot Guards (for the war only). This of course was a heaven-sent opportunity for me. You know that I have never believed much in the possibility of any <u>extensive</u> cavalry work here – nothing more than a dash now and then. Perhaps I'm quite wrong. Anyhow, I would always have taken an infantry job, Territorials or anything. So now this does seem to be a golden opportunity, in every way. There must be the real pressing need there for officers; and if one is to go footslogging, who could one go to, better than the Guards. And who could do anything but approve of one's going, on an appeal like that? I never <u>really</u> hesitated, though I thought it over for a day and a night. Then

---

[415] Misquotation from the poem by Percy French (1854-1920) entitled variously 'Slattery's Light Dragoons' or 'Shlathery's Mounted Fut'. One version of the chorus is: 'An' down from the mountains came the squadrons an' platoons, / Four-an'-twinty fightin' min, an' a couple o' sthout gossoons, / An' whin we marched behind the dhrum to patriotic tunes, / We felt that fame would gild the name o' Shlathery's Light Dragoons' (http://www.traditionalmusic.co.uk/folk-song-lyrics/Slatterys_Light_Dragoons.htm)

I wrote to the Colonel (today, by mounted orderly) asking him to put in my name. I wonder if he'll be angry about it? Anyhow, I don't see how he can refuse.

It will be a great step for me, because I expect they will give me sooner or later a job of my own (instead of being 3rd in Command of a Squadron, as I am now). I don't quite know <u>how</u> short of officers they are. It is obviously the "pushing" thing to do. And just think of the unthinkable glory of being a Guardee, and being privileged to create an uproar in a box at Florodora[416], and to marry a chorus girl, not only with impunity but with added lustre!

Of course the disadvantages are equally clear – giving up something one knows by heart, for something one knows nothing about; giving up people one loves for people one knows nothing about; and horses, for smelly feet; and men who know one, for men who don't. It has almost broken my heart already. And I'm so bad at picking up new things. But think, too, of the <u>fun</u> of starting a new thing in the middle.

I long to know what you think. And I'd got some other <u>thrilling</u> things to tell you. But I'm afraid I shan't be able to now, because they've stopped leave from March 1st.

I heard from Casie, back at Boulogne – no, she was going back next day. How is Daddy? How is Moggie? When does Billa-boy think he is coming out?

Do send out some more of those good cakes, and some port. You don't know how much they were appreciated last time.

Are you well, Mummy? How well the family is bearing up and staying on through this great European war, isn't it? Do write and tell me any bits of news.

Best love to Daddy Moggie & Ivo.

I wish I'd been a militiaman[417], and that I were at home now. It's so dull here J.

---

[416] Florodora was one of the first successful Broadway musicals of the 20th century. Originally opened in London on 11 November 1899 at the Lyric Theatre, where it ran for 455 performances, it moved to New York in 1900 and ran for 552 performances – the first instance of a London production achieving such a Broadway run, and the second longest on Broadway of any theatre piece up to that time. There was a successful London revival in 1915 (http://en.wikipedia.org/wiki/Florodora)

[417] A member of the military force raised from the civilian population of a country or region, especially to supplement a regular army in an emergency, as distinguished from mercenaries or professional soldiers (OED)

254   26 Feb 1915   Western Front   DE/Rv/C1135/699

Darling Mother

Could you please send me a <u>luminous wrist watch</u>, with strap, <u>as soon as</u>
<u>possible</u>. Mine has gone bust; and they are so absolutely necessary. I heard
today from the Col saying he had sent in my name for the Toe Guards.
Best of best of love J.

255   3 Mar 1915   Western Front   DE/Rv/C1133/84

My dear Dad

Thank you very much for your letter. You must be having a tremendous lot
of work with the Volunteers. It is a good thing that they are taking over the
bridges, etc, and it will relieve a lot of men for the other things. But it must
be a great undertaking to have to deal with so many of them. They certainly
ought to make you a general. Why haven't they?
Life has been very quiet for us here. I went to see General Putty yesterday,
and found him in great form – also Londonderry[418], who is charming. They
were devising bombs and infernal engines of all sorts for the Boches. Putty
said he would help me about getting into the Foot Guards; because I had
written to George Paynter to get me into his batt[alion]n (2ⁿᵈ Scots Guards) –
and they are in Putty's army.
I wish that I had brought out your .303 rifle with the telescopic sight, which
you said that I might take. Do you think you could possibly get it out to me?
Leave having stopped now, it makes it rather hard to get it out. But perhaps
Col Charlie Burn, or one of the despatch carriers, could bring it out to me? I
would be <u>awfully</u> glad to have it, and to have it soon. It is just what one
wants for shooting at their loopholes, now that we are close up. I suppose it
will take this pointed Govt ammunition all right?
I have also written to Mr Bart to send out my little Colt repeating pistol, and
some extra ammunition for it. It is .42 or .48 bore, I forget which. Could

---

[418] Charles Stewart Henry Vane-Tempest-Stewart, 7ᵗʰ Marquess of Londonderry
(1878-1949). He had succeeded his father as marquess in February 1915 but was
sometimes still known under his former title of Castlereagh. He served as a staff
officer and later as adjutant to the 'Blues' on the Western Front. He ended up as a
lieutenant-colonel and was twice mentioned in dispatches (ODNB)

you please tell Mr Bart where to get the ammunition.

I hope that you are fit and well, Daddy? I suppose Casie is hard at work again at the London Hospital. I am very fit, and longing to get at it again. Best love from Julian.

256   7 Mar 1915   Western Front   DE/Rv/C1133/85

My dear Dad

Thank you very much for your letter. It was good of you to write so quickly. As a matter of fact, they have <u>withdrawn</u> the scheme for the transference of officers. They said that the cavalry had sent in all their worst names; and I believe that a lot of regiments did do that!

What I thought about it was this – that the very fact that they started the scheme meant that they were not going to do anything with the cavalry for the immediate future; and that, as they wanted officers so badly for the Foot-Guards, it was obviously the right thing to do. So I decided, and sent my name in.

I think it would be a very different thing if one <u>applied</u> for a transfer; but when the Army asked for it, I had no hesitation in sending my name in.

I wish that I could think there is a good prospect of cavalry work here or elsewhere; I only hope that there will be! What you say is very interesting; but it's a long way to Tipperary, and we have got so many troops nearer there. Knowing absolutely nothing, I am rather sceptical about it.

Maurice Baring and Evan[419] turned up today here – Maurice looking <u>young</u> and <u>handsome</u> and <u>athletic</u>, but as mad as ten March hares. He came into our squadron mess for 10 minutes, during which time I filled him with Sloe Gin and Brandy mixed. He eventually balanced the liqueur glass on his bald head (whence it fell with a crash), and sang a Maori Love Song! Philip Hardwick said that he was the only man that he had ever seen as mad as me; and that no wonder I called him "Mother" (I had called him "Mullah").

I saw Putty the other day, and he was very good to me, and put in an

---

[419] During the First World War Maurice Baring (see also letter 188) was attached to the Royal Flying Corps branch of the British expeditionary force, and for four years from August 1915 was 'mentor and guide' to Hugh (later Viscount) Trenchard. He became a staff officer of the Royal Air Force in 1918 (ODNB); Evan: possibly Evan Charteris (1864-1940), seventh son of Francis 10th Earl of Wemyss and uncle of Ego and Guy Charteris (see also letter 65)

application for my transfer. I saw Londonderry and Pembroke[420] there too. Goodbye, Daddy. I hope you're fit and well. Best love from Julian.

257   7 Mar 1915   Western Front   DE/Rv/C1135/700

Darling Mother

Thank you awfully for all your letters. Although I agree absolutely with a lot of what you say, I really never had a moment's <u>doubt</u> about what I did. However, they have now cancelled the whole scheme; so the Gods have settled it. They said that the cavalry had only sent in their rubbish (which I believe was quite true in a lot of cases). Anyhow, for whatever reason, they have called it off.

When I first heard of the scheme, I thought that really it was Amen to any cavalry work in the near future – or they would surely never have done it. Besides, it was so obviously the <u>right</u> thing to do. After all, loyalty to the Army must override loyalty to the regiment. Yes, I never really hesitated – though <u>fully</u> realising the big big objections.

I love thinking of the Arabian Nights schemes; and I think that the stopping of this transference certainly shortens the odds against them.

Putty was such a darling about helping me. I went once to luncheon and once to tea with him. I <u>do</u> like him, and his cheerfulness, and his laugh, and his straight watchful eye. He wrote to Gen Lambton about it. Another man who was awfully nice about it was George Paynter, who moved heaven and earth to get me into his battalion.

If they still try to get me now, I shall <u>not</u> go; because it's a very different thing, if the Army <u>ask</u> for volunteers, to leaving one's regiment more or less on one's own bat.

I'm back here now with jolly old "B" Sq[ua]d[ro]n, after 12 days with the 11[th]. It is certainly good to get back to one's own kith and kin. How is your Waiting going? I hear that you got Charlie Lister in alright. How splendid, and what a good job for him. I <u>do</u> love him, I will write to him. Peperharow & Stanway sound great fun. I'm glad that Casie is back to her slogging. I got Brooke's poem[421], and liked it very much – <u>awfully</u>. I am sending you

---

[420] Reginald Herbert, 15th Earl of Pembroke (1880-1960) (*Burke's Peerage*, 106th edn, vol 1, p78)

[421] Possibly 'The Soldier' (1914), Brooke's elegy to England, which was probably the best-known sonnet published in English in the 20th century

under separate cover, a poem of mine. Don't show it to Charlie Castlereagh. How nice he is; and why shouldn't people drive about in limousines; they probably like it as much as I like being in the trenches. And to each man his job.

I have got the luminous watch; and Columbine; thank you awfully. But no more cakes or jam have come, after the first lot. Yes, one cake has just arrived, from Stewart & Co, 50 Old Bond Street. Is that from you?

About the Victoria Street things – I cannot make out that the men have got any cigarettes from the fund for months and months, and I do think that it is the most awful shame. The Colonel is at home at present; I'll see him again about it as soon as he comes back. But he is very hard to extract information from. The other things in your list, soup, cake, sweets, coffee etc, I have never heard tell of in the regiment. The shirts, socks etc, I am not sure of. About the Panshanger things. Yes, please send the cigarettes regularly, at present anyhow. The cigarettes & tobacco have arrived. Also the pipe-lighters. But not the matches, cocoa and milk, vests, pants, or electric torches.

How is Billa-boy, and when does he come out. There are rumours here of tremendous transportations already? I never dare to tell you any news, because of the Censor; and I'm simply bursting with news, largely critical. Are you welly, Mum? I knew I sh[oul]d get a splendid letter from you about the Toe Guards. Do you agree with me, or not? I mean, can you possibly imagine my decision as sound from my point of view? Because one can only say that a judgement is right when it is according to one's own standards & point-of-view, whether these are right or wrong.

Goodbye & bless you.

I'm writing to Dad. J.

258   8 Mar 1915   Western Front   DE/Rv/C1135/701

Darling Mother

Could you please send me two footballs for the men, as soon as poss, out of the Pans[hanger] money?

I'm sending a letter to Tap[low] to Charles Lister. Could you forward to him?

All love J.

Could you please send me

      A box of "relief" pen-nibs

A <u>larger</u> block of writing paper (twice the size of this sheet)
Envelopes. J.

259   8 Mar 1915   Western Front   DE/Rv/C1135/702

Darling Mummy

Who is y[ou]r Canadian friend?[422]
Please send 2 extra bladders with the footballs (asked for in letter of today's
date). J

260   9 Mar 1915   Western Front   DE/Rv/C1133/86

My dear Dad

I have been asked by the brigade to get hold of some "Nottingham" fishing
reels, to be used by snipers. When they go out of the trench they take the
line out with them, and tie it up at a place about 50 yds out. Then when they
want to come back they jerk the end of the line, and that clicks the reel and
warns the sentry in the trench that they are coming back: and he tells the
others not to shoot.
Do you think that you could get me a couple of reels, with a good long length
of line on them? If you send me the bill, I will recover it from the brigade.
Best love from Julian.
Rex just been here – in his motor – with Alan and Hubert Hartigan, all in
great form.

---

[422] Julian's exploits are described in letter 234 but were ascribed to a Canadian
officer (see also letter 265). Extracts from at least two of Julian's letters (numbers
229 and 232, for example) were published in the press; number 229 appeared in *The
Times* on 4 November 1914

261   9 Mar 1915   Western Front   DE/Rv/C1135/703

Darling Mother

Could you please send me out my old red Diary, which I gave you some time
ago to lock up. I want to write out my war diary, as it's a very good
opportunity now that there is nothing to do. Can you send it <u>soon</u>? Bind it
up carefully, as it's nearly in bits.
All all love & blessing
How is Moggie? J.
Can you send me another map-measurer? Mine broke. Can you send 1 doz
more pipe lighters.
I was wrong when I said that the <u>cigarettes</u> had come, from the Panshanger
money. It was the packets of tobacco sent by the Taplow servants.
The pipe-lighters are the only things that have come out of the Pans[hanger]
money.
I've sent you today, with this, a letter to Charlie Lister.
Rex & Alan have just been here, in great form.

262   14 Mar 1915   Western Front   DE/Rv/C1135/704

Darling Mother

I got your splendid letters today, of March 10th and 12th. How capital about
Constantinople! But do you know, I was talking to a man here the other day,
who really seems to know about things, and he said that the great idea was to
disguise the Cavalry Corps as reindeer, and to send them up by Norway, and
in that way. The only thing I am afraid of is our African horses, that they
will be discouraged by another and still colder move.
What did you make out from the Colonel about all your things? This is <u>all</u> I
can make out, but I do not in the least vouch for it as correct – a lot of
cigarettes from the Regtl Fund at and before Christmas, but <u>none</u> since; 72
prs of vests & pants in February; and several boxes of Balaclava hats,
mittens, gloves etc. I cannot trace anything else. The men have had <u>very</u> few
cigarettes since Christmas – hardly any, and what they had were Government
issue. <u>No</u> cakes, sweets, coffee, pies etc have arrived at all, and no writing
books.
Two cakes and two bottles of port arrived for me today, and were awfully
good; thank you very much for them.

Of the things you sent from the Panshanger fund only the pipe-lighters and the vests and pants have arrived so far. Could you ask them to send some spare lengths of tinder for the pipe-lighters every fortnight?

I wrote you a letter about this last week. Did you get it?

We moved up on Thursday as reserve to the attack last week, and billeted behind there for two days, listening to the guns. It was horrible to sit there doing nothing, while the foot-sloggers were running into Machine Guns. We came back here again yesterday. Our whole atmosphere was filled throughout with rumours and almost expectations of the wild joy-ride schemes – which <u>do</u> sound ridiculous, and impossible, in the crude form in which we got them. Philip said that we should get so much quicker to the Rhine by <u>train</u>, when also the restaurant cars would do away with the difficulty about supplies. All the horse-soldiers I have seen are boiling with indignation at the idea of being treated as an <u>experimentum in corpore vili</u>[423] and prefer the Norway idea infinitely.

I'm glad you liked the "Staff"[424] poem. It had a great succès out here. "Punch" w[oul]d never take it, because of its religious tone.

How are you liking the Waiting? Do you know Lady Ida Sitwell?[425] She <u>does</u> sound good. She ought to be introduced to little Watkin, who, though "not addicted" to certain vices, would have helped her to get her money much quicker than those friends of hers.

How did you like the Colonel?

All love & blessing J.

Please give my best love to Dad, and tell him that the pistol arrived quite safe. Please thank him very much, and ask him if he can send another box of ammunition (Colt automatic .380).

Poor George Paynter has been hit at last. Yes, he has commanded that battn practically all through.

Can you please send me the following, <u>urgently</u> needed.

> A big foolscap size Note Book
> Writing paper
> Relief nibs
> Shaving soap ("Williams'" stick)
> Tooth paste in tube
> Soap

---

[423] The experiment by/in a humble/worthless body

[424] Julian's poem, 'Prayer for those on the staff' (Mosley, p372). See Appendix 2

[425] Wife of Sir George Reresby Sitwell, 4th Baronet (1860–1943)

Towels (2)
A good map of the Eastern Front (large general map)
A good map of the Western Front (d[itt]o)
"Land & Water"[426] each week
Matches
An old kit-bag to hold my spare stuff
Labels
Please stop Daily Mail (we get papers now)
Methylated spirits.

263   20 Mar 1915   Western Front   DE/Rv/C1135/705

Darling Mother

Thank you awfully for your letter, also 2 footballs, 2 extra bladders, 2 large
blocks writing paper and heaps of envelopes, relief nibs, & 2 more cakes;
also (slightly before) 2 very good bottles of port, which was awfully good;
also the diary. The only thing that has not arrived is the 3,000 cigarettes.
Did you send them to me? Please send on the next lot, anyhow, as the men
are frightfully short. Do you think that they bag[427] cigarettes in the post? I
wonder? The other things arrived alright (pipe-lighters, electric torches, vests
& pants).
I wish I could write to you more about things; but I simply dare not. But
certainly all they wished was not achieved – very far from it. And really
what a waste it seems, doesn't it, when really nothing was gained. Because
nothing was gained.
I love Bill's poem about John[428].
I am simply bursting with things to tell you, and it does seem hard not to be
able to. I wish I could have any optimism about your Dardanelles theory; or
did you only put that forward as "argumentum ad hominem". Did you see
that Army Corps Order which they published in yesterday's (or the day

---

[426] A weekly journal. For the duration of the war, it changed its emphasis from sports
and natural history to the reporting of the war. It retained its numeration while
adding a separately numbered series title called *The county gentleman & Land and
water*. *War series* (University of Cambridge Library, serials catalogue)
[427] Steal
[428] Billy's poem about John Manners, written after the latter was killed. Monica
quotes it in full in her book *Bright Armour* (pp211-212)

before's) papers, having got it through Berlin? That was actually published and distributed right through.

Wasn't it <u>the</u> worst!

I don't think myself that we shall ever make a hole through their line; simply because of the <u>impossibility</u> of attack under these conditions. If they could not get through our line at Wipers[429], how shall we get through theirs now? That is, of course, if conditions remain more or less the same as now. <u>All all</u> love from J.

Can you tell Mr Bart <u>not</u> to send any more methylated. He can't have got my letter.

264   22 Mar 1915   Western Front   DE/Rv/C1133/87

My dear Dad

Thank you very much for your letters, and for the Nottingham Reels[430], which are splendid, and just what I wanted. You must have had great fun with the Epée[431] at Folkestone. Did you have a pool? And did you win? It is very good of you to send me some more cartridges for my automatic pistol. I have been practising a lot with revolvers lately, to the great personal danger of all the French villagers, and I have now become fairly accurate; it's simply a matter of practise, isn't it? About the telescope rifle, as we are apparently not to go into trenches at present, there would be no good in having it; but if we do go into trenches again, it would be invaluable. I wish I could have seen Frederick as a Staats Artilleryman[432]; I expect he is very good. I wonder when the Durhams and Yorkshires, and the rest of K's army, are coming out? Do they shoot with [*sic*] at the Boathouse range? That is the only thing I feel nervous about with them; because shooting is so tremendously a matter of practise, and it's the thing which all the <u>regulars</u> have done most thoroughly of all. You must have put in a tremendous lot of work with the Volunteers to get them on so far and so quick.

I very much doubt any more of us from this sphere of operations; but probably that is because I know nothing about it.

George Paynter was hit very badly in the lungs the other day. But I heard

---

[429] Ypres, Belgium
[430] Fishing reels (see letter 260)
[431] A duelling or fencing sword
[432] Member of the South African army

today, from a doctor, that he is going on very well.

We are living a very lazy life again here, but the country has dried up wonderfully, and one can get about now and do things.

Best love from Julian.

265   24 Mar 1915   Western Front   DE/Rv/C1135/706

My darling Mother

Thank you awfully for your letter; also for the 2 <u>splendid</u> maps, which were just what we wanted. You always send just the things that I want. Also arrived today kit bag, towels, tooth powder, shaving soap, labels, nails for boots, matches, other soap, and Land & Water. Also Moggie's good letter about the knew guneas [*sic*] ("two white ones and a black, that makes 7" – she ought to be in the Army Intelligence Department, for estimating German casualties). I told you that I had got the writing blocks and nibs. But the first lot of the 3,000 cigarettes have <u>not</u> arrived; and of course the second 3,000 (of course) not yet. About the Mrs Steele things, the men have certainly not received <u>any</u> cigarettes since Xmas, as far as I can make out, and no eatables soap cocoa chocolate etc. I do think that it's a shame. Don't you think it would be better to send the things straight to me?

It's splendid about the Russians taking Pchemize[433], isn't it? It does look as if salvation were coming from the East.

Did you have fun at Ascott[434] with Marion Manie? Where are the Bucks Hussars, with all the long-nosed Grenfells and short-nosed Yidds?

Did you send the "Canadian Officer's" letter to the Morning Post? Did you get that letter of mine enclosing it?

Is the new Maurice Hewlett novel good? [435] Do send it to me. And some more of that good port?

---

[433] The Siege of Przemyśl was the greatest siege of the First World War, and a crushing defeat for Austria-Hungary. The investment of Przemyśl by the Russians began on 24 September 1914 and was briefly suspended on 11 October due to an Austro-Hungarian offensive. The siege resumed again on 9 November and the garrison surrendered on 22 March 1915 after holding out for a total of 194 days. (http://en.wikipedia.org/wiki/Siege_of_Przemysl)

[434] Ascott House, Wing, Buckinghamshire. It was acquired by Baron Mayer de Rothschild (of the neighbouring Mentmore Towers estate) in 1873

[435] Maurice Hewlett published at least three novels in 1915: *A Lover's Tale*; *The Forest Lovers: A romance*; and *The Little Iliad: a novel*

We have had a wonderful <u>boiling</u> hot Spring week, with all the birds shouting. It makes me feel terribly restless! Goodbye Mummy darling. I wish I could see you. What urgent "business" reason can I give to get another week's leave J.

266   28 Mar 1915   Western Front   DE/Rv/C1135/707

Darling Mother

Thank you awfully for your "birthday" letter, and the <u>very</u> good cake and Tiptree jam; and chocolate from Casie and a bottle of port from Moggie. Also one lot of 3,000 cigarettes <u>have</u> arrived for the men, (today), to their great delight. Also extra tinder for the pipe-lighters. You must have had a very good Sunday at Ascott. Yes, I love the country between Tap[low] & Aylesbury; it is much prettier than the real hunting country in the Vale[436]. I loved the letter from Moggie; she seems to have had a great joust at Melbury[437]. Can you make out why the people in England (and the generals here) say that the war is going to end directly? I cannot for the life of me make out How or Why. Can you? I think it would be <u>too</u> awful to leave them where they are without having the Big Go at them for which we have been waiting and reserving ourselves all along.
I <u>do</u> so agree with you anti the Grousers. Although I think that there are a good many large and obvious criticisms that could be made.
Life here rather dull, and varied only by sudden spasms of the worst Spit-and-Polish peace-soldiering energy. I am exercising the Scouts again now; but for a long time we have done nothing but exercise the horses for a short time every morning.
We had four wonderful <u>hot</u> Spring days; and now again bitter cold.
Goodbye & <u>all</u> love from J.

---

[436] Vale of Aylesbury, Buckinghamshire
[437] Melbury could be one of two houses: Melbury House, Evershot, Dorset, house of Lord Ilchester or, Melbury House, near Cobham, Surrey

267   2 Apr 1915   Western Front   DE/Rv/C1133/88

My darling Dad

Thank you so much for your letters. I should like to have seen the Moran-Wells fight[438]; but I think that Wells is always rather a poor creature, don't you? The Volunteers have been a most successful undertaking, haven't they? The Bradford meeting must have been magnificent. As to Edward Lyttelton, I must say that I think he got no more than he deserved; what call 'ad 'e (as Barnes says) to talk about politics, about which he knows nothing? And the pathetic part is that his critics tell him to get back to his Greek, about which he knows, if possible, less still! How is the Likkie-Man?

Things are rather boring here, and we do all the regular peace-soldiering things, and grumble at the men if their spur-buckles are dirty – rather ridiculous, when the real thing is going on 15 miles away. I can't help wishing that I were fighting now with the foot-sloggers; especially when there is quite a chance of us doing nothing more.

We've got a boxing show on here tomorrow; I wonder if I shall find an opponent!

Goodbye, & best love from Julian.

268   5 Apr 1915   Western Front   DE/Rv/C1135/708

Darling Mother

Thank you awfully for your letters, & Mrs Steele's enclosed. I still don't think that it is quite satisfactory; although I have no doubt that the things do start off alright. But what is the good of sending things if they are to be stacked in a room out here? The Col[onel] is so funny about it. He seems to resent anybody asking about it; so that I had to find out what I could, most inadequately, through the Adjutant & the Quartermaster. Again, he seems rather to resent the men getting things at all; or else why should he stack them in a room? And why should he take up the attitude that "they've got plenty of things, and should not have more"? (O Christ, I hope this letter is not opened by the regimental censor!) I must say, I do not see why they should not have a fair supply of cigarettes and small eatables; which they

---

[438] Boxing match on 29 March 1915, between the Englishman "Bombardier" Billy Wells and the American Frank Moran, "the fighting dentist". Moran knocked Wells out in the 10th round (http://www.cyberboxingzone.com/boxing/wells-bb.htm)

have not got at present.

Only <u>one</u> of your 3,000 cigarettes lots has arrived; and was vastly appreciated. I suppose that they bag them all in the post; it's rather sickening. I am longing for some more, but I hardly like asking, when the other ones did not arrive. What do you think?

Could you please send me <u>a dozen more electric torches, and a dozen more matchlighters</u>? Also some more <u>tinder</u> for the lighters? And with the torches, <u>2 dozen</u> refills (besides the 12 in the torches). I will give them to the Scouts as well to my troop. They <u>love</u> them; like children with toys, and they are so useful too.

We've had <u>boiling</u> hot weather lately, and no snow at all. In fact, it's rather trying weather with winter trench-clothes and no outlet for one's energy! I wonder if you are at Pans[hanger] now? Margot seems to be in terrific form; I should think she was just one of the people who are at their best in war, and try to raise a state of war even in peace-time to help themselves out. I don't know Simon, or much about him.

Diana Wyndham & Rosemary motored up to a place quite close here last week, & Alastair & I went over and spent the day with them; it was rather amusing. My world, what a nether millstone that Rosemary is! Have you ever seen anyone so little touched by any softer emotion? But I don't think that some of the things which she laughs at are very amusing; do you? Alastair in his best "My dear girl" form. Yesterday Alastair & I went over to Dunkirk in Millie's motor, which she sent for us. It was great fun, after these very dull billets; all the picture-postcard celebrities were there – Wilding[439], Maurice Elliot, Bend Or, Millie, Fitzgerald[440], Lady D Fielding, & Col Bridges. Millie looking <u>too</u> lovely, lovelier than anything I've ever seen; how much prettier she is than anything of the young generation! And <u>how</u>

---

[439] Anthony Frederick Wilding, tennis player. The outbreak of the First World War brought a halt to his tennis. He joined the Royal Marines, and in October 1914 was gazetted second lieutenant at headquarters intelligence corps. His knowledge of European roads was potentially valuable, and he was keen to work with armoured vehicles. He volunteered for an auxiliary armoured squadron in the Royal Naval Air Service, and in March 1915 was posted to France with the rank of lieutenant. In early May 1915 he was promoted to captain, and his team was moved to the front line near Neuve Chapelle, France. Just one week later, on 9 May 1915, he was killed when a shell exploded adjacent to the dug-out in which he was sheltering (ODNB)

[440] 'Bend Or' is probably a nickname as 'Bend Or' was a thoroughbred horse that won the 1880 Epsom Derby (http://en.wikipedia.org/wiki/Bend_Or). 'Millie' is the former Millicent Sutherland-Leveson Gower, duchess of Sutherland, widow of the 4th

fascinating. I simply loved seeing her, and had great fun with her. She looks radiant, and tremendously in love with Fitz, who treats her in rather a cavalier manner. Fitz rather too too, don't you think? But I like her.

We all motored up – it was quite funny to see trenches again. Apparently they go anywhere and do anything; which I suppose is possible when anybody has got that absolutely natural and unconscious amount of nerve, cheek, & face as all of them.

We had a boxing show on Saturday; and another ASC private volunteered to fight me, called Hay. When we went into the ring, and stripped, in deadly silence, a loud voice suddenly came from the back of the room, (from one of his friends)

"PORE OLD 'AY"

It was rather a good omen for me, and I landed him a terrific thump with my second punch, which shook him up so that I outed him in the second round. The same voice came again

"OO'S THE NEXT?"

I wish I could find out who it was; he would be a very good man to hire as a bravo to give me moral support whenever I fight.

I loved Moggie's letters, & Vovo's. I wish I could see the Pans[hanger] broadwater and all those trees thick and brown with spring; I do <u>love</u> that warm spring brown of the trees, don't you?

Mummy, could you send some more <u>cocoa and chocolate and eatables</u> for the men? How is the fund money holding out?

Another glorious cake arrived the other day. And a bottle of port and a bottle of Brandy today; were they from you?

Goodbye, & <u>all</u> love & blessing from J.

Duke of Sutherland and mother of Geordie and Alastair. She was one of the 'Souls'. On 17 October 1914, she had married Percy Desmond Fitzgerald, an army officer. On the outbreak of the First World War she organized a Red Cross ambulance unit, and served in France throughout the war (ODNB); see also Lyn Macdonald, *The Roses of No Man's Land* (1993), pp 28-35

269   15 Apr 1915   Western Front   DE/Rv/C1135/709

Darling Mother

Thank you awfully for your letter. Yes, Bridges looks too thrilling, &
amusing, and devilish. The cakes are <u>just</u> right, and we love them; <u>do</u> send
some more. The port not quite strong enough, but very good; and the Tiptree
jams wonderful. No more cigarettes arrived for the men – only the one lot;
and they are tremendously wanted.
We have moved billets again, but only a little way, into rather a good little
village; but off the hill, where we were before, & down into the flat again. I
am billeted with a <u>lovely</u> girl (and her Mother), and we sit solemnly for hours
(with the Mother) kicking each other under the table. We do a lot more
military work now, which is a good thing. Walter Hodgson has just come
back to the regiment, from the Yeomanry; he is a great dear. He has not gone
to this squadron, but to "A", when he has charge of Watkin and Alf. Watkin
lost £600 to Tubby Simon (the sapper who was with us in Africa, & who
part-owned "Kangaroo" with me) on the National; and Tubby came over
today to collect. Watkin saw us coming, and got into a ditch, thinking he was
unobserved; but we rounded him up eventually. He had won £1200 on the
Lincolnshire, so he's alright.
I <u>do</u> love the spring, don't you? I love your story about Nancy Cunard[441]; is
she a good girl? How is Billa-boy? Who was at Picket with you? Anyone
else?
Best <u>best</u> love.
I do wish I could see you J.

270   27 Apr 1915   Western Front   DE/Rv/C1133/89

Field service post card: I am quite well. I have received your letter dated -.
Letter follows at first opportunity. Julian.

---

[441] Nancy Clara Cunard, poet and political activist. During the early 1910s, she was
a glamorous and wild society girl among the artists at the Eiffel Tower restaurant in
London and a member of a group who called themselves 'the Corrupt Coterie'
(ODNB)

271   27 Apr 1915   Field Post Office   DE/Rv/C1135/662

Pre-written postcard: I am quite well. I have received your letters
(3)/parcels (2). Letter follows at first opportunity. Julian.

272   29 Apr 1915   Western Front   DE/Rv/C1133/90

Field service post card: I am quite well. Letters follow at first opportunity.
Julian.

273   29 Apr 1915   Army Post Office   DE/Rv/C1135/663

Pre-written postcard: I am quite well. I have received your parcel. Letters
follow at first opportunity. Julian.

274   30 Apr 1915   Western Front   DE/Rv/C1135/710

Darling Mother

I haven't written to you for ages and ages. First I went to Paris for four days
(and saw Casie on the way back) – and then we have been up here to assist at
the fighting. We've been up just a week doing Fire Brigade, which has
meant lying all day in fields, with the horses, and in the most wonderful hot
summer sun – except for the first two days, which were as cold as anything
which we have had for the whole winter. We only once left our horses and
went up into support, for two days, when we got shelled a bit, but nothing
much. The Greys had taken their horses right up there, and the horses were
in the field next us, with a few men, (the rest being in trenches). Three or
four shells suddenly came from the blue into the middle of them. They
stampeded, and the few Greys men, helped by our men, were wonderfully
good, and got them all away, riding one horse and leading about 4, through
all the pandemonium. They were shelling the road pretty hot at the time; and
wagons were galloping down it, and the usual amount of people had lost their
heads. We only had two men hit, and two horses. We "made" a mule, which
was immediately put in with the other 3 horses to pull our lumber; and off
they went, as happy as anything, looking irresistibly comic. We also had an
aeroplane bomb into our garden that day, which got 2 men (Canadians, not
ours). It was a funny mixture in that house, just off the big road – Canadians,
and doctors, and refugees, and Greys, and Yeomanry, and all our officers, all

crammed together anyhow, and "mucking in" together. The road itself was really a wonderful sight, all the two days; wounded in ambulances going back, wounded walking back (Turcos, Zouaves[442], Indians, Canadians, French, and our men); supplies going up, and reinforcements; doctors & generals and ambulances to and fro; and the constant piteous stream of refugees, old women and old men and young children, carrying all they can, with little carts and trollies pulled by themselves and their dogs, flowing back all the time. The road was shelled intermittently. I was asleep in the sun when they started the heavy bit of shelling; and they ragged[443] me terribly because they said I slept on through the first 3 shells that fell in the garden. I don't believe I did; anyhow when I got up a man staggered into me, very white and gibbering, saying he had been hit in the legs. I carried him to a doctor: I never heard what happened to him. Our men were very good; they fell in outside their barn, and began betting when the next shell would pitch. We were turned out quickly that night, to go to a gap; but after half an hour we got a message to say that things were better, & that we were not wanted. The next day we marched back the 6 miles to our horses.

It's been such <u>glorious</u> hot sun these 4 days, and with you too? It's been <u>tremendous</u> fighting?

I <u>did</u> love seeing Casie; I've never seen her looking so well and radiant and <u>pretty</u>, and we had the greatest fun. She was <u>so</u> good with the wounded Tommies, who all seemed to <u>love</u> her; she was just exactly "right there" with them. I was tremendously impressed by the cheeriness and comfortableness of the hospital, and by the happiness and easiness of the Tommies there; they seemed so absolutely content and at home.

And Paris! I can't imagine how I have lived so long without being there. I was absolutely fascinated by the <u>whole</u> thing. I had four divine spring days there. Isn't it gloriously light and gay and beautiful? The view down from the Arc de Triomphe to the Champs Elysées is as good as anything in the world, isn't it? I loved Versailles, too; but not frightfully; I think it is just a little blatant, just a little vulgar in its "grand-seigneurishness". What do you think? What I liked most about Paris was the light-heartedness of it all, the

---

[442] These were light infantry in the French army, originally recruited from the Algerian Kabyle tribe of Zouaoua, but afterwards composed of French soldiers distinguished for their physique and dash, and formerly retaining the original Oriental uniform. Turcos is another word for 'Zouaves'. A body of native Algerian light infantry in the French army; a Zouave soldier (OED)

[443] Teased (OED)

complete joie-de-vivre of the place and the people. They are so much lighter of heart than anything of ours, and really much more natural. And such artists in "fun". Isn't the Sunday crowd in the Jardins des Tuileries good, walking about and watching each other and enjoying each other? Aren't the Revues witty and amusing and unlike ours? And the tremendous tension of War running through all the gaiety and throwing it into relief. I saw a bit of everything – 'igh society, and the artists, and included the racing set (not the Lord Derbys[444] but the real racing push) included – the boxers, too, and the nuts, and the actresses, and the mannequins, and all the different very strictly defined classes of girls, all in their own particular places. I had the two best possible Cook's Guides[445] (quite by chance); Hubert Hartigan, of the 9th, also on leave, who knows Paris like a book, from racing there; and Henri Bardac, who used to be at Oxford, and who is convalescing from seven wounds, poor devil. It was the biggest "experience" of New Things I've ever had in my life; bigger than India, because it's more like our things and so more comparable – but really how much further removed from anything of ours! I do like the French people.

No more paper, as you see; and I've got such oceans more to say! All our baggage is left behind.

I do love getting your letters, and you've been awfully good in writing such a lot. I got another tonight, dated 27th, and the shirts & socks, which my men loved & wanted badly. What fun your Stanway & Grimsthorpe must have been.

Here is a poem, if you can read it. I rather like it. Publish it, if you think fit, with "JG". Can you send me a typed copy; and 3 typed copies of the "staff" one?

Goodbye, Mummy darling. Best love to Dad and all the family.

How sad about R[upert] Brooke[446]. J.

[*Envelope has* 'Into Battle' *written on it in ballpoint pen*]

---

[444] The Earls of Derby were famous for their commitment to horse-racing. In 1779 the Epsom Oaks race was renamed the Epsom Derby after the 12th Earl

[445] Tour guides produced by Thomas Cook, the international travel company, that is still one of the best-known businesses in the world

[446] See letter 85 with footnote

275   5 May 1915   Western Front   DE/Rv/C1133/91

My dear Dad

Thank you very much for your letters. Also for the port, which was greatly appreciated. We should simply love some Black Strap[447], if you could send some, 2 bottles a week. A leather telescopic-sight <u>case</u> has arrived, but not the rifle or the sight yet.

It must have been very interesting to see Bill's lot. I expect they are jolly good I wish they would hurry up and get them out quickly. It would be great fun to meet Billy suddenly at the corner of the road somewhere! The wounded Canadians are very comfortable at Cliveden[448], I expect. They seem to have fought most awfully well up here.

We are still up here, "near handy". We have twice been up in support since we arrived here, and were shelled a bit, but nothing to matter; and tonight we are going up again to dig trenches. It has been the most lovely warm sunny weather. They are damn good, these Huns; I wish that we didn't lie so much in all our reports; it is difficult to see the point of it.

Will you please thank Mother for the

12 electric torches	)	
chocolate	)	for the men
cigarettes	)	
pipe-lighters	)	

and the Respirators[449], which all arrived quite safely.

We are all tremendously fit and well. It is astonishing what a difference the weather makes to men and horses. The horses are looking fit and hard, for the first time since Africa. I sleep out every night now.

I hope the Likky Man had good holidays. I saw Casie at Wimereux the other

---

[447] An inferior kind of port wine, also a mixture of rum and treacle taken as a beverage (OED)

[448] Cliveden, from 1893 the home of the Astors; the neighbouring estate to Taplow. It was used as a hospital during the war

[449] Gas masks. The Germans had introduced poison gas in 1915 in the second battle of Ypres; 168 tons of chlorine gas were released on 22 April over a four mile front. Around 6,000 troops died within ten minutes from asphyxiation; the gas affected the lungs and the eyes causing respiration problems and blindness. Being denser than air it flowed downwards forcing the troops to climb out of trenches. (http://en.wikipedia.org/wiki/Second_Battle_of_Ypres)

day, looking so well and happy. I had 4 days leave in Paris; which was great fun, & did me a world of good. I just got back in time for this show.
I hope that you are fit and well, Daddy. I wish I could see you again soon.
All love & blessings from Julian.
I've got a great big horse now, thorobred, a sort of cross between Buccaneer and your old bay Goliath.
Please tell Mother to send <u>always more cigarettes</u> for the men.

276   8 May 1915   Western Front   DE/Rv/C1133/92

My dearest Dad

Thank you very much for your letter. The Gibbs rifle arrived today, with the telescopic sight. It <u>is</u> fun having it. I shot with it this afternoon, at 150 yards, 20 shots. Nobody would believe me when I showed them the target – all the shots in a 4 inch ring, and most of them cutting each other! What a wonderful thing it is, the telescopic sight! Mr Gibbs said on his directions that it shot 1 inch high at 100^x; but I thought that it shot dead at 150. Thank you very much for sending it. It will be just the thing for loophole shooting – waiting till the face appears, & drawing a bead. I shall carry it on my back; could you send me a good <u>broad</u> sling for it. It is deliciously light, too, after the service rifle.
You will have great fun with Casie at Wimereux. I <u>must</u> manage to get over to see you. It would be splendid if you could come up to Putty[450].
I'm glad that the Volunteers are going so well.
We got back to our old billets in the middle of last night, after 15 days wandering. But we never got up to first-line trenches, which was disappointing.
Goodbye, Daddy. I <u>do</u> hope we meet this month.
All love from Julian.

---

[450] Visit General Pulteney at his headquarters of the Third Division (Mosley, p386)

277   8 May 1915   Western Front   DE/Rv/C1135/711

Darling Mother

Thank you awfully for your letters. You will be finishing your fortnight's
waiting now? Stanway must have been delicious; and interesting to see all
the "heads" in London during this bad time. The men <u>did</u> love the things so
much – the lighters, and the lamps, and the chocolate, and the cigarettes; they
arrived while we were "up", at different places, and I just had time to throw
them at the troop as we were starting off somewhere, mounted or
dismounted, and loaded up with every kind of weapon and ammunition; they
said "Ho Lord, we'll ave to put this in our mouths – but always managed to
stow it away somewhere. <u>Cigarettes</u> are what they really want, always; they
have only got 2 packets of 10 cigarettes each per week, since Christmas.
We went up once more since I wrote to you, to dig second line trenches, all
through the night. We billeted a good distance away, and it made quite a
long expedition, going up on the horses, and then leaving them, and then
walking on, with 2 bandoliers of cartridges, (150 rounds, & you can't
imagine how heavy, cutting into one's shoulders.) I stayed to look after the
horses this last time – the first time I have ever done it! They shelled round
them, & never into them. There were some of our big guns in the next field,
blazing away all the night. They said that our men dug <u>too wonderfully</u>, on
their empty stomachs, poor dears, (we had left at 2 pm), from 9 pm till 1 am.
The Sappers[451] said that 1 cavalryman digs more than 2½ infantry men. They
got shelled a bit, but we were lucky again, and we only lost 1 man hit. We
got back to our farm at 6.30 am on a lovely spring morning, with
nightingales singing round us all the way home. And yesterday we did our
20 miles back here, in the rain, to our old billets.
It is great fun to wander about the country with no baggage or impediments,
not knowing or caring where you are going or how you are going to fetch up
– a great feeling of independence, and no personal property to tie you down,
which Plato said is the ideal state. We had left all our belongings (including
my dogs, and the puppies) here – and we were utterly uncertain whether we

---

[451] Soldiers employed in working at saps, the building and repairing of fortifications,
the execution of field-works, and the like. The non-commissioned officers and
privates of the Engineers were formerly called the (Royal) Sappers and Miners, but
in 1859 they became the Royal Engineers (The privates are still unofficially called
sappers) (OED)

should ever return, or see them again. I really like the wandering existence, & sleeping in fields, better than standing billets – or anything else. But I don't imagine that we shall stay here for long.

It will be the <u>greatest</u> fun if you get up to Putty; or if I can get down to Boulogne. But I imagine it will be difficult to get leave from now onwards. But we <u>must</u> fix it somehow. Poor Casie, I expect she is working plenty just now. What fun it will be for you to be out there with her.

I'm so glad that you like the verses[452], because I liked them a lot; although I thought afterwards that they were slightly meretricious[453], due no doubt to a recent visit to Paris and the earlier influences of other people; but "good meretricious", which is after all no bad quality. Yes, send them to the "Times" – I don't think it is too long.

The long dogs were very good when I got back here. A kind woman at the farm had kept and fed them for me. One had been run over by a motor bus, but was none the worse. We arrived in the middle of the night, and when they heard my voice they came out of the yard like shrapnel bursting. "Comrade" jumped up onto the horse's shoulder; and when he fell back they all started fighting like hell, from sheer joy.

I went into one of the "forward dressing stations", that night when I stayed with the horses. A tiny hovel of a farm, 5 doctors, and the bad cases coming in and going out on the stretchers, everything choc-a-bloc. How <u>marvellously</u> brave and cheerful the wounded English Tommy is! And what a fine class of men, the Territorial Tommy – quite different to our men, of course.

Bless you J.

---

[452] 'Into battle', which had been sent with letter 274. The poem was published in *The Times* on 27 May, along with news of his death the previous day. Two copies of the poem are in D/EX789/F23a (items abstracted from his diary) and one of these could well be the one sent with the letter, but later abstracted; DE/Rv/F119 contains two typescripts of the poem. It was published in a number of newspapers and journals

[453] Showily or superficially attractive but in reality having no value or integrity (OED)

278   14 May 1915   Western Front   DE/Rv/C1135/712

Darling Mother

Isn't it wonderful and glorious that at last after long waiting the Cavalry have
put it across the Boches on their flat feet and have pulled the frying pan out
of the fire for the second time. Good old "iron ration". We are practically
wiped out; but we charged and took the Hun trenches yesterday. I stopped a
Jack Johnson with my head, and my skull is slightly cracked. But I'm
getting on splendidly. I did awfully well. Today I go down to Wimereux, to
hospital. Shall you be there?
<u>All</u> <u>all</u> love Julian of the 'Ard 'Ed.
Longing to see you and <u>talk</u>!!
Bless you!
[*Envelope has* 'From No 10 Casualty Clearing Station BEF' *written on it in
ballpoint pen*]

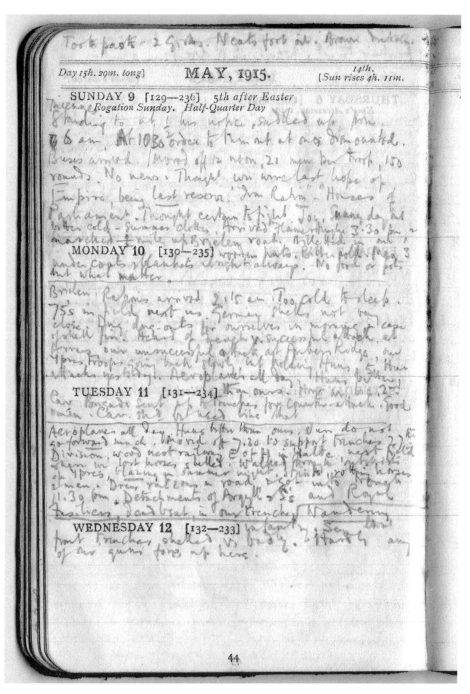

The last entries in Julian's diary, May 1915.

Appendix 1

The diaries of Julian Grenfell and Lady Desborough

Julian Grenfell's diary, 1915 [HALS: DE/X789/F23]

Sunday 24 January: Leave. Got to Hazebrouck 7.30 pm and had dinner.
Went on by the 8.45 train and slept in the saloon on the boat. Sailed 9.30 am.

Thursday 28 January: Hunted with South Berks at Lodden Bridge, Reading,
riding a ch[ar]g[er] belonging to Saunders. We had a poor day in the big
woods near Maiden Erlegh.

Saturday 30 January: Hunted with Bron with NF Fox hounds at Backley.
Arrived late, coming by 8.55 train from Waterloo. I rode Bron's Irish
thorobred. Fox scent. Ran a fox to ground in the afternoon.

Sunday, 31 January: <u>Absolute perfect week at home</u>. Hunted colts with
Bron. I rode Tartlet Bron the grey Welsh stallion. Found bay mare & foal
under Sawley beeches, stalked [?] them in through Bratley Soldiers Bog
Backley enclosure. Excitement of officers & men at going back to battle,
after awful boredom. Fun of seeing old Ypres again. Cathedral & Cloth Hall
in ruins.

Monday, 1 February: Marylebone 10.5 Aylesbury 11.20. Norah - Petrograd
Hotel – Audley St. Rumours of cavalry back in trenches.

Tuesday, 2 February: Returned from leave having heard that we are now in
trenches. Motored from Boulogne to St Omer with Rex & Alan, heard
reg[imen]t is at Blaringhem. Motored on but could not find Royals. Banging
doors everyone in bed. Slept at farm, found woman. Drove on in farm cart
next morning, & found B eventually; at La Belle Hotesse.

Wednesday, 3 February: Paraded 12.15 pm. Marched to Steenbecque 12.30
pm. Moved off in motor buses (the brigade) at 2 pm for Ypres. Halted N
side Hazebrouck till it got dark. Arrived Ypres market square 9 pm and went
into billets. We had left our horses behind at La Belle Hotesse with 1 man

to 3 horses. ½ 8th Ca[valry] Brig[ade] and 7th Cav[alry] Brigade in trenches now. We go in next for 5 days.

Thursday, 4 February: Went round Ypres Cathedral & Cloth Hall. Saw Giles Courage. German aeroplane dropped bomb near Somerset Yeomanry. A little shelling every night but not much. Population don't care much. Ordinary life. Some of them have stopped being the whole time. The shops do a roaring trade with the soldiers. One lady told me that she had had Jamais aussi du plaisir dans la vie que pendant cette guerre. Indeed the ladies of Ypres are very fond of pleasure, and some of them very pretty. We had good billets in the big streets S of the square. Food very dear but good and plenty of it in the town.

Saturday, 6 February: Wonderful <u>excitement</u> of getting up to the firing line again and to business. Men tremendously excited too. Funny how tired the war feeling and the sound of guns makes one. Nerves? No, just strain of excitement. Officers going up 2 by 2 to the 1st L[ife] G[uards] trenches, staying there for a night and a day, and returning the following night. Very good plan. 8th Cav[alry] Brigade and ½ 7th Brigade in trenches now for 5 days then us for 5 days, then other Cav[alry] Divisions, 1½ Brigades at a time. Germans throw bottle to Blues saying "Why fight with bl[ood]y English. French & German people brother socialists. <u>Alsatian</u>.

Sunday, 7 February: Very hot day for me in Ypres. All these people take Free Love as a matter of course and habit. The daughter says Ask Mother if she will give us a bed. In evening I went out to the 1 LG trenches. Awful walk in the dark; loaded up with food and stuff. James came to meet us and took us a long way through the wood.

Monday, 8 February: 1 LG very good to us. I brought 2 bott[le]s wine for them. <u>Capital</u> trenches like in papers & fairy tales. A quiet day. 2 sappends from German lines to ours, ours being old German trenches. Signs of work in one of them. Made loophole. Sappers started sap, but did not finish. Reg[imen]t arrived 11 pm.

Tuesday, 9 February: Germans had dug another new line of trenches 100 yds nearer us, to avoid fire of the 75s behind us? Col[onel] would not open up sappend running to German trench. No smoking! <u>No aggression</u>!! Trench v good for snipers.

Wednesday, 10 February: Germans had dug new embrasure about 30 yds from our salient on the right. In afternoon they sent 5 minnenwerters just each side of our trench. Can see them in air. About 8 in long, 2 in thick. Big explosion. 3 of our dug-outs knocked in. I replied with 3 rifle bombs, & the 75s with shrapnel further out. Then Huns stopped. I sleep with Philip, share watches 6.30 – 12.30, sleeping in little front dug out. Uncomfortable in trenches, but always exciting. Our men good, but one or two [?] bad. They Roared with laughter when bombarded.

Thursday, 11 February: Quiet day. Found embrasure when Germans fired bombs yesterday, in thick patch of wood (fallen trees) 50 yds in front of A Sq[ua]d[ron] to our right. Our sentries look & fire thro small loophole day and night. Useless for night attack. Huns all have stands, shoot over parapet. Night attack unobservable till enemy on top of trench. Hun flares much better than ours. Huns have front trenches; only way of warning for night attack.

Friday, 12 February: Germans played drum and bugle band in morning. Some sleet & snow. Getting tired of our 5 days. 75s shelling 3rd Huns line of trenches in front of us. Thrush singing in wood every morning. Poor mating season. Cat along our trenches at night. Lucky so far. <u>Run</u>. Flares & firing all night.

Saturday, 13 February: Huns dug new trench last night. They have now got about 4 diff[erent] lines of trenches. Much better either for attack or defence. Raining like Hell. Hear our billets last week in Ypres were shelled last night, with 20 casualties to 1 LG, who are in them now. Luck for us & them. Hope I get a chance to do some damage to the Huns before I get killed in some stray way like that. I boil cocoa for self & Philip in my billy at 12.30 and 5.30 am (when we stand to for an hour). Bad thing to hold trenches 5 days only, then a new lot to come in, not used to them. Rained most of day. NB Dead bodies buried in parapet of trench, & washed out when rain came or bombs.

We were supposed to be relieved at 10 pm, but not until 12 midnight, by 3rd Hussars. Walked back to Ypres, carrying all our loads. Wagons did not meet us at Zillebeke to take loads as arranged. Foul state of decaying flesh in Zillebeke. All houses bashed in. Got back to Ypres square and motor buses about 3 am.

Monday, 15 February: Started 4 am. Got in 7.30 am to Steenbecque. Chicken & clams provided in motor bus by Hopper. Wonderful to get back to rest, out of bullets.

Tuesday, 16 February: Bath – 7 days beard off. Even 5 days (not fighting) a great strain. Even the moderate Estaminet civilisation a wonderful change. People who like being dirty best take being clean best. Although I like trenches, I love getting back. Slept 9 am – 6 pm. NB Night when I heard noise of bomb dropping on top of dug out. Petrified. Lost self control – lay still, clenching my hands, for 20 secs. Asked what it was. "Rum jar thrown away".

Friday, 19 February: Went out with dogs. "Sandon" "Comrade" and "Rocket" ran a hare under Moulin Fontaine, but she beat them. I walked a long way over plough before finding her.

Saturday, 20 February: NB Germans only hold front line trenches with 2 men & a boy, snipers and machine guns. Best way. Can avoid shells, if we ever shell them. Means less casualties than us, when they are not attacking in ordinary trench warfare. If first trench taken MGs from 2nd trench & counter attack.

Wednesday, 24 February: Rode over to Lynde with the dogs, and had a run after a hare which got up very wide and beat them.

Tuesday, 9 March: La Belle Hotesse. In evening news arrived that we are to stand in readiness during attack by British near La Bassée.

Wednesday, 10 March: Standing in readiness all day. Heard about 9 pm that we are to start at 4 am. Order from Haig to 1st Army "48 batt[alion]s to German 4, & heaviest guns ever known". Slightly boastful?

Thursday, 11 March: La Belle Hotesse. Breakfast 3.0 am. Sq[ua]d[ro]n parade 4.15 am. Brigade rendezvous at Steenbecque. Marched to La Motte, and waited there till late in afternoon. News that the La Bassée attack is going well but 2000 casualties yesterday. Filthy dull cold day, on edge of wood. Coffee & omelette in little farm house. In evening marched on through Merville. Into billets in dark. Tiny cottage, after turned out of measles farm. 3 boiled eggs for dinner. Slept on kitchen floor. Very misty up till 12 m[i]d[night]. Bad for an attack.

Friday, 12 March: Standing to all day 1 m E of Merville. The curry-edded fucker told me that we had very nearly been shoved through the hole yesterday. News of 100 prisoners in am; 600 in pm. Saw about 30 marched along road into Merville; they looked well fed – a little pale – some of them very young, about 17 yrs old. News that attack goes well. Lovely sunny morning. Rumour that we have taken La Bassée. Subsequently confirmed that we have not taken La B, and 4,000 casualties. Bad to wait doing nothing while all friends killed.

Tuesday, 16 March: La Belle Hotesse. Sandon & Comrade killed a hare in the field behind the house in the a.m.

Thursday, 18 March: Coursed a hare in field behind house

Tuesday, 23 March: Had a good course near Moulin Fontaine with Comrade & Sandon. Comrade ran wonderfully, and nearly killed, but Sandon would not help him.

Friday, 26 March: Coursing. High ground Bille Hoterne. Comrade runs beautifully, but Sandon will not back him up, or he w[oul]d kill.

18 – 22 April   Details of stay in Paris, including hotels, places visited; includes 'Peggy (fair hair) 82.34'.

Friday, 23 April: Paraded 1.15 pm (brigade) marched to Abeele (division). Heard of French territorials going back 3 miles from Langemarck & Canadians, in air, fighting like hell. Billets back at Eecke, got in at 1 am.

Saturday, 24 April: Eecke. Moved off 10 am, & marched to place E of Poperinghe[454]. Lots of French troops moving up. Turcos in motors, rough men, cheered by our troops. Tremendous chock-a-bloc on roads. We had moved without our echelon B, and so without our rations. Men had no rations with them when we started yesterday (no time or means of carrying

---

[454] During the First World War, Poperinghe was part of unoccupied Belguim and developed into the nerve centre of the British sector

them) – and none today, & no prospect of getting them, apparently. Back to billets at Boeschoote 10.30 pm. Bitterly cold these 2 days. Bitterly cold $\underline{1^{st}}$ 2 days, then warm & lovely. Rations <u>at last</u> arrived (7 am Sunday).

Sunday, 25 April: Boeschoote. Moved at 9.30 to field S of Poperinghe. Waited. Moved on in afternoon, NW of Poperinge. Went into billets 6.30 pm at Outkerke Houtkerke. Refugees flying on all the roads. Slept in barn, men in field.

Monday, 26 April: Stood to 5.30 am, and moved to brigade rendezvous soon after 6. Waited there till 10 am, & moved to field SW of Poperinghe. Waited then till 11 pm. Tremendous gunning. News good & bad. Looks as if they must get Ypres. Shells into Poperinghe. We went up 2 miles on the horses, tied them up, left 1 man to 4, & walked through Pop to Vlamertinghe, arriving 2 am. Slept in loft 3 am & men in barn of factory.

Tuesday, 27 April: Slept till 8. All sorts in this house. Canadians, Yeomanry, Scots Greys, & us. Quiet morning. Shells started 5 pm. About 2 dozen. Stampede of Greys horses, in field next road. 12 killed, 2 men (Greys in trenches). Men wonderful, collected horses & moved them all down road. Wagons, wounded, galloping, refugees running & crying, man knocked 10 yds by loose Grey horse. Our men collected & waited quietly outside factory. Road scene amusing. Battledore and shuttlecock between Pop & Vlam. French supply col[umn] coming up. English mule jibbed, French white horse bit him & he ran away. Aeroplane bomb into garden, hit 2 Canadians, 2 of our men hit by shell. Mil[itary] police gallop back, walk forward. Aeroplane bomb killed 2 men in our garden. Rodgered last night. Turned out about 9 pm to go & help Turcos on Iser. But as you were after ¼ hr.

Wednesday, 28 April: Flamertinghe. Quiet day, no shelling. 12 noon long walk back to horses, then back into billets farm near Wattou at 9 pm. Kindness to refugees, always given best places, not to be disturbed. Lots of boys selling chocolate to troops. Horses, their patience. Mule instead of our lost (shelled) horse running with horses in limber.

Thursday, 29 April: Nr Whatho. Moved off 8 am towards Pop. Brigade rested in field. Rested all day and got back to our farm at 7.30 pm. Pork chops for dinner. Wonderful sunny lazy days – but longing to be up and doing something always. Slept out. Wrote poem "Into Battle".

Friday, 30 April: (E of Wathou, farm). Moved off at 8 am, and stopped all day in field 2 m W of Pop. Lovely day again. Slept all day. Good grazing for horses. Steam Plough in his element, getting like barrel. Back to our farm 7 pm. Pork chops. Slept out.

Saturday, 1 May: Farm E of Whathou. Exercised on blankets 5 – 6 am. Moved off 8 am, rested all day in same field E of Pop. Back to our Wathou farm 7 pm. I did gymnastics and contorsions and shadow-boxing in evening to get some exercise. Another glorious hot spring day. Slept out.

Sunday, 2 May: Farm E of Whathou. Exercised on blankets 5 – 6 am. Moved off 8 am, and rested in same field all day. Went back at 3.30 pm to new billets, near Proven. Pork chops. Ran ¼ mile ag[ain]st James in evening, & did shadow-boxing. Slept out.

Monday, 3 May: Exercise in morning. Started at 7 in evening to go up in reserve, while we were returning the line. Left horses SE Poperinghe in field. 1 man to 4. Marched on to field just W of Wipers, arriving about 2 am. Wet night and cold. Walked in concentric circle.

Tuesday, 4 May: Staff work. Drew rations about 3.30 am, and rum. On empty stomachs, everyone cheerful and slightly drunk. At 5 am we were told that the line had been successfully withdrawn & we walked back to horses, & so back to our farm. Stables, arms, food, & sleep. Breakfast in farm before we started with horses. Nightingales singing all way back (first time heard). Nearly went to sleep on my horse.

Wednesday, 5 May: Exercise in morning. News at midday to go up & dig trenches in reserve line. Started 4.30. Left horses in field between Flam & Ypres about ½ mile from Ypres, 7.30 pm. Stayed with horses. They say the men dug <u>awfully</u> well, 1 cav[alry] man same work as 2 infantrymen. We come fresher to it. Went into dressing station in farm. Cases kept coming in. 30 men died of gas. Kitchener affair. Everyone smoking. Dead & wounded lying on stretchers in barn waiting for ambulances. Men dressed on the small kitchen floor.
Men back at 1 & rode back to our farm near Proven. Stables, arms & slept all day. Staff officer told me we are going to hold line just round outskirts of

Ypres. Told me also Hill 60 taken by gases. NB "Shattered" look of wounded & men going back.

Friday, 7 May: Exercise 8 am. Plato's idea of Happiness realised – no personal property or ties, just as ready to move or to stay. Saddle up 2 pm. In to billets at Thiennes, via Steenvoorde & Hazebrouck, at 7.30 pm, in the rain. Dogs all right except Sandon run over by motor, shot him. Puppies grown out of knowledge.

Saturday, 8 May: New rifle with telescopic sight arrived. Tried it in afternoon. Wonderful. 20 in 4 in radius circle. Shall carry it with me, over shoulder. News of attack by us at Aubers Ridge. No news from Ypres.

Sunday, 9 May: Thiennes. Standing to at ½ hrs notice, saddled up, from 6 am. At 10.30 order to turn out at once dismounted. Buses arrived. Moved off 12 noon, 21 men per troop, 150 rounds. No news. Thought we were last hope of Empire, being last reserve. "Iron Ration" – "Houses of Parliament. Thought certain to fight. Joy. Sunny day but bitter cold – summer clothes. Arrived Flamertinghe 3.30 pm, & marched ½ mile up Brielen road. Billeted in our wooden huts. Bitter cold. Men 3 under coats & blankets alright always. No food or pots but what matter.

Monday, 10 May: Brielen. Rations arrived 2.15 am. Too cold to sleep. 75's in field next us. German shells not very close. Dug dug-outs for ourselves in morning in case of shell fire. Heard of French v successful attack at Arras, our unsuccessful attack at Aubers Ridge, our Ypres troops going back slowly, but holding Huns, 5 Hun attacks yesterday. Aeroplanes all day. Huns better than ours. How we lie. 2nd Cav[alry] Brigade sent up to trenches for counter-attack. Good omen. Cav[alry] sh[oul]d be used like that.

Tuesday, 11 May: Aeroplanes all day. Huns better than ours, ours do not go forward much. Moved off 7.30 to support trenches 27th Division, wood next railway E of H in Halte, next field where we lost horses shelled. Walked through outskirts of Ypres, blazing on summer night. Stink, rotting horses & men. Drew rations on road, & got into trench 11.30 pm. Detachment of Argyll & S[utherland]'s and Royal Fusiliers, dead beat in our trenches.

Wednesday, 12 May: Wandering infantry. Say that front trenches shelled v badly. Hardly any of our guns fire up here.

Lady Desborough's diary, May 1915.

Lady Desborough's diary, 1915 [HALS: DE/Rv/F61]

[Rough notes, lists, accounts, etc not included]

15 May   Got Mon's telegram at 11 that Julian slightly wounded in head & at Boulogne & prob[ably] coming over tomorrow.

16 May   Telegram at 4 summoning us to Boulogne from Commandant at Julian's Hospital. No steamer till tomorrow, got leave from Admiralty to cross in ammunition-boat. Seven minutes to pack & start. Flew up to London in motor…Caught train Victoria, Newhaven 9.6. Authorities so kind, gave us din[ner], got Ca[sie]'s telegram, rather consoled. Started at 11. Calm night.

17 May   Got to Boulogne 5 am. Straight to Hospital, Ca[sie] there, dear Julian operated on yest[erda]y – his skull was fractured & a splinter was 1½ in into his brain. Sargent did it & Holmes & Lister were with him. He was doing well but cannot be out of danger for 11 days. At Hospital only all day…saw Julian twice for second.

18 May   To Hosp[ital] w[ith] W[illy] & Ca[sie] 8.45. Julian very good night, saw him. Back to breakfast…Back to see Ju[lian], he said "So much better". Saw Col Sargent, <u>good</u> account…sat w[ith] Julian. To Wimereux w[ith] Ca[sie].

19 May   To Hospital. Julian good night.

20 May   Billa came out w[ith] Regiment. Julian fair night…Sat w[ith] Julian & Bill saw him…We fancied Julian a shade stronger.

21 May   …to Hospital early. Julian seemed shade stronger. Much with him…To Hospital late…<u>Slightly</u> less anxious.

22 May   Too lovely day, much w[ith] Julian, he seemed really a shade better…Hospital at 4…To Hospital late.

23 May   We all had Communion with Julian at 7. Darling Julian less well, a second operation sole chance, performed at 11. Saw him at 1. With him from 4 straight on & all 3 there all night. He slept after 1.15 & from 20 to 5 very soundly.

24 May   Home at 6.30. Lay down for an hour. Back to Hosp[ital]. Lister. Sargent at 11 gave us one thread of hope. We had quite given up hope. Ca[sie] & W[illy] stayed there. I slept till 2. With him whole aft[ernoon]. Shade better. Slept there. He had fair night.

25 May   With Julian the day long. Less well. Talked a little in morning, but did not speak again after 2.30 pm. With him all night. Very peaceful & looking so happy.

26 May   We thought Julian was dying at 7.30 am but he lived till 20 minutes to 4 pm. We thought he knew us till the very end. "Phoebus Apollo".

27 May   W[illy] & Mon & I came to Hardelot, to the lovely green woods & Sea & peace. We went first to the little mortuary tent, where Julian lay under the Union Jack.

28 May   Julian's funeral, in the burial ground at the top of the hill at Boulogne.

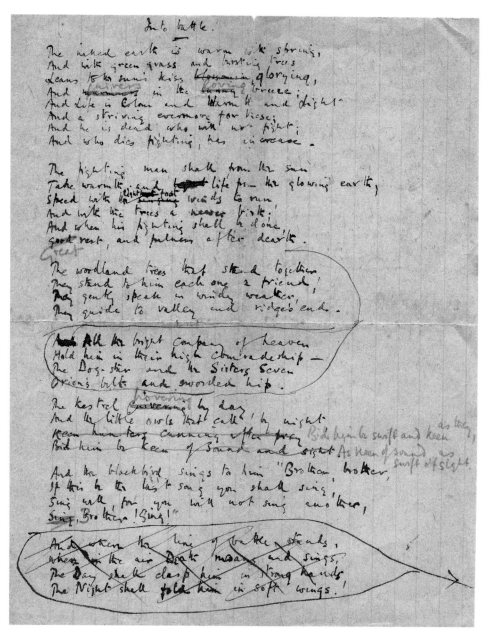

Draft manuscript of *Into Battle*, 1915.

Appendix 2

A selection of Julian's poems

To a black greyhound

Shining black in the shining light,
Inky black in the golden sun,
Graceful as the swallow's flight,
Light as swallow, winged one;
Swift as driven hurricane –
Double sinewed stretch and spring
Muffled thus of flying feet,
See the black dog galloping
Hear his wild foot-beat.

See him lie when the day is dead,
Black curves curled on the boarded floor.
Sleepy eyes, my sleepy-head –
Eyes that were aflame before.
Gentle now, they burn no more;
Gentle now, and softly warm,
With the fire that made them bright
Hidden – as when after storm
Softly falls the night.

God of Speed, who makes the fire –
God of Peace, who lulls the same –
God who gives the fierce desire,
Lust for blood as fierce as flame –
God who stands in Pity's name –
Many may ye be or less,
Ye who rule the earth and sun:
Gods of strength and gentleness
Ye are ever one.

Hymn to the fighting boar

God gave the horse for man to ride
And steel wherewith to fight,
And wine to swell his soul with pride
And women for delight:
But a better gift than all these four
Was when he made the fighting boar…

Prayer for those on the staff

Fighting in mud, we turn to Thee
In these dread times of battle, Lord,
To keep us safe, if so may be,
From shrapnel snipers, shell and sword.

Yet not on us – (for we are men
Of meaner clay, who fight in clay) –
But on the Staff, the Upper Ten,
Depends the issue of the day.

The Staff is working with its brains
While we are sitting in the trench;
The Staff the universe ordains
(Subject to Thee and General French).

God, help the Staff – especially
The young ones, many of them sprung
From our high aristocracy;
Their task is hard, and they are young.

O Lord, who mad'st all things to be
And madest some things very good
Please keep the extra ADC
From horrid scenes, and sights of blood…

Into battle

The naked earth is warm with spring,
And with green grass and bursting trees
Leans to the sun's gaze glorying.
And quivers in the sunny breeze;
And life is colour and warmth and light
And a striving evermore for these;
And he is dead who will not fight;
Ad who dies fighting has increase.

The fighting man shall from the sun
Take warmth, and life from the glowing earth;
Speed with the light-foot winds to run,
And with the trees to newer birth;
And find, when fighting shall be done,
Great rest, and fullness after dearth.

All the bright company of Heaven
Hold him in their high comradeship –
The Dog-star and the Sisters Seven,
Orion's belt and sworded hip.

The woodland trees that stand together,
They stand to him each one a friend;
They gently speak in the windy weather,
They guide to valley and ridge's end.

The kestrel hovering by day,
And the little owls that call by night,
Bid him be swift and keen as they –
As keen of sound, as swift of sight.

The blackbird sings to him 'Brother, brother,
If this be the last song you shall sing.
Sing well, for you will not sing another;
Brother, sing!'

In dreary doubtful waiting hours,
Before the brazen frenzy starts,
The horses show him nobler powers;
O patient eyes, courageous hearts!

And when the burning moment breaks,
And all things else are out of mind,
And only joy of battle takes
Him by the throat, and makes him blind,

Through joy and blindness he shall know,
Not caring much to know, that still
Nor lead nor steel shall reach him so
That it be not the Destined Will.

The thundering line of battle stands,
And in the air death moans and sings;
And Day shall clasp him with strong hands,
And Night shall fold him in soft wings.

Appendix 3

Various letters and other documents relating to Julian

1. Letters regarding his actions in November 1914

DE/Rv/C1230/1, 18 November 1914, from Philip Hardwick, Royal Dragoons

Dear Lord Desborough

I thought you might like to hear how Julian is getting on from an independent source, in case he himself is modest. He is doing very well indeed, as I always knew he would, but it is more especially of what he has done the last two days that I thought might interest you. We were in the trenches on a 48 hour turn of duty & where we were, in a wood, less than 100 yards from the German trenches, we were very much bothered by snipers who were doing a lot of damage.

The day before yesterday Julian crept through the undergrowth right up to one of the German trenches & shot one of them dead through his own loophole. Yesterday he crawled out in the same direction & found the trench evacuated so he crept on some little way beyond. He put two more Germans in the bag & then came back with the most useful information that the Germans were advancing. Within half an hour they attacked the line very heavily & were repulsed with great loss. Both acts were not only extremely plucky, but it showed great resource & presence of mind not to say cunning. I have reported the matter to the Colonel who will send it on. He is very fit and well & cheery in spite of many unpleasant conditions. I won't let him do anything too rash, but so far he has shown that he is quite capable of looking after himself and more than a match for a whole lot of damned Germans[455].

DE/Rv/C384/1, 20 Nov [1914], from Col David Campbell [*typed extract*]:

…Julian Grenfell has done awfully well. On the 16th he crawled through a wood and shot a German through the loophole of his own trench. On the 17th he went out again from the trenches and shot 2 Germans and found them concentrating for the attack…

---

[455] See letter 234 for Julian's account of the incident

APPENDICES

D/EX789/F30: 29 Dec 1915, from Alan [Lascelles?]

My Dear Ettie
On being ordered into action again, I have been looking through some old
"kit" I had laid by, and have found this disc. I am ashamed that I didn't send
it to you before, but we were fighting when I found it, and I forgot afterwards
where I had put it. There is a story attached to it – last November, Julian's
squadron "took over" from mine in Zillebeke Wood, and it was the morning
after that, he crawled out and won his DSO – last February I again held
practically the same line (by then, very much improved). On the 3rd Night
one of my "listening posts", who had crawled out along a ditch towards the
German line, brought this disc back, which he had found. Dear Julian must
have lost it on the actual morning when he was out scouting in November, as
he had not been there since. I do most humbly beg your pardon for not
having sent it before, but it was stowed away in a letter-case that I thought
lost. Julian was always a very great friend to me; the calamity was too great
for me to write to you at the time and afterwards I <u>couldn't</u> trespass on your
great sorrow. Please forgive me.
Y[ou]rs affect[ionatel]y Alan.
[*Julian's identity disc enclosed*]

2. Telegrams and letters regarding his wounding and decoration

DE/Rv/C1979/1: 15 May 1915, from OC, 7th Stationary Hospital

Telegram: Son wounded in head better come show this for permit

DE/Rv/C2303/37: 15 May, Monica Grenfell to Lord Desborough

Telegram: Julian arrived Seventh Stationary Hospital Boulogne this morning
with slight scalp wound received Thursday Condition excellent no
Complications Have been with him no cause whatever for anxiety going to
England tomorrow will wire name Hospital Ship Monica

DE/Rv/C2303/38-39: 6 May, from Monica Grenfell to Lord Desborough

Telegram: From miss Monica Boulogne decided keep Julian here for few
days know you will both come tomorrow; with telephone message

DE/Rv/C1231/1, 17 May 1915, Philip Hardwick to Lady Desborough

I am very grieved to have to write and tell you that poor old Julian was hit last Thursday. He was hit in the head by a shell. He was quite conscious when I saw him and on enquiry at the hospital yesterday we were told he was going on well and had been passed on which means he was fit to travel. So I hope by this time that he has reached England & that you have got him under your care. It is idle to pretend that a wound such as he got is anything but serious, but I pray that he will soon mend and be his old self again…We had a desperate day, in fact two days. Twelve officers out of fifteen killed and wounded. Colonel Steele desperately wounded in the head…Julian did very well – he was wounded at an observing station whilst talking to the General. After the Colonel was hit I found myself in command of the Right & in that capacity I have recommended Julian to the notice of the General for excellent work done on that day. I shall be very anxious to get news of him, so I hope you will be kind & let me know how he goes on. Please give him my love.

DE/Rv/C2454/1: 14 May 1915, from Ven H K Southwell [chaplain]

Dear Madam
Your son gave me the enclosed to post, & I was obliged to put it into an envelope, as it was not safe for post as he gave it me. You may be glad to know that Sir Anthony Bowlby saw him here [*casualty clearing station*] this afternoon, & at once said that he could go on to Boulogne without any risk

DE/Rv/C2681/1: 16 May 1915, from War Office

Telegram: Regret that Capt Hon J H F Grenfell 1st Royal Dragoons was wounded 13 May nature and degree not stated

DE/Rv/C2681/3: 13 October 1915, from War Office

My Lord

His Majesty the King having been graciously pleased to confer the Distinguished Service Order upon Lieutenant The Honourable Julian Henry Francis Grenfell, late 1st Dragoons, now deceased, in recognition of his services with the Expeditionary Force in France, I have the honour to forward to you as next-of-kin, the Insignia of the Order, together with the Royal Warrant of appointment and a copy of the Statutes.

3. Some letters from Lady Desborough, May 1915

DE/Rv/C1071/11: to Julian, 12 May 1915, Washington Hotel, London

My darling Julian

Daddy was so delighted to get your letter yesterday. You don't know what a joy your letters always are, and how we look forward to them, and you have been such an <u>angel</u> about writing.

I sent your poem by hand on Friday night to Geoffrey Robinson, and could not make out hearing nothing, so this morning I telephoned to him, and hear he has been away and is expected back this morning. I sent you the copies of it yesterday I cannot tell you how I love it, and am simply longing to see it in print.

The alternative to <u>The Times</u> is, I think, the <u>English Review</u>?

After unspeakable difficulty, we have got leave to go to Boulogne on Saturday, and shall be there all next week. What a joy if you possibly <u>could</u> get down to see us? I fear it is absolutely hopeless any chance of our getting up to you, and I suppose if this tremendous fighting is still going on there will be no chance of your getting even an hour's leave.

Dad saw Lord Kitchener yesterday, who was cheerful. The account of dear Edward last night was much better, and I believe dear Francie returns to England to-day, as of course they cannot allow people to take up room up there. He is in one of Bowlby's hospitals at Bailleul.

Ock is shot through the leg, but no danger to life or limb. Charles Lister's wound is not serious, and he telegraphed that he is doing famously. We are deeply grieved at Wilding's death; I did like him so much.

Billy goes almost immediately but we don't know yet what day.

I dined with Mr Asquith and Sir Edward Grey last night. I don't think one realised until the last day or two how intensely anxious they were about the Dardanelles until the landing was actually accomplished.

Did you ever get Chesterton's poems which I sent you? I thought some of them so good, but yours is the war poem I like best of all.

My own own dear. Your Mother.

[*Note on envelope:* Wounded 13/5/15]

DE/Rv/F150/8: to Monica, 12 May 1915, Washington Hotel, London

My darling Casie

One line to say that after simply unspeakable difficulties, which at one time seemed final, that angel Lord K has got us permission to go to Boulogne, and we hope to come by the midday train from London on Saturday.

I expect you will have got my letter asking you to engage us rooms at the Hotel Folkestone, unless you can find anything decent at Wimereux. Two small bedrooms for Daddy and me, and a room for Gaston.

I cannot tell you how relieved and delighted I am at getting permission to come out, only ten minutes ago.

I don't believe there is the faintest chance of our getting up to the Front with this heavy fighting going on, but I do hope Julian will get down to us.

I will bring your nursing shoes and the other things you want.

How too delightful that Betty and Elsie are going out to you. I am so delighted, though worry for poor Iris.

I am sending this to Fitz and do hope it will get to you quickly.

Your most loving M.

PS I am bringing out such a lovely poem of Julian's to show you. Daddy heard from him yesterday. Darling Bill goes out quite soon now. We don't yet know which day.

DE/Rv/F150/8: to Monica, 14 May 1915, Washington Hotel, London

My darling Casie

We have been so tossed to and fro about plans, as darling Billa does really go now next week, and thinks he can get one more day at Taplow first, and of course I could not bear not to remain with him on that chance, as you will understand better than anyone in the world.

He will either come tomorrow or Sunday, so we shall cross either Sunday or <u>Monday</u>, and I will telegraph to you directly I know, and meantime send this out by Venice tomorrow, as I feel you will begin to be bewildered by our changes.

I enclose Julian's poem, and a letter from Iris, and have got your nursing shoes, and all your things.

It is too divine to think of seeing you in two days, or three. With quite indescribable difficulty we have got all the permits, and shall come over by the midday boat; you know, the one arriving about four on either Sunday or Monday.

Probably <u>Monday</u> now.

Your own M.

DE/Rv/C1102/5: 17 May 1915, from Boulogne to unknown recipient

Julian was wounded on 13th. Sir A Bowlby saw him at clearing-station and said he was fit to be moved to Boulogne. His temperature and pulse were so good on arrival that they did not at once X-ray him, thinking it only a scalp wound, and that he could travel to England Sunday – Hence Monica's good telegram. Slight signs of brain pressure made them X-ray him early Sunday fracture of the skull was revealed, and a splinter of bone penetrating 1½ inches into his brain. They operated instantly, it took two hours. Sergeant performed the operation, Holmes the neurologist was with him, and Colonel Lister (the oculist.) Col Lister said no operation could have been more <u>perfectly performed</u>. Willy and I have both seen Julian, and he is <u>quite sensible</u> when he speaks, and very quiet. His temperature and pulse are very good. There is no paralysis at present, and he has not been sick, but at the best he cannot be out of danger for eleven days. He could not be under better specialists. We are only four houses away, in same street. Monica has been splendid, she never left him, and slept at the hospital last night. Edward Horner is still very ill, and they fear must have another operation tomorrow. Alastair Leveson-Gower is going on well. They are all in the same hospital, No 7 Stationary. We shall of course stay here straight on.

DE/Rv/C1085/90: 21 May [1915], to Lord Balfour, written in Boulogne

I think he is a <u>shade</u> less weak today, but the doctors won't admit it yet. He is so good…Billy went up to the Front last night, with his Regiment. He saw Julian for an instant. Monica has simply held us all up…Julian is <u>quite conscious</u>. The paralysis they firmly believe only temporary.

4. Letters from Lord Desborough to Lord Kitchener, May 1915

DE/Rv/C1170/1: 25 May 1915, from Boulogne

My dear Kitchener

I am so grateful to you for your two letters which Stavordale has just given me. It is most kind of you.

Julian is I deplore to say <u>very</u> bad: there is little or no hope now. I quite thought yesterday that he was going to pull through – but I am afraid it is not to be. He has just been dressed, and the original trouble which the second operation was to remove is still there, & his temperature is 104. I will give him your message.

Yours sincerely <u>Desborough</u>

DE/Rv/C1170/2: 28 May 1915, from Boulogne

My dear Kitchener

Dear Julian is to be buried today: his end was quite peaceful & he looked very happy. He had everything done for him that could be done: the Doctors & nurses were so good to him, and loved him & said he was the bravest of the brave. The most trying thing was that we were told not to let him talk, and he was longing to talk: there was some particular bit of work he was very pleased about, but I never heard what it was. He was too bad to let me tell him about your enquiries – the last ones, but I did let him know that you had often asked after him, which pleased him much. His soul was in the war and he loved the fighting, and every one tells me how grandly he was doing, and we shall always think of him with love & affection & great pride.

Ettie sends you her love: she was with him night & day, & is quite knocked up. We come home on Monday. Yours sincerely <u>Desborough</u>

DE/Rv/C1170/3: 30 May 1915, from Hardelot

My dear K[itchener]

You cannot think how grateful Ettie and I are to you for your letter, it takes away one's sorrow.

You were so fond of Julian that you will be pleased to read what Billy's Colonel Maclachlan wrote to him.

'Julian has set an example of light hearted courage which is famous all through the Army in France, and has stood out even above the most lion-hearted'.

There was one piece of work he did the last day which pleased him very much, some observation he took under a heavy fire which he thought turned the situation, but we were told not to let him talk about the war so we shall never really know. However I think it made him quite happy.

Ettie has had almost no sleep since we have been here till last night. We get home tomorrow night.

All that can be done now is to see that Julian and his like shall not have laid down their lives in vain: each in the way that is open to him.

Yours ever Willy.

5. Letters from Billy Grenfell, May and June 1915

DE/Rv/C1110/461: Friday [21 May 1915], Western Front

Darling M[other]. It was a joy to see you yesterday so wonderfully brave and calm & strong. One feels that Ju must repose now on the strength of those that love him as much as on his own, & that all strangling influence of fear or misgiving should be cleared away from him. it was sad to see his "dear delightful head" brought so low, but I really do feel the most complete confidence & trustfulness. Casie is so marvellous, a tower of strength - & Daddy too…

DE/Rv/C1108/54: Tuesday [25 May 1915], Western Front

My dear Daddy

I got your second letter today with the less good account of dear Ju. The issue lies with God alone now, & He will decide for the best – I pray to Him to be with you all in these days of trial, & to uphold the splendid courage you have shewn through all.

I thank Him too for having allowed the dear boy to show his glorious valour to all the world before he was struck down.

What better fate could one desire for a loved one – "Sed miles, sed pro patria."…

DE/Rv/C1110/464: nd, Western Front

Darling [Mother]. Just one word of blessing and good hope. I know how strong you have been and will be.

How can we feel anything but serenity about our darling J – whether the trumpets sound for him on this side or the other.

DE/Rv C1110/465: nd [1 June 1915], Western Front

Darling [Mother]

The more I think of darling J, the more I seem to realise the nothingness of death. He has just passed on, outsoared the darkness of our night, "here where men sit & hear other groan", & how could one pass better than in the full tide of strength & glory & fearlessness, so that there is no interruption even in the work which God has for him.

Our grief for him can only be grief for ourselves.

How beautiful his poem is. It perfectly expresses the unity & continuity of all created things in their Nature. I pray that one tenth of his gay spirit may descend on me…

DE/Rv/C1111/21: nd, Western Front

Darling Casie

…Our sorrow must be swallowed up in the thought of his glorious life – splendid example…

6. Letters from Ivo Grenfell, May and June 1915

DE/Rv/C1125/298: Wednesday [19 May 1915], Eton College

Darlingest Mummy

…I feel the worst is over now, don't you? and I am sure Juju's wonderful bravery and calmness would pull him through any wound or disease…Do give my best love to darling Juju; I feel sure he will get well now, because God could not spare him from this world. Hawa told me that a very good surgeon at Nancy's hospital told her that to be conscious after an operation is the very best sign of all…

DE/Rv/C1125/297: Sunday [23 May 1915], Eton College

Darlingest Mummy

Thank you <u>so</u> much for your letter, and do thank Casie and Daddy for their dear ones, they have been such comforts. Everyone has been so kind here, and on Friday Mrs Warre Cornish came and saw me, and I told her all the news about dear Juju. It is good so far, isn't it? and one of the surgeons at Juju's hospital wrote and told Mabel Ogilby's sister (whom he knew) that Julian Grenfell, he didn't know if she knew him, would get well...It was nice Billy being able to see Juju, I am sure it cheered him. Juju must be too brave and good for any words and he must love having you with him...But I do feel that Juju is well on the way to recovery, don't you? ... I am sure Juju will pull himself well wonderfully quickly now by his courage ...

DE/Rv/C1126/5: Friday 28 [May 1915], Taplow Court

Darlingest Casie

Juju is in peace and happy for evermore, and no one could have died so bravely. The blow seems almost too cruel, but we know how brave you all are out there, and we know what darling Juju would wish us to do. The world will never be quite the same again, but God does everything for the best...Juju has so nobly done his duty, and has died as I am sure he wished to die, fighting for his country...We must all try and be like Juju. He has triumphed over all, and he would never wish us to feel sad but rather what a glorious thing death is...

DE/Rv/C1125/299: Friday [28 May 1915], Taplow Court

Darlingest Daddy and Mummy

We have just got your telegram and we know that darling Juju is in peace. God bless him for all his wonderful life on earth, and what a joy he has been to us all. He died, as I am sure he wished to die, for his country and he has left a life behind him that none can equal. ... We are all trying to copy Juju's glorious example of bravery here, and we know what he would wish us to do...

DE/Rv/C1123/11: Saturday [nd, 29 May 1915]

Dearest Daddy
I have just got your letter and I know you are right about darling Juju…You know how much we are thinking of you and Mummy and Ca[sie] here, and how we are sending you our dearest dearest love. Juju would not wish us at all to grieve but only to think of him in his peace and great glory…Juju has lived and died so so gloriously and no one will ever be like him again…If we could only all live and die like him, how beautiful a place the world would be…

DE/Rv/C1125/300: 6 [June 1915], Eton College

Darlingest Mummy
…I had seen the poem about Juju in the Times and I really thought it too wonderful. It had really the right idea, the ringing note of joy and glory, and I thought the poetry good. I do wonder who wrote it, he must have known Juju awfully well, and have just the same beliefs as us…Death is absolutely vanquished now. One knows that it never again can be anything but only just the separation of our bodies. What a wonderful life Juju led, never a moment wasted, and never a moment given to anything else but nobility and unselfishness. How he was loved, and how his example seems to have stirred everyone to the roots…

7. Letters from Monica regarding Julian's grave

D/ERv/C2305/422: nd [May 1915?], to Lady Desborough:

[*description of Julian's grave*]…I was so comforted to be able to be there today, & I thought of you all at home the whole time. What I could do today seemed a tiny symbol of our great tribute to him. There can never have been anyone so <u>wonderful</u> as Julian: or so much loved

D/ERv/C2303/16: nd, to Lord Desborough:

[*beginning missing*]…I often go up to see darling Julian's grave – it looks very nice and is well kept. I could hardly bear to go there at first, but I often go now. There is an oak cross at the head of the grave with

Captain J H F Grenfell
1st Royal Dragoons

on it – DSO has been omitted altogether. I wonder if you will want me to do anything about this? It is all very well kept and looked after…

D/ERv/C2305/428: Saturday [nd], to Lady Desborough:

I have been to see Colonel Kiddle – he was charming & said he would do anything he could to find out for me: but he said <u>none</u> of the arrangements were made through him or through the hospital & he could not tell me when I ought to go to have the alteration made. I am sure Daddy will know? Will you tell me when you next write.

At present the inscription is

Captain The Hon J H F Grenfell
1st Royal Dragoons

Will you say what exactly you w[oul]d like, as I suppose the whole inscription will have to be re-done. Julian is such a lovely name, wouldn't it be <u>much</u> <u>nicer</u> to have it in full, (and with the DSO added, of course)

Captain The Hon Julian Grenfell DSO
1st Royal Dragoons.

I went to see Colonel Kiddle at once about it - & then waited for Daddy's letter, as I thought he might tell me in it, but as he did not mention the place he must have thought that Colonel Kiddle knew all about it…

8. Documents mainly relating to *Into Battle* [HALS: DE/Rv/F119]

Three typescript copies of poem
Three cards with printed copy of poem, issued by RSPB

Typescript of letter from Sir Walter Raleigh[456] to Lady Desborough about poem, 11 Sept 1916:

I don't think that any poem ever embodied soul so completely as "Into Battle". The other poems are good, but not in the same world. This thing has hardly ever been done – an anthology of the adequate poems on real

---

[456] In letter 129 Julian refers to Raleigh and this is probably the same man.

things would be tiny.

Remember I didn't know who wrote it when it first knocked me down. It was like a dream come true. Those who glorified war had always, before this, been a little too romantic; and those who had a feeling for the reality of war had always been a little too prosaic. It can't be done again.

I was so thrilled to-night that I had to scribble this.

Extract from *The Times* relating to an anthology of war poems it had published; quotation from first verse of *Into Battle* + 'So sang that very gallant soldier Julian Grenfell before he joined the glorious company of England's sons who up the steep crimsoned by the life blood have borne, and still bear, the honour and good fame of the Motherland to the everlasting gates of heaven'.

12 printed copies of *Into Battle*, with *Out of Battle* by William M Hardinge, and an unattributed poem entitled *Julian Grenfell*:

> Because of you we will be glad and gay,
> Remembering you, we will be brave and strong;
> And hail the advent of each dangerous day,
> And meet the great adventure with a song,
> And, as you proudly gave your jewelled gift,
> We'll give our lesser offering with a smile,
> Nor falter on that path where, all too swift,
> You led the way and leapt the golden stile.
> Whether new seas, new heights to climb, you find,
> Or gallop through the unfooted asphodel,
> We know you know we shall not lag behind,
> Nor halt to waste a moment on a tear;
> And you will speed us onward with a cheer,
> And wave beyond the stars that all is well.

On the back is an extract from a letter from Lt Col Maclachlan, 8th Service Battalion Rifle Brigade, to 2nd Lieut The Hon G W Grenfell:

"Julian set an example of light-hearted courage which is famous all through the Army in France, and has stood out even above the most lion-hearted."

Press cuttings of *Into Battle* from various newspapers and journals

APPENDICES

Extract from *The Spectator* of 5 June 1915:

[*Referring to Rupert Brooke*] We find the same thing again in the remarkably beautiful lines which were written by the late Captain Julian Grenfell and were published in the *Times* last Saturday. Deep feeling and art – something of the art of Chaucerian simplicity – are joined in these lines. Like Brooke, Julian Grenfell did not make death seem preternaturally glorious by contrasting it with hollow life and cruel Nature. He saw life full of companionship and Nature full of smiles and beauty. But these things supported and taught him. [*with quote from poem*]

Extract from *The Saturday Review* of 11 Dec 1915 [*with poem*]:

JULIAN GRENFELL
"I was ever a fighter, so – one fight more,
The best and the last!"
No family has given of its best more generously in the war than have the Grenfells, and no individual record is more moving to consider than the glorious one of Captain Grenfell, DSO, Lord Desborough's eldest son, who fell in France on 26 May. It needs the pen of the Royalist historian who drew the portraits of Lord John Stuart and of Falkland to do justice to the theme; for in Julian Grenfell was a rare union of what that historian called the "cholerick" soldier, who did not disguise his love of battle, with the writer of magical English verse. Oxford has turned out of late years no completer Englishman. "Julian", writes one who can speak of him from the most absolute intimacy, "was a fighting man and not a poet"; and that is so, essentially; he was the professional soldier, the amateur poet. And his brief and splendid story was largely one of physical prowess. He was a good rider, and a boxer of renown. In South Africa Julian Grenfell won many races, and brought off the record high jump at the Johannesburg horse show – 6 ft 5 in. He defeated the champion boxer of South Africa, after a severe fight, and "was always ready to take on anybody with the gloves if he could get the chance". In the week in which he wrote in Flanders, last April, his famous poem on the fighting man ministered to by all Nature – the stars, the sun, the winds and the birds – he was employed in knocking out two professionals at boxing meetings at the Front!
Julian Grenfell then was the casual, strictly the amateur, poet; and his scattered lines, when presently they are collected, may be too slight to describe as "works". But one at least of his verses will live on and make a

sure appeal when perhaps the great bulk of printed matter, poetry and prose, of our day has been completely forgotten. There is not the faintest doubt about the quality of his lines on the fighter and the glory of fighting. They are matchless among the verses of to-day; and we believe they will pass into the living body of English literature, partly through pure poetic merit and partly through the high renown of Julian Grenfell. They were printed for the first time some months ago, and lately the Society for the Protection of Birds has given them in part on its Christmas card. We are glad of the privilege to reprint the lines here, so that readers who have been haunted by their beauty and strength, and by their glorious sense of surging youth, may enjoy them once again in full. Hitherto they have not been quite accurately printed as regards the arrangement of the lines; the first verse, as Julian Grenfell wrote it, should consist of eight lines, the second of six, and the rest of four apiece.

Typescript notes (in French) – extract from conference on English poets of the war, 8 May 1919, with biographical information on Julian

Extract from *The Athenaeum*, **30 July 1921**: 'What pride they have is of another kind, the kind which made Julian Grenfell write the poem which is always quoted by the martial-minded against the war poems of the Sassoon school. But it seems to me that, surrendering to a conventional mood, he only wished us to believe that poets may make first-rate soldiers; though a doubt that they would not would never have occurred to anybody but the sort of practical poltroons who never feel safe unless they are surrounded by battleships, boys compelled to bear bayonets, and a Business Government'.

Extract from *The Saturday Review*, **16 July 1921**: 'Can his [Sassoon's] warmest admirers pretend that posterity is likely to rank anything of his with that wonderful song of Julian Grenfell's, like the passionate trilling of the larks in the air above "No Man's Land," that we heard on a summer's day in Artois? No, they cannot. And Grenfell was an unregenerate man, who dared to write of "joy of battle," as his cousin Francis dared to say with his last breath: "I die happy."

Extract from *English Review*, article entitled 'Soldier poets' referring to Julian and quoting from his letters/diary. It finishes:
A piece of bursting shell has deprived us of a great leader, with the characteristics of the finest kings of men. And though wealthy enough to travel with dogs and horses wherever he went, he could not bear to think that

a friend had deserted the Socialist cause out of respect for the "loaves and the fishes." This friend writes – "I don't suppose many people knew what an ardent love he had for honesty of purpose, and intellectual honesty, and what sacrifices he made for them – sacrifices of peace-of-mind abhorrent to most Englishmen…caused himself no end of worry and unhappiness." Yes, facing discomfort clears the will as facing physical danger clears the head, and wrong within can be defeated by braving evil abroad. And now while intellectual honesty is at a premium I will confess that the last two lines of his "Into Battle" always disappoint me. They ring hollow and empty; it is as though he had been disturbed and scribbled in haste something that looks like an end but is not, and never given his mind to the poem again. The other poems published since are slighter in mood and more boyish in execution. Though they are not bad, they are not good enough to enhance the effect of "Into Battle."

Physically, mentally and morally splendid he might seem to have done little in this world but be and be destroyed. Yet to have been, and to be known to have been such as he was may well in time seem one of the grandest facts of these times. Such admiration as we owe to him is an experience as rare as it is beneficent, and will outlast a vast number of topics and crazes. Two phases of his worth he revealed even to those who never met him, the one in his poem, the other in his letters, and they tally as the like aspects have rarely tallied in other men. This proves the density of the integrity that was destroyed by a fragment of iron. He lay wounded a few weeks before he ceased to suffer.

…And Grenfell cheers this hope as few can, foreshowing a better proportioned life. The limpidity and strength of his emotion, though it creates beauty and reveals wisdom, was seconded by no matured art; yet those who have this at command are so liable to fail just where he succeeds, in sureness of aim.

Typescript of letter from Sir W Raleigh, nd:

I don't know if you really know that Julian's poem is one of the swell things in English Literature. It is safe for ever, I know it by heart, and I never learned it. It has that queer property which only the best poems have, that a good many of the lines have more meaning than there is any need for, so that new things keep turning up in it.

9. DE/Rv/F120, Julian's other writings

Typescript of poem, 'To a Black Greyhound'
MS of 'Lines suggested by the earthquake of San Francisco', Apr 1906
MS of 'Elegy on the death of Mr Warre's dog'
MS of 'Short historical survey of the Germanic people'
MS of 'Prayer for those on the staff' [*in envelope addressed to Lady Desborough*]
Typescript of same poem
MS of 'To the Missouri Race Club', *with note in pencil* – Written by Julian at Chakrata, May 1911
MS of 'Epitaph on Turner'
MS of 'Mistaken Identity' with sketches
MS notes – '20th century Guide to Love'
MS of untitled poem
Typescript of 'Hymn to the fighting boar'

10. DE/Rv/F121, Papers re life and death

Rough sketch of area around Ypres
Cuttings from various national and overseas newspapers reporting Julian's death, obituaries, etc
Newspaper cutting entitled 'Life in the trenches' – unattributed but assumed to be written by Julian (three copies)
Newspaper cutting entitled 'Cavalry subaltern's vivid experiences' - unattributed but assumed to be written by Julian (two copies)
Typescript of biographical details
Typescript of poem about Julian's death
MS biographical notes
Receipt for payment for newspaper cuttings

Appendix 4

Letters from Julian to Flossie Garth[457]

Flossie Garth out riding, 1915.

29 Jan 1915
Telegram: Will be at meet hulcott 12 Monday hope you had good hunt
Wednesday Julian.

Feb 1915
My darling Flossie
One line, to thank you a thousand times for my very jolly day with you on
Monday, which I enjoyed enormously, in spite of your low cunning in cutting
me down at that damn brook place (an action for which I shall never forgive
you).
I hope you're having good sport now. We are at the front again, fighting for
the Empire. God Save the King. It's quite good to hear the noise of a shell

---

[457] Florence Garth (1896 –1980), married Henry Mather-Jackson in 1920

bursting again. We had almost forgotten what it sounded like.

Take care of yourself, Flossie, and mind you don't go out in that Mercedes with anyone who doesn't know how to wind it up. You <u>will</u> remember to send me that photograph, won't you?

Goodbye now & bless you Julian. Lt Col 1st Royal Dragoons.

Will you please give my best respects to your Mother[458], and please thank her very much for the toothbrush, and other little things? Please tell her how sorry I was not to see her.

16 Feb 1915

My darling Flossie

Thank you awfully for your letter, photograph, and drawing. They reached me in the trenches, and they cheered me up ever so. It was very dear of you to remember to send me the photograph and it's a very jolly one. I do hope that your cold and throat are better by now. Are they? You are quite right about hot port, it's the best cure for almost anything, if you drink <u>enough</u>.

[This French pen is impossible]

As I was saying, the best cure for almost anything, if you drink enough. Just consider what it has done in your case! Not only has it cured your cold, but it has also cured (apparently - for so you say) the perverse and uncomfortable attitude which you adopted about the subject which we were discussing last time. Hooray, Flossie, I am glad! I have put in for leave immediately, out of my turn, to see whether you mean what you say. But they will not give it me yet awhile.

I loved your drawing. You were quite right in the prophesy which you wrote underneath it ("Horrible thought, perhaps you are in the trenches"). So we were. About a quarter of an hour after I got your letter the Boches started sending bombs into our trench. I starting sending bombs back at them; and I threw the first three clean into their trench! So you can see what good it did me to get the photograph!

Oh Flossie, I <u>am</u> looking forward to having another hunt with you. I can't tell you how much I enjoyed our last day. Have you been getting good sport lately?

I had a most exciting time on Tuesday, the day after our hunt. I heard in the morning that my regiment had moved, and that nobody knew where they had

---

[458] Lily McComb, married (1) Granville Garth, (2) Hubert Hartigan. Hartigan belonged to a family of racehorse trainers (see letter 164)

gone to. Probably into trenches. So I arrived in France not knowing what to do or where to go or how to go. Rex Benson luckily had a motor, and he kindly motored me all over France looking for the Royals! About midnight I gave it up, and woke up a kind woman in a farm, who gave me a bed (which she was quite ready to share with me, had I pressed her). Rex drove on to his regiment. At 6 o'clock next morning my woman gave me a pony-cart, and eventually I found my regiment, who were starting for the trenches in an hour's time! The first thing I saw was my 3 greyhounds being exercised in a field; they came slap over the hedge into the road, and into the cart, when I holloaed to them!

Goodbye, Flossie, & bless you.

I shall not forgive you for cutting me out at that open ditch, unless you [are] terribly nice to me next time.

Please send me the big photograph.

Goodbye XXXXX Julian

24 Feb 1915

My darling Flossie

How are you? I am very angry with you. You are a bad wicked girl, and you will certainly go to Hell when you die.

I had dinner with Hubert the night before last, and he told me that you had said that I was "madder than ever". How dare you speak like that about a man old enough to be your father, and a man of very high rank in His Majesty's Army? How dare you say such a thing, when you yourself have admitted that you were entirely convinced by the arguments on morality which I put forward to you on that occasion?

I am very angry with you, and I shan't let you ride my horses any more. Hubert is a great darling, and I'm very fond of him. He used to dislike me in the old days, but now I think he is overcome by my exalted position, and has turned towards me. He went into the trenches yesterday, poor chap; but it didn't seem to worry him any.

I am over in the next billets to him now, looking after horses for a regiment who have gone into the trenches – but only for a week.

Flossie, are you having good hunting. Write and tell me about it. I am going to give up horses, wine, and women. I am, really. I am going to join the Foot Guards, with the sons of the Gilded Aristocracy. They want officers badly and have sent round asking for officers from the cavalry. So I've sent in my name. Fancy me in the Guards! God Almighty!

Why haven't you sent that photograph?

We shan't have that hunt together, Flossie. Not this year, anyhow. Because they've stopped all leave.

Goodbye, my dear, & take care of yourself and drink lots of Hot Port. Bless you XXXX Julian.

26 Feb 1915

My darling Flossie

Thank you for your letters. You are a most disreputable and disrespectful little girl, and I shall tell Hubert about you directly he comes out of trenches. I had always thought that you were one of those quiet, modest, bashful well-brought up children. But I have now discovered that you are one of the FAST SET of girls; one can see it from your letters; you show no respect for your elders and betters. I always promised my mother to have nothing to do with fast girls.

Ask Hubert if he saw what was in my pocket-book.

O Flossie, I wish I could see you again. But I love your letters, and they cheer me up a lot, so just sit down and write me another! Please.

Thank you for the photograph of the damned brook place (I wonder you dare to send me one) – and also of Domino. God bless you, Miss, I know that sort of horse. I've ridden hundreds of them. I feel sorry for you, about that £2,000 bet. I've entered it in my pocket book, with the other things. But I suppose FAST girls, like you, never bother about paying a bet?

Will you ever be respectful to me, Flossie? You will have to, when I am in the Guards. If you are not, I shall show everyone that pen-and-ink sketch which you did of the bedroom scene, when under the influence of strong drink.

What you want is a <u>good talking-to</u>; I shall have to ask for an amnesty, for me to get leave to come and administer it to you. Flossie, please send me another good letter, and the photograph of you jumping the wall at Navan[459]. [But don't be conceited about it, because I've jumped much bigger walls than that, on £15 horses. You are one of the idle rich. I am poor but <u>honest</u>]. Also send me photographs of you being kissed[x] by Hubert and other loose young men.

You're a <u>bad</u> girl, as I've said before.

(Signed) J.H.F.G. x

XX The Guards'

x I'd very soon show you the sort I like.

---

[459] County Meath, Ireland

29 Feb 1915

Field service postcard [*obviously a joke*]. Signed 'Captain Kidd'. I have been admitted into hospital. I am being sent down to the base. I have received your letter dated Feb 29, telegram Feb 30, parcel Feb 31. I have received no letter from you <u>for a long time</u>.

4 Mar 1915

My darling Flossie

Thank you awfully for your letter. It's very good of you to say that my letters cheer you up – because your letters have done me a deal of good, and I love getting them. I'm writing to you quick, to catch you for your birthday; it's not my fault if this letter doesn't get to you in time, because I only got yours today. Many happy returns, my dear. I had no idea that you were so <u>old</u>. I had always thought that you were 16, 15 off or rising 16. Of course, if you are really as old as all that, you can be as wicked as you like. I only wrote to rebuke you because I thought you were so young that somebody ought to look after you; and who better suited for the job than myself; because Hubert and all that racing crowd are bad tutors for a young girl. But as you are so <u>very</u> old (past all mark of tooth) I will give up the job. Anyhow, I'll drink a bottle of wine to your very best on Monday; the hottest port I can get hold of. I wish I could drink it with you, talking all the time about the principals of morality, like last time. Did you have bad flue, Flossie? That must have been a great hunt with the Whaddon[460]. What do you think I would have added to that famous Bedroom scene? I daren't think. I daren't guess to what depths of iniquity your mind can descend. It's like arithmetic.

> If a herring and a half costs $1\frac{1}{2}^{d}$,
> What does a whale cost?
> If a girl of 18 off has a mind like a sink,
> What does a young lady of 19 think of?

I always mean to write you nice sensible letters about the Progress of the War and the Economic Situation; and I always finish by writing this drivel. I suppose it's your evil influence on me. You write very good letters, Flossie. Just write to me now about the Moral Progress of the Young, with especial regard to the Female Sex.

No news much. We have got some gigantic guns out here, but everybody is

---

[460] The Whaddon Chase hunt, later amalgamated with the Bicester; it hunted in north Buckinghamshire and surrounding counties

much too frightened of them to shoot them off. So they are just shown off, like prize fat bullocks, and everybody looks at them, and says "Ah…ah…My God…Eh?"

They are not taking any of us 'oss-soljers now for the Foot Guards. I am rather sorry. I had seen George Paynter and he was going to apply (had applied) for me to go with him. But they've knocked it all on the head know [*sic*] – I don't know why. Perhaps it's a good thing, because I don't know how to walk. But I can run some; and that w[oul]d be useful.

Why didn't you send me your extra-special photograph? I shall sue you for breach of promise. But I really like the ones of you riding best[x] – or the ones of you being kissed in public by Hubert and other people. Don't forget to send me these - a <u>large</u> selection.

When this war's over we'll go and fairly knock them with the celebrated Leicestershire packs of fox-dogs.

Goodbye F & bless you; and here's a <u>very</u> big extra X for your birthday, from poor lonely J.

x Not that you can <u>ride,</u> oh no.

Look at the poor grey's mouth in the picture!

15 Mar 1915

My darling Flossie

Thank you awfully for the photographs of yourself on horseback. I was most impressed by them – especially by the charming way in which you display the Odol[461] Smile whilst in mid-air. You must have been taking lessons from Mrs McB; (except that she never jumps fences). Did I ever thank you for the magnum of champagne which you sent me? I drank it all at one fell swoop. Ever since the day I got it we have been hurried all over the country, all day and all night, so there has been no time for writing. We were always expecting to fight the next moment, but we never did. The billeting is rather amusing, because we never get in to a place till about 10 or 11 pm, and then we are suddenly stuck down in a strange place with all the men and all the horses, and told to make ourselves comfortable for the night. I generally sleep in a cottage kitchen, on the floor; because then I can always secure coffee & eggs in the early morning, and, as you know, the Englishman always fights best on a full stomach. We peg out the horses in a field, and generally get barns for the men. But I wish we did a bit more fighting. They have stopped the scheme for sending horse officers to the Foot Guards, so I

---

[461] A brand of mouthwash

remain a heavy dragoon for the time. Poor George Paynter was hit very badly this week; I am awfully sorry, he is such a good man.

Flossie, I love your photographs. What horse is it? You say that you are "flying off the saddle". When I go show-jumping a certain portion of my anatomy is always at least 2 ft off the saddle; but I always hoped that this was the right way to do it! You certainly can ride some. I think that it is a very good plan of yours, to come and be cook, as long as you don't cook anything except linseed for the horses on Sat nights. But we won't go to Leicestershire; we'll go to India and pigstick. You would like the Anglo-Indian ladies; they are almost as abandoned as you are. I wish I could see your big new chestnut horse. If he is really too much for you I will surely ride him to quieten him down for you at a purely nominal charge. I'm glad you had a good hunt on Saturday; but be very careful not to get caught up in the gates when you open them. And don't kill yourself in that motor.

Flossie, send me more photographs, because I love getting them. If you don't, that cook situation will go to one of these French beauties (who, by the way, do not exist in these parts).

Goodbye, F, and write to me.

What shall I give you for your birthday? I am very rich. My birthday is March 31 when I am 30[462]. It's terribly old. You are very rich. Bless you XX J.

[*Pencil drawing of British cavalryman in sunset*]

We all wear 3 coats, and so many things strapped around us and on the saddle, that we cannot fall off. The horses are as fat as pigs. So are the men. Don't miss the lovely sunset.

[*Last page has (upside down)*): 10 Mar 1915. Darling Mother. Darling Flossie. Please excuse this, but I'm short of paper, and always starting letters & never finishing them]

19 Mar 1915

My darling Flossie

Thank you for your letters. I'm glad you had a good day with the Pytchley – I wish I'd been there. I'm sorry that you've been falling about such a lot lately – out of taxis in Bond St, and off the old brown horse. What you want is someone strong and capable, with a strict sense of duty and morality to look after you.

---

[462] His birthday was *30* March and he was 27 in 1915

You ask about photographs, F. Yes, I've got quite a fair supply of them with me. I always carry them about. Which would you like? No 35, leading a charge into the German trench, with a revolver in each hand and a sword between my teeth? Or No 57, which is a very good likeness – receiving the Order of Leopold from the King of the Belgians for saving Ypres from the Prussian Guard? Or 68 – home life, swinging a golf club, in a neat check suiting? They are yours for the asking; but only one of them, because there is such a large demand.

I'm glad to note that you're becoming more respectful in your letters, with advancing age. What shall I give you for your birthday; (your next one, I mean, when I shall have come into my money)?

Thank you for your valuable present of shamrock, which I wear next to my heart, and only remove once a fortnight (when I have a bath).

What were you doing in Bond St? Buying a trousseau? Or being manicured? It's very dangerous for a young girl to go dashing about London like that.

Nothing doing here much. We went up the other day for the attack on Neuve Chapelle, all the cavalry. But they did not want us, so after waiting there for two days we came back again into our farms and pubs here. I ride over the country bareback, over gates and brooks and canals and wheat and all sorts, just to show the French what a good rider I am.

Can you ride bareback?

I don't believe you can.

I will teach you one day, dv [*deo volente,* God willing].

Flossie, are you having fun. Write and tell me. How's your big new chestnut horse? Is he still too much for you. Send me some more photographs. I believe that you and Elsie Janis[463] are the two most photographed people in the world at the present minute.

I've just written to a lady who advertised in the Times that she was willing to write to any officer who was lonely and wanted letters. I wonder if she'll write to me? She is perfectly lovely. She looks like this.

Goodbye F XX

Heaps & heaps of love from Julian.

[*With sketch of woman's head*]

---

[463] An American actress

2 Apr 1915

My darling Flossie

Thank you for your letter from somewhere in Liverpool. The pink ink and mauve paper are very good; it's a pity you couldn't keep it going the second time round. I have always thought what you say about the National fences; you and I think nothing of fences twice that size, with wire along the top on one of our real Who Shall days in the Vale. Hubert must have had a great ride on Meridian. He came over here the other day, but I missed him. He is very popular with all the bloody and licentious soldiery (Quotation, so it's alright, and you needn't blush. Would anything make you blush?). By the way why wasn't your horse running? I am always seeing its name in the papers in the list of probable starters, but never anywhere else. Isn't this rather odd? Please explain.

O Flossie darling, I'm so bored here and I've got the old complaint of "Spring in the blood". I wish I were fighting with the footsloggers. Horses are such dangerous animals. I think it's quite likely that we shall never fight again.

I will give you several strings of pearls on July 10th. You can go and choose them, and tell them to put them down to me. I've also got a fawn-and-white greyhound bitch puppy, born here last week, who will certainly win the Waterloo[464]. Yours for the asking.

Flossie send me some more photographs to cheer me up. I'm so dull. How are you? And your morals? Just you be a good little girl, & remember the words of y[ou]r father, Julian.

30 Apr 1915

My darling Flossie

Thank you awfully for your letter. I'm so glad you had a win at Cheltenham. I missed it in the papers, so I have only your word to go on; and Bad Luck to you if you are pulling my leg! What are your colours? What is the name of the steed? Of course I will buy him. Please reserve him for me at once. £800 or £8,000 – all the same to the rich. Do you remember when you tried to sell me that nice horse with his hock down to his fetlocks. I remember you producing the Books to look up the animal's form, and how hard it was to find – never placed in those bright £15 Irish steeplechases. I remember the

---

[464] The Waterloo Cup, a greyhound race run since 1836 at the Altcar estate, near Formby, Merseyside

amused look on your face that evening; and on mine! Flossie, did you really have a fall on the flat? Poor little girl! But if you have really taken to that golf, I shall never speak to you again. Have you been to Ireland?

Hubert and self had a great Who-Shall in Paris the other day. I had a very difficult task in keeping him out of trouble; he is so immoral and excitable. It is a lucky thing that I am of a staid and balanced temperament, or the poor fellow might have got into mischief. Did he tell you of the cab-driver whom we took into the Ritz, and introduced into high society?

We will have great fun after this war, you and Hubert and me. We will fairly knock them in the Old Kent Road.

We've been up here assisting at this battle for the last week, but have been no nearer the fighting than getting shelled a bit. I'm writing this in a Belgian farm, where we are billeted. It's full of refugees – old men and old women and young children. You see them all day streaming down the roads, carrying everything they can in their arms, and with little carts drawn by dogs; it is too pathetic.

I wish we could get some fighting. The only fighting I can get is boxing. A private in the A.S.C. challenged me at a show the other night, but I hit him with great violence below the fifth rib (as the Bible says) and he subsided with a nasty groan.

Thin or fat women? Ah! Who was it compared your mind to a sink? Please tell me the answer. And send me some more photographs, or I will exhibit the ones you have sent me in a public place. God bless you Flossie. Good night.

XX J.

Letters from Monica Grenfell to Flossie Garth and Hubert Hartigan

24 May 1915, from Boulogne

Dear Miss Garth

This is one word to thank you ever so much for the charming letter you wrote me about Julian: it was so nice of you to write, and he talks so much of you & Mr Hubert. I told him this morning that I had heard from you and that you had asked for news of him.

We have had a dreadful time of anxiety about him as he has been in a very grave condition. He stood the first operation (they trephined [*sic*] his skull & removed a small splinter from his brain) very well, at first: but yesterday morning they thought that the wound was showing serious symptoms and they operated again at once to try & relieve the pressure round the wound. He had a bad night, but they really think him slightly better this morning, and he has had a good long sleep now and is not in much pain for the time being. We can but <u>pray</u> that all will be well and just watch and await results. He has been so wonderful and good and brave through it all – and he has been conscious almost all the time. He was talking today about you & Mr Hubert and of the happy hunting days – he is so devoted to you both and has spent some of his happiest times in your hunting country.

Thank you again for your letter.

Yours sincerely

Monica Grenfell.

Please let Mr Hubert know this news of Julian.

30 May 1915, from Hardelot

Dear Mr Hartigan

Thank you so much for your telegram and your charming letter about darling Julian – I was so pleased to get them & they reached me eventually out here. I had such a dear letter too from Miss Garth. Julian talked <u>so</u> much of you both during the last days, and it was such a happy theme for us to talk about – almost his happiest times were spent with you in your happy hunting country: and he was so devoted to you both – you were indeed a companion after his own heart.

I gave him your messages & he was very pleased with them. I don't think he suffered much while he was lying ill at Boulogne, and he died very calmly & peacefully just as a soldier should. He was conscious all the time until the last day, so we had some lovely talks and some divine times together. He said he knew you w[oul]d be disappointed to have been in England and so to have missed this "show" at Ypres!

Please give my love to Miss Garth, as I know she will be sad: but I think it will be comforting for you as well as it is for us to think of his <u>splendid</u> life and death.

Y[ou]rs ever, Monica Grenfell.

11 June 1915, from Taplow Court
Dear Miss Garth
I have been looking through the unopened letters which did not reach Julian,
& I think this one must be from you? I am returning it to you on the chance.
Y[ou]rs affectionately, Monica Grenfell.

Saturday [12 June]
And this is another one I found in his pocket book last night – I think it is
from you?

Appendix 5

Sources outside Hertfordshire

The National Archives [Public Record Office], Kew

WO 95/1153, regimental diary:
16 Nov 1914: Lt Grenfell with a patrol got close up to the German trenches
and shot 2 through their loopholes
13 May 1915, 1.30 pm: About 1.30 Grenfell and the brigadier who had been
observing were both hit by a shell; the former severely in the head and the
latter slightly in the back

WO 339/7684 [15710], Julian Grenfell's personal file
[Sparse] includes copy of his birth certificate (born 4 St James's Square);
details of grave (no 2272); telegram from Lord Kitchener, 27 May,
expressing sympathy to Lord Desborough; telegram, 16 May notifying Lord
Desborough that he had been wounded; telegram, 17 May – 'Capt Hon J
Grenfell 1st Dragoons admitted 7 Stationary Hospital Boulogne yesterday
suffering gunshot wound head seriously ill'.
[*Rest mainly to do with effects and accounts*]

WO 389/1, 26; WO 390/2:
Date of appointment of DSO: 27 Dec 1914; date in *London Gazette*: 1 Jan 1915; insignia and warrant forwarded to Lord Desborough: 13 Oct 1915. 'On the 17th November he succeeded in reaching a point behind the enemy's trenches and making an excellent reconnaissance, furnishing early information of a pending attack by the enemy'.

Balliol College, Oxford
Balliol College war memorial book, 1914-1919, vol I, *1924*
Balliol College register
John Jones, *Balliol College. A History*, 2nd edn, OUP, 1997
J M Winter, 'Balliol's "Lost generation"', *Balliol College Record*, 1975

Bedfordshire and Luton Archives and Records Service, Bedford
Diary of Madeline Whitbread, 23 January [ny]: '…Julian…has overworked and therefore had a touch of nerves…'; June : 'Julian Grenfell, King of Athletes & beloved among his brother officers & men dead'.

Centre for Buckinghamshire Studies, Aylesbury
D11/16/2: Further copy of *Into Battle*
D11/16/3: Viola Meynell, *Julian Grenfell*, reprinted from *The Dublin Review*, nd:
D86/22: Typescript copy and slip proof, both incomplete, of *Pages from a Family Journal*; correspondence with publishers
About 80 letters of condolence on Julian's death, including one from Queen Alexandra
31 photographs of Julian & Billy
43 photographs of Lord & Lady Desborough and children
(*All returned to depositor, 1970*)

Somerset Archive and Record Service, Taunton
DD/DRU 103: Letters (undated) from Ettie Desborough to Evelyn Charteris, Viscountess de Vesci, and copy of memorial service sheet.

West Sussex Record Office, Lewes
MAXSE/460/f 339, f 394: two letters from Julian, dated 30 July and 7 September 1909, to Leopold James Maxse, editor of the *National Review*, about submitting his essays for publication. (According to Mosley they were rejected.)

Viscount Gage, Firle Place, Sussex
Two game books kept by Julian:

Volume I begins in 1895 and contains information about hunting at Taplow, Panshanger and Eton up to 1905; he wrote: 'My first day's hunting I rode "Kitty"…'. There is also information on shooting and fishing in Taplow, Panshanger and other places, many of them in Scotland. He records when he shot his first stag, caught his first salmon, etc. There are a number of photographs, some of them taken by Julian, and sketches by him. He noted: 'This book was first kept regularly Christmas, 1904'. When he was at Eton and Oxford he recorded details of rowing, horse racing, etc in which he was involved. The last entry is dated October 1907.

Volume II contains sketches, photographs, newspaper cuttings, race cards, etc, as well as details of hunting, shooting, horse racing, pig sticking, stalking, otter hunting, coursing, polo, boxing, ostrich-catching, baboon-hunting, etc.
Entries begin on 27 October 1907 and record activities in many venues, including Taplow, Panshanger, Knebworth, Balliol College, Castle Ashby, Avon Tyrrell, Stanton Woodhouse, Picket Post, Wigglesworth, Gisburne, Nairn and other places in Scotland, India and South Africa.

There are some 'diary' entries. For example, late in 1910 he wrote: 'On Nov 4 I left England for India on HMTS "Rewa"'. At the end of the pigsticking season, 1911, he noted that the total bag was 400 boar. When he was about to leave India for South Africa he placed an advertisement in the local paper, offering his horses for sale – The Hawk, Caesar, John Kino, The Girl and Kurta. On 21 September 1912 he noted that he was arriving in England on six months' leave and recorded his sporting activities at Sawley Lodge, Clitheroe, Panshanger, Taplow, Aldershot, Bletchley, Aylesbury, etc. On 12 April 1913 he sailed for Africa and in August the following year he wrote:

'Sailed from Cape Town in "Dunluce Castle", the regiment and horses. In same convoy 10th Hussars, Gunners, Queen's Regt, Essex Regt, some Bedfords, and Staffords'. Almost the last entries record the exploits for which he was awarded the DSO in 1914. There are two entries, written E of Klein Zillebeke near Ypres:

Nov 16   1 pomeranian
I went out sniping in the thick wood in front of the Tenth Hussar trenches. When I got to the German trench, about 40 yds in front of ours, it was unoccupied. But there was a party of Germans about 10 yds behind it in the wood, and I shot one over the parapet of the trench.
I went out again in the afternoon in front of our lines. Found German trench about 60 yds in front but saw no Germans, after waiting there for an hour.

Nov 17   2 pomeranians
I went out again next morning, same place. Nobody in German trench, so I went on further into the wood. Heard a man coming. He walked straight up to me, & I shot him. About 5 minutes afterwards the Pomeranian Guard came along, passing me about 40 yds away, making for the salient in our line. I dropped the one who looked like an officer, and retired hurriedly. They attacked in force ½ hour afterwards.

He was on leave in the winter of 1914-15 and, on 25 January, wrote: 'All hunting and coursing stopped, because the French grumbled'. The final entry is for 28 January, when he was on leave in Reading.

THE HERTFORDSHIRE RECORD SOCIETY

The Hertfordshire Record Society exists to make Hertfordshire's historical records of all kinds more readily available to the general reader. Since 1985 a regular series of texts has been published.

HERTFORDSHIRE RECORD SOCIETY
ALAN RUSTON, Chairman
HEATHER FALVEY, Hon. Secretary
GWYNNETH GRIMWOOD, Hon. Treasurer
SUSAN FLOOD, Hon. General Editor

Membership enquiries and orders for previous publications to the Hon. Treasurer, 190 Lonsdale Road, Stevenage, Herts SG1 5EX

Annual Subscription (2007-2008)   £17.50

Previous publications:

I: *Tudor Churchwardens' Accounts*. Edited by Anthony Palmer (1985) O/P

II: *Early Stuart Household Accounts*. Edited by Lionel M Munby (1986) O/P

III: *'A Professional Hertfordshire Tramp' John Edwin Cussans, Historian of Hertfordshire*. Edited by Audrey Deacon and Peter Walne (1987) O/P

IV: *The Salisbury-Balfour Correspondence, 1869-1892*. Edited by Robin Harcourt Williams (1988) O/P

V: *The Parish Register & Tithing Book of Thomas Hassall of Amwell* [Registers 1599-1657; Tithing Book 1633-35]. Edited by Stephen G Doree (1989). Price £6.00

VI: *Cheshunt College: The Early Years*. Edited by Edwin Welch (1990). O/P

VII: *St Albans Quarter Sessions Rolls, 1784-1820.* Edited by David Dean
O/P

VIII: *The Accounts of Thomas Green, 1742-1790.* Edited by Gillian
Sheldrick (1992). Price £6.00

IX: *St Albans Wills, 1471-1500.* Edited by Susan Flood (1993). O/P

X: *Early Churchwardens' Accounts of Bishops Stortford, 1431-1538.*
Edited by Stephen G Doree (1994). Price £6.00

XI: *Religion in Hertfordshire, 1847-1851.* Edited by Judith Burg (1995).
Price £6.00

XII: *Muster Books for North & East Hertfordshire, 1580-1605.* Edited by
Ann J King (1996). Price £6.00

XIII: *Lifestyle & Culture in Hertford: Wills and Inventories, 1660-1725.*
Edited by Beverly Adams (1997). Price £6.00

XIV: *Hertfordshire Lay Subsidy Rolls, 1307 and 1334.* Edited by Janice
Brooker and Susan Flood, with an introduction by Dr Mark Bailey
(1998). Price £18.50 (£15.00)

XV: *'Observations of Weather' The Weather Diary of Sir John
Wittewronge of Rothamsted, 1684-1689.* Edited by Margaret
Harcourt Williams and John Stevenson (1999) Price £19.00 (£15.00)

XVI: *Survey of the Royal Manor of Hitchin, c1676.* Edited by Bridget
Howlett (2000) Price £18.75 (£15.00)

XVII: *Garden-Making and the Freeman family A Memoir of Hamels, 1713-
1733.* Edited by Anne Rowe (2001) Price £18.50 (£15.00)

XVIII: *Two Nineteenth Century Hertfordshire Diaries, 1822-1849.* Edited by
Judith Knight and Susan Flood (2002) Price £19.50 (£15.00)

XIX: *"This little commonwealth": Layston parish memorandum book,
1607-c1650 & 1704-c1747.* Edited by Heather Falvey and Steve

Hindle (2003) Price £21.00 (£15.00)

XXI: *The Hellard Almshouses and other Stevenage Charities, 1482-2005.*
      Edited by Margaret Ashby (2005) Price £21.00 (£15.00)

XXII: *A Victorian Teenager's Diary: the Diary of Lady Adela Capel of*
      Cassiobury, 1841-1842. Edited by Marian Strachan (2006)
      Price £17.50 (£15.00)

Maps:

*The County of Hertford From Actual Survey by A. Bryant In the Years 1820
and 1821* (2003) £7.50

A Topographical Map of Hartford-Shire by Andrew Dury and John Andrews,
1766 (2004) £9.50

For more information visit www.hrsociety.org.uk

Note: references in **Roman numerals** refer to pages in the Introduction; references in **normal type** refer to the numbering of the letters in the main text; references in *italics* refer to page numbers in the Appendices; **fn** signifies footnote to the letter indicated

Note: references in **Roman numerals** refer to pages in the Introduction; references in **normal type** refer to the numbering of the letters in the main text; references in *italics* refer to page numbers in the Appendices; **fn** signifies footnote to the letter or page indicated.